Time and Relative Dimension

Time and Relative Dimensions in Faith

Religion and *Doctor Who*

Edited by Andrew Crome and James McGrath

DARTON·LONGMAN + TODD

This edition first published in 2013 by
Darton, Longman and Todd Ltd
1 Spencer Court
140 – 142 Wandsworth High Street
London SW18 4JJ

ISBN 978-0-232-53021-6

A catalogue record for this book is available from the British Library.

Phototypeset by Kerrypress Ltd, Luton, Bedfordshire
Printed and bound by ScandBook AB

Contents

Acknowledgements

Just before he regenerated, David Tennant's Tenth Doctor took the TARDIS on one last trip, thanking all of those who had meant something special to him. These acknowledgements give the editors an opportunity to do something similar. Thanks must first go to David Moloney, Editorial Director at DLT. We are deeply grateful to all the work that David and all at the publisher have put into the volume, and their quick, friendly and remarkably efficient working practice. We would also like to express our thanks to all of our colleagues and students at Manchester and Butler for their interest in the book and being willing to endure our obsession with the show.

All of the contributors to this volume, who have provided such a rich and wide-ranging collection of viewpoints, also deserve special thanks. They have made what could have been a stressful process into one that was hugely enjoyable through their level of insight and willingness to work to deadlines. We would also like to thank all of those who expressed an interest in contributing to this process in its early stages. We were staggered by the response we received when we first floated this project, and hope that all who had an interest in it at that early stage enjoy this book.

A number of other heroic individuals helped in a variety of ways. In particular, Crawford Gribben, Gordon Blows and David Butler have all offered useful advice or material at key moments in this book's development. Jon Ainscough, Stef Elstub, Helen Hardwick and Lizzie Slingsby provided insightful discussions on individual episodes (and lots of tea) during the final editing process. Their contributions to the debate over whether we called this book *Time and Relative Dimension in Faith* (as our inner-fans demanded) or whether to go with (as we eventually did) *Dimensions* were particularly helpful, as were the opinions of Sam Carey and Daniel Rozday as non-fans. The reasoning behind our fan-baiting title is laid out in our introduction.

Finally, our thanks go to our families and friends, and to all those who share a love of *Doctor Who* with us, or have had to endure our addiction. When he was nine years old, Andrew Crome's mother grew so frustrated with her son's obsession that she told him to focus on learning about something useful ('like history') rather than things like UNIT dating controversies. This book is, in many ways, a (very) belated response to that challenge. In its many forms *Doctor Who* inspires, challenges, excites and asks us important questions about who we are. This book tries to examine, from a variety of perspectives, why *Doctor Who* is so good at asking these questions, and why they continue to appeal to us today. As *Doctor Who* increasingly grows its fanbase (now including Andrew's mum!), this book tries to look at why its appeal is so wide. *Time and Relative Dimensions in Faith* is therefore dedicated to anyone who has ever been moved, thrilled and excited by the Doctor's adventures. As the show celebrates its fiftieth anniversary this year, we look forward to seeing exactly where it goes next.

Introduction

Andrew Crome

At one time, generations stood entranced by it. Knowing its key texts and the enemies vanquished by its hero was a part of every English childhood. The stories of demons defeated and people set free; of ordinary men and women swept into a story greater than themselves; of a man who died and was raised from death captivated all those who came across it. Those gatekeepers left in charge of this phenomenon looked out with growing confidence. It would continue to go from strength to strength; it was destined to be embraced by generation after generation. But then, suddenly, interest began to decline. The confidence of an earlier era was revealed to be complacency as those who had shown weekly commitment began to drop away. Children were no longer interested in what (to them at least) appeared dull and dated. Desperate measures aiming to rekindle interest through nostalgia failed miserably. Revamps, modern music, even esoteric clothing were all tried with little effect. And by the early 1990s it seemed dead in the water.

Then something unexpected happened. The most committed followers continued to believe. New texts, different approaches and fresh voices suggested that it could be reimagined for a new century. Unsurprisingly, there were disagreements – how should their hero be represented? What were the acceptable boundaries he could transgress? And, of course, which of his adventures should be considered part of the canon? While the answers to these questions differed, the core followers revealed that they never gave up the faith. And like its hero, quite suddenly, interest began to rise again. The phenomenon was reborn and appeared more alive and relevant than ever. And by 2013, the concept that had been confidently written off as a throwback to a forgotten age twenty years earlier was more visible and influential than ever before.

This is, of course, the story of *Doctor Who*'s triumphant return to our television screens, first in the UK and then across the world. However, it could just as easily be a description of the role of religion in British life, at least according to one recent wide-ranging survey of the subject by a group of sociologists, historians and theologians.[1] Whether you agree with this reading of religion's fortunes in the UK or not (and plenty do not),[2] *Doctor Who* itself has always contained a rich current of religious themes and ideas at its heart. In its very first episode, the programme asked how humans rationalise the seemingly supernatural, as two snooping school teachers refused to accept that the TARDIS was real ('This is nothing more than a game that you and your grandfather are playing ... but you can't expect us to believe it'). On their travels, Ian and Barbara (now reluctant believers) served as the prototype for the companions who would confront false gods and eternal beings; robot messiahs and strange cults. Above all of this stands the figure of the Doctor himself. The ultimate mystery, beyond time, the force above all those imaginary deities, only *he* has truly experienced the mysteries of creation. As he recently reminded us, he had seen the creation of the universe and its destruction 'until nothing remained, no time, no space, just me'. The Doctor is therefore unique in the universe; the guardian of terrible truths and secrets 'that must never be told, knowledge that must never be spoken, knowledge that will make parasite gods blaze!'[3]

Time and Relative Dimensions in Faith: Religion and Doctor Who is a collection of academic (but accessible) articles which examines these (and many other) religious themes and ideas within *Doctor Who*, as well as looking at responses to religion in audio adventures, online communities and wider fandom. Much like the TARDIS itself, this book offers a way of exploring a number of different worlds; a variety of communities, philosophies and historical periods. Yet while the TARDIS's initials stand for 'Time and Relative *Dimension* in Space', studies of religion often suffer by being narrowly confined to particular faith traditions or academic approaches. The worlds of different faiths and faith communities which have used *Doctor Who* are as wide as the universe the Doctor traverses, and this calls for a similarly eclectic approach. This collection therefore examines the history and relative *dimensions* across the landscape of contemporary Religious Studies, Religious History and Theology.

Readers might, of course, be sceptical of the benefits of examining religion and *Doctor Who* side by side. Indeed, at first glance they might appear to have little connection with one another. We are certainly not suggesting that *Doctor Who* should be viewed as focused *primarily* on religion. Even the editors of this volume do not sit down to watch *Doctor Who* in the expectation that it will deal with deep religious issues – which is not to say that we aren't very pleasantly surprised when it *does* focus on such things! As Robert Pope notes in his work on religion and film, people usually watch movies and shows like *Doctor Who* to be entertained, not to engage with deep philosophical and theological issues. This is an important point which can easily be forgotten in academic work on religion and popular culture. Nonetheless, as Pope's own work shows, just because something exists primarily to entertain, does not mean that religious themes cannot be dealt with in highly complex ways, and those themes later debated, reinterpreted and engaged with in fandom and in wider popular culture.[4] Indeed, digging a little into *Doctor Who*'s own rich history reveals that different presentations of religion, religious themes and critiques of religious positions have been present in the series from 1963 until the present day. We would therefore suggest that there are a number of reasons for examining religion and *Doctor Who* together.

First, it allows an appreciation of the changing ways in which religion has been presented on British television and in wider popular culture from the 1960s until the present day. *Doctor Who*, with (an admittedly loose) educational remit in its early days, therefore presented images of other cultures to British viewers, inviting them to think through the implications of different behaviours and belief systems. To take one example, the different ways in which Buddhism has been presented in the series suggests something about changing conceptions of non-Christian religion in Britain from the 1960s onwards. The 1964 serial 'Marco Polo', for example, saw the titular explorer suggesting that the TARDIS crew might be Buddhists because of their apparently magical blue box. 'At the Khan's court in Peking, I have seen Buddhist monks make cups of wine fly through the air unaided and offer themselves to the Great Khan's lips', reveals Polo, 'I do not understand it, but I have seen it.' While this might seem to invoke Arthur C. Clarke's 'third law', that advanced technology appears indistinguishable from magic, it in fact offers a subtle modification of this. For Polo, advanced technology appears indistinguishable from religious power.

Buddhism in fact appeared relatively regularly through the series' original run. Patrick Troughton's Second Doctor stopped off at a Tibetan monastery in the 1967 serial 'The Abominable Snowmen' and encountered the Great Intelligence and robotic Yetis, as well as monks going about their daily routine of meditation and prayer. In Jon Pertwee's final story, 'Planet of the Spiders' (1974), UNIT regular Mike Yates cleared his mind through meditation after a run-in with apocalyptic environmentalists in 'Invasion of the Dinosaurs'. Here, Buddhist practice is no longer semi-magical, as in 'Marco Polo', or restricted to Tibet as in 'The Abominable Snowmen'; we find Tibetan meditation centres have now sprung up in rural England. If the journey of monks from Tibet to the Home Counties might have seemed like a long one for the average viewer in the 1970s, then spare a thought for the Doctor's former mentor, who had journeyed from Gallifrey and lived on Earth as Buddhist Abbot K'Anpo (and, somewhat confusingly, as a projection of his future incarnation Cho-Je). Viewers concerned about the impending regeneration of Pertwee into Tom Baker could be reassured through K'Anpo's wisdom: 'All things pass away, as you will learn in your meditation. This world of samsara, the world of appearance, is the world of change'. Producer Barry Letts, a Buddhist himself, intentionally worked many of these themes through the series in the Pertwee era, but the show also returned to the subject in later years, particularly in Peter Davison's 'Kinda' (1982) and 'Snakedance' (1983), in which scriptwriter Christopher Bailey wove complex Buddhist allegories into his tales of the alien Mara.[5]

To talk about the presentation of Buddhism is merely to scratch the surface of the way in which the series has dealt with religion. The show's science-fiction basis has offered writers and producers opportunities to explore contemporary religious challenges in abstracted contexts. To provide just one example, in 'The Aztecs' (1964), the First Doctor's companion Barbara attempted to change the beliefs of those she encountered when she was mistaken for the god Yetaxa. Written in a Britain that was facing the challenges of increasing immigration, and the resulting clashes between British Christianity and new forms of faith, Barbara's desire to remove 'primitive' aspects from Aztec faith by opposing human sacrifice is perhaps the understandable response of the 'civilised' Westerner confronting an unfamiliar faith. Yet her plan fails when the victim, horrified that he has been denied the honour of serving his god, kills himself to complete the sacrifice. The story contains a warning from the Doctor that attempts to change beliefs without understanding them will lead only to disaster: 'Human sacrifice is their tradition. Their religion. There's nothing we can do about it'.

This was far from the universal position of the series, and *Doctor Who* can also be open about challenging religion. The Doctor certainly doesn't profess any sort of faith himself. Indeed, it is fun to speculate on what would have happened had the planned second serial 'The Masters of Luxor' made it to our screens in 1963. The decision to replace it with 'The Daleks' may have been wise in hindsight, but it tragically denied us not only the worst double entendre in the show's history,[6] but also the Doctor kneeling in a prayer of repentance and his condemnation of Karl Marx's statement that religion was 'the opium of the masses'. 'I think he was wrong,' notes the Doctor. 'It would have been truer to say, "Religion sneering at scientific progress ... or scientific progress sneering at religion ... either of them can lull people to sleep". Each needs the other.'[7]

In later episodes, *Doctor Who* encourages viewers to confront false belief and reveal its regressive character. Whether this is through the unmasking of false gods (as in 'Pyramids of Mars' (1975) or 'Four to Doomsday' (1982)), the discovery of demonic/alien cults ('The Masque of Mandragora' (1976) and 'Image of the Fendahl' (1977)), or the exploration of the nature of religious faith ('The Curse of Fenric' (1989)), *Doctor Who* suggested that false faith should be revealed wherever it was found. As the Doctor exposes the god Xoanan as nothing more than a computer with a split personality, so he criticises those who refuse to accept his conclusions: 'You know the very powerful and the very stupid have one thing in common. They don't alter their views to fit the facts. They alter the facts to fit the views.'[8]

By the time of the revival of the show in 2005, religion again worked its way through the episodes of the newly popular series. The Daleks, for a long time a purely secular enemy of the Doctor, found faith in their Emperor-God (or, as the Doctor put it, 'They're insane!').[9] The Tenth Doctor was offered an early chance to become a God ('School Reunion' (2006)), before encountering a society which based its existence on solidarity created through hymn singing ('Gridlock' (2007)). The Eleventh Doctor discovered that the Church of England still exists in the far future as a paramilitary organisation sometimes fighting for him ('The Time of Angels/Flesh and Stone' (2010)); sometimes allying with orders of 'Headless Monks' to battle against him ('A Good Man Goes to War' (2011)). The fact that religion works itself out in this way suggests that it remains a concern of producers, writers and viewers.

This extremely brief overview has merely scratched the surface of the religious themes which have been used by the programme.

Countless other examples could be (and, indeed, are) offered in the course of this book. And here we can move beyond the television series. As fans know, *Doctor Who*'s world is much wider than its televisual context. The vast range of novels – starting with Virgin's *New Adventures* and continuing through the BBC's Eighth Doctor and 'Past Doctor' adventures – provided opportunities for writers to address increasingly complex themes and issues in much greater detail than on television. A similarly deep analysis was possible from 2002 onwards through Big Finish's range of audio plays, of which around 170 have been produced at the time of writing. Plays like Rob Shearman's 'The Holy Terror' therefore acted as open critiques of organised religion in a much more nuanced way than had been possible on television, while Caroline Symcox's 'The Council of Nicaea' allowed the Fifth Doctor and his companions to take part in early Christian debates on the nature of the Trinity. This is before we think about the spin-offs, graphic novels, *Doctor Who Magazine* comic strips, webcasts, and video games. *Doctor Who* is truly a vast transmedia franchise.[10] But merely highlighting examples of religion in *Doctor Who* achieves very little. It is not enough simply to say that religious themes are present; what is important is that we analyse *why* they are present, and what they tell us about the society that produced the show and the viewers who engaged with it.

The writers in this collection therefore attempt to answer these questions through an in-depth analysis of the various treatments of religion throughout every era of the show's history, and through the various media of which it has made use. While the majority of chapters here focus on televisual *Doctor Who*, the authors also look at audios, novels and the response of fandom in their chapters. Their analyses reveal that examining religion in a long-running series such as *Doctor Who* can contribute to a number of key debates within faith communities and religious history. Changes in the level of religious content and the background knowledge that producers assumed viewers would have regarding faith-based themes can offer valuable perspectives on the controversy over the supposed secularisation of British society since the 1960s. With Callum Brown's highly influential study *The Death of Christian Britain* highlighting 1963 as the year in which full-scale secularisation set in, *Doctor Who* presents an obvious tool through which we can examine the outworking and impact of secularisation, if it in fact can be said to have happened at all.[11] Indeed, the increasing prevalence of spiritual themes in the revived series, used both positively and negatively, might locate

Doctor Who as part of a wider spiritualised, rather than religious, 'occulture'.[12]

A further advantage to considering religious themes in the programme is that it provides fresh ideas and illustrations for those teaching Religious Studies in universities and schools. As the example from 'The Aztecs' above shows, *Doctor Who* has never shied away from the difficult effects religion has on those who follow it. This is true not only of *Doctor Who*, but also other popular science-fiction programmes and films – we need only think of similar themes running through the various *Star Trek* series or *Battlestar Galactica* to see this. Popular science fiction therefore offers a way in which complex religious and philosophical ideas can be presented to students in such a way that it enables them to see their relevance in contemporary culture, rather than as merely 'academic' questions. One of the aims of this book is to encourage those teaching Religious Studies and related subjects to make fuller use of science fiction in this area, and to explore the ways in which an interaction with popular culture can be used creatively in these studies.

Of course, the question of how these religious themes were received by the audience is as important as the interrogation of the themes themselves. To those on the outside looking in, *Doctor Who* fandom might well appear to be semi-religious in nature, with its debates on canonicity and arguments about whether recent portrayals of its central figure fit with preconceived notions of how the Doctor 'should' behave. A quick glance at the various fan forums available online will reveal a great disparity between different fan reactions to religious themes (and, in fact, everything else) in *Doctor Who*. A search of online fan fiction reveals a number of stories suggesting the Doctor's involvement with the life of Jesus (vying for readers' attention alongside the Doctor/Master slash-fics). Indeed, the idea of a mysterious individual with the ability to die and rise again automatically suggests certain comparisons with Christ. While Christian writers are unlikely to join fan fiction in asking whether Jesus was in fact a disguised Time Lord, they have often co-opted the Doctor as a Christ-figure. Reverend John D. Beckwith, chaplain to the Bishop of Edmonton, wrote in 1972 that while the programme was fiction:

> Doctor Who, as a character [*sic*] is essentially a good man and, although even he has his setbacks and the situation often hangs in the balance, Good in the end triumphs over Evil. This is the

most important connection between *Doctor Who* and religion: the recognition that there is one basic Truth in God's Creation and this is that the most valuable and worthwhile thing is GOODNESS.[13]

For others, *Doctor Who* could serve as a more direct tool for understanding faith. This has been even more common since the return of the series to our screens in 2005. 'Does *Doctor Who* feature a God for our times?' asked Stephen Kelly in a 2011 article for *The Guardian's* website, while in 2013 Liel Liebovitz suggested that the Doctor was 'the greatest Jewish character in the history of television ... it's been a very long time since a television show took metaphorical questions so seriously and answered them in a way that was so profoundly Jewish'.[14] At times, these religious readings of the show fired up evangelism. In 2008 the Church of England's 'Church Army' organised a '*Doctor Who* and Spirituality Day', in which fans were encouraged to explore religion through the series.[15] For those ministers present, the day offered a way to connect with popular culture. As Bishop of Sherwood, the Rt Revd Tony Porter commented: '[the conference] is a great idea as *Doctor Who* is hugely popular and it's critical to identify with where people are'. Other attendees took a more literal approach to the subject matter. The Revd Andrew Meyers concluded that 'We saw the Doctor persuaded to save a family of Pompeians in one of the most recent episodes, surely a reference to Genesis and Abraham's bargaining with God over the fate of Sodom and Gomorrah ... Even the more cynical have been convinced that this immensely successful series provides a wonderful toolkit'.[16] Even the then Archbishop of Canterbury, Rowan Williams, referred to the series in his preaching, illustrating the dangers of a society built around the wrong kind of fulfilment by quoting the 1987 episode 'The Happiness Patrol' in his 2011 Easter sermon.[17] For Christians wanting to explore theological themes in the show, it was possible to pick up books like Baptist minister Anthony Thacker's *Behind the Sofa*, which used the 2005 and 2006 series as the launch pad for theological and ethical discussions on issues such as sexuality, reincarnation and the occult.[18] This Christian interest in the evangelistic potential of the show reached a bizarre peak in 2007, when Russell T. Davies's 'Gridlock' was nominated for the Epiphany Prize, an award for 'television programs which are wholesome, uplifting and inspirational and which result in a great increase in either man's love of God or man's understanding of

God'.[19] The nomination was withdrawn when the prize committee realised Davies's background was not in line with their interpretation of what constituted family values.

The case of 'Gridlock' is interesting, because Davies later revealed that he explicitly wrote it *against* religion. While initially including the sequence in which a disparate community unites around hymn singing to 'show how good faith could be, regardless of the existence of God', as the production proceeded he revealed that 'the real me came bleeding through, because it transpires that hope stifles the travellers. It stops them acting ... the Doctor realises that no one is going to help them. There is no higher authority'. As he concludes, 'That's what I really think about a ton of things: religion, superstition, mysticism, legends, all bollocks.'[20] The Epiphany Prize committee would probably not be amused.

'Gridlock', then, can be taken as a good example of the complex way in which religious themes in popular culture can be reinterpreted by fans. What Davies intended as an anti-religious text becomes, in the hands of those who consume and interact with it, something which in fact promotes their belief. To see how fans have used *Doctor Who* in this way, both to promote and to attack religious positions they either hold to or disagree with, is to see the active reworking of these texts in action. It offers a fascinating window into the way in which fans consume texts, and the way in which religious (or, indeed, anti-religious) communities reinterpret the products of popular culture.

The Book

Time and Relative Dimensions in Faith tries to examine these issues through adopting a number of different methodological approaches across its nineteen chapters. At this point, it is important that we say something about the nature of the approaches taken by the contributors to this book. This volume as a whole does not take a uniform approach to religion. It does not aim either to promote a particular type of religious faith, or to attack any tradition. Some contributors write from a particular faith background, while others approach the subject from an explicitly secularist viewpoint. While each author has certainly been influenced by their particular religious (or non-religious) background, the intention of this collection is to provide a scholarly overview of the many complex uses of religion in *Doctor Who*, rather than to promote any particular form of belief. Reflecting the popularity of *Doctor Who* across the English-speaking world, contributors are drawn not just from the United Kingdom, but also from the United States and Australia. The approaches used are similarly diverse. Chapters have been written by film scholars and sociologists; theologians and historians; rhetoricians, philosophers and anthropologists. This makes for a diverse collection, which aims to appeal to a broad disciplinary range. While scholars from each of these fields use their own approaches, they have written their essays to be both academically engaging and accessible for fans without specialist knowledge of Religious Studies or Theology. Where technical terms are used, they are explained clearly. This is a book that aims to be, at one and the same time, a valuable academic resource and something that will appeal to fans interested in the issues it raises.

The book is structured into four sections. The first explores religious issues within *Doctor Who* itself. Courtland Lewis opens this by examining the way in which *Doctor Who* has dealt with immortality. Lewis shows how immortality leads the show's characters, from Omega to the Master, to madness and depression. An acceptance of death is always part of *Doctor Who*, and calling on ideas found in a variety of faith traditions and philosophical positions, Lewis shows how we might all benefit from a notion of 'objective' immortality based on the shared memory banks of the Time Lords' 'Matrix'.

Claims that the Doctor represents a messianic figure are among the most popular in works on religion and the show. Gabriel McKee explores them in a creative way as he writes about the Doctor's ethics. Denying that the Doctor can be characterised as either an authoritarian or anti-authoritarian figure, he shows how *Doctor Who* has always looked beyond simple resolutions and dualistic either/ or solutions to moral problems. What matters is our ethical and humanist response – if the Doctor is messianic in any way, it is that he shows us how to be truly human.

Continuing the theme of Christ figures, K. Jason Wardley offers a thorough theological reading of Paul Cornell's 'Human Nature', both in its early form as a novel and its 2007 adaptation on screen. Wardley examines the Doctor's *kenosis* (self-emptying) in the story, comparing it to Christ's incarnation and applying the categories of René Girard to analyse the role of mimetic violence in the Doctor's incarnational journey. This, argues Wardley, does not provide an image of the Doctor as a simple analogue of Christ, but allows the viewer/reader a creative exploration of the idea of incarnation.

Tim Jones, meanwhile, offers a stimulating look at the faith that the Doctor inspires through a close reading of two episodes which explore the theme in detail: 'The Curse of Fenric' (1989) and 'The God Complex' (2011). Comparing these episodes offers very different perspectives on faith, and allows Jones to consider the wider changes in British attitudes to religion between the airing of the two episodes.

Michael Charlton examines time in his chapter, making use of rhetorical and theological concepts of Chronos ('clock time') and Kairos ('God's time') to explore how the Doctor has faced his own moments of decision and judgement when facing the challenges of time travel. In an accomplished analysis, Charlton examines the differing treatment of the theme in 'The Waters of Mars' (2009) and 'A Christmas Carol' (2010), as the Doctor falls foul of the laws of time in one episode, while seemingly re-writing them in the other.

The section closes with Brigid Cherry's chapter, which offers a detailed reading of Martha Jones's story arc in the 2007 series of the show. While acknowledging the difficulties of reading the Doctor as a Christ-figure, Cherry shows the way in which Martha's story can be read as apostolic. As she concludes, Martha's agency is restored at the end of her story arc, a significant 'development for a black female character in popular culture'.

In the second section of the book we turn to look at the way in which religion has been used to deal with encounters with the unfamiliar and the alien in *Doctor Who*. Laura Brekke's chapter examines the way in which the uniqueness of humanity has been dealt with in post-2005 *Doctor Who*. Taking an explicitly theological approach, Brekke argues that the Doctor's conception of 'humanness' is not tied to *Homo sapiens* alone. Rather, it is based on ideas of empathy and emotions which are equally applied to aliens. Where these qualities are lacking – in Cybermen and Daleks for example – so is humanness. Indeed, Brekke argues, the image of God is itself denied through the removal of these qualities.

Taking a different approach, Jennifer L. Miller asks whether we can view *Doctor Who* as saying something about humanity's capacity for turning evil. While acknowledging a potentially messianic reading of the Doctor in the post-2005 series, Miller argues that we are perhaps more justified in viewing the Doctor as a representation of the monstrous. Employing Freud's notion of the uncanny to explore the way in which Christian imagery was used in Russell T. Davies's tenure as Executive Producer, she presents a reading of the Doctor's character which sees him as more bestial than divine.

Searching for figures representing both 'otherness' and (mis) representing the divine, we can turn to many false gods or 'Celestials' who appear in the series. John Vohlidka looks at the way in which God-like beings were represented in the 1970s and early 1980s era of the programme. While on occasion seen as positive messianic figures, he finds on the whole an attack on those who falsely claimed divinity. Such attacks are not necessarily symptomatic of the secularisation of society, but as Vohlidka argues, had always been a part of the Christian tradition. The presentations of these 'Celestials' in this manner therefore suggests the strength of a form of diffusive Christianity in British culture in the 1970s and 80s.

Kieran Tranter develops this in a chapter which demonstrates the way in which *Doctor Who* has constantly shown an antipathy towards divinity throughout its history. Reading *Who* through H. G. Wells and Thomas Huxley, he shows the way in which the show helps provide us with a model of how to live as humans in a universe without divinity.

Karma Waltonen, meanwhile, turns to the question of how cults and their ethical positions have been portrayed in post-2005 *Doctor Who*. From Pompeii to the Cult of Skaro, brainwashing, blind belief and unquestioning obedience are condemned on the show. But what, asks Waltonen, of the cult of the Doctor? What are the implications of his ethics for those who follow him? Her chapter presents a stimulating analysis of the ethics of the programme, teasing out ambiguities and challenges to the viewer.

Science has often been seen as one of religion's many 'Others', especially in the popular image of a conflict between science and faith. David Johnson argues that science-fiction television provides an abstracted way for contemporary society to address controversial issues of science and religion. Looking in detail at this issue in *Doctor Who*, he finds the Doctor plays the role of a mediator, who is capable of building bridges between those who rely purely on science and those who believe in the supernatural. Such a mediator, he concludes, is exactly what we long for today in disputes between science and belief.

Closing this section, Kristine Larsen applies a fascinating Buddhist reading of the Tennant years to explore themes of loss, karma and death in the revived series. Using the work of Tsong-kha-pa, she offers a rich analysis of the way in which key themes in Tennant's episodes reflect Buddhist concerns, highlighting strengths and weaknesses in the Doctor's character as she does so.

The book's penultimate section then turns towards the question of what *Doctor Who* can tell us about the religious positions of the society it was produced in, and the utility of using the programme in its historical context. Andrew Crome's chapter looks at the way in which apocalyptic ideas can be explored through *Doctor Who*. He finds that apocalyptic fears can reveal much about wider cultural concerns at times when episodes were produced, and that the often playful treatment of apocalypse can serve to reveal some of the ambiguities and challenges of apocalyptic thought itself. For those teaching courses on the apocalyptic thought or British religious history, *Doctor Who* is therefore seen to be a useful tool through which to engage students.

Alexander Cummins examines the way in which magic has been portrayed in the programme. Looking at 'The Dæmons' (1971), 'Battlefield' (1989), and 'The Shakespeare Code' (2007), he emphasises the similarities and differences between magical practice on screen and in historical practice. While magic is often portrayed as a primitive interpretation of technology in science fiction (as per Clarke's third law), Cummins shows an increasingly nuanced approach to the subject in *Doctor Who*, which culminates in the subtle presentation of the subject in 'The Shakespeare Code'.

Marcus Harmes, meanwhile, considers different portrayals of the Church of England in the Russell T. Davies and Stephen Moffat eras. Whereas Davies's episodes featured the Church both literally and metaphorically under attack, Moffat portrays a reconstructed, active and militarised (if theologically vague) Church of England. Reading this through Iris Murdoch's novel *The Time of the Angels*, Harmes offers important insights into the way religion is portrayed in *Doctor Who*, and the institutional Church is seen in science fiction in general.

Taking a more contemporary view, Russell Sandberg poses one of the most interesting questions in this volume – Could *Doctor Who* actually become a religion? Sandberg answers this question as a scholar of religion and law, asking whether belief in concepts found in *Doctor Who* would be considered as religious under the UK's 'Equality Act' of 2010. The result is a fascinating tour of the case law that will appeal not just to fans of the show, but to all who are interested in law and religion.

The book draws to a close by looking outwards towards fandom and the audio adventures of the Doctor. Noel Brown examines the way *Doctor Who* audio dramas have dealt with religion. Although sometimes seen as primarily based in nostalgia, Brown shows how a number of Big Finish's earlier audio plays – 'The Holy Terror' and 'Bloodtide' – explore religious issues in a critical and controversial manner. Both plays construct a positive image of secularism through showing its ethical nature and poetic capabilities, while attacking the dangers of religious fundamentalism.

Joel Dark's chapter closes the book by exploring the way in which fans reacted to the cancellation of *Doctor Who* in 1989 through an imaginative engagement with its world. The novels and audios produced in the 1990s and early 2000s showed a creative exploration of hidden voices and continuity issues found in the original televisual material, creating new texts overflowing with different approaches to the programme. Dark argues that these approaches reflect the rabbinic process of Midrash, in which biblical texts are creatively interrogated and reimagined. This is a useful approach to non-televisual *Doctor Who*, and Dark's chapter will be of interest to all examining how fans engage with televisual worlds.

Throughout this book, *Doctor Who* episodes have been referenced simply by their titles and the year of their production. Early serials, which included different episode names for each individual instalment, have therefore been referred to using the serial title as a whole, rather than their individual titles (the episode 'World's End' is therefore referred to as 'The Dalek Invasion of Earth', Part one). Those interested in full details of the writer and director of each episode will find them included in the Appendix at the end of this book.

In summary, this collection is designed to enhance our understanding of how religion interacts with popular culture; how people make use of science fiction in their religious practice and what religious themes in this culture say about secularisation. Most importantly, it provides another way of looking at why *Doctor Who* continues to inspire, to engage and to excite generations of passionate fans, whatever their position on faith. Whether the reader of this book is an academic looking at contemporary religion or a fan wanting to explore the themes and history of the show they love, we hope that *Time and Relative Dimensions in Faith* will prove stimulating, thought provoking, and exciting reading.

1.

Why Time Lords Do Not Live Forever

Courtland Lewis

One might think that a race as powerful as the Time Lords could find a way to live forever. The 1983 serial 'The Five Doctors' shows that at least one Time Lord, Rassilon, did discover the secret of immortality. The most intriguing feature of this serial is that immortality is portrayed as something undesirable, as something proper for only the corrupt and evil. 'The Five Doctors' is not unique. Other examples include: the Master's propensity towards evil, which is partly due to his fear of death and his ability to steal and manipulate regenerations; the Cybermen's desire to be free from death resulting in conquest and destruction; and Omega's entrapment that fosters a hate-filled desire for revenge. The vast majority of Time Lords are content with their limited mortal existence, and this appears to be the result of an acute awareness concerning the dangers of living forever. They hold a position similar to Bernard Williams, who claims, 'There is no desirable or significant property which life would have more of, or have more unqualifiedly, if we lasted forever.'[1] Not only do they share Williams' concerns about the boredom of an immortal life and how death brings value to life, but they are also concerned with the hatred, depression, and desire for destruction that seem to result from being immortal. Time Lords, then, do not live forever because such an existence is both undesirable and dangerous.

Most religions and their respective followers hold a different intuition about the desirability of immortality, and offer intricate positive explanations describing immortality and afterlife. These explanations are meant to inspire good behaviour, assuage the fear of death, and among other things, ensure that those who suffer injustices in this life find justice in the next. As a result, many people proclaim a confidence in and sometimes longing for immortality.

Doctor Who, on the other hand, suggests that such accounts fail to fully consider what an immortal existence, where an individual continues to have subjective personal experiences for all eternity, is like, and fail to adequately provide answers to the question of what *you* would do for all eternity. How would you spend your time? Would you work? Would you set goals? What happens when you run out of goals? How many millions of times could you watch every episode of *Doctor Who* before you get sick of *Doctor Who*? Could you retain your personal identity over such a long period of time? What do you do when you get tired of those around you? More importantly, what do you do when you get tired of yourself?

In the following pages I will examine the themes of immortality found in *Doctor Who*, and will show that it teaches viewers that a continual subjective immortality is undesirable. I will use the phrase 'subjective immortality' to describe a form of existence in which subjects (i.e. individual persons) continue to have personal subjective experiences, in ways similar to their subjective existence on Earth, for all eternity. I will begin by providing a brief survey of how several different world religions describe immortality and afterlife. Next, I will present Charles Hartshorne's three arguments against the desirability of a subjective immortal existence, and will use *Doctor Who* to provide support for each. Finally, I will present a positive account for the desirability of an objective immortal existence where individuals cease to have subjective experiences. I will use the Matrix, as featured in several *Doctor Who* episodes, to suggest that since such an immortal existence is freely accepted by Time Lords, then we as humans might find such an existence preferable to the two alternatives (complete nothingness and subjective immortality).

Before beginning, let me make some important distinctions that will better focus my chapter and help prevent confusion. First, I will be using 'immortality' in a very loose sense to mean 'a life that appears to exist without end'. Because human minds are finite, it is impossible to fully imagine an infinite existence. Also, we do not know enough about many of the characters in *Doctor Who* to determine with certainty whether or not they are immortal. For instance, Captain Jack Harkness appears to be immortal, and both *Doctor Who* and *Torchwood* talk as though he is, yet the 2007 episode 'Gridlock' suggests that the Face of Boe (the being that we are led to believe he will eventually become) is capable of dying. Also, Daleks and Cybermen seem capable of immortality, if they would stop trying to conquer the universe and learn how to get along with others. I will leave conclusions about such matters to someone else.

Second, the way in which I understand the desire to be immortal is as a desire to have an existence similar to the *subjective* one we currently have, yet free from pain, suffering, injustice, and the other features of mortal life that are undesirable. So, when considering immortality, I will do so from a position that takes an idealised version of our current human existence as its hallmark, which is the same approach *Doctor Who* takes. I will focus on how we, as finite beings who perceive the world from a particular point of view of time and space, should understand the desirability of an eternal existence; for this is the issue of immortality that *Doctor Who* is concerned with. The issue of what sort of entity (e.g. soul, pure energy, atoms, etc.) exists as an immortal being will not be addressed. For such an account, I would suggest Paul Edwards' book *Immortality*[2] and Michael Hand's essay 'Regeneration and Resurrection' in *Doctor Who and Philosophy*.[3]

Fear and the Need for Immortality

Death is a mysterious aspect of human existence. As Hiroshi Obayashi states, 'Questions about death and afterlife ... seem thoroughly futile because there are no criteria and no empirical evidence on which to assess the relative merits of the variety of ideas held to be true by people of various cultures.'[4] In an age of advanced technologies and exotic treatments, we seem to fear death more than ever. Medicine increasingly treats death as a disease to be cured, and continues to create new technologies capable of keeping us 'alive' decades after our internal organs cease functioning. In addition, theologians and philosophers continue to work on new strategies to comfort those who fear death and to provide possible explanations for what happens after one dies. The simple fact is the finality of death is scary. Even the Doctor, who gets to regenerate twelve times, does not 'want to go'.[5]

The Tenth Doctor's sentiment towards not wanting to die is shared by most people, which is why explanations of immortality and afterlife feature prominently in various world religions. In Africa, the Mende of Sierra Leone understand death as a social construction that occurs twice in one's life. The first death occurs when a child reaches the age in which she or he can enter one of the community's secret associations.[6] At this important stage of life, the child's spirit leaves the body and is accepted by the spirits. When recognised, the child is born anew as a social person who can enter into the society's communal associations. The second death occurs when the body dies. Upon the death of the body, the spirit continues its existence in another realm, performing many of the same actions the living person did on Earth.

Ancient Mesopotamians believed that upon death the ghost of the dead journeyed to a netherworld, where it would be judged by its earthly credentials. These credentials were determined by how well the living presided over the deceased's corpse. The proper offerings had to be made and the body had to be properly interred, or it could not be accepted into the netherworld. Even if one's credentials were judged favourably, one's immortal existence would be quite grim. As Obayashi points out, except for the account offered in the poem 'Gilgamesh, Enkidu and the Netherworld', where those who have large families or suffered untimely deaths get to enjoy music and other pleasures, most accounts of afterlife suggest a form of existence devoid of any emotional ties and only dimly resembling life on Earth.[7]

Egyptians used elaborate burial rituals and practices to help overcome death and aid the deceased on their journey through afterlife. The three major monotheistic religions have a variety of explanations. The Hebrew Scriptures lack any clear concept of afterlife. Life begins when God breathes the breath of life into an individual, and life ends when that breath is gone. The physical body turns to dust, and the deceased descends to Sheol – a place where the dead remain lifeless and inert.[8] Sheol also appears in the Christian New Testament, under the guise of the Greek notion of Hades – a place where the dead reside. Hades was used to translate Sheol in the Septuagint, the Greek translation of the Hebrew Scriptures. However, the Christian Scriptures also discuss a different sort of afterlife, Gehhenna, where unworthy souls are punished with fire, brimstone, and gnashing of teeth. In both cases, there is disagreement over whether hell is an eternal or temporary residence of the dead.

Christians also maintain that one can avoid hell by having faith in Jesus Christ. Since the formation of Christianity as a religion there have been many attempts to describe the nature of heaven. All appear to agree that heaven is a place where God reigns and it is populated by those whom God finds righteous. Where accounts differ is in the nature of such an existence and who is justified. Some envision heaven as a place where the resurrected are eternally rewarded. Many early Christians envisioned the creation of a new heaven and new earth, with those found righteous populating the new earth. The Christian scriptures describe heaven in many different ways: as a feast, as being filled with mansions, and as a place of justice. As for who is justified, accounts vary greatly. For some, only those who believe in Christ, as the son of God, will enter. Others maintain that God predestines individuals, while some argue that God's forgiveness of sins is universal; so in the end, all will be welcomed into heaven.

Islam accepts the concepts of resurrection, heaven, and hell, but offers a different explanation of how one is judged. For Muslims, Allah creates people for a specific purpose, and their success in carrying out their respective purpose determines the mode in which they return to Allah. Since Allah creates individuals for specific purposes, individualism is a key characteristic and emphasis of Islam, and even though individuals have free will, each is supposed to surrender him/herself to Allah, thereby releasing themselves from all other forms of slavery that are part of one's earthly existence.[9]

For Islam, the human soul is immortal. When a person dies, his or her soul enters the first stage of death, which is known as the Innerworld. In the Innerworld, souls are only in relation to themselves. It is a place of solitude and reflection. The soul stays in the Innerworld until the Day of Resurrection. This second stage of death is a period of judging, where souls encounter their Reckoning. Each soul's fate is determined by the success or failure it had in carrying out its purpose. If the soul is successful, it will enter the heavens (sometimes referred to as the Garden), but if it fails, it enters the hells (often referred to as the Fire). Both judgements determine the soul's proper separation from Allah. In the Garden, souls are 'treated to fountains, cool shades, and chaste *houris* [virgins]...; to carpets, cushions, goblets of gold, and sumptuous food and drink.'[10] In the Fire, souls are treated to 'burning garments, molten drinks, maces of iron, and fire that splits rocks into fragments.'[11] More importantly for both existences, in the Garden souls are in the presence of Allah, which brings great happiness; whereas, in the Fire souls are veiled from Allah, which brings misery. There are some disagreements among Muslims about Reckoning. For instance, some maintain that Allah gives everyone solace eventually, since eternal punishment is inconsistent with Allah's nature.[12] Others avoid this possible inconsistency by maintaining that Allah does not judge souls; instead, souls judge themselves. In other words, Allah gives individuals free will, and if they choose not to follow His plan, then they have freely chosen an afterlife in the Fire.[13]

There are many polytheistic religions, and several ways of understanding each of them. Three of the most familiar polytheistic religions are Jainism, Hinduism, and Buddhism. As A. Chakrabarti describes, all suggest similar systems of saṃsāra (the continual cycle of death and rebirth) and the eventual release from this cycle; though each one refers to this release by a different name: *mokṣa* (Jainism), *apavarga* (Hinduism), and *nirvāna* (Buddhism).[14] According to Charkrabarti, there are four ways of understanding what happens to the soul when one achieves release. From the school of theological thought called Advaita Vedāntin, the soul experiences intense joy at being liberated and sharing in the joy of 'the bliss-breathing company of his truly beloved Lord (a personal God of some sort)'. The Naiyāyika school of thought maintains that the soul does not enjoy any special happiness beyond the 'absolute absence of pain'. For them, happiness is a hindrance to release. The third school of thought suggests that happiness is part of release, but that such happiness should not be sought, and the fourth suggests that even though there is no happiness involved in release, one might imagine its inclusion to help overcome worldly desires.[15] Regardless of the approach one takes to liberation, saṃsāra suggests a form of immortality of the soul, where the soul continues to exist in a cycle of death and rebirth until it is liberated. As seen in the four schools of thought just described, there is much debate about what happens to the soul upon liberation.

Philosophy has just as many explanations for what occurs when one dies. Here are two, one offered by Plato and the other by Friedrich Nietzsche. In Plato's *Apology*, Socrates argues that two possible things occur when one dies: either we cease to be, or the soul changes and migrates.[16] *Ceasing to be* is merely the loss of all consciousness, which is not any different from being in a very deep sleep; whereas *change* allows souls the chance to migrate closer to the Good. For Socrates, neither of these outcomes is undesirable, and so, death and afterlife are nothing to fear. In another dialogue, *Phaedo*, Socrates argues that the soul is immortal and that there is strong evidence to believe in reincarnation.[17]

On the other hand, found throughout Friedrich Nietzsche's writings is the notion of existence continually repeating itself for all eternity, in what he calls the 'eternal recurrence'.[18] For Nietzsche, we are destined to repeat for all eternity the things we do (or do not do) in this life, so we better get it right.

Besides Socrates' suggestion that death is the end of all existence, each of the above accounts offers an explanation of one of two types. The first type provides individuals with an explanation of how they can continue their subjective existence, in some way or another, for all eternity, and is exemplified by all except the polytheistic religions (and possibly Nietzsche) mentioned above.[19] The second type provides an explanation of how we should live our lives while on Earth, so that we will one day escape our individual subjective existence. This type is illustrated by Jainism, Hinduism, and Buddhism, all of which suggest an ideal state of existence where the individual self, which is only illusory, ceases to exist.

As I will show in the next section, though sharing some similarities with the second type, *Doctor Who* offers a third type of explanation. It suggests that even though death can be extremely sad, and sometimes devastating, death is good. It brings value to life, it inspires us to live each day to its fullest, and it challenges us to fight for what is right. This is exactly what Rose tries to get across to her mother Jackie and boyfriend Mickey in 'The Parting of the Ways' (2005): 'It was a better life. And I – I don't mean all the travelling and … seeing aliens and spaceships and things – that don't matter. The Doctor showed me a better way of living your life.'

The Undesirability of Subjective Immortality

The undesirability of subjective immortality (or, at least, scepticism towards its desirability) is seen throughout *Doctor Who*. Take, for example, Omega from the 1973 serial 'The Three Doctors'. Omega (the 'solar engineer') is the first Time Lord, and is honoured for his sacrifice which allowed others to master time-travel. Omega was thought to have died while turning a star into a black hole, but unbeknownst to everyone, he survived the transformation and found himself trapped alone for eternity in a universe of antimatter. His only contact with others was with beings he created using his mental powers, and after millions or perhaps billions of years, he changed from a being who was willing to risk his life for the benefit of others to one who was wanting to destroy that life. His never-ending subjective experience of loneliness and feeling abandoned made him bitter and vindictive, sustained by hatred, and wanting to be worshipped as a god.[20] His knowledge, power, and subjective immortality caused him to see himself as a god – a creator and destroyer of life; and the pain of living forever made him desire the latter. In fact, when Omega removes his protective helmet it is revealed that the only part of himself that still exists is his will's desire for revenge. This is the sort of existence that *Doctor Who* illustrates time and again as representative of subjective immortality, and serves as the basis of why being immortal is undesirable.

How would such an existence change us? Would we become like Omega, who starts off as someone good and engaged in creating, but in the end, seems no better than Sutekh the Destroyer ('Pyramids of Mars' (1975)) or the Master, both of whom wish only to cause suffering and destruction? Omega's example suggests we can live too long, and that an immortal life would eventually become a life of torment. The Master illustrates the same concern: his continued subjective existence, mainly due to his fear of death, drives him to steal regenerations, which only makes him angrier and more determined to destroy. *Doctor Who* shows that if we live forever, we run the risk of creating a world (whether actual or metaphorical) in which we come to see ourselves as a god, tormented by the eternity of our immortal subjective existence, and willing to become destroyers of what we once loved, even ourselves.

Doctor Who is not alone in being sceptical of an immortal subjective existence. Based on Randall Auxier's essay 'Why One Hundred Years is Forever: Hartshorne's Theory of Immortality', philosopher and theologian Charles Hartshorne offers three arguments for why subjective immortality is undesirable.[21] Hartshorne's first argument concerns the spatiotemporal status of humans, and how a subjective immortal existence would eventually lead to humans and God being indistinguishable. For Hartshorne, like humans, God is limited in knowing only actual events and is subject to natural laws.[22] Unlike humans, God is eternal – has no beginning or end. If humans had a subjective immortal existence, then they would be substantively indistinguishable from God. Hartshorne says, 'If our capacity to assimilate new future content and yet remain ourselves, as much untied to our past selves as in contrast to them, is unlimited then in that respect we are exactly as God is'.[23] With the capacity for subjective immortality, humans would cease to be uniquely created beings; they would rival the abilities of God. To avoid such a conclusion, Hartshorne maintains that humans should be spatiotemporally limited, and the best way to do this is to deny a subjective immortal existence. Without subjective immortality humans become incapable of rivaling God because, unlike God, humans would be *beings that die*.

Support for a version of this argument is seen throughout *Doctor Who*. In *Doctor Who* the fear is not so much maintaining an actual distinction between individuals and God; instead, the fear is that individuals who live too long begin to see themselves as God. I already detailed how Omega's subjective immortality led to him thinking he was a god, but we also see the same phenomenon with the Master, Rassilon, and, in the 'The Waters of Mars' (2009), the Doctor. For each individual, their subjective existence is so incredibly long that they cease to identify themselves as being the same type of being they were and, instead, begin to see themselves as a god.

By limiting the subjective existence of humans, Hartshorne lays the foundation for a type of objective immortality, where humans cease both to gain knowledge and to have new experiences. Instead, the entirety of each individual's life is retained in the memory of God. I will hold off on providing a description of Hartshorne's objective immortality until the next section, where I will both examine and show that a similar account is found in *Doctor Who*.

Hartshorne's second argument is directly tied to the first but focuses on the exhaustibility of finite existence. For humans, it is our limited ability to perceive the world from one subjective viewpoint that allows us to have unique identities. If humans, like God, gained the ability to see the world from multiple viewpoints over an infinite amount of time, then we would lose our personal identity and eventually cease to be recognisable as what we once were.[24]

Again, Hartshorne's suggested change is seen in the case of Omega. Let us turn our attention to two different cases. First, the Doctor has only been around for twelve hundred years, yet he must continually fight the urge to transform into something similar to Omega. Hardened by the Time War, the Ninth Doctor is more-than-willing to gleefully watch people be punished ('The End of the World' (2005)). The Tenth Doctor struggles with knowing when to stop killing in 'The Runaway Bride' (2006), and he gives in to his god-like powers to shape existence in 'The Waters of Mars' (2009). The Eleventh Doctor becomes judge, jury, and executioner in 'Dinosaurs on a Spaceship' (2012) and without Amy Pond's help he would have done it again in 'A Town Called Mercy' (2012).

Captain Jack, who is not a Time Lord, fares no better. His immortality is, most of the time, viewed as a curse. He loses the excitement of life, he is forced to watch his friends die, and his life lacks the meaning that death provides. His life is contrasted nicely with his *Torchwood* companion Gwen Cooper, who is acutely aware of the value of life and the deadly vulnerabilities of the ones she loves. Jack must continually fight the temptation to become bitter and hateful. The Doctor and Captain Jack show that even the best heroes are apt to morph into something unrecognisable, if given enough time.

Hartshorne's third argument is that immortality inevitably leads to boredom and monotony. If we lived forever, our experiences would eventually cease to be enriching, we would become disinterested, and would eventually long for death. To imagine the monotony of an eternal existence, think of the lives of elderly individuals who have lost their zest for life and wait in anticipation for death's release. A gripping example of the monotony of an immortal existence can be imagined from the perspective of Ursula, from the 2006 episode 'Love & Monsters'. At the end of the episode the Doctor 'saves' Ursula by preserving her as a paving stone. For the episode, this creates a happy ending where Ursula and Elton Pope get to remain together (and even have a love life).

Setting the storyline aside, think of how terrible Ursula's life will be for the next several eons. Elton will be long gone, and if she is lucky, she will be preserved somewhere nice, instead of being buried in a dump, cracked, placed back on a street, or possibly abused by someone who finds her after Elton dies. Even if she were well taken care of, she would eventually reach the limits of all possible experiences, and inevitably, life would become monotonous. There is no release from her existence, and though Ursula is happy at the end of the episode, it is hard to imagine her continued happiness beyond a certain period of time. At some point, Ursula's existence needs to end, and for Hartshorne 'death is the solution'.[25] Death is what brings value and 'definiteness' to human existence. It allows us to avoid the boredom and monotony that is the result of existing too long. We can only hope the Doctor will one day revisit Ursula and rectify what he has done.

Based on Hartshorne's arguments detailed above and the supporting examples provided by *Doctor Who*, subjective immortality has three shortcomings. First, if humans are immortal, then it appears we would eventually become indistinguishable from God. Hartshorne suggests humans would share the same attributes; whereas, *Doctor Who* suggests a psychological state where we see ourselves as indistinguishable from God. Second, since humans perceive the world through their limited (i.e. finite) perspective, the infinity of experiences would eventually lead to the loss of our human identity. We would forget who we are, and as seen in the first shortcoming, we run the risk of seeing ourselves as gods and/ or becoming miserable in our own existence, the third shortcoming. The third shortcoming suggests that a subjective immortal existence would become a life of boredom and monotony, leading to an overwhelming desire to be released from existence. It is now time to look at a possible alternative, one supported by both *Doctor Who* and Hartshorne.

An Objective Existence We Can Live With

Time Lords do not live forever, nor do most of them want to. The ones who seek immortality typically end up being eternally tormented. For instance, in 'The Five Doctors' Lord Borusa creates an elaborate ruse in order to achieve Rassilon's secret of immortality. However, when he finally receives the promised immortality it is revealed that such an existence is a curse. Borusa must live for all eternity as a living stone bust on Rassilon's tomb. For almost every other Time Lord, the thirteen lives they have are enough, and they appear to be satisfied with their objective immortal existence as part of the Matrix.

Viewers of the new series of *Doctor Who* might be unaware of the Matrix and its role in the life/death of Time Lords. First introduced in the 1976 serial 'The Deadly Assassin' and prominently featured in the 1986 serial 'The Ultimate Foe', the Matrix is a data storage computer that is part of what is called the Amplified Panatropic Computer Network (APC Net). The APC Net connects the Matrix to various TARDISes, which allows them to collect the bio-data extracts of all Time Lords. The Matrix, then, stores all of this data, which includes every experience, memory, and bit of knowledge, and keeps it on file for all eternity. When Time Lords use up their twelve regenerations their subjective existence comes to an end, but the entirety of their experiences as subjective beings continues to exist within the extra-dimensional framework of the Matrix. They are not simply stored, like we might imagine data stored on a computer, but their lives are continually replayed as a form of virtual reality. They do not experience this 'playback', for they no longer have a subjective viewpoint in which to experience it. Rather, they exist in a state where others can learn, remember, and be enriched by the lives of those who are deceased. So, upon death Time Lords do not cease to exist. They merely shift from a subjective to an objective existence, to an existence where they stop having new experiences as individuals (assuming no one tampers with the Matrix), yet continue to exist as part of the sustained virtual reality of the Matrix and as contributing to the creative forces of the universe.

Similar to the Matrix, Hartshorne maintains that when humans die, instead of continuing to exist subjectively or merely ceasing to exist, they stop having subjective experiences and exist objectively in the mind of God – each person is perfectly preserved in the memory of God as objective beings.[26] Auxier describes objective immortality as '...the view that God loses nothing of the past ...', and for Hartshorne, it means that '...the past, including its subjective immediacies, is perfectly had and retained, and that there is no limit on this activity in the future'.[27] In other words, God perfectly remembers each person's existence, including the subjective feelings each person experienced while alive.

Hartshorne maintains that objective immortality not only avoids the shortcoming of subjective immortality, but also prevents the meaninglessness of total annihilation. As a positive account, Hartshorne suggests that with an objective existence, if one engages in a life of creative enterprises, then one's life will bring joy to God and become a source of God's creative force. If one chooses to live a destructive life, then one's life will be a source of pain for God and, therefore, contribute nothing positive to the universe. So even though the subjective individual ceases to experience new phenomena, their objective existence continues to exist and have creative influence for all eternity.

To put it in _Doctor Who_ terms, the Doctor will one day run out of regenerations and cease to have a subjective existence. At that time, he will only exist as an objective being within the Matrix. However, because of the type of life he lived – one filled with excitement, passion, creating, etc., he will forever be remembered and studied by the Time Lords. Of course, the Time Lords will also study the Master and Omega, but they will do so in sadness, as a means to avoid contributing to the creation of such individuals.

To think of it more practically, imagine if the BBC cancelled _Doctor Who_ (for some readers, this is not hard to imagine – we have already experienced it!). If this occurred, there would be no more new episodes, just as when we die there are no more new subjective experiences. However, there would remain an impressive catalogue of past episodes. These past episodes exist objectively, and can be watched and enjoyed again and again; and just as after the show's cancellation in 1989, they can serve as a source of joy to inspire the creation of new fan fiction and non-fiction. The objective existence Hartshorne supports works in the same way, except we do not seem to have the ability to be rebooted like *Doctor Who*.

Is such an immortal existence more desirable than subjective immortality? As shown above, a subjective immortal existence is undesirable because it threatens the relationship between humans and God, it threatens the identity of humans, and it appears to lead to boredom and monotony. An objective immortality avoids all three of these implications – our status as created does not change, our individual personality cannot change since we cease to have new experiences, and there is no subjective self to experience boredom and monotony. So, in regards to these three implications, an objective immortality is superior to subjective immortality.

On the other hand, one might complain that objective immortality is nothing more than a façade of complete nothingness, since only memories of the self, and not the subjective self, continue to exist. However, the nature of the Matrix, or in Hartshorne's case the nature of God, prevents it from becoming mere nothingness. I understand the fear of nothingness in terms of Albert Camus' discussion of the absurd in *The Myth of Sisyphus*.[28] For Camus, human life is analogous to Sisyphus's punishment to push a rock up a hill, to only have it roll back down. We as humans spend our lives doing a variety of things (e.g. making friends, crafting goals, getting degrees, etc.), but all of these things, in the end, appear to be meaningless, since we will one day die and eventually – no matter how great or memorable we were – be completely forgotten. Camus appears to capture what people fear most about nothingness: if we simply cease to exist, and all of our accomplishments are eventually forgotten, then life seems meaningless. Objective immortality and the Matrix avoid this conclusion in one important way: we are never forgotten.

It is true that our subjective selves cease to exist, and even though other humans might forget us, we are never completely forgotten. Due to the nature of the Matrix/God, our lives are eternally sustained as objective markers of our existence, which can then be reflected upon, in order to influence the creative forces of those reflecting on us. As a result, objective immortality is different and more desirable than mere nothingness.

Some of the explanations of immortality described above provide similar accounts. The polytheistic religions mentioned above suggest that an existence free from the suffering of individuality is desirable, and other than nothingness, the only way to achieve such an existence is to become one with something beyond human existence. These accounts differ from Hartshorne and the Matrix because they suggest a cessation of all individuality. The objective immortality suggested by the Matrix retains one's individuality, but denies the torment that comes from an immortal subjective existence. Nietzsche's eternal recurrence is also similar, but differs in the sense that it assumes that our subjective experiences will be repeated for all eternity, which is not the objective existence of the Matrix or Hartshorne.

The objective existence that the Matrix offers, for some, might appear to be no better than non-existence. However, such a sentiment seems based on our inability to adequately imagine an objective existence. Our status as subjective beings prevents us from imagining an existence where we no longer have subjective experiences. Our best attempts to do so result in something like an imagined existence of being stored on a computer or being in some sort of persistent vegetative state, where we find ourselves 'trapped' and unable to have new experiences. Such imaginations are fundamentally flawed, for they assume a subjective self 'trapped' in some way, not allowed to have new experiences. An objective existence maintains there is no longer an individual subjective *self* that is capable of being trapped.

Even though such an existence is difficult for some to accept, if it is better to exist than to not exist, and existing subjectively is undesirable, then our best option appears to be some sort of objective existence. The Matrix provides such an existence, and for Time Lords this appears to be enough. Granted, *Doctor Who* is fiction, but its conclusions about immortality are supported by both philosophical and theological arguments. The conclusion might not be the one we are used to, but maybe with this explanation of why subjective immortality is undesirable, it is a conclusion we can learn to live with.

The End

Doctor Who teaches viewers that death brings value to life, whether it happens once, or in the case of Time Lords, thirteen times. It makes the things we do during the precious moments of our finite mortal life meaningful, because we know we only have one chance. It shows us that even though living a little longer might be preferable to the short existence we currently have, being immortal is a nightmare that leads to suffering, madness, and the desire to destroy. Instead of dedicating our limited time and energy to gaining immortality, *Doctor Who* challenges us to ignore how our lives will end and what the afterlife might consist of, and instead, focus our energies on living each day as though we are immortal – taking advantage of the opportunities and relationships we as mortal beings have now. As the Ninth Doctor tells Rose, 'You lot, you spend all your time thinking about dying, like you're gonna get killed by eggs, or beef, or global warming, or asteroids. But you never take time to imagine the impossible. Like maybe you survive.'[29]

The survival that the Doctor refers to here is one of taking advantage of the opportunities life offers in the here-and-now, instead of worrying about how we will die and live our immortal existence. We should live our subjective life on Earth similarly to the Doctor – developing meaningful relationships, helping those who are vulnerable, and striving for and achieving great things. Furthermore, we should be satisfied with the objective immortality that the Doctor will one day experience. Though the objective immortality *Doctor Who* envisages is probably completely different from what we first thought we desired, both *Doctor Who* and Hartshorne maintain it is one with which we can be satisfied; one that allows for a rewarding life on Earth and one that is free from the dangers of living too long.

2.

Pushing the Protest Button: *Doctor Who's* Anti-Authoritarian Ethic

Gabriel McKee

In the 2010 *Doctor Who* episode 'The Beast Below', the Doctor and Amy find themselves in London, but not the London we know – thousands of years in our future, the city has been removed from Earth to space in order to protect its populace from certain destruction due to massive solar flares. The Doctor detects something strange about Starship UK, which he suspects is a well-disguised police state. And little is stranger here than the spaceship-nation's 'voting booths', which show the ship's citizens a video explaining something awful about the nature of their world. They are then given a choice of two large, red buttons to press: one, labelled 'Forget', will erase their memory of the video's contents and allow the status quo to go on unchanged. The other, labelled 'Protest', records their objection to the state of affairs revealed in the mysterious video, with unspecified consequences for the voter. The voting booth won't show the Doctor the video – it can tell he's not human, and thus not entitled to vote – but he chooses the 'Protest' button, sight unseen. 'This is what I do', he explains, 'every time, every day, every second.' This sums up the Doctor brilliantly – a being who will always, always push the 'Protest' button. And by the episode's end, this instinct to protest has freed the people of Starship UK from their self-imposed amnesia. The Doctor is a revolutionary messiah, capable of transforming simple protest into outright liberation.

Since its inception, *Doctor Who* has displayed a strong opposition to violence and tyranny. The Doctor's greatest enemies – the Daleks, the Cybermen, the Sontarans – represent militarism, oppression, and the suppression of the individual to the collective. Moreover, he has consistently, and successfully, opposed these highly symbolic villains through non-violence, using instead his wits and ingenuity to turn the villains' destructive impulses loose upon themselves. The Doctor is anti-authoritarian, and occasionally even an anarchist, and his adventures put the ethical application of his anti-authoritarian ideals at the forefront. His very character represents the disruption of dehumanising, violent, and tyrannical systems.

For the Doctor, individual liberty is the greatest – perhaps even the only – good. In the Second Doctor story 'The Macra Terror' (1967), he and his companions travel to a space colony whose populace is hypnotised into blind obedience of their rulers. When they sleep, they are programmed by eerie recordings: 'Everything in the colony is good and beautiful. You must accept without question. You must obey orders. The leaders of the colony know what is best. In the morning when you wake up, you will be given some work. You will be glad to obey. You will question nothing in the colony.' When he finds the hypnosis machine that has been indoctrinating his companion Ben, he disables it. When Ben complains that it's 'against the law' to interfere with the equipment, this prompts the Doctor to smash the machine even more furiously. The Doctor encourages his companion Polly to outright rebellion against her hypnotic programming: 'Now, Polly, I want you to forget everything that you've been dreaming … It's just possible that you've been given a series of orders while you've been asleep. You know, do this, do that, do the other thing. My advice to you is don't do anything of the sort! Don't just be obedient! Always make up your own mind!'

This rebellious spirit is particularly pronounced in Patrick Troughton's tenure as the Doctor. In his first story, 'The Power of the Daleks' (1966), this incarnation of the Doctor travels to a space colony called Vulcan where a crashed Dalek vessel has been recovered. The colony is in the midst of a power struggle between its hidebound administrators and a group of violent rebels, who wish to use the Daleks to overthrow their government. The Doctor does not choose sides in this conflict, but rather plays both sides against each other. By the serial's final episode, the Doctor has defeated the Daleks, but only after they have murdered most of the colony and left both the reigning governor and the rebels powerless (literally and figuratively – their power system is destroyed and will take months to rebuild). The Doctor is rather flippant about the shambles he has left the colony in: 'I did a lot of damage, didn't I?', he asks, then adds with a chuckle, 'I think we'd better get out of here before they send us the bill'. There is a playfulness about this appetite for chaos, but it is not without its purpose: there is a strong implication in these concluding lines that the Doctor deliberately destroyed their infrastructure, not just to defeat the Daleks, but to give the two factions a clean slate and force them to cooperate.

A similar situation unfolds in the Tom Baker-era story 'The Sun Makers' (1977). In this serial, the Doctor finds himself on the planet Pluto in the far future, where the entire planet is ruled by a heartless corporation with a byzantine system of bureaucracy. The citizenry is subject to crippling taxes, paid by a populace that is kept docile with mind-controlling drugs. The planet also contains a large band of outlaws that has dropped out of society entirely, living a vagabond existence in the Undercity. But at the outset, these outlaws are not much better than the Company – the leader of the band, Mandrel, is a thief and kidnapper who, at one point, threatens to torture the Doctor with a branding iron. But the Doctor awakens what can only be described as a sense of class consciousness in the outlaws, prompting them to question the nature of the Company and its control over their world. The thieves' selfish greed turns into a thirst for freedom, and thus transformed they overthrow the Company (the surface radicalism of 'The Sun Makers' earned it some criticism: fan writer Jeremy Bentham wrote that the story was 'laced with left-wing propaganda').[1] Without the Doctor's guidance, the state of affairs on Pluto would likely have remained unchanged. He brings liberation, but his salvation does not free the people of Pluto from their responsibility for their future. Rather, he is a catalyst whose presence turns the potential for change into actuality.

The Doctor's rebellious impulses were muted in the earliest episodes featuring William Hartnell as the Doctor, who defined himself in 'The Daleks' Master Plan' (1965-66) as 'a citizen of the universe, and a gentleman to boot'. Compared to later incarnations, the First Doctor seems downright conservative, even assisting the people of the planet Marinus in rebooting the Conscience of Marinus, an all-powerful computer that they have allowed to control their minds to combat crime and war. 'They no longer had to decide what was wrong or right', the machine's caretaker explains, 'the machine decided for them' – and the Doctor does not protest. Nevertheless, *Doctor Who*'s first producer, Verity Lambert, intended Hartnell's Doctor to represent a voice outside of accepted political divisions. In their book *Doctor Who: The Unfolding Text*, John Tulloch and Manuel Alvarado conclude that Lambert had cast William Hartnell instead of a more conventional, square-jawed hero 'to represent ambiguity and contradiction' rather than 'uncontradictory patriarch and law-giver'.[2]

Nevertheless, the Jon Pertwee era offers a powerful challenge to the idea that the Doctor is an anti-authoritarian pacifist. It was in this period of *Doctor Who* that the Doctor served as a full-time advisor to UNIT, which was, essentially, a paramilitary organisation. Tulloch and Alvarado quote Lambert as criticising Pertwee's Doctor for being 'very moral, very upright, very dependable... always ringing up heads of state'.[3] *Doctor Who* stories would occasionally include references to, say, class inequalities, 'but generally *Doctor Who* stepped back from this and displaced stratification through the Doctor's wit and action into a cool "establishment" superiority'.[4] The Doctor, this suggests, cannot be a true rebel; his easy association with figures of power, and his general detachment from societal strife once the alien invasions are quashed, would seem to cast him as a defender of the status quo.

But it is important to note that even the 'upright and dependable' Third Doctor in fact had quite tense relations with UNIT commander Brigadier Lethbridge-Stewart, and opposed his decisions as often as he supported them. The Doctor frequently used his advisory role to guide UNIT *away* from the use of force. In the story 'Doctor Who and the Silurians' (1970), for instance, the Doctor dissuades a species of subterranean reptiles from invading the planet. Following his negotiations, however, Lethbridge-Stewart destroys their underground base, and the Doctor is furious. (The Silurians' aquatic cousins become embroiled in a similar situation in the loose sequel to this story, 'The Sea Devils' (1972)).

He sees this practical use of violence as the veritable undoing of his exhausting efforts at preventing war between the two species: after all his promises of peace, the humans have insisted on solving the problem with a one-sided war. In working with UNIT, the Doctor is working from within the system to change it, to replace the humans' knee-jerk resort to violence with a more diplomatic approach in conflicts with extraterrestrials, monsters and villains. His position with UNIT is almost a kind of camouflage similar to that of the TARDIS itself. The Doctor's time machine has the exterior form of a metropolitan police box, a symbol of law and order; but inside is something alien, bizarre, and constantly changing – chaos masquerading as order.

Underlying the Doctor's advocacy of rebellion is a powerful ethic of nonviolence (or, at the very least, an abhorrence of any potentially fatal violence). In 'Genesis of the Daleks' (1975), Tom Baker's Fourth Doctor finds himself on the planet Skaro, at the time of his greatest enemy's creation. He has been ordered by the Time Lords to either find the Daleks' weakness, alter their makeup so that they are less evil, or destroy them outright in their infancy. Placing explosive charges outside the incubator room containing the mutated beings that are to become the most evil creatures in the universe, he is faced with a concrete example of a common hypothetical dilemma. The Doctor wonders aloud: 'Do I have the right? Simply touch one wire against the other and that's it. The Daleks cease to exist. Hundreds of millions of people, thousands of generations can live without fear, in peace, and never even know the word "Dalek".' Sarah Jane Smith argues in favour of destroying the Daleks, comparing them to a plague – something the Doctor would not hesitate to eradicate. 'But if I kill,' the Doctor continues, 'wipe out a whole intelligent life form – then I become like them. I'd be no better than the Daleks.' Ultimately, the Doctor has the choice taken out of his hands. But the mere act of questioning the decision implies its conclusion. For the Doctor, no act of murder can ever be truly justified, no matter how beneficial its result might be.

Recent series have seen a darkening of the Doctor's character, resulting in an apparent shift in this nonviolent ethic. For instance, the Matt Smith episode 'Dinosaurs on a Spaceship' (2012) is, on the surface, a light-hearted episode, full of wise-cracking robots, amusing banter and the eponymous dinosaurs. But at the episode's conclusion, the Doctor essentially executes an enemy, placing a missile-attracting homing beacon on the spaceship of the pirate Solomon. It would seem that the Doctor may not be so pacifistic after all – until the very next episode, 'A Town Called Mercy'. Here the Doctor finds an alien living in the Old West – a doctor named Kahler-Jex who has provided the struggling frontier town of Mercy, Nevada with electricity. But Jex is no simple altruist – the Doctor learns that he is a war criminal who has committed countless atrocities, and is hiding in the town to avoid the vengeance of one of his victims, a botched cyborg named Kahler-Tek. The Doctor attempts to turn Jex over to his pursuer, bringing him to the edge of town at gunpoint. It appears he is going to allow Jex to be killed, just as with Solomon, until companion Amy Pond stops him. 'What's happened to you, Doctor?' she asks. 'When did killing someone become an option?'

The Doctor argues that Jex has to answer for his crimes, prompting Amy to ask where that logic ends: 'And what then? Are you gonna hunt down everyone that's made a gun or a bullet or a bomb?' The Doctor's response indicates remorse for not taking a harder line in the past – for instance, in 'Genesis of the Daleks'. 'Every time I negotiate, I try to understand. Well, not today. No. Today I honour the victims first – His, the Master's, the Daleks', all the people who died because of my mercy!' But Amy's response reminds the Doctor of the reason for his past leniency: 'See, this is what happens when you travel alone for too long. Well, listen to me, Doctor. We can't be like him. We have to be better than him.' In 'Genesis of the Daleks', the Doctor raises the dilemma, while a human encourages him to solve a problem with violence. Here, it is the Doctor that is threatening violence, and a human who calls him back to his moral centre. Later, the Doctor states unequivocally: 'Violence doesn't end violence. It extends it.' It would be better to let a criminal like Jex live as a fugitive than to submit him to a justice that would have him killed, and so the Doctor attempts to help Jex escape Tek – until Jex's own sense of guilt leads him to provide his own ultimate punishment, detonating his ship rather than using it to escape. Justice that is brought by violence, this episode argues, is no justice at all. Redemption cannot be brought about by punishment, but must emerge from within. The similarities between the cases of Solomon and Jex are striking, and it's notable that Amy and Rory were not present to witness the Doctor's decision to let Solomon die; it seems unlikely that they would have allowed him to act as he did had they been there. Rather than a simple example of the Doctor committing violence, then, an action like the killing of Solomon is part of a larger moral arc that underscores the Doctor's commitment to nonviolence, albeit showing that he needs close contact with humans to keep him humanistic.

Melissa Beattie makes a case that the Doctor's character arc in the Russell T. Davies era shows his struggle to return from a 'wartime morality' that he adopted during the Time War – a morality that led to his decision to destroy both the Time Lords and the Daleks. In this context, the darkness of the Doctor's character in this period reflects the difficulty of shifting from a temporary moral code that justifies violence back to a peacetime, nonviolent ethic: 'Series 1 through 4 represent a healing process, complete with backsliding and missteps, such as the regression into solitude to protect others suggesting a re-entry into a state of emotional lockdown much as was seen in Series 1 of the revival'.[5] And the signs for a more calculating ethic are seen earlier, as well, particularly in the Sylvester McCoy era and the *New Adventures* novels. Vincent O'Brien discusses the Daleks' mythologising of the Doctor as the Ka Faraq Gatri – the Destroyer of Worlds.[6] This term (hinted at in Davros' reference to the Doctor as 'the destroyer of worlds' in the 2008 episode 'Journey's End') first appeared in the *New Adventures* novels, but it likely has its root in the serial 'Remembrance of the Daleks', when the Doctor tricks the Daleks into destroying their home planet Skaro. The facts of these instances of rather extreme, even genocidal, violence in the Doctor's history make difficult any argument for his nonviolence. However, shifts in character – even rather extreme ones – are inherent in the Doctor's character and the concept of regeneration.

But even in these cases, contingent factors – the presence of human beings to question the Doctor's actions; the grander arc of the character – leave room for the possibility of the audience being led to different ethical conclusions than those the Doctor himself reaches. It could even be argued that actions like the destruction of Skaro or the scorched-earth conclusion of the Time War are indicative of the Doctor's shift toward a place of true moral darkness suggested by the introduction of the Valeyard, an evil future incarnation of the Doctor, in 'Trial of a Time Lord' (1986). Further evidence of this progression appears in the episode 'The Name of the Doctor' (2013), in which the Great Intelligence – referring specifically to the case of the pirate Solomon, among others – states that 'the Doctor lives his life in darker hues day upon day, and he will have other names before the end: the Storm, the Beast, the Valeyard.' The darkening hues of recent seasons of *Doctor Who* have served to undermine the Doctor's role as a moral authority, but this merely gives the programme a richer and more complex moral fabric. Una McCormack argues that '*Doctor Who*, in [its] most recent incarnation, is sceptical of all those who claim the ability to perfect or deliver us – prophets or doctors, religious visionaries or scientific utopians, anyone who promises escape from the here-and-now into eternal life, anyone offering consolation in place of action – including, occasionally, the Doctor himself.'[7] The Doctor's actions are no longer held up as singularly heroic and ethical; the audience is led to question his choices rather than simply accepting that he, as the hero, will do the right thing. This injection of moral ambiguity complicates the Doctor's personal role as hero or saviour, but it only enriches the moral tapestry of the grander canon of *Doctor Who*. We can now look at actions like the destruction of Skaro or the conclusion of the Time War as dark moments in the Doctor's past from which he is struggling to recover, moral traumas that occasionally lead him to regress. But, as in 'A Town Called Mercy', we the audience are led to cheer the Doctor's return to nonviolence, understanding, and mercy. Even if the Doctor's traditional heroic and/or messianic role has become more ambiguous, this does not mean he can no longer be a salvific figure – rather, it leads us to question our understanding of what to expect of a saviour.

The Doctor's insistence on new ways of thinking and a search for nonviolent solutions puts him in the territory of Leo Tolstoy, whose book *The Kingdom of God is Within You* identifies 'the non-resistance to evil by force' as the central, albeit generally neglected, tenet of Christianity. Christ's doctrine, Tolstoy states, 'consisted not only of the prohibition of resistance to evil by force, but gave a new conception of life and a means of putting an end to conflict between all men, not by making it the duty of one section only of mankind to submit without conflict to what is prescribed to them by certain authorities, but by making it the duty of all – and consequently of those in authority – not to resort to force against anyone in any circumstances'.[8] For Tolstoy, this was the true essence of the Sermon on the Mount. It is essentially a philosophy of anti-authoritarianism and rebellion, for the machinery by which the entire state functions is based on either violence or the tacit support of violence: 'All state obligations are against the conscience of a Christian – the oath of allegiance, taxes, law proceedings, and military service. And the whole power of government rests on these very obligations.'[9] The state depends on the participation of its subjects, and it is this refusal to participate, rather than any revolutionary sentiment, that is destructive to government. Thus 'Christianity in its true sense puts an end to government'.[10]

Other Christian pacifists have also linked nonviolence directly to anarchism. Jacques Ellul even makes pacifism, rather than simple rejection of the state, the defining feature of anarchy.[11] William Lloyd Garrison, best known today as a central figure in the American anti-slavery movement, was a strong advocate of non-resistance, and in 1838 drafted a statement decreeing not only war to be unchristian, but also participation at any level in the entire machinery of state that leads to violence – including the manufacture and ownership of weapons, holding any political office connected to war or imprisonment, seeking the protection of the law in criminal or civil matters, and voting in public elections.[12] For Garrison and others, pacifism is by necessity connected to the outright rejection of any government that uses violence as a tool.

In the *New Adventures* novel *No Future,* an anarchist rebel in 1976 Britain describes the Doctor as 'the purest sort of anarchist', which prompts a smirking dismissal from Lethbridge-Stewart, who proposes instead 'that the Doctor symbolises the best values of British life. Eccentricity, the creative amateur, and civilisation'.[13] The Doctor himself does not take a side in their argument. But despite his anti-authoritarian leanings, it would be difficult to class the Doctor as an outright anarchist.[14] The Doctor's attitudes and actions are closer to the territory of one of the most influential Christian rebels in history: Martin Luther King, Jr. Tolstoy's philosophy had a strong influence on Mahatma Gandhi, who in turn influenced King, who turned nonviolent resistance into a major transformative force in American society. In the essay 'My Pilgrimage to Nonviolence', King rejects the term 'non-resistance', which both Garrison and Tolstoy used:

> My study of Gandhi convinced me that true pacifism is not nonresistance to evil, but nonviolent resistance to evil ... Gandhi resisted evil with as much vigor and power as the violent resister, but he resisted with love instead of hate. True pacifism is not unrealistic submission to evil power, as [Reinhold] Niebuhr contends. It is rather a courageous confrontation of evil by the power of love, in the faith that it is better to be the recipient of violence than the inflicter of it, since the latter only multiplies the existence of violence and bitterness in the universe, while the former may develop a sense of shame in the opponent, and thereby bring about a transformation and change of heart.[15]

This is, essentially, the doctrine of the Doctor as well, for though he eschews violence, he is always an active resister of evil. As he says in 'Genesis of the Daleks', to use his enemies' tools against them cannot bring victory, for it is precisely those tools that make them evil. The Doctor's struggles against fictional monsters extrapolate from the very real struggles of his earthly predecessors, embodying the philosophy of nonviolence in a form more easily comprehensible to a young audience. Though the Doctor's fight against the Daleks and the Cybermen pales in comparison to the fight against real-world discrimination, injustice and war, this sort of fiction can nevertheless be a tool in those struggles as well.

Much pacifist thought – and particularly that of Gandhi and King – depends on an inversion of commonplace logic where defeat becomes victory. This kind of reversal has scriptural roots, for instance in Paul's insistence in 1 Cor. 1:27 that 'God chose the foolish things of the world to shame the wise'. This is reflected, too, in the Doctor's choice of companions and his attitude to the powerful figures he encounters on his journeys. Rather than choosing to travel with political leaders, military commanders, or brilliant scientists, the Doctor tends to choose far more humble companions: a rookie investigative reporter (Sarah Jane Smith), a bright teenager (Adric), a shop assistant (Rose Tyler), a temp (Donna Noble). His companions, generally speaking, are unremarkable on the surface. Moreover, in his encounters with the powerful people of the universe, the Doctor is frequently cool, even dismissive. Witness his irritation with billionaire technocrat Henry van Statten, who 'owns the Internet' ('Dalek' (2005)); his lack of deference to the similarly-wealthy Kazran Sardick, the richest man in Sardicktown ('A Christmas Carol' (2010)), his snubbing of the Time Lords on Gallifrey when they attempt to make him their President ('The Five Doctors' (1983)). The Doctor much prefers to hear the insights of those whom societal hierarchies, prejudices, and assumptions leave out. In this, he echoes George Fox, the founder of the Society of Friends, commonly known as Quakers. Fox considered a refusal to honour society's ideas about respecting high and low station as part of his religious mission. In his autobiography he writes, 'when the Lord sent me forth into the world, He forbade me to put off my hat to any, high or low; and I was required to Thee and Thou all men and women, without any respect to rich or poor, great or small ... neither might I bow or scrape with my leg to any one; and this made the sects and professions to rage'.[16] These signs of radical egalitarianism led to great scandal and persecution in the early days of the Quakers.[17]

Other radical religious figures of the period surrounding the English Civil War similarly embraced the idea of radical equality – cutting down the haughty and raising up the low. This is one of the possible origins of the term 'Leveller', which described one of the more radical politico-religious groups of mid-seventeenth-century England. A typical figure of the era is George Foster, an unaffiliated mystic whose 1650 pamphlet *The Sounding of the Last Trumpet* describes a vision of a figure on white horse 'cutting down all men and women that he met with that were higher than the middle sort, and raised up those that were lower than the middle sort, and made them all equal; and cried out, "Equality, equality, equality" … I will … make the low and poor equal with the rich'.[18] The Doctor's approach lacks the eschatological angle of Foster's vision, but he too treats all those he encounters on their own merits, frequently finding those who appear most ordinary to in fact be the most remarkable. Thus is the wisdom of the world proved foolishness, and vice versa.

This logic, too, upends the meanings of 'defeat' and 'victory'. In the David Tennant episode 'The Last of the Time Lords' (2007), we see a successful nonviolent revolution that makes this reversal manifest. The Master has conquered the Earth, with the help of the British electorate and an army of deadly alien creatures called the Toclafane. For a year, he has held the Doctor prisoner – artificially aged hundreds of years until he is a withered homunculus trapped inside a birdcage. His companion Martha has spent the year travelling the world in secret to organise a resistance force against the Master. But, when the moment for that resistance to act finally comes, we learn that she has not been organising an army, but rather something more akin to a worldwide prayer circle. 'I told a story', Martha says, 'That's all. No weapons, just words. I did just what the Doctor said. I went across the continents all on my own. And everywhere I went I found the people and I told them my story… I told them about the Doctor, and I told them to pass it on. To spread the word so that everyone would know about the Doctor.' At an appointed hour, the people of the world chant the Doctor's name, imbuing him with power and restoring his body and mind. And at the culmination of this moment of reversal, where the Doctor's utter defeat at the hands of the Master becomes the triumph of the people of the Earth, the Doctor grants his greatest enemy forgiveness. Here it is weakness that has prevailed – the Doctor's weakness as a wretched prisoner, Martha's weakness as a revolutionary who eschews violence, the weakness of the human race in the face of a foe too powerful to ever defeat by force.

The events at the conclusion of 'The Last of the Time Lords' embody an on-going theme in *Doctor Who*: the Third Option. On the surface, we see two possibilities in Martha's situation prior to the Doctor's revival: either her victory over the Master (through what we have been led to believe is her organisation of a worldwide uprising) or the final defeat of humanity at the hands of his Toclafane minions. Instead, we are surprised by the introduction of a third option: that the Master can be defeated through the nonviolent action of the human race as a whole. 'The Beast Below' presents a similar disruption of an apparent binary: the secret at the heart of Starship

UK is that their city is built on the back of an enormous star whale, the last of its kind, and that they have been torturing this creature to keep it moving. The Doctor sees only two options: he can either free the star whale from its bondage, thereby destroying the city; or he can lobotomise the creature, allowing the city to survive but committing an unredeemable crime against a spectacular creature. Companion Amy Pond introduces a third option: free the whale from its bondage, but seek its consent in the survival of the city (a proposition which the star whale happily accepts). From the Jon Pertwee era on, *Doctor Who* frequently featured stories directly inspired by political conflicts of the day, but the Doctor rarely if ever 'took sides'. Instead, appearing in the midst of a conflict divided into a binary opposition, the Doctor generally represents a third way – often moderate, but sometimes simply outside that left-right opposition. This advocacy of new solutions to old problems is inherently anti-establishment, viewing the entire concept of binary oppositions as a sign of an ossification that prevents real growth.

This rejection of both sides of a black-and-white division is a disruption of programming, the programming that encourages (or even allows) us to view any subject from only two angles. The Doctor's history is rife with programming rewritten, hypnotism defeated, and controls smashed. The Fifth Doctor's companion Turlough, when first introduced, was a saboteur trained by the Black Guardian to destroy the Doctor, until the Time Lord's kindness changed his outlook. In 'Victory of the Daleks' (2010), the humanoid bomb Edwin Bracewell, who was created by the Daleks but believes himself human, is convinced by the Doctor that he is more human than machine and thus averts his detonation. 'Asylum of the Daleks' (2012) introduces Oswin Oswald, a human mind trapped in a Dalek body who believes, like Bracewell, that she is human. The Doctor, in this case, believes she is beyond redemption, that her Dalek form will ultimately win out over her human mind; she too asserts her humanity and defeats the Daleks, allowing the Doctor to escape their asylum planet.

But it is the Eleventh Doctor's companion Rory Williams who offers the most powerful example of disrupted programming. Rory dies in the episode 'Cold Blood' (2010), shot by a Silurian and then sucked through a crack in reality that erases every trace of his existence from history. We watch as Amy's memories of him slip away, her grief being replaced in mere moments by forgetfulness and then fear about the crisis at hand. Rory mysteriously returns in

'The Pandorica Opens' (2010) an event that the Doctor is at a loss to explain – he describes it as 'a miracle', which is saying something on a show where the impossible occurs every week. Rory – or a being bearing an uncanny resemblance to him – is stationed with the Roman legion at Stonehenge in the year 102CE, and has full memories of two lives – that of a bumbling twenty-first-century nurse, and that of a first-century Roman centurion. As the episode progresses, we learn that this isn't really Rory, but an Auton – a plastic alien android programmed with Rory's memories. He was also programmed, it turns out, to kill his twenty-first-century self's fiancée Amy Pond, which he does despite his conscious, human mind's protests.

At the opening of next episode 'The Big Bang', the universe has been all but destroyed, rewritten out of existence just as Rory was in 'Cold Blood'. Rory, now revealed as a machine, is cradling Amy's lifeless form, his human grief having overtaken his android heartlessness. When the Doctor finds him, the Time Lord downplays that grief in light of the destruction of the universe: 'Do you know how many lives now never happened, all the people who never lived?' the Doctor asks. 'Your girlfriend isn't more important than the whole universe.' Whereupon android-Rory rises up and punches the Doctor in the jaw, shouting, 'She is to me!' Rory thereby passes the Time Lord's test: in the Doctor's eyes, he has now proven that he's the real Rory Williams. For the Doctor, there is no qualitative difference between the real Rory and an android programmed to believe he's Rory, provided that the android displays appropriate, human emotions. This, indeed, is the very definition of humanity: the ability to overcome programming, to make a choice outside of those prepared for us, to exceed our operational parameters. In the face of mechanical determinism, *Doctor Who* loudly proclaims that machines, even those designed only to kill, can will themselves into humanity with the right amount of *caritas*.

The Doctor's disruption of dangerous programming extends to the core of our system of ethics: whether the ends can ever justify the means. In our society, we frequently hear about survival, about 'existential threats' justifying the suspension of otherwise ironclad restrictions on our behaviour as individuals, nations, and a species. In the audio drama 'Spare Parts' (2002), which recounts one version of the origin of the Cybermen, we see *Doctor Who*'s response to teleological ethics. The Cybermen originate on the planet Mondas, an exact twin of Earth hidden from us by its position on the opposite side of the sun. Mondas is slowly drifting out of this orbit, however, and as its surface has grown colder, its people have retreated underground. A mission has been undertaken to create a planetary propulsion system to return the planet to a warmer orbit, but conditions on the surface are extreme. Subterranean life has taken its toll on the inhabitants of Mondas – disease is endemic, leading to a booming trade in organ transplants and replacements. Medical technology has allowed the creation of an artificial replacement for virtually every organ – and, for those brave explorers who seek to return to the surface of the planet, 'full conversion' is available. The results of this process are what come later to be known as the Cybermen. Mondas is beset with entropy – its surface freezing, its people slowly dying. And in the face of this entropy, they have made survival their highest ideal. The Doctor confronts Doctorman Allen, a scientist in charge of the conversion of the people of Mondas into cyborgs, demanding to know how she could put her own people through this horrifying transformation. Allen offers a pragmatic response: 'Because we're dying! … We've been trapped down here so long, we daren't even step out on our own planet's surface. Just the thought of the vast, empty sky drives us insane. Only Cybermen can go out there and save us…: No Cybermen, no life. Unless you have a better solution.' Allen sees transformation into Cyberman as the only hope for survival. But if survival is the only measure of the good, then all other considerations fall away. What remains is no longer human, but something less. Doctorman Allen's refusal to consider any other factors beyond mere survival doom the people of Mondas to 'full conversion' into the cold, heartless Cybermen, which exist for no other purpose than to extend their lives and to create more creatures exactly like themselves. Survival is not enough: we must survive as moral beings as well as mortal ones.

This privileging of the perseverance of our moral ideals over the survival of our bodies is perhaps the farthest-reaching reprogramming of all, for it asks us to overcome the imperatives of our very biology. Our bodies and minds are both wholly devoted to survival, to continuing our existence, both as individuals and as a species. An ethic that asks us to suspend this imperative, to risk or even sacrifice ourselves for something abstract and intangible, represents a complete rewriting of the laws by which everyday life is lived. And yet this is what the Doctor does every week: risking himself, and on ten occasions to date actually sacrificing himself, not just for his friends, not even for mere strangers, but for *aliens*. And in this radical upending of the laws of everyday life, the

Doctor embodies the Christian ideal as well. As Tolstoy stated, Jesus' message was not simply a new or revised ethical code, but 'a new conception of life' – a completely new understanding of the relationship between individual human beings, societies, nations, and worlds. And it is an inherently rebellious understanding, for it calls into question the entire basis of our politics, our international affairs, our interactions as individuals. To truly and fundamentally replace self-interest with other-interest requires a shift in every level of human life. Jesus' message is therefore a new definition, or perhaps the first true assertion of the definition, of humanity. If the Doctor is a fictional messiah, this is the form that his salvation takes: he liberates us from our assumptions, our intellectual and ethical dead-ends, and our dualities.

The episode 'Cold Blood' remains one of *Doctor Who*'s strongest statements on the ethical basis of what it means to be human. Ambrose Northover, a woman whose husband and son have been kidnapped and father poisoned by the Silurians, threatens to torture a reptilian prisoner unless she provides an antidote. When the Silurian doesn't answer, Ambrose shoots her with a taser, and the wound soon proves fatal. In the moral calculus of most TV and movies, the Silurian 'deserves' it – shows like 24 build much of their suspense around precisely this kind of ticking-bomb torture scenario. But when Ambrose's father, Tony Mack, enters the room to find his daughter standing over the writhing form of the tortured reptile-woman, he is furious, even though it is his life she was trying to save. Through gritted teeth he admonishes her: 'We have to be better than this!' Tony's message is clear: he will not support the torture of anyone in his name, no matter the reason.

The Doctor later echoes Tony's moral message, telling Ambrose: 'In future, when you talk about this, you tell people there was a chance, but you were *so much less* than the best of humanity'. The Doctor phrases this sentiment a bit more eloquently than does Tony, and the Time Lord expresses it even more succinctly in his later order to his human friends to 'Be extraordinary'. But it is important – and a sign of *Doctor Who*'s all-around moral optimism – that this message comes from a human being first. Dee Amy-Chinn uses a similar cases to argue that 'perhaps the real lesson… is not that the Doctor is a metaphor for Jesus, but that mercy and compassion are most fully embodied in the very human companions that accompany the Doctor on his travels'.[19] Surely the Doctor is not simply a 'metaphor for Jesus', but the moral role of the Jesus of the Sermon on the Mount is to awaken this kind of merciful behaviour in human beings. The mercy that truly matters is not that which God shows to human beings, but that which human beings show to each other. The same applies to *Doctor Who*. The alien Doctor may be this show's *de facto* messiah, but the ethical message he brings originates in and finds its ultimate expression in human action. If we simply hear the Doctor telling us to 'be better', we have the opportunity to write off that call to moral improvement as an impossible bit of science-fantasy. But if it comes from an earthbound elder like Tony Mack in 'Cold Blood', then maybe we do have a chance.

Despite his best efforts, however, Tony is unable to salvage the agreement between the humans and the Silurians over sharing the surface of the earth. The process is derailed by the violence of extremists – that of the human Ambrose, who has killed her prisoner, and of Restac, the Silurian military commander who refuses to forgive that death. Emotions override reason, neither side backs down, and the peace deal is scuttled. As the episode concludes, the Silurians are returning to hibernation, but the Doctor still struggles to create the peace that has been deferred. 'This planet is to be shared', he states, and urges the humans to encode this message in a form that will last: 'legend, or prophecy, or religion'. Humanity may not be ready now, but through proper preparation, they may be able to shape a future where peace is a possibility.

And this, ultimately, is the role that *Doctor Who* itself plays. The legends of our era – television programmes – are rightly connected to popular religion, as 'Cold Blood' suggests. Legend and religion are both things of the imagination, and imagination is where our experience of reality takes shape. It is in the imagination that we create a better future. *Doctor Who* encodes a message of a nonviolent, individualistic, anti-authoritarian ethic in one of our popular culture's most enduring legends, and thereby rewrites *our* programming, turning us into beings that can better approximate the impossible ease with which the Doctor solves the insoluble and turns ordinary rebellion into revolution. The rewiring of the imagination is no small thing: indeed, that is precisely what was done when Dr King shared his dream with the world. Imagining a universe in which our apparently-impossible dilemmas can be solved brings us closer to making that universe real. There is still a lot of work to be done to realise it, but nothing is possible unless it is first imagined.

3.

Divine and Human Nature: Incarnation and Kenosis in *Doctor Who*

K. Jason Wardley

Introduction

Theologians have employed a variety of metaphors to identify God's activity *pro nobis*: victory (over the devil, powers or principalities); expiation of a legal debt; sacrifice; and the enabling of human participation in the divine life. This chapter aims to explore two aspects of that Christian salvific tradition – incarnation and kenosis – by way of *Doctor Who*. Specifically it will examine the Hugo Award nominated 2007 television episodes 'Human Nature' and the 'The Family of Blood', and the original 1995 novel by Paul Cornell from which they were adapted. In this story the Doctor sheds his Time Lord attributes and, with a back story provided by the TARDIS and a new identity as 'John Smith', a schoolteacher at a public school, he assumes human form, thus setting the scene for a violent confrontation with a family of alien shapeshifters:

> 'What a strange predicament your friend's got into. Why do you think he wanted to be human?'

> 'I'm not sure. I think he wanted a change, to have a holiday from being him.'[1]

My contention here is that these themes can be profitably explored through the theory of 'mimetic violence' proposed by the anthropologist René Girard, which upsets traditional notions of sacrifice and the 'ontology of violence' to which they relate. At issue is whether Christianity became locked into a pernicious sacrificial interpretation caused by its transition from Hebraic to Greek cultures, the victim of a metaphysics that reinscribed that violence by subsuming the story of Christ and his church for that of 'Christianity'.[2]

Girard's assertion that violence is 'the heart and secret soul of the sacred' made the notion of sacrifice problematic for Christian theology. Girard proposed a tripartite theory that sought to reveal what causes societies to cohere successfully in the first place, why they disintegrate, and the role of religion in these processes. First, there is the mimetic or imitative (competing and thus potentially violent) nature of desire; secondly, the scapegoating mechanism (the victimisation of an individual or group) as a source of social order;[3] thirdly, the possibility that the Jewish and Christian traditions can help enlighten our understanding. For Girard the root of conflict lies in competition – the mimetic rivalry between persons, countries and cultures and the desire to imitate the other in order to obtain what they have, by violence if necessary. Moreover, this anthropology suggests that awareness of the self and the other arise simultaneously, as part of the same process of violent desire; here, promethean modernity is not celebrated but lamented as humanity's greatest idol.

Theology maintains that God relates to humanity through the medium of material creation – first and foremost, 'through the medium of human nature itself. Eventually, God relates to humankind through the medium of God's own humanity, in the Word made flesh and crucified'.[4] For Girard, Christ's incarnation dismantles both the violence of the sacred and the identification of this violent god with the God of metaphysics: God's self-abasement in Jesus Christ to the level of humanity means that the God of Christianity is neither the violent God of natural religion nor is he the abstract and omniscient 'first cause' of metaphysics.

A specifically kenotic Christology (from κένωσις [*kénōsis*] meaning 'emptiness'; here a 'self-emptying') describes the incarnate Word of God as having either withheld or temporarily relinquished certain divine prerogatives during his incarnation. Scriptural warrant for this is found in the Christ-hymn of Philippians 2 where Christ is said to have 'emptied himself [*ekenōsen*]' in order to take 'the form of a slave in … in human likeness … obedient to death'. The extent of this divine 'forgetting' or 'withholding' has been the subject of debate: while the 'locus of salvation is the sphere of ordinary personal existence in which God establishes fellowship with man'[5], theological thinking about redemption may not do justice to its complexity, sometimes forgetting that its language (recorded in its scripture) is not merely a 'metaphysical' but also a moral and eschatological one.

Canon and Apocrypha

Originally part of the *New Adventures* series issued by Virgin Books, *Human Nature* featured the Seventh Doctor (played on television by Sylvester McCoy) and Bernice Summerfield, a companion created for the books by author Paul Cornell in 1992; in the 2007 television adaptation their roles were taken by Tenth Doctor, David Tennant, and companion Martha Jones (Freema Agyeman).

Maintaining Leavis's notion of canon[6] is difficult for a drama series which now stretches across half a century and includes not just television episodes but original novels and audio drama. As the authors of the *Discontinuity Guide* (including Paul Cornell) said back in 1995, '[S]ometimes references gel with a kind of beautiful serendipity ... [s]ometimes continuity has to be beaten into place with a sledgehammer'.[7] Reconciling differences can be awkward: for instance, in one scene in the television serial of *Human Nature*, 'Dr Smith' is seen eating a pear – one of the things that, in the original book, Bernice was specifically instructed not to allow him to do while in human form.[8] Elsewhere, one of the boys at the school where the Doctor is teaching absorbs some of the Doctor's memories and personality from his biodata, assuming a Doctor-like role (whereas in the television story his acts of bravery seem to be his own). His experiences with the Doctor lead that boy – Timothy (scapegoat for the other pupils' violence) – to become a conscientious objector and Red Cross medic.

Although the *New Adventures* were the officially licensed continuation of *Doctor Who*, they also tried to tell stories beyond the scope of the small screen. While the first three in the range were written by experienced authors from the television novelisations, 'the book that set the agenda' was by Cornell.[9] Indeed, the *New Adventures* (NAs) represented an attempt to tell stories of an emotional and physical scale beyond the constraints of the original series, which was dismissed as a family serial. However, with the new series, Cornell observes how producer Russell T. Davies was looking for a 'voice' that was 'about emotion, about evoking strong emotional response from what happens to real characters. [...] The NAs put human drama high on the list.'[10]

Lance Parkin refers to the 'absence' from *Doctor Who* of a 'pope' who 'can state officially what and what isn't canon', a term which for him describes something 'imposed by a central authority'.[11] In contemporary television drama this role might be filled by its executive producer.[12] However, Davies has stated that 'canon' is 'a word which has never been used in the production office'.[13] Parkin's comment misunderstands the development of the biblical canon (a better term might be library) to which it alludes, in which there are differences between the Jewish and Samaritan canons, and between those that emerged in the Western, Eastern Orthodox, and Oriental Orthodox traditions of Christianity. While writings attributed to the apostles were in circulation amongst the earliest Christian communities, there was as yet no *accepted* definition of canon. The Christian New Testament is the result of internal debates over what constitutes canonicity – debates that were perhaps even more contentious than those found in *Doctor Who* fandom.[14]

As Girard observes, 'the "mimetic process" that produces this sort of conflict … is prior to language'[15], so here, where there are two versions of a story, it makes sense to treat the novel as properly belonging to the genre of extra-canonical or 'apocryphal literature' and then read the two narratives alongside one another, with added reference to other relevant texts (such as the audio dramas) and with differences indicated.

Incarnation and Kenosis

Apotheosis or kenosis?

'It was your friend the Doctor, with a great sadness about his shoulders. He wanted to be human...'[16]

According to 'A Brief History Of Time (Travel)'[17] Cornell's original story was inspired by Joseph Campbell's 1949 work on traditional mythologies, *The Hero With A Thousand Faces*. Specifically mentioned is the notion of *apotheosis*, in which the protagonist surrenders everything in order to gain enlightenment. In *Human Nature*, the Doctor's companion Benny had endured the death of her lover in the previous *New Adventures* novel, and so the Doctor transforms himself into a human being in order to try and comprehend his companion's grief. As he laments:

> 'Recently, I thought I had become wiser than him, but found that I was still hurting people terribly. [...] I'd climbed back on the wheel. Become a bully. Which is why I decided to stop.'

> 'Being a bully?'

> 'Being me.'[18]

This mimetic cycle of bullying is challenged by apotheosis and kenosis which instead articulate a dispossession – a humbling of the promethean in pursuit of something more humane. Kenotic Christology describes Jesus Christ relinquishing certain divine prerogatives or attributes when he took on human flesh during his incarnation, and early Christians found themselves mocked by Hellenic culture for the importance that they then placed upon the material body. The church, meanwhile, had to endure its own disagreements regarding the nature of the incarnation.

Incarnation and conflict

The Council of Nicaea, apparently with the Fifth Doctor in attendance, was convened in 325AD in order to settle the question of the divinity of Jesus Christ. Although few fourth-century Christians would have doubted that Jesus Christ was a divine being, for them the question was whether his divinity was equal to that of God the Father. In the liner notes to her *Big Finish* audio adventure based on the events of the council (written while she was a doctoral student at the University of Oxford) author Caroline Symcox expresses her own surprise at the level of common interest in doctrinal debates in the fourth century, when theology was 'a spectator sport'.[19] This 'interest' sometimes flared into rioting and mob violence outside the halls where bishops debated the meaning of philosophical terms such as the Greek *homoousios* ['of one substance'].

This dispute could be caricatured as a mimetic clash between rival personalities – a popular legend relishes how Nicholas, bishop of Myra (later mythologized as Santa Claus) was seemingly so incensed by the views of Arius (a priest from Alexandria) that he slapped him. Arius promoted his own argument in songs popular among the sailors and dock-workers of the Mediterranean, while his bishop Athanasius – whom Constantine at one point declares one of the '[l]oudest voices in this endless church argument' – led a ferocious opposition against Arius and his supporters.

In its fictional retelling Symcox's portrayal of Arius is quite flattering: his cause is taken up by one of the Doctor's companions, a fellow Egyptian, Erimem, who provides a useful idealistic narrative foil, arguing on Arius's behalf at the council rather than making any concession to *realpolitik*. As far as Erimem is concerned, Constantine is merely 'a tyrant!' who 'speaks of forgiveness and reconciliation' yet resorts 'to assassination'. Meanwhile the Doctor finds himself recruited by the Emperor to keep the troubled empire intact.

In the final episode, Constantine makes an impassioned plea to the mob gathered beneath his balcony, that the church should not be 'ripped apart by squabbles from within. She must be strong, unified, one church'; Constantine announces that he will 'keep the peace while the debates go on', expressing his desire for 'a swift resolution to the eternal debates of the church. I pray for all of us that this conflict will be over soon and the church may be whole once again'. In fact, as the Oxford theologian Maurice Wiles points out, there is evidence of a certain deliberate ambiguity that suited his interests and 'that the Emperor was ready to allow the greatest latitude' in the interpretation of doctrine.[20]

Following on from these debates, the Trinitarian doctrine of the equality of the Holy Spirit with the Father and the Son was only finally affirmed at the Council of Constantinople in 381. Their co-divinity having been established, further debate arose concerning the relationship between the divinity of Christ the Son and the humanity of Jesus of Nazareth. This was finally resolved at the Council of Chalcedon in 451. In order to explain the 'two natures' of Christ (understood as both human and divine), the church fathers appealed to a *communicatio idiomatum* ('communication of properties') to explain how the eternal God could die on the cross. This *communicatio* was grounded in the belief that the same person (Jesus Christ) is the metaphysical subject of both natures.

Kenosis and mimetic violence

'There's this great misconception that the Slitheen are for kids, and episodes like *Human Nature* and *The Family of Blood* are for adults...'[21]

For Girard modernity represents a revolutionary loosening of the constraints upon mimetic desire, which then has to be channelled into safer forms of competition such as the capitalist market and parliamentary democracy if open aggression is to be avoided.[22] For his part the English philosopher Thomas Hobbes shared this opinion of human nature, observing that: '[I]f any two men desire the same thing, which nevertheless they cannot both enjoy, they become enemies; and ... [they] endeavour to destroy, or subdue one an other'; life is the continuous 'Warre of every one against every one'.[23] Indeed, neither the television serial nor the novel minimise the violence committed in pursuit of the Doctor's biodata.

What Girard terms 'mimetic desire' – that is, desire as an imitation of 'the desire of the other' – represents an overwhelming metaphysical imperative to '"Imitate us!" "Imitate me!" "I bear the secret of life, of true being!".'[24] This is captured in the desire of the Family of Blood to be like the Time Lords (paradoxically, at the same time as the Doctor desires to be human); the object of desire is what is desired by the other.[25]

Here violence plays out as 'rivalry' for an object of mimetic desire – the Doctor's Time Lord biodata – which 'acquires the status of a disputed object' as the story progresses. The longer it is disputed, the more envy it arouses, events becoming 'more and more heated'.[26] The quest of the Family for a Time Lord's regenerative capacities captures Girard's argument about 'mimetic desire' – their reasons amount to a litany of unfulfilled desires: their genetic material has been 'drawn too thin' and for a family which has devoted their 'lives to the pursuit of power and pleasure ... a sort of lethargy sets in'. With 'no political or sociological goals beyond [their] own pleasure' they have swiftly reached a point where they have 'no goals left at all'. '[I]t does not take a dozen planets to serve our greatest desires', observes one member of the Family, Serif, '– even Greeneye's perverted sexual appetites.'[27] Having assimilated the attributes of a Time Lord, they intend to increase their family to the size of an army. Moreover, with Serif's skills at influencing a child *in utero* 'we'll be able to create individuals suited to particular tasks. The Aubertides, once ignored as a race, will become a major force in galactic affairs.'[28]

Their victims are themselves caught in the same cycle of violence – confronted by the arrival of the Family and the rejection of the truce being offered by the school bursar ('Damn soft tactics', murmurs one boy disdainfully) the headmaster decides to 'break out the arms' belonging to their army cadet force and 'make a show of it' until help arrives:

> 'Get up! Buck up and play the game!' [...] 'We're going to show them that [we're] made of old English stuff! The stuff that built the Empire, the stuff that doesn't back down to threats and bullying! Who's with me?'[29]

This decision delights the boys clustering around their form masters, while the school captains salute their headmaster, Rocastle, as he prepares to do his duty regardless of the cost, organising what even he concedes could prove merely to be a futile and bloody gesture of defiance. Here the notion of mimetic violence found in Girard's analysis will be borne out in the rival pedagogical claims of the Family and the school. As Girard observes:

> The child possesses no perspective that will allow him to see things as they are. He has no basis for reasoned judgements [...] The future orientation of his desires – that is, the choice of his future models – will be significantly affected by the dichotomies of his childhood. In fact, these models will determine the shape of his personality.[30]

Centuries ago Giambattista Vico speculated that children have an ingenuity that adults lose. 'Children excel in imitation; we observe that they generally amuse themselves by imitating whatever they are able to apprehend.'[31] Thus it is that, seemingly indifferent to the subsequent loss of life, having been schooled for war[32] and having managed to kill one and trap another member of the Family, the surviving boys, clutching rocks and clubs in scenes reminiscent of William Golding's *Lord of the Flies*, and led by sadistic school captain Hutchinson (whose attempts to speak degenerate into 'roars' and 'shrill cries' as he seizes one of the Family's weapons) form a circle around the pit as the alien climbs out of it, his own face 'a mask of rage and sorrow' following the death of a Family member. He is bent on revenge, thereby perpetuating the cycle of mimetic violence: 'You animals! I'll cover this hill with your blood!'[33] The boys descend upon the trapped Greeneye, by now struggling for his life 'felling boys to the left and right with his fists'; and yet, caught up in the cycle of violence the boys persist, closing in, swinging their rocks and clubs. Here Benny intervenes to break the cycle, pushing the crowd aside to get to Greeneye to stop him detonating an explosive capsule:

> 'You can't stop us!' Greeneye was roaring. 'I – will – see you all die...' Benny felt something give inside her, an internal explosion of some vast rage she'd never known. 'Nobody else dies!' she shouted.[34]

Having averted the immediate threat, in the momentary calm that follows the boys fall back and Hutchinson, having recovered Greeneye's sword, tries to behead the alien – Benny is able to finally stop the boys' attack only by throwing herself onto Greeneye's body, 'clutching him tightly to her, slamming her head against his. [...] "Do you hear me?" She glared up at Hutchinson. "Do you understand?"'[35] Hutchinson nonetheless persists with his dead teacher's rhetoric[36]: 'It's time for some good old British grit. Play up and play the game, chaps!'[37] Fortunately for their sake none of the surviving boys takes heed of him.

   Besides this exploration of the mimetic legacy of violence, *Human Nature* offers another side of Girard's anthropological investigation, namely that 'the eating of sacrificial flesh' might represent 'a veritable cannibalism of the human spirit'.[38] This Girardian reading suggests that in their confrontation with the Aubertides the boys – in imitating their teachers – are at risk of consuming their own humanity.[39] Girard's point is that '...cannibals are always eager for their victim to demonstrate by a show of courage that he is the incarnation of supreme violence'. Of course, the victim is eaten only after he has been killed, 'after the maleficent violence has been completely transformed into a beneficent substance, a source of peace, strength, and fecundity'.[40] 'Very true', agrees one of the Family, 'We'll kill you both quite humanely before we eat you.'[41] This cannibalistic account of sacrifice is contradicted by the logic of the Christian celebration of Eucharist when properly understood as an act of hospitality, thanksgiving and remembrance by human beings who are defined by communion rather than consumption.

Kenosis and metaphysics

> 'I tried to give up so much – my responsibilities, my past, my guilt. But [...] I [...] will be the Doctor again, and go on an

adventure, and defeat the monsters. [...] It takes determination. And hope for humanity. And love.'

Benny went to him and held him. 'What you said about sacrifice, John. It doesn't have to be like that. There's always another way.'

'Not this time.'[42]

The *kenotic* denial of the attributes of power and dominance – omniscience, omnipresence, and eternity – (attributes not dissimilar to those of the 'cosmological wizard' which the Doctor renounces)[43] undermines the notion of a violent God of personal sacrifice co-identified with the *ipse esse subsistens* ['subsistent Being itself']. For postmodern and postmetaphysical philosophers such as Gianni Vattimo, a rediscovered Christian doctrine of salvation is neither a set of doctrines nor an attempt to find solid ground among a 'sea of uncertainty'.[44] With the demise of notions of sacral violence, conflict is no longer resolved through the extreme behaviour exemplified by that of the Family. Against this background lies the question of whether the Doctor should take up his Time Lord mantle in order to defeat them, or whether to follow through with the instinct of his human self in the novel, and let them have the biodata in the expectation of them leaving. Such self-abnegation cannot continue indefinitely and, in the end, for both the novel and the television serial, the Doctor's ethical responsibilities outweigh his personal happiness. Thus his answer to Joan's belief that she 'must seem so very small' to him: 'No. We could start again. I'd like that, you and me. We could try, at least. Because everything that John Smith is and was, I'm capable of that, too'.

For Girard the innocence of the victim ultimately permeates its surrounding culture. In *kenotic* terms, the descent of God to humanity confirms the innocence of every victim, in a final rejection of attempts to disclose the divine merely as power and law. Thus the rejection of the principal characteristics of a metaphysics of violence. In a Girardian reading, the innocence of Jesus reveals the innocence of *every* victim; something hard to dispute given the collateral damage that accompanies the Family's pursuit of the Doctor – as Joan Redfern demands of the Doctor at the end of 'The Family of Blood', 'Answer me this, just one question. That's all. If the Doctor had never visited us, if he'd never chosen this place on a whim ... would anyone here have died?'

The self-limitation of God in the incarnation means that the divine is truly disclosed in its self-abandonment, in the vulnerability of taking on human form. This exposure and weakness is explored to particular dramatic effect in the novel:

> He was only human [...] the most precious thing in Smith's life was now at risk. What were his principles beside that?

> Now [...] he felt impotent and lost once more. He was only a small Scottish schoolteacher. He didn't have any heroics to save Joan. All he could do was what any human could: bargain. Bargain ethics against everyday life, the image of how life should be against how it really was. [45]

Kenosis and forgiveness

There remains the question of the fate of the Family once they have been defeated: will the restored Doctor exercise mercy, or extract a terrible 'godlike judgement'? As 'John Smith' observes, '[t]here are monsters out there, yes. Terrible things. But you don't have to become one in order to defeat them. You can be peaceful in the face of their cruelty. You can win by being cleverer than they are.'[46] But is this enough? And can cleverness be reconciled with mercy? The survival of one of the Aubertides presents the Doctor with a quandary:

> He wandered around the tree and smiled gawkily up at the naked Greeneye. 'What are we going to do with you?'

> 'I don't care. You can torture me –'

> 'No. I think I'll have you locked up [...]'

> 'But we can't have him getting away,' Hutchinson objected. 'He ought to be bloody well hung!'

> Alton wandered up. 'I appreciate how you feel, but don't you think that this man's powers go beyond the army's ability to hold him? We could just shoot him and bury him here.'

> 'Don't be barbarous. Oh, he might get away' – the Doctor tapped his umbrella handle against his chin – 'but what will he do? He's got no weapons, no technology, and a life span of, what, ten

more years at the most? That's the thing about such powerful biosystems. They burn themselves out.' His face darkened. 'I think killing him would be far too merciful.'[47]

So does the Doctor elect to be merciful? As Colin Gunton notes, '[t]o be victorious does not mean butchering your opponent with weapons but refusing to exercise power demonically in order to overcome evil with good'.[48] But there is a decided ambiguity[49] in the Doctor's response; in fact, Greeneye is ultimately undone by his own inability to control his appetites and dies in the slaughterhouse.[50]

The finale of the television serial is no less ambiguous, with a soliloquy from one of the Family narrating their fates and the Doctor's reaction: 'He never raised his voice, that was the worst thing. The fury of the Time Lord. And then we discovered why, why this Doctor; who had fought with gods and demons, why he had run away from us and hidden. He was being kind. [...] We wanted to live forever, so the Doctor made sure that we did.' The Family's onscreen reaction – 'screaming, bound in thick metal chains [...] pulled backwards' – are in marked contrast to that of the Doctor who 'watches coldly, no emotion on his face', before finally walking away.

Conclusion: *homo eucharisticus*

'I'll think of another way. Even if it kills me.'[51]

For Girard a 'non-sacrificial reading'[52] of the Cross 'discredits and deconstructs all the gods of violence, since it reveals the true God, who has not the slightest violence in him'.[53] And as Gunton argues, 'the language in which the story is told is one of the ways in which we are enabled to speak of God. We learn ... that God is the kind of being who makes his presence felt in our world in the way in which the life and death of Jesus takes shape'.[54] For some Greeks salvation meant *theopoiēsis* or *huiopoēsis* – that is, 'divinisation' or 'filiation' (the making of gods or sons) – not in the sense that humanity become gods in the same way as Christ is the Son of God, but that they are saved through participating in the divine nature. In an essay[55] written around the same time as *Human Nature* is set, future Archbishop William Temple proposed an account of God as humble, self-forgetting and self-sacrificing love. However, this 'self-humbling and self-emptying sacrifice' is part of the '*eternal* glory of God'; God is simply a fellow sufferer of humanity. Temple's Christology offers a moral resolution of divine-human relations which sees Jesus merely as an exemplary human being rather than the vulnerable incarnate Word. While the Doctor might claim that 'I won't feel the loss. I've gained so much, being human. I know I have',[56] in the end – however genuine the sense of jeopardy – the reader and viewer expect 'Doctor Smith' to revert to his true nature, become the Doctor, 'make the villains fall into their own traps, and trick the monsters'.[57]

For Girard though, the 'Gospel does not provide a happy ending', merely two options – exactly what ideologies 'never provide, freedom of choice: either we imitate Christ, giving up our mimetic violence, or we run the risk of self-destruction'.[58] The advantage of a kenotic account is not that it allows God to wallow in suffering, but that it reminds humanity that God's experience of the world would 'remain radically different from ours unless he has somehow entered into the human condition'. Having done so, 'he can then come alongside the sufferer, and offer grace from the inside[59] ... showing how the situation might, potentially at least, be transformed, or at the very least, be endured'.[60] In *Human Nature*, the object[61] of 'John Smith's' affections, the widowed Joan Redfern, finds *any* minimisation – or celebration – of the noble qualities of sacrifice troubling, and her scathing assessment at the end of the television serial of the Doctor's actions undercuts any presumed sacrificial dignity: 'I see. Well then. He was braver that you, in the end. That ordinary man. You chose to change. He chose to die'.

Ultimately, neither his incarnation nor his self-abnegation is that of Christ: a Time Lord is too 'Inhuman', too 'Dangerous', someone who loves 'greatly but not small-ly', more like Merlin than anyone else.[62] By contrast, for Girard 'there can be no victim who is not Christ, and no one can come to the aid of a victim without coming to the aid of Christ'.[63] *Eucharistic* humanity – *homo eucharisticus* – the new way of 'being human' inaugurated at the incarnation (and articulated by the Anglican Benedictine thinker Gregory Dix) and which participates in the divine nature is grounded in thanksgiving, that is, liturgical remembrance[64] of the incarnation as a gratuitous gift rather than as a mimetic sacrifice ('This is my body, *given* for you...'). If humanity's failure is its inability to recognise the place of that victim, then conversely its hope – which is founded upon the incarnation through the kenotic self-identification of God with human condition – comes from the acknowledgement that however 'ghastly the things that humanity and God experience' the divine mind cannot be 'blown' or 'stumped' by them, instead recontextualizing those horrors in joy, delight and love.[65]

4.

Breaking the Faiths in 'The Curse of Fenric' and 'The God Complex'

Tim Jones

Two of the thematically closest stories across the arguably somewhat artificial divide between 'classic' and post-2005 *Doctor Who* are Ian Briggs's 'The Curse of Fenric' (1989) and Toby Whithouse's 'The God Complex' (2011). Central to both is the concept of faith, specifically its benefits and its dangers. Faith, especially, is key to which characters die at the hands of each story's respective monsters: 'Fenric''s vampiric Haemovores and 'The God Complex''s Minotaur, allegedly a distant relative of the eponymous villain from the classic series' 'The Horns of Nimon' (1979-80). What's more, neither story depicts faith as simply a religious phenomenon. Both parallel religion with a range of secular, or non-religious faiths. The Christianity of Reverend Wainwright in 'Fenric', for example, is placed alongside Sorin's faith in the Russian Revolution and Ace's in the Seventh Doctor. In the later 'The God Complex', meanwhile, Rita's faith in Islam is equated with an even larger variety of secular alternatives, including faith in the power of surrender (as held by the alien Gibbis, from the ill-fated planet Tivoli), luck, grandiose conspiracy theories, and, not least, Amy's in the Eleventh Doctor, which is contrasted here with her husband Rory's more rational scepticism. Even the climactic scenes of each story hinge on hugely similar moments in which the Doctor demonstrates himself to be an unworthy subject of the faith held in him by his companions. But much more important than these vivid similarities are the ways in which a crucial cultural shift between the production of these two stories fuels what could be described as their ultimate stance on faith – or whether holding an unconditional faith, be it secular or religious, can be described as a good thing. 'Fenric' would answer absolutely yes, 'The God Complex' absolutely not.

Before going any further, it is worth examining what precisely these two episodes understand by the concept of 'faith'. How, exactly, can all the disparate belief systems that feature in these stories be grouped under this one banner? Clearly, faith here has little to do with religion per se. Ian Briggs is clearly aware of his story's overt juxtaposition of different varieties of faith, explaining on a DVD extra that 'there's Ace's faith in the Doctor, which has to be broken. There's Wainwright's faith, which ultimately cracks. [And then] there's [Sorin's] faith in the Revolution'.[1] Within the episodes themselves, the Eleventh Doctor is, in this respect, slightly clearer about the precise nature of faith than the Seventh. While his predecessor merely describes faith somewhat vaguely as producing a 'psychic barrier', without detailing exactly how this is so, or how the disparate belief systems within the story even qualify as such, the Eleventh clarifies to Amy that compulsive gamblers such as Joe possess a belief in luck as 'a force that makes them win or lose' and that all holders of faith alike imagine 'there's something guiding them, about to save them'. What the Eleventh Doctor describes here as 'luck' is not quite the same as what mathematician and game theorist Richard A. Epstein describes as the prime ingredient of betting systems, which for him is a notion of 'primitive justice ... which embodies the notion of balance', overseen 'by an eminently equitable god of symmetry ... who ensures that for every Head there is a Tail.'[2] While we never hear Joe's own views on his mindset or behaviour, by Epstein's model what Joe holds faith in is perhaps the opposite of the luck envisaged by the Doctor, having more to do with luck's opposite, inevitability. But either by the Doctor's description of gambling or Epstein's, what links both religious faiths and this secular alternative, then, is a belief in some invisible force (whether luck or balance) that influences external events and, specifically, the fate of the believer.

It is not just the secular faiths held by compulsive gamblers that can be compared with religious faiths in such a way. The philosopher and theologian Paul Tillich, for one, describes faith as 'the state of being ultimately concerned' and goes on to argue that 'it demands the total surrender of him who accepts this claim, and it promises total fulfilment even if all other claims have to be subjected to it or rejected in its name.'[3] Notice the lack of any religious element to this model: the prime ingredient a belief requires to be considered a *faith* is intensity, which is demonstrated via the subordination of the whole of a believer's life around a single subject or guiding principle. Whether or not this subject or principle is God appears for Tillich irrelevant. It is easy to see how a number of the secular faiths in both episodes fit Tillich's criteria. The historian Richard Hofstadter explains that individuals such as Howie in 'The God Complex', with his faith in the existence of 'messed up CIA stuff', imagines 'a "vast" or "gigantic" conspiracy as *the motive force* in historical events.'[4] David Aaronovitch, a British journalist, confirms these links when he argues that a 'believer in a conspiracy theory or theories becomes, in his own mind, the one in proper communion with the underlying universe, the one who understands the true ordering of things.'[5] Again, a faith is essentially a belief-system that has become all-consuming. That Gibbis and his race's faith in the act of surrender fits this description too is confirmed by their city-planning focusing on making areas pleasant for aliens who have yet to invade. Future invasions that might not even happen appear, nonetheless, to govern every aspect of their lives.

Captain Sorin's faith in the Russian Revolution, and in the communist ideology that was at its forefront, is the clearest example of a non-religious belief system that parallels its religious cousins. Perhaps controversially, particularly since the episodes in question would have aired while the single-party Soviet Union was still in existence, this faith appears in 'Fenric' to be stronger than Wainwright's Christianity, which falls under Jean and Phyllis's attack while Sorin's own faith holds, even without the symbolic badge (a hammer and sickle) that underpins his faith the first time it is needed. Political philosopher Eric Voeglin influentially levelled religious and political belief systems when he coined the term 'political religion' in 1938, to describe both Communism and Nazism. As summarised much more recently by Hans Maier, Voeglin discerned that 'the modern dictatorships are based on an inner-worldly religiosity that elevates the collectivity of race, class or state ... and thereby "divinizes" them.'[6] Once more, a single, non-religious idea ends up mirroring religion by becoming a deeply guiding principle, though in this case, unlike with Howie's faith in conspiracy theories, or Joe's in luck, this particular guiding principle of class collectivity is one that in countries such as the Soviet Union became entrenched across a whole society, proliferating as deeply as Christianity did in our less secular past. Klaus-Georg Riegel directly links the fall of this older society-wide faith with the rise of its Communist alternative when he argues that 'the loss of Christian truth led to the Communist church'.[7] This is possibly why, in 'Fenric', Wainwright's Christian faith has to fail while Sorin's secular alternative repeatedly succeeds, since the very existence of the latter depends on a world in which the former has become obsolete.

A faith, then, is basically a belief in a higher power able directly to influence the fate of the believer, and which also, because of this, becomes the prime organising factor of a believer's ideology and life. Both 'Fenric' and 'The God Complex' feature a wide variety of faiths, levelling both religious and secular examples alongside one another in a manner that isn't too dissimilar to the writings of various big-hitting historians, philosophers and cultural theorists. But beyond the broad similarities sketched above between the types of faith included within both stories, the ways in which these stories actually treat the theme of faith become very different.

Noted sociologist and Marxist literary critic Terry Eagleton presents a picture of faith's redemptive powers that cuts to the heart of how it appears distinctly within these two *Doctor Who* stories. Eagleton argues that while many critics of faith deplore, for one, the fact that it often works in ignorance of verifiable evidence that might prove a particular faith valid or invalid, what these critics do not see is that faith 'is not primarily a belief that something or someone exists, but a commitment and allegiance' to a larger power that 'might make a difference to the frightful situation you find yourself in'.[8] Rather than Wainwright or Rita believing in the existence of a Christian or Islamic God, then, Eagleton would stress that this belief is not the main component of these faiths as much as is these deities' ability to act as saviour. Obviously this presupposes that both faiths must propose that such a God exists, but this proposition is just one component of a faith, and not the main one. The non-religious faiths throughout both stories can also be understood by this model, with luck, number systems, the act of surrender, Communist doctrine and conspiracy theories all carrying the potential to save believers from a place of darkness, whether through guaranteeing a more successful betting experience the next time around, safeguarding from obliteration by alien invaders, or rescuing the proletariat from capitalist oppression.

In 'Fenric', this process is seen to work almost exactly as Eagleton would describe. The respective faiths of Wainwright and Sorin, which posit that the Christian God or Communism can deliver them from a world of evil, indeed prove powerful enough to form what the Doctor describes as a 'psychic barrier' that protects them from the attacking Haemovores. When Wainwright is eventually killed, this is because Jean and Phyllis have convinced him that the world has grown so corrupt that no deliverance is possible. Ironically, this supports Eagleton's model; Wainwright's crisis of faith *is* his failure to believe that any greater force can save the world from its current state, made deplorable both by English bombs killing innocent German children and by the manifestation before Wainwright's eyes of two young women who successfully convince him they were 'lost the day [they] were born'. Wainwright's fate also questions those critics of faith who, as will shortly be explained further, decry followers of religion for continuing to hold faith in denial of all evidence against it: the moment Wainwright sees what he regards as incontrovertible, empirical evidence against Christianity's potential for salvation, he gives it up! It is interesting to speculate exactly how the Doctor's faith in his companions would work by Eagleton's theory of salvation. Perhaps it falls in line with later comments made to the Tenth Doctor by Donna in 'The Runaway Bride' (2006) regarding his need for a companion to be present in order to save him from his own proclivity for violence. His faith in his companions is his faith in their ability to rescue him from the darkness within himself. The Eleventh Doctor's morally questionable actions in both 'Dinosaurs on a Spaceship' (2012) and 'A Town Called Mercy' (2012), during a phase of his life with no regular companionship, go far in supporting this view. Witness Amy asking him 'When did killing someone become an option?' in 'Mercy', also written by Toby Whithouse. The answer, clearly, is at some point while travelling alone, without Amy and Rory's humanising influence.

But by 'The God Complex', produced over twenty years after 'Fenric', the process described by Eagleton has run off course. Faith still basically functions here much like he suggests and as is demonstrated by 'Fenric'. The inhabitants of the hotel see a sight they intensely fear: for Howie, this sight is a group of teenage girls mocking him for his stammer; for Rita, it is her overbearing father; and while we do not see what lies in the Doctor's particular hotel room, the Daleks, the Master, or even the Doctor himself are several intriguing possibilities. Or perhaps it's John Hurt delivering a powerful reminder of the time that the Doctor broke the promise represented by his chosen name. The fear these sights generate encourages each character to fall back on his or her faith in whichever all-encompassing subject they believe has the power to save them, much like Wainwright and Sorin fall back on Christianity or Communism to save them from the Haemovores. So far, so similar. The key difference is obviously that the Haemovores have no vested interest in encouraging such a fall back to a subject of faith, for it works successfully against them and not to the detriment of the believer. In 'The God Complex', conversely, faith is actively encouraged as a means to an end, for the Minotaur is able to convert a disparate array of faiths into a faith in himself, which he then devours.

The most obvious departure, then, and the one that I think most tellingly signifies a shift in cultural attitudes between the moments of each story's production, is that the strong faith that protects the characters in 'Fenric' is what dooms them in 'The God Complex'. What was once a guarantee of safety has become, instead, actively fatal. To demonstrate this vividly, we just need to consider how a character from one story might fare in the other. Rory is protected from becoming the Minotaur's food source because he doesn't have a strong enough faith in anything or anyone, including, it would seem, his wife. But what saves him from the Minotaur would doom him to the earlier story's Haemovores. The failure of Wainwright's faith that sees him killed in 'Fenric', on the other hand, would instead be what saves him in 'The God Complex'.

The presentation of faith as valuable in 'Fenric' but dangerous in 'The God Complex' runs deeply through each respective story, beyond the stark distinction described above. 'Fenric' demonstrates holders of faith to be continually correct in their beliefs, while 'The God Complex' shows them to be mistaken. Right after the latter's pre-titles sequence, Amy has clearly been given evidence of the Doctor's fallibility, since she is seen muttering despondently that he promised to take the trio to 'Ravenscala' rather than to 'a rubbish hotel'. Amy's subsequent assurance to Gibbis that the Doctor has 'never let [her] down' is starkly at odds with her having complained about exactly this at the start of the very same episode. She slightly qualifies this remark by bringing up the time 'when [she] was a kid' and he failed to return to pick her up as promised (as depicted in 2010's 'The Eleventh Hour'), but does not allow this suggestion of a lapse in her faith to stand as she explains to Gibbis that the Doctor 'came back' and 'saved her'. Amy's defence here, of both the Doctor and her faith in him, appears wishful thinking: though the Doctor did of course return for her, this was an entire twelve years later and after her visiting a number of psychiatrists to help deal with the negative effects his abandonment had on her childhood. Her faith in the Doctor thus appears extremely unreasonable, only tenable because any evidence that challenges him being deserving of such unquestioning belief is either minimised or completely ignored. And after Rory has sceptically (but quite reasonably, given the evidence *he* has seen) stated that 'every time the Doctor gets pally with someone' he 'has the urge to notify their next of kin', he remembers that last time he showed such doubt Amy hit him with her shoe. Not only is Amy's faith preserved by her minimisation of evidence to the contrary, but she appears ready to use violence against anyone who reads the same facts in a manner that leads to a more balanced conclusion!

Indeed, in 'The God Complex' alone the Doctor is continually shown to be unworthy of an unconditional or all-compassing belief, beyond his failure to get Amy and Rory to Ravenscala. Around halfway into the episode, the Doctor promises that 'no one else dies today' – shortly before the tragic deaths of Howie and Rita. The inability of the Doctor to save the latter is stressed by him having to watch her die, at a distance, from inside the hotel's surveillance room. Here the Doctor literally mirrors the God which the faith of characters like Ace and Amy depicts him to be, his ability to see via the camera system into every area of the building effectively making him similarly omniscient, or all-seeing. But this omniscience is proven to be functionally useless in helping him save Rita, the victim of the Minotaur about whom he appears to care the most. Even if there is a God, this scene perhaps implies, there is absolutely no guarantee that He will be able to help you in your hour of need. Demonstrating a worse oversight still, earlier in the episode the Doctor has triumphantly observed that the Minotaur 'feeds on fear'. Clearly this mistake is dangerous in that it prolongs the situation by preventing the Doctor from being able to deduce the Minotaur's true *modus operandi*, but it pales in comparison to the terrible advice that he later derives from this hypothesis and offers to Rita while she is facing the monster down. By telling her to 'block out the fear and stay focused on [her] belief', his mistaken theory about the Minotaur's feeding habits actually leads him to encourage its latest victim to bring to the surface exactly what it is looking to devour.

Rita, too, is demonstrably wrong regarding at least one key deduction drawn from her faith in Islam. She is convinced that the Hotel is 'Jahannam', or the Islamic equivalent of Hell, described in the Qur'an repeatedly as a place of 'blazing fire' and referred to also as 'that which breaks to pieces'.[9] But the location in which she finds herself is, of course, revealed to be a sophisticated prison-ship built by a race who had outgrown their God and so sent him into exile. The description of Jahannam as 'that which breaks to pieces' does, on the other hand, accurately describe how the prison works by breaking down a person via his or her individual fears, so perhaps Rita is not entirely misguided in reaching this conclusion, even though the complex clearly contains none of the other features described in the Qur'an, such as the omnipresent fire itself and the seven gates that sort people out according to the nature of their sins.[10] This is definitely not to say that the episode demonstrates that Rita is wrong to hold faith in the existence of Jahannam, just that where she finds herself is clearly *not* it, and so her faith causes her to reach a conclusion that the prison-ship is something it only very marginally resembles. Unlike Amy's faith in the Doctor, the content or subject of Rita's faith is not condemned, so much as are its effects upon her ability to reason regarding the situation in which she has found herself. Sam Harris has sharply criticised faith's 'very nature' for working as 'an impediment to further inquiry' and this at least appears true for Rita as well as Amy, the faith of one in Islam and the other in the Doctor working to stifle thought processes that might lead them to more verifiably correct conclusions, Amy going as far as physically chastising people like Rory who seek to inquire rather than to hold an unconditional faith.[11]

A close reading of 'The God Complex', then, sees both the practice of having faith and the subjects towards which these faiths are directed powerfully brought down a peg or several. But how does faith fare in the story from twenty-two years earlier, 'Fenric'? Clearly much better, and for reasons well beyond the obvious contrast, already mentioned, that when marshalled by a believer as a 'psychic barrier' faith proves powerful enough to shield the Seventh Doctor and Captain Sorin from Fenric's Haemovores. Again in opposition to 'The God Complex', every conclusion that is reached via a character's faith also appears perfectly justified, while the sort of scepticism embodied by Rory in the later episode is proven consistently misguided. These distinctions become apparent from the story's opening scene, in which Sorin dismisses the fears of his crew as 'stupid Armenian superstitions' – his incredulity is mistaken, for his crew are correct to believe that their lives are in danger from the supernatural forces that have been following their boats. Doctor Judson similarly dismisses Commander Millington for 'wasting time on superstitions', only for Millington to retort that 'the Viking legends' concerning the eponymous curse will 'come true'. Once again, it is the sceptic that is proven wrong, even falling victim himself to the very curse in which he refuses to believe, while the faith-based believer is proven correct in his fears. And Mrs Hardaker warns her two young evacuee wards, Jean and Phyllis, that there is 'nothing left' for them 'but pitiless damnation'. Considering that they are about to be transformed into Haemovores, her strongly superstitious reading of the situation, for which she appears to possess no concrete evidence, proves entirely valid.

But what about the faith of Ace in the Doctor? Unlike Amy's in his older counterpart, it is presented as entirely well-founded. When the Doctor instructs her not to 'go into the water', she instinctively obeys, despite him giving no explanation or evidence whatsoever as to why he believes the sea to be dangerous; that she should not enter the water simply because the Doctor has decreed that she should not is entirely a matter of faith. And her faith is completely justified by the aforementioned fates of Jean and Phyllis, who rush into the sea mocking Ace with jeers of 'there's evil in the water!', a possibility in which they clearly do not believe, but yet nonetheless is soon established to be fatally true.

The same practice of holding faith that appears so dangerous in 'The God Complex', and which fuels so many falsehoods, instead genuinely saves people in 'The Curse of Fenric', often by leading to remarkably correct deductions. But is this shift in the treatment of faith indicative of a wider cultural and societal shift, across the twenty-two years between the two stories' transmission, towards a fundamental distrust and scepticism towards faith and its worth? An argument that this is indeed the case might start with the attacks on religious faith made by one Richard Dawkins (husband of Lalla Ward, aka earlier *Doctor Who* companion Romana II). Much of what he has to say against faith clearly parallels the distrust of its worth that we have seen within 'The God Complex'. *The God Delusion* (2006) is certainly his most famous and extended attack on faith, but in a much earlier text the same opinions can be detected, with *The Selfish Gene* (1976) describing faith as 'blind trust, in the absence of evidence, even in the teeth of evidence.'[12] While the original edition of this text might lay my argument here open to questioning by dating from over ten years *before* 'Fenric' and still denigrating faith, the above attack is little more than a passing aside, or a sign of things to come, rather than the primary purpose, as it is for the much later *The God Delusion*. Here, 'religious faith' in particular is singled out for an extended assault, described as 'an especially potent silencer of rational calculation', a quality that 'discourages questioning, by its very nature.'[13] Shortly afterwards, Dawkins asserts that 'faith is an evil precisely because it requires no justification and brooks no argument'.[14] Dawkins *does* extend his attack to faith itself, rather than merely religious faith, though it is apparent that this, for him, represents the most extreme example of everything inherent to the wider practice that he regards as dangerous.

The huge popularity and resultant bestselling status of *The God Delusion* attests to the fact that, by 2006, there was a huge audience at least sceptical enough about faith to be willing to give Dawkins' hugely vitriolic arguments and delivery the time of day. Similar to this text is Christopher Hitchens' *God is Not Great* (2007), which attacks faith from a very similar angle by describing it as 'grounded on wish-thinking' and opposes it to a scientific method which, to the contrary, works through 'evidence and reasoning'.[15] It is worth mentioning that these two books have been followed very quickly by a glut of titles that use a very similar popular and journalistic style to defend faith. These include Alister and Joanna McGrath's predictably titled *The Dawkins Delusion* (2007) and Keith Ward's *Why There Almost Certainly is a God* (2008). But such texts are clearly a defensive counter-move against the popular thrust of preceding works like Dawkins' and Hitchens', or even against the trend made popular by Dan Brown's hugely successful novel *The Da Vinci Code* (2003), which portrayed Christian faith as being founded on cover-ups and lies. They do not appear to be books that appeared under their own steam. That the general thrust of British society around the turn into the twenty-first century is indeed one against religion and towards secularism, is explored thoroughly by Callum G. Brown. Indeed, in *The Death of Christian Britain* (2001) Brown argues that by 2000 Britain has *already* experienced 'the demise of the nation's core religious and moral identity.'[16] Brown positions this decline as starting 'quite suddenly in 1963', entirely coincidentally (or not?) the same year that saw the beginning of the alternative great British institution explored in the very book you are now reading.[17] By 2000, less than a quarter of the population belong to a specific church and fewer than one in ten children attend Sunday school, while religious forms of marriage have become perhaps surprisingly uncommon.[18] Both Dawkins and Hitchens, then, can be understood as an example of what Brown (amongst others) has identified as a deeply pervasive trend that, a decade before the production of 'The God Complex', has already fundamentally undermined the religious makeup of Britain.

It is worth stressing that Brown's arguments centre on religion rather than on faith itself, so his theories regarding secularisation are perhaps only directly relevant to *one* of the many examples of faith described in this chapter. We can account for the decline in *all* faith by moving temporarily away from Dawkins, Hitchens and Brown and towards the deeply entrenched cultural movement known as postmodernism. One of the first critics to write about postmodernism, French philosopher and sociologist Jean-Francois Lyotard defines it in 1979 as 'incredulity towards metanarratives'.[19] Put simply, these metanarratives, in which we no longer trust, can themselves be defined as any ideal or theory that attempts a comprehensive tying together of all the disparate qualities or characteristics of life itself into a nice, neat bundle. And any faith – especially according to the definitions offered at the start of this chapter that focus on different faiths' shared totalising impulses – loosely qualifies as a metanarrative. So if postmodernity is characterised by scepticism towards such modes of thinking, then faith is perhaps an inevitable casualty. What Brown has observed regarding the decline of religious faith, and the arguments Dawkins and Hitchens make that focus on religious faith but move also towards faith in general, can therefore all be levelled as consequences of a wider cultural movement fiercely sceptical towards all ideological comprehensiveness or neatness. Postmodernism, like secularisation, predates both 'Fenric' and 'The God Complex', but it is hard not to see that during the twenty-two year interval between these stories its characteristic scepticism has ratcheted up several notches.

Moving back from postmodernism to the denigrations of faith made by Dawkins et al, it is not the purpose of this chapter (and perhaps not even realistically possible!) to come down on one side of the debate or the other, or to agree with either Dawkins or Ward regarding the redundancy or otherwise of religious and secular faiths. One fair caveat from Ward's *Why There Almost Certainly is a God* is that the belief of Dawkins that everything is (or will eventually be) explainable by science 'goes so far beyond the available evidence that it might be seen as a passionate commitment to a preferred worldview ... made in conditions of objective uncertainty', or, in other words, as much a faith held 'in the teeth of evidence' as those Dawkins attacks.[20] The dialogue between these two recent sets of texts, and the roots from which they have arguably developed, has been evoked simply to convey the sense of a renewed debate about the worth, and even about the safety, of holding faith that simply was not anything like as active in wider cultural circles during the time of

'Fenric', but which can be said to set the stage for the far more cynical portrayal of faith that is central to 'The God Complex'.

The two diametrically opposed portrayals of faith traced here throughout the two stories come to a head in the two stories' strikingly similar final scenes. At the close of 'Fenric', the Seventh Doctor is forced to break Ace's faith in him so that the Ancient Haemovore might sacrifice himself in order to destroy Fenric; unaware of this plan, Ace imagines the Ancient Haemovore is about to attack her and the Doctor instead, and so uses her faith to freeze him in place. Towards the end of 'The God Complex', meanwhile, the Doctor is forced to break Amy's faith in him so that the Minotaur does not claim her as its next victim and is able to lay down its role for good by starving itself. While these scenes might initially appear almost identical, a thorough examination of what's going on in both actually confirms the two distinct versions of faith that belong to the two cultural moments pre- and post- the emergence of the extreme cynicism demonstrated by Dawkins and Hitchens.

The Seventh Doctor's dissolution of Ace's faith may appear necessary within the context of the scene, but is nonetheless remarkably cruel in its execution. After denouncing her as a 'social misfit' and an 'emotional cripple', he then asserts that he 'wouldn't waste [his] time on her' unless he 'had to use her somehow', suggesting that he only ever allowed her to travel with him following their meeting in Briggs's 'Dragonfire' (1987) due to his fore-knowledge that she might one day prove a valuable pawn. Such remarks naturally render Ace a sobbing wreck. But while the Seventh Doctor breaks Ace's faith by ostensibly revealing the truth about his impressions of *her* via a brutal personal attack, the Eleventh Doctor breaks Amy's faith by leaving her alone and, conversely, denigrating *himself*. He informs her, seemingly with genuine regret, that he 'stole [her] childhood' and 'led [her] by the hand to [her] death'. What's more, he admits that his motive was simply vanity and that he is 'not a hero'. Unlike the Seventh Doctor later revealing to Ace that he was merely acting, the Eleventh appears to believe every word he is saying. The focus of the Doctor's denunciation being here not his companion but himself means that Amy feels none of the trauma of Ace, perhaps even experiencing this moment of truth as a profound emotional release. While Ace, then, experiences a loss of faith in her own particular God as profoundly painful, Amy instead experiences the same enforced move to faithlessness far more comfortably. The actual process of losing one's faith has shifted from a negative experience to a positive.

The second important distinction between these two superficially similar moments arises from their aftermaths. It becomes clear that the Seventh Doctor envisages Ace's loss of faith as a temporary emergency measure, rather than a situation that he intends to last beyond Fenric's defeat. Almost immediately afterwards, the Doctor stresses that each of his statements was a lie and begs for Ace to 'believe' him, his use of this specific word suggesting that he is literally asking for Ace to resume the belief that he has just asked her to give up. The very final scene of 'Fenric' involves Ace diving into the newly-safe waters and strongly resembles a baptism, as though Ace is being sworn back into the faith that was temporarily forsaken (actress Sophie Aldred specifically describes this final scene on the DVD commentary as 'a baptism of sorts').[21] Not only does the logic requiring Ace to give up her faith only really attest to its genuine power in warding off monsters, these final scenes demonstrate too that the act of giving up one's faith can hardly be said to be portrayed positively within the episodes when it is only ever conceived of as a temporary measure, to be reversed literally as soon as the situation allows.

'The God Complex', on the other hand, portrays Amy's loss of faith as not only a positive experience, but a lasting one. Most obviously, the Doctor does not ask for Amy's faith back, but realises that his influence has lastingly damaged her and so leaves her on Earth to attempt a normal life with Rory. The Doctor has already explained to Rita that if you 'offer someone all of time and space' then, like a child accepting a 'suitcase full of sweets', he or she will 'take it', which, the Doctor concludes, 'is why you shouldn't'. The Doctor's self-awareness here of the dangerous faith he encourages veers startlingly close to Dawkins' own withering equation of encouraging religion in a child with abuse.[22] Throughout this episode, the Minotaur's devouring of those who wind up holding faith in it is paralleled with the Doctor's own proclivity for placing his companions in extreme danger. The connections between these two characters run deep. On first encountering the Minotaur, the Doctor describes him as a being who has 'lived so long, even [his] name is lost', anticipating the reveal at the close of the upcoming season finale 'The Wedding of River Song' (2011) that the question from which the Doctor is running – and that the Silence are desperate he never answer – involves his own concealed identity. But the salient point here is that it is the Doctor's realisation that he and the Minotaur *both* place others in danger, through the faith held in them, which catalyses the Doctor's benevolent severing of Amy's faith. It could even be argued that the Minotaur urging the Doctor to help it cut off its food supply sets such a righteous example that the Doctor could not do otherwise than respond by cutting off his own. That the Doctor's severing of Amy's faith is motivated by the Minotaur's own example, which demonstrates to the Doctor how encouraging faith in others can be so incredibly dangerous, means that the loss of Amy's faith, unlike the very temporary loss of Ace's, simply has to be permanent. The lasting nature of this breaking of faith is attested to not only by Amy's aforementioned incredulity regarding the Doctor's growing propensity for violence in Whithouse's next episode, 'A Town Called Mercy', but also by her urging the Doctor in her very final episode, 'The Angels Take Manhattan' (2012), that he avoid travelling alone, Amy seemingly having learnt by her last moments with him that he requires constant companionship for the darkness within him to remain safely contained.

So while breaking Ace's faith appears a temporary but harsh cruelty, breaking Amy's appears a merciful release for herself, the Minotaur and not least the Doctor himself, freed from the burden of leading others blindly into danger. We should also look closely at what actually happens to the god complex described by the story's title – a title particularly fitting, for it describes both the messianic mindset of the Doctor (as pointed out to him by Rita) and the literal, concrete complex that is the prison-ship built to house the Minotaur. And at the same time as the Doctor lets go of his own god complex by revealing his true, somewhat mundanely selfish self to Amy, the physical environment in which this adventure takes place is similarly dismantled and its true nature finally revealed. Its appearance as a twisting, multi-levelled labyrinth is exposed as an illusion, the stripping away of which leaves nothing more than a bare room. The opulence and complexity of the hotel, like the nobility of the Doctor, and by extension the value of all subjects of faith, is simply the result of a trick. Perhaps this revelation sees the episode arguing that a delusionary faith appears most enticing when the reality lying beneath its false splendours remains bereft of its own attractions.

Either way, this unveiling of the empty space that lies beneath the ship's facade appears the perfect metaphor for cutting to the heart of how this episode's portrayal of faith is so distinct from 'Fenric''s. The earlier story's constant affirmation of faith's genuine powers of redemption and the re-stoking of Ace's belief in the Doctor almost immediately after its suspension both suggest one of two alternative possibilities, depending upon your own point of view. Either the story is unwilling to expose the illusions dissolved in the closing moments of 'The God Complex' and prefers instead to keep the viewer in the dark about faith's true nature, or, conversely, the story triumphantly preserves faith's true values by continually underlining what it can really do for us in our times of need. Whichever reading of 'Fenric' a particular viewer might favour, it is clear that Dawkins, Hitchens and their many fans would far prefer the later episode's obvious and extreme scepticism.

5.

The Doctor Working on God's Time: Kairos and Intervention in 'The Waters of Mars' and 'A Christmas Carol'

Michael Charlton

Kairos and Chronos

> Then Jesus said: 'My time is not yet come: but your time is always ready.'
> (John 7:6)

In Greek mythology, Chronos was the personification of time. An ancestor of the more familiar figure of Father Time, Chronos or Khronos would also become the root of words such as chronology and chronometer. Essentially, 'chronos' referred to 'time in the sense of duration' – time as measured by clocks and calendars. However, the Greeks had another word for time, which would come to be crucial in both rhetoric and theology. This was *kairos*, which could literally mean 'climate' or 'weather' but had a more esoteric meaning as well:

> Kairos is time in the sense of particular time, especially right and proper time, as in Romans 5:6 where Paul says that while we were yet helpless, at the right time (*kairos*) Christ died for the ungodly. Therefore in Christian studies there is endeavour not only to have an appreciation of the long sweep of history but also to identify the particular points by which that history is notably punctuated.[1]

Though the word first appeared in sources as early as Hesiod and Homer, *kairos* is crucial to the New Testament. As Phillip Sipiora notes, 'the first words of Christ call attention to the importance of timing: "The time [kairos] is fulfilled, and the kingdom of God is at hand" (Mark 1:14)'; other Biblical mentions of timing abound, perhaps most famously in Ecclesiastes.[2]

Ultimately, kairos came to mean 'something like "God's Time", uninfluenced by the rhythms and cycles of chronological, earthly time':

> Kairos always contextualises or mediates circumstances, usually in making situations conducive for the persuasive act of belief and trust, which lead in turn to changes in conviction, emotion, and action.[3]

In other words, kairic time was a 'time of crisis' or 'judgement' or 'special opportunity' in which human beings, especially believers, were called upon to act in the interests of divine providence. *Chronos* or chronological time is allowed to move forward in its normal fashion until the 'ultimate kairic moment' of decision, which can lead on to salvation or condemnation.[4]

It is worth stopping to think about the Christian conception of time and temporality in general. As William Gallois puts it, Christian time as set forth in the New Testament and expanded upon by later philosophers is 'deeply anti-linear' and a deliberate rejection of 'biology and materiality' as opposed to the redemptive narrative of the Gospels:

> History . . . acquires meaning as destiny and as a form of judgment. Its purpose is the judging of souls to assess whether they are deserving of eternal life, of living beyond human history. Jesus and God's mastery of time enables them to move between old days and new times in a manner which assures men that their immediate apperception of time (from, for example, the changing of the seasons) is but one of the modes of time that exist in our lives. Faith is the belief in that which is not obvious, and a belief in the otherness of God's time is one step towards a life of faith ....[5]

The conception of the divine as omnipresent and omniscient – knowing and being in the past, present and future – and the conception of human history as essentially a long preface to and judgement for the afterlife, makes human history and material conceptions of time pale reflections of spiritual time. God's time is, by definition, not chronological time – or, at least, a version of chronological time not readily comprehensible to the average believer. For example, 2 Peter 3:8 famously presents a temporal paradox of the very timey-wimey variety: 'that one day with the Lord is as a thousand years, and a thousand years as one day'.[6] While Gallois does not consider the concept of *kairos* in detail, it is easy to see how a belief in time which stresses not clocks, calendars, and other human measurements of time but divine plans and interventions is essentially kairic. History and chronological time are only a background to the primary narrative of salvation, which progresses to moments of crisis and decision.

Kairos as an important religious concept would survive into the twentieth century, when it became central to the theology of, among others, Paul Tillich, who sought to integrate the notion of kairic time with history:

> Tillich distinguished . . . the notion of Kairos from that of Chronos in order to indicate that certain times have a unique and specific qualitative nature; that there are times in history which constitute 'turning points,' demanding our decision, our response in some special way . . ..[7]

Describing Tillich's view of *kairos* as 'that point in which eternity invades into time' and history as a 'succession' of kairic moments in which human events intersect with the divine, William Warren notes the connection to the concerns of liberation theology, which sees 'history [as] the locus of God's purpose in terms of God's liberating purpose and liberating activity' and which argues for 'a very close parallel between the manner in which God is revealed in the Biblical witness and the manner in which God is revealed in the struggle for liberation'.[8] Central to these theologians was the idea that religion and the religious are always a part of historical tragedies and struggles, not separated from them; to live in the world in time was to face moments of decision plagued by doubt and illuminated by belief. In a rhetorical reading of Martin Luther King's final sermon and its relationship to *kairos*, Richard Benjamin Crosby noted much the same theme. As one popular preaching handbook titled *Kairos Preaching* put it, 'when we preach in the face of injustice, we will need to do so with an acknowledgment of our own enmeshment and without any plausible claim to purity or perfection'.[9] The intersection of time as perceived by humans – historical events, natural cycles – and time as conceived of by scripture – spiritual crises, divine omnipresence – continued to make time and history problematic concepts for the believer, who is asked to perceive both simultaneously and to know when historical events call for spiritual decisions.

Classical rhetoricians tended to have a more pragmatic view of *kairos*, and focused on it as a tool for the persuader. Indeed, *kairos* was sometimes seen as synonymous with propriety or good taste.[10] Greek orators like Gorgias believed that timing was important because 'an oration's timeliness adds to its force and effectiveness'.[11] A speech on an issue which has already been decided or which has not yet become significant will obviously fail to capture an audience preoccupied by the present moment. However, even in rhetorical studies there were ethical dimensions to *kairos*, such as Aristotle's insistence that the 'most beneficial way to perform an act is in the "right time"'.[12] Modern scholars have tended to note the slippery nature of *kairos*: 'Kairic time . . . marks opportunities that might not recur, moments of decision. Whereas chronos-time is absolute, universal, and objective, kairos is interpretive, situational, and, thus, subjective'.[13] While Aristotle confidently asserts that accusation and defence and praise and blame 'each . . . has its own time'[14] and Isocrates declares that the educated are those 'who possess a judgment which is accurate in meeting occasions as they arise and rarely misses the expedient course of action',[15] rhetoricians in a less certain world have tended to argue about how one is to know when expedience is called for and which action will, in fact, be expedient. In many ways, rhetorical and religious theories of *kairos* have both come to their own kairic moment in which a recognition that 'right action' and intervention are important has been coupled with a knowledge that decisions to act, to preach, or to believe are fraught with dangers and surrounded by complications.

Modern Conceptions of Time and *Doctor Who*

And he saith unto me, seal not the sayings of the prophecy of this book: for the time is at hand.
(Revelation 22:10)

Of course, the concept of time itself reached a turning point with developments in relativity and other areas of physics. Einsteinian space-time smashed the perception that clock-time was the constant and objective reality it appeared to be. Where *chronos* had been defined as 'the successive occurrence of global nows or presents', relativity insisted on a simultaneity that made it impossible to select a 'particular set of simultaneous events as constituting the now or the present'.[16] Space and time were no longer separable and the perception of time could be based on the positions, speeds, and natures of the observer and the object being observed, leading to any number of theoretically accurate but mind-bending sentences such as the following: 'In the history of some material object or person an event not on its world line can at some earlier times be in its future and at some later times be in its past without ever being present'.[17]

Apparent paradoxes abounded, such as the 'twin paradox' in which 'an astronaut who makes a journey into space in a high-speed rocket will return home to find he has aged less than his twin who stayed on Earth' due to the twisting of time at extreme speeds.[18] As the great physicist Richard Feynman put it in a statement that would effectively eliminate a quarter of the *Doctor Who* plots in the series' history:

> There are fortune-tellers, or people who tell us they can know the future, and there are many wonderful stories about the man who suddenly discovers that he has knowledge about the affective future. Well, there are lots of paradoxes produced by that because if we know something is going to happen, then we can make sure we will avoid it by doing the right thing at the right time, and so on.[19] But actually there is no fortune-teller who can even tell us the present! There is no one who can tell us what is really happening right now, at any reasonable distance, because that is unobservable.[20]

In vulgar terms, *chronos* lost its mojo. The certainty that human beings could remember something confidently termed the past, live in something absolutely perceptible as the present, and meaningfully affect a singular future disappeared.

Unsurprisingly, along with the increasing ambiguity of time in science came attempts to tie time back into religious conceptions of eternity and spiritual time, such as Lawrence Fagg's concluding remarks in his *The Becoming of Time*: ' . . . a more complete comprehension of time can only be achieved by incorporating a spiritual perspective with the physical view in a harmonious view of faith and reason'.[21] The new understanding of time reintroduced age-old questions about time, including the question of determinism. Consider famous time travel paradoxes, such as whether one can go back in time to kill one's own grandfather, or whether a time traveller can bring an object back to the past and so cause it to be invented before it should have been invented because it has already been invented.[22] A new understanding of time forced questions about how freely human beings were allowed to act in relation to time and whether there were any outside constraints or larger narratives that must be preserved. In many ways, these debates were not dissimilar from religious debates about the freedom to act in a universe created by an omnipresent, omniscient deity who exists apart from time. The time traveller of paradox was always faced with a kairic moment of one sort or another: meeting up with a twin years older than himself, or deciding whether or not to shoot grandpa.

Doctor Who has usually dealt with a version of *chronos* which nods to Einsteinian space-time with the very name of the TARDIS. The Doctor is a Time Lord, capable of visiting the past, present, and future at any physical location in the known universe. There is a running idea that the Doctor is adverse to, or possibly even forbidden to, alter history. As early as 1964's 'The Aztecs', the Doctor admonished his companion that, 'You can't rewrite history! Not one line!' Especially early in the series, when the Doctor and his companions met up with historical figures such as Marco Polo and Nero, or revisited events such as the Reign of Terror or the Crusades, there was a normally unexpressed rule that the course of known human history would be preserved.[23] The most the Doctor could do was observe and perhaps rescue someone like Dodo, who plays no major part in the history of the world. Serials like 'The War Games', in which aliens kidnap soldiers from across human history and force them to fight each other, or 'The King's Demons', in which the Master tries to prevent the Magna Carta from being signed, reinforce the idea that interfering with human history in any fundamental way is villainous.

As *The Discontinuity Guide* notes, there are no clear guidelines: 'There seem to be acceptable and non-acceptable areas of interference, and many grey areas, and these are constantly evolving. An unmentioned, but vital, code of conduct seems to exist'.[24] Paradoxically, sometimes the Doctor's attempts to not interfere cause the already-accepted history to happen in the first place; the Doctor manages to be behind both the burning of Rome (in 'The Romans') and the great fire of London (in 'The Visitation'). Most of the time, there appears to be an 'accepted' narrative of the past and future – the ways things were 'meant to be' – though it is never clear who or what determines what is acceptable. Even the Time Lords, who seem to stand aloof from time and seek to preserve it, have been known to interfere (such as in 'Genesis of the Daleks', where the Doctor is sent back to stop the eventual victory of his mortal enemies). It appears that history can, in fact, be rewritten. Stories like 'City of Death' require the Doctor to intercede before humanity is wiped out in the past or the future.

There are beings who live apart from time, most notably the Black and White Guardians. These quasi-divine beings are said to 'maintain balance', and yet their motives and means remain fairly inscrutable. They seem to show up only when their own interests are threatened (such as in the 'Key to Time' sequence). The ability to move within time and to alter events does not seem to have a moral prerequisite. For example, the time-and-space transversing Tharils in 'Warrior's Gate' turn out to have been decadent slave owners before they were enslaved themselves, and the Eternals in 'Enlightenment' (1983) are willing to murder hundreds of kidnapped human sailors in order to stave off what is essentially the boredom of their unchanging existence.

The idea that there is a 'limitation effect' for time travel, which prevents the Doctor from continually retrying to alter the same series of events or 'crossing his own timeline' to revisit an event he has already witnessed, first appears explicitly in 'Day of the Daleks', though a similar idea had been hinted at many times before in the series. Partly, this is obviously a storytelling device to prevent certain paradoxes and to add suspense; if the Doctor could constantly repeat events until he achieved what he desired or if he could jump in the TARDIS to go back five minutes and prevent a sudden death, what tension would be left in the series? Yet this 'limitation' remains the series' major rule for time travel, particularly in the revival. Arguably, the overarching story of the first four years of the revival depends on the Time War, which wiped out the rest of the Time Lords, being a 'fixed point' in time which cannot be revisited or rewritten. 'Father's Day' shows the dire consequences of allowing someone to try and save a person who is 'meant' to be dead, as well as the consequences of two versions of the same person existing in the same space. In multiple stories, the Doctor insists that he cannot go back and change things once he has become 'part of events'. As with the original series, attempting to interfere with history can actually cause the original 'intended' events to take place (most notably in 'The Fires of Pompeii', where the Doctor's confrontation with the Pyroviles directly causes the eruption of Vesuvius). In 'The Wedding of River Song', the Doctor's death itself turns out to be a 'fixed point' in history. When River refuses to kill the Doctor according to the timeline, time itself comes to a stop and all of human history begins to co-exist simultaneously.

As we have seen, time in *Doctor Who* is mostly conceptualised as chronological or historical. Time is a sequence of events which may or may not be altered. Yet there are moments when the series confronts the rhetorical and theological notion of *kairos*. The remainder of this chapter is concerned with two particular moments of intervention from the revived series, 'The Waters of Mars' (2009) and 'A Christmas Carol' (2010). In both stories the Doctor is confronted with an unusual enemy. While both feature an external threat, the threat in each is really time itself. In the first, the Doctor is torn between preserving the 'correct' course of human history or preserving the human lives under threat. In the second, the Doctor chooses to rewrite history in order to change the life story and personality of a miser who holds lives in his hands.

In these twin battles with time, the Doctor takes on traditionally divine powers because he believes it to be the kairic moment of choice. While one adventure becomes a story of salvation through time redeemed, the other becomes a story of damnation through time lost. *Doctor Who* and the viewer are confronted with complex religious questions of determinism and freedom as the series reveals the thorny moral questions at the heart of the Doctor's interventions in time.

'The Waters of Mars' and Time Lost

> For man also knoweth not his time: as the fishes that are taken in an evil net, and as the birds that are caught in the snare; so are the sons of men snared in an evil time, when it falleth suddenly upon them. (Ecclesiastes 9:12)

Given co-writer Russell T. Davies's well-known hostility to organised religion, it may seem like a stretch to read 'The Waters of Mars' (co-written by Phil Ford) as a religious text. Certainly neither story under discussion here is meant primarily as a sermon on Christian religious tenets or ethics. While 'A Christmas Carol' takes place during one of the central events of the Christian calendar, it is based on the world's most famous secular Yuletide tale. Yet both stories play with images and concepts crucial to the Judeo-Christian traditions, and both tangle with philosophical and moral questions that are relevant to both Christians and those with other beliefs.

In fact, one of the earliest scenes in 'Waters of Mars' evokes Judeo-Christian tradition, as the gardener for Bowie Base One (the first off-world human colony) comments on his domain: 'Everything brand new. Eden – that's what we should have called this place.' Obviously, Eden is a fitting name for humanity's first outer space garden and yet the line is also a foretelling of the choices the Doctor will face once he lands near the doomed base. For what is Eden but a symbol of knowledge gained at the cost of paradise and the temptations of breaking divine rules?

The Doctor knows from the beginning that he is breaking the rules of non-intervention. As soon as he discovers his actual location and the date, he realises that Bowie Base One will be destroyed before the end of the day. His knowledge of human history tells him that this colony is doomed and that there will be no survivors. The series' long-standing rule of 'non-intervention' and leaving major historical events as they were 'intended' to occur tells him that he should go. Yet from the beginning he alternates between begging to leave and recognising that leaving goes against every instinct in his body, which normally prods him to save human life whenever possible – especially humans as brave and noble as these space pioneers: 'I'm sorry with all my hearts. But it's one of those very rare times when I've got no choice.' Choice will be the word he returns to over and over again. Early in the story, he insists that leaving is not a decision he wants to make but one forced on him by circumstances. When prodded for more information by the crew, who quickly realise he knows more about the developing crisis than he admits, he chooses to plead ignorance ('I just open my mouth and words come out. They don't make much sense.').

The Doctor is held hostage by his pilfered spacesuit, which prevents him from walking back to the TARDIS. But he is also held hostage by curiosity. He wants to know more about these heroic individuals. When talking to Adelaide, the no-nonsense commander of the mission, he asks a simple question: 'Was it worth it? They say you sacrificed your whole life to get here.' The question comes from a humane place. There is nothing the Doctor consistently admires more than courage and the willingness to sacrifice for others. Adelaide responds in a moment that reveals her own buried idealism, contrasting the 'chaos' on Earth with their ability to 'fly above it'. It is a moving image of transcendence – of escaping the 'smoke' and 'extinction' of her old life to her new life in Eden. More than anything else, it is this emotional connection between the Doctor and Adelaide which will result in tragedy and her eventual death. Later, when she tells of losing her parents and her childhood encounter with a Dalek, the Doctor calls Adelaide remarkable for wanting to explore the universe for its own wonders, not for 'revenge' against the alien invaders. It is clear that, in other circumstances, Adelaide is just the sort of person who would make a fitting companion for the Doctor, who describes himself as the 'maintenance man of the universe' and also seeks to fix things and 'fly above it' all.

They both dream of the future. Yet the Doctor knows from the beginning that Adelaide has no future. His admiration for her becomes a trap. The more he likes her, the harder it is to leave. He tells her that she will inspire her granddaughter to fly out to the stars and that this, in turn, will inspire all of humanity to explore the universe. When she asks him why he is sharing this information about the future, he tells her simply that it is for 'consolation'. The obvious dramatic moment in the story comes later, when the Doctor explicitly tells Adelaide that Bowie Base One is doomed, and yet that one word – 'consolation' – seems to signal a turning point in itself. The Doctor has already told her his theory of time and that there are 'tiny, precious moments' in the sweep of history that have to 'stand': 'What happens here must always happen.' He tries to diffuse this dire warning, claiming that 'something wonderful' is about to come, but it is clear that Adelaide does not believe him. In his sympathy and admiration, he has already gone too far. 'Consolation' is itself a word with religious connotations of spiritual comfort – but a comfort grounded in great loss and suffering.[25] Adelaide, who is nothing if not attentive and intelligent, seems to understand from this moment that her tragedy is fixed and inescapable. She traps the Doctor into telling her the entire truth about the destruction of Bowie Base One at her hands mostly as confirmation of this moment, despite her avowed certainty that this is the 'moment we escape'.

It is important that the Doctor approaches his moment of spiritual crisis with what are normally considered noble principles. His respect for human life causes him to regret his inability to act and further spurs his admiration for Adelaide, whom he notes fails to shoot Andy when given the opportunity. He understands that the people of Bowie Base One will sacrifice themselves to spare Earth from invasion by the Flood, the water-based parasites who consume the crew members one by one. Yet, when forced by Adelaide to tell her of her doom, he stresses that he has no choice in the matter. By this point, though, the terms have notably changed. In previous discussions, the Doctor stresses that the matter is out of his hands and that all he can do is leave. Now, he stresses the futility of trying to act against the course of history: 'Imagine you knew something. Imagine you found yourself somewhere – I don't know, Pompeii. Imagine you were in Pompeii. And you tried to save them. But, in doing so, you make it happen. Anything I do, just makes it happen.' This is a more telling shift than it might first appear. While the Doctor's original argument is based on principles set down by the Time Lords, this is an argument based on pragmatics. He now knows that he wants to act – that he wants to violate the laws of time – but insists to himself that this is not just immoral but actually impossible: 'Your death is fixed in time forever. And that's right.'

The villain in 'The Waters of Mars' is not really the Flood but time itself. This is what separates the story from most of *Doctor Who's* time-honoured 'base under siege' stories.[26] The real threat is not alien invasion but the possibility that the intended course of history could be fractured. *Chronos* even sounds like a suitable name for a *Doctor Who* villain.[27] It is after his conversation about Pompeii and Adelaide's death, when the Doctor is walking away from the base and listening to the crew as they die one by one over the audio in his helmet, that the Doctor himself realises the true nature of his villain. The Doctor faces his kairic moment as Bowie Base One faces a literal, chronological countdown in the form of the self-destruct sequence.

As we have seen, there are two competing definitions for *kairos*. In rhetoric, it might be seen as the ability to perform the right action at the right time. In theology, it might be seen as the ability to determine when the time has come for moral and spiritual action according to the divine plan. The tragedy of the Doctor in 'The Waters of Mars' is that he embraces rhetorical *kairos* while violating its spiritual cousin. In normal moral terms, it would be difficult to argue against the Doctor's behaviour once he returns to Bowie Base One and attempts to save the three remaining crew members. This moral decision has been building from the beginning of the story, when the Doctor began to notice the qualities of courage, sacrifice, and compassion in the crew. The Doctor does his best to save three people who have proven to be moral themselves and, temporarily at least, he succeeds. When the kairic moment came – the choice to continue on to the TARDIS and save only himself or to turn back and attempt a rescue – the Doctor made the choice that most members of the audience would normally applaud. In fact, given his indecision and insistence on his impotence throughout the story, most members of the audience would normally applaud the Doctor for finally making any choice.

Yet the story insists that the Doctor was wrong in terms of what I have called spiritual *kairos*. If *kairos* is indeed the moment of judgement, when people are called upon to act according to a grander design, then the Doctor finally makes a choice only to make the wrong choice. There is a sophistication to this moment and a recognition of moral dilemmas. The 'right' course of action can become wrong if the moment in time asks for what would normally be considered cowardly and self-serving.[28] The idea that the Doctor is wrong for turning around and helping others flies in the face of most human principles, but this is the morality imposed by the idea of 'fixed points'; in this scheme, the value of individual human lives is less important than the preservation of the historical plan. This is an uncomfortable notion both in science fiction and in religion, where believers may be called upon to act in ways that benefit ineffable, inscrutable divine plans and that cannot be easily understood by mundane humans.

When the Doctor approaches *kairos* or 'God's time', he begins to claim godhood for himself. His claim that time will 'obey' him because he is the 'winner' is pure, undiluted hubris. He follows up his realisation that they are fighting 'time itself' with the boast that he is going to 'win'. Adelaide becomes an enemy when she decides to question him, even though it was her curiosity and strength that first drew his admiration. She faces her own kairic moment when she decides to activate the self-destruct – choosing to sacrifice herself and the remaining crew but ensuring that Earth will be safe from invasion. Indeed, by this point the Doctor and Adelaide have switched moral positions. While he originally took a deterministic stance that history was written in stone and she insisted that they could act to save themselves, he now insists on his free will while she accepts the need for self-negation in order to preserve history and her legacy.

The Doctor has become a raging ego. Upon returning them all
to Earth, he pouts that they do not thank him quickly enough and
callously remarks of the defunct robot that, 'He's lost his signal.
Doesn't know where he is.' On the contrary, it is the Doctor who
has lost his own moral signal and his own sense that time is precious
rather than the enemy. Adelaide slams the point home, appalled
at his dismissal of her crew as 'little people' and articulating the
deterministic argument for preserving the course of history first
posited by the Doctor himself when he insists that history will bend
to his whims: 'You can't know that. And if my family changes, the
whole of history could change. The future of the human race. No
one should have that much power.' Unable to grasp that his decision
to intervene has been disastrous, the Doctor proclaims himself the
'Time Lord Victorious' and asserts that no one can stand against him
any longer. He is proven wrong almost immediately and in tragic
fashion. Adelaide kills herself in order to prove that the 'fixed point'
of her death will remain and that the glorious human future will be
preserved. There is a moral murkiness to this moment, as victory
comes at the cost of a human life and in a fashion that many would
consider immoral in itself. There is also a philosophical murkiness to
this moment, as the viewer is presented with a conundrum: did the
course of history itself deterministically force Adelaide into her tragic
choice or was she able to choose a path which preserved history?

Confronted with this rebuke to his claim of god-like powers over
time, the Doctor realises that he has 'gone too far'. As in theology,
the kairic moment is a moment of judgement and even death. The
Doctor immediately perceives the benevolent and even mystical alien
Ood and interprets it as a sign that his death is imminent and that his
own actions have brought him here, having already been told that
his death is approaching in 'Planet of the Dead'. He flees into the
TARDIS to hear the ringing of the cloister bell, which in stories such
as 'Logopolis' was tied into moments of impending disaster and can
foretell the Doctor's demise. Yet the Doctor is not willing to submit
to judgement. His last word in the story is an emphatic 'No!' as he
frantically causes the TARDIS to dematerialise. In 'The Waters of
Mars', the Doctor loses his battle with kairic time. What began with
noble motives and sympathies devolves into a self-centred assertion
of power and control over the course of history. Faced with this final
kairic choice – to go to the Ood and face his appointed judgement
or to flee – he falls into self-preservation mode and again makes the
wrong decision at the right time.[29]

'A Christmas Carol' and Time Redeemed

> And that, knowing the time, that now it is high time to awake out of sleep: for now is our salvation nearer than when we believed. (Romans 13:11)

In many ways, Kazran Sardick is the opposite of Adelaide Brooke: selfish, cowardly, concerned only with himself, and obsessed with past wrongs. A tyrant over an entire planet, Kazran has inherited his father's technological ability to control the skies and the descent of swarms of fish that swim within its crystalline fogs. He has also inherited Elliot Sardick's collection of iceboxes, in which people are cryogenically frozen as security for the massive loans their families have taken out with the Sardicks. Whereas Adelaide valiantly struggles to save her people, Earth, and history itself, Kazran is an old miser who spends his Christmas Eve gleeful over the prospect that a spaceship filled with thousands of innocent bystanders will crash because he refuses to help them. Yet while Adelaide is doomed to a tragic end, Kazran will be redeemed. Time itself will be the decider, with the Doctor on hand to recreate Dickens and serve as the ghosts of Christmases past, present, and yet to come. As the writer Steven Moffat notes in the *Doctor Who Confidential* episode about 'A Christmas Carol', Kazran, whatever his faults, is 'saveable' and it is time travel itself that saves him (much as it does for Scrooge with his ghosts). Such are the difficulties of *kairos*. Sometimes the right action at the right time is performed for the person who appears least deserving of mercy and grace.

After the prologue, in which the Doctor's companions Amy and Rory are endangered by their crashing spaceship, the episode proper begins with a reflection on time: 'On every world, wherever people are, in the deepest part of the winter at the exact midpoint everybody stops and turns and hugs as if to say: well done. Well done, everyone. We're halfway out of the dark. Back on Earth, we call this Christmas, or the winter solstice.' In this narration, Christmas itself becomes a kairic moment – the turning point between the darkness and death of winter and the light and renewal of spring. If 'The Waters of Mars' built its narrative partially on images of Eden and paradise lost, 'A Christmas Carol' builds its narrative on images of light and music. Throughout the episode, light becomes a metaphor not only for the time of the year but for the state of Kazran's soul, which grows lighter as his bitterness is lessened. Music serves a similar redeeming function, with Abigail's songs moving from reflections on the season caught between darkness and light (when she first awakes, she sings 'In the Bleak Midwinter') to full-out redemption in her final song, which saves the inhabitants of the spaceship and accompanies a joyous and long-delayed snowfall.

The Doctor's first confrontation with Kazran is a crucial moment in the progression towards the kairic decision. At first appearing comical, sliding down the chimney like Santa and joking about staying off the 'naughty list', the Doctor turns cold when Sardick casually dismisses the girl in a nearby icebox as nobody important: 'Nobody important? Blimey, that's amazing. Do you know, in nine hundred years of time and space I've never met anyone who wasn't important before?' Unlike the Doctor of 'The Waters of Mars', who himself spoke of 'little people', this Doctor stresses that all life is important and does so by emphasising his own great age and experience. Time has taught him the value of apparent nobodies.

He flares with anger at Sardick: 'Whatever happens tonight, remember: you brought it on yourself.' This hints that the Doctor's plans for the tyrant are far from benevolent or benign. Yet these plans turn in a moment. When a young boy throws something at Sardick, the old miser rises from his chair and rushes to strike the child – only holding back at the last moment. This act of restraint is what convinces the Doctor that Kazran is worth saving ('Because you didn't hit the boy. Merry Christmas, Mr Sardick.'). He instantly notices that Sardick's chair is angled away from a portrait of his father and intuits the abusive relationship that will later be confirmed by videos of the past. Intent on saving Sardick and the crashing spaceship, the Doctor struggles to come up with a plan for the hour he has left before disaster. Tellingly, it is the striking of a clock which gives him the idea. As a mechanised choir begins to sing Christmas carols on the hour, the Doctor makes the connection not only to 'A Christmas Carol' itself as a story about redeeming a miser, but the need to travel into the past to understand the roots of Kazran's behaviour. In a certain sense, time is the villain in 'A Christmas Carol' just as much as it is in 'The Waters of Mars'. Time is counting down for Amy, Rory, and thousands of other souls; time is running out for Abigail. Yet there is a crucial difference: time can also be an ally, starting with the striking of this clock and the spark of inspiration.

It is central to the moral meaning of 'A Christmas Carol' that it rejects the traditional rules of time and intervention in *Doctor Who*. As he begins to travel back into Kazran's childhood, the Doctor makes a simple statement: 'Times change'. This is a radical revision of the idea of 'fixed time' or an intended history which must be preserved. The Doctor rather cavalierly informs Sardick that changing time will mean changing his memories – something that Sardick quickly realises is true as he watches videos recorded by his younger self in which the Doctor suddenly appears. There is a massive contradiction built into all of this. The Doctor is rewriting the personal history of this man. Realistically, this should mean that Sardick instantly remembers the new version of events, since they have already happened decades in the past.[30] Yet the present and the past seem to exist simultaneously, so that the miser only remembers this 'new' past as it happens on the video ('That never happened ... But it did.'). Later, Sardick seems to remember the 'new' past an instant before it happens on the video. Obviously, this makes very little literal sense. However, it is crucial to Sardick's development as a character. In order for him to be redeemed and to make the correct choice when the kairic moment comes, it is necessary for him to remember both pasts simultaneously – the one in which the Doctor never interfered and the one in which he did. Only by contrasting himself with the man he used to be can Sardick hope to change.

As a young boy, Kazran turns out to have a compassionate nature, even wanting to save a shark that had previously tried to eat him. Deciding that an icebox will preserve the shark, the Doctor and Kazran race down to the vault but are stuck outside because Kazran will not be told the keycode until he is older. The Doctor jumps forward into the future to learn the keycode from the elderly Kazran, then returns to the younger Kazran and opens the door. Note that this is another violation of how time traditionally operates in *Doctor Who*, as the Doctor is quite obviously bouncing back and forth in events in which he is a central participant. As with the simultaneously occurring past and present, this violation is done with a view toward Kazran's moral development. Having seen that the miser was once a kind soul, the Doctor is not going to let a little thing like the laws of time and dictates about not criss-crossing timestreams interfere with this first generous gesture of saving the shark.

Opening the door leads them to Abigail, a frozen girl with a beautiful singing voice and the future love of Kazran's life. Kazran's family has attempted to control time-as-money by freezing all of these people as collateral and stealing their lives away. Abigail is untouched by this greed – a genial soul who loves Christmas and can soothe the savage shark through song. But she is not untouched by

time – a counter on the front of her icebox indicates that she only has
a few days left to live before illness claims her, though both Kazran
and the Doctor fail to notice this. Infatuated with her, Kazran pledges
that he and the Doctor will spend every Christmas Eve with her. As
with the opening narration, there is an insistence on Christmas as a
particularly crucial time and a time in which joy and redemption are
possible. The Doctor and Kazran spend a whirlwind of Christmases
with her, still oblivious to her rapidly dwindling hourglass.

Tellingly, when Abigal is given the choice of any Christmas to
experience across all of time, she picks 'this one' – the present moment
– and to spend it with her family as well as the Doctor and Kazran.
The Doctor abuses the timeline, melding past and present. Kazran's
family attempts to control people's time through the iceboxes and the
manipulation of the atmosphere. It is only Abigail who truly values
the moment in which she is living, in part because her impending
mortality has made time more precious to her.

Kazran approaches his kairic moment when he discovers how
little time Abigail has left. Crucially, his kairic moment is a choice not
only to be made at the right time but a choice about the right time.
Upon learning that he has only one day left to spend with Abigail,
he immediately slides back into the bitter and miserly old man he
was in the beginning. Rather than telling the Doctor the truth, he
turns against him and decides that his attempts at redemption were
actually cruel ('As a very old friend of mine once took a very long time
to explain: life isn't fair!'). The painting on the elderly Kazran's wall,
which had turned into a glowing portrait of Abigail, is transformed
back into his dour, abusive father. He is as bad as he ever was and
still willing to let the ship crash.

The final 'ghosts' appear to him: Amy and the other people
doomed to die because of his selfishness. She assures him that 'time
can be rewritten' but he rebukes her, reminding her that she will soon
die and 'tonight's as good as any other night' to do it. The attempts
to rewrite history and to redeem time seem to have failed. Even
Christmas, that time halfway out of the dark which signalled his rare
and precious periods with Abigail, has been rejected.

This is Kazran's moment of decision. His kairic choice is a bitter
one, in which more time for the people aboard the spaceship means
the final sacrifice of his remaining time with Abigail ('Would you do
it? Would you do this? One last day with your beloved. Which day
would you choose?'). Yet the Doctor assures him that this marks an
improvement over the man he used to be ('Better a broken heart than

no heart at all.'). Utterly torn, he is confronted with the one person who can make him see the change within himself: his younger self, who the Doctor has brought forward in time to witness the horrid miser his choices have made him. It is a moment that shatters the last remaining conventions of time in *Doctor Who*, by allowing two versions of the same person to occupy the same space at the same time. According to the conventional rules, there should be dire consequences. Yet it is this confrontation that leads on to Kazran's salvation. He learns to let go of his bitterness about lost time and to release Abigail, who gently tells him that he has 'hoarded [her] days like an old miser' and that it is time for him to move forward in his life. After all of the Christmas Eves they have spent together, 'it's time for Christmas day'. Time must be allowed to move and the people in the spaceship saved, even if it means that Abigail and Kazran have only one last day together.

Time in 'A Christmas Carol' seems to have taken a holiday from the rules: it can be rewritten, the past and the present can be one, and the past and the future can even touch. This is not accidental but rather another dimension of *kairos*. Early on there is a sneering suggestion to 'pray for a miracle', and this is precisely what appears to happen. Christmas itself becomes a kairic moment, when the rules are suspended in the interests of redemption. When it comes time for judgement, Kazran proves to be worthy of his choice. The Doctor's timely intervention has made him into a man who understands not only the bitterness of loss but the promise of the time remaining. While the story jokingly posits the Doctor as a stand-in for Santa, he fulfils a role closer to the deity in Christian conceptions of time and *kairos*: a being capable of existing in the past, present, and future who creates a grand narrative pointing toward choice and redemption.

It is crucial that Kazran be free to make this choice. The Doctor's most fragile moment is when he is rejected by the young man, who has just learned about his beloved's fate, and realises that Kazran will grow to be as bitter and isolated as he was before his intervention (Kazran: 'Times change.' Doctor: 'Not as much as I'd hoped.'). While he can do his best to intervene and to persuade, the Doctor is ultimately powerless to force Kazran to change. His change must come in time and with recognition of love and charity.

If Adelaide represents the negative side of *kairos* – the ways in which decisions can seem strait-jacketed or choices can seem unfairly constrained – then Kazran represents the positive side of *kairos*. Wholly undeserving, he benefits from a recognition that he can be guided into becoming a man who makes the right choice at the right time. Rather than fleeing from judgement, he embraces the grace and mercy represented by Abigail even in the face of death.

Conclusion

> Whereas ye know not what shall be on the morrow. For what is your life? It is even a vapour, that appeareth for a little time, and then vanisheth away.
> (James 4:14)

In theological terms, *kairos* is a concept at once eternal and ephemeral. While assuring believers that there is a plan and a reason behind the grand schemes of time and history, it also insists that each tiny moment can also become hugely significant and that decisions have to be made without full knowledge of the future. The Doctor is able to cross all of time and space and yet it is in these tiny kairic moments – the moments which force him to confront time itself, the morality of his actions, the uncertainty of his future, and the call to judgement for his successes and failures – that he comes to seem awfully human and mortal for a Time Lord.

6.

'You're this Doctor's companion. What exactly do you do for him? Why does he need you?': *Doctor Who*, Liminality and Martha the Apostle

Brigid Cherry

Given that Christianity is an important constituent of traditional British culture, it should not be surprising to find Christian themes encoded within examples of British popular culture. As Anton Kozlovic states, 'secular film can engage in religious storytelling without appearing "religious".'[1] This can be extended to television, and *Doctor Who* is, of course, no exception. In fact, the high status accorded the programme within British culture reinforces this. Although *Doctor Who* is sometimes considered to be a cult programme and devalued by dint of it being both science fiction and aimed at children, it is – as Matt Hills argues – 'thoroughly part of the cultural mainstream'.[2] On the one hand the programme itself has provided iconic imagery to British popular culture: the TARDIS (very much a traditional British police box), the Daleks and perhaps a very long scarf have become instantly recognised symbols of British popular culture; the Doctor himself is the epitome of British eccentricity. On the other hand, and of more interest here, components of British cultural identity have been incorporated into the series.[3] Amongst these are religious, specifically Christian, themes or backdrops, and these can be identified in *Doctor Who* from early on in its run ('The Time Meddler' (1965) and 'The Dæmons' (1971) for example). As Barry Letts (producer from 1970 to 1975) has said, 'it is inevitable because of Britain's cultural heritage that a long running programme about the fight between good and evil will have some Christian

themes as a backdrop'.[4] References to Christianity, particularly as
an aspect of British social history, have been explicit in the series
reboot as overseen by Russell T. Davies, among these the unifying
and uplifting power of hymns in 'Gridlock' and the Church as the
site of family events and sanctuary in 'Father's Day'. Whilst he is
a declared atheist, Davies recognises that religion is 'a very primal
instinct with humans, a very good one, part of our imagination'.[5]
As David Rafer recognises in his discussion of mythic identities in
classic *Doctor Who*, 'Promoting the mythic...supplies a modern need
since civilization and science continue to demythologise the world.'[6]
Such mythic storylines draw on and reflect instinctual human
mentalities. In terms of ideology, we would expect that a writer
imbued with British cultural identity would draw on Christianity,
amongst many other aspects, in his writing regardless of personal
faith. Discussing 'Gridlock' in *The Writer's Tale*, Davies says that big
issues – or what he calls 'that social/political/religious thing' – are
related to life, people and 'what you think about the world'.[7] In this
respect, as a writer 'they are all in there, in one huge continuum' and
are constantly being examined. One of the more explicit references
to Christ in the series under Davies's producership is the Doctor as a
messianic figure.[8]

   There is, to borrow a term employed by Matt Hills to describe the
themes in the *Doctor Who* spin-off series *Torchwood* (also created by
Davies), 'atheistic ambivalence' at work in the series.[9] This tension
between atheism and Christian themes demands to be explored
further. As Davies recognises: 'The series lends itself to religious
iconography because the Doctor is a proper saviour. He saves the
world through the power of his mind and passion.'[10] Examples of
these Christian themes have certainly been picked up by various
religious groups of Christians, and whilst some reactions have been
negative (e.g. the complaint by Christian Voice that it 'subverted
religious iconography'),[11] other church organisations have embraced
and celebrated these representations. Faith publishers have released
books which include examples drawing on *Doctor Who*[12] and the
Church of England has organised a conference exploring themes of
evil and redemption in the series. The *Telegraph*'s religious affairs
correspondent Jonathan Wynne-Jones reports that clergy were
urged to 'use examples from the programme in their sermons in an
attempt to make Christianity more relevant to teenagers'.[13] Themes
addressed in such critiques include examples of resurrection and

sacrifice, similarities between the Doctor and Christ, whether the Daleks are capable of change and the TARDIS as an ordinary object pointing the way to something higher. Church Army spokesman Andrew Wooding has pointed out that 'there are countless examples of Christian symbolism in *Doctor Who*'.[14] In a more general sense, this can be attributed to the fact that *Doctor Who* is particularly polysemic in relation to many socio-political readings and its incorporation of British cultural traditions is wide and fluctuating (David Layton draws on Frazer's *Golden Bough* in his analysis of mythic and religious elements in 'Last of the Time Lords' for example).[15] Nevertheless, these responses demand further discussions of the text to analyse and contextualise such representations. As Hills states, the series 'can hybridise, deconstruct, and cross over all these fixed, unhelpful discourses of cultural value.'[16]

Although messianic themes have always been clear in the character of the Doctor – his role in saving humanity and his ability to regenerate – the Doctor as a Christic figure is strongly developed in the Davies era and particularly in the third revived series. It is nevertheless too simplistic to conclude that the Doctor is a straightforward encoding of Christ. After all, the Christian myth cycle is based upon myths that went before it and viewers might read the Doctor as another mythic figure, recalling the archetypal hero and god – saving humanity, righting wrongs and returning from the dead; he is King Arthur, Robin Hood and the Oak King.[17] That said, however, given the context of the quotes by producers and writers and the cultural background of the text, it presents itself as a valid reading that deserves to be discussed in more depth. Secular texts can sustain a religious interpretation[18] and Christ-figure research suggests that sacrifice and resurrection motifs are common in popular film and television.[19] And it is in the third series that the Christian and Christic representations are most developed, specifically around the Doctor becoming human ('Human Nature/The Family of Blood'), dying, resurrecting and ascending ('Utopia/The Sound of Drums/Last of the Time Lords'), cleansing the temple of New New York of mood drug sellers ('Gridlock') and ministering to the poor and disenfranchised ('Daleks in Manhattan/Evolution of the Daleks').

These textual developments are not straightforward, however, and in particular they render the role of companion problematical. It is significant in this respect that Martha Jones, companion during the third series, has a rather different relationship to the Doctor than other companions of the Davies era. Rose Tyler has a fond and loving relationship with the Doctor, even a romantic love, and Donna is the good friend who lends him her conscience and moral compass.[20] Martha, however, lacks this closeness with the Doctor and is a much more temporary and overlooked companion. After they meet in the hospital ('Smith and Jones') he takes her home, and only as an afterthought is she offered one trip in payment for having helped him on the moon (to Elizabethan London in 'The Shakespeare Code'), extended not just once more but twice (to New New York and 1930s New York in 'Gridlock' and 'Daleks In Manhattan/Evolution of the Daleks'). He returns her home once again, involving her in a further adventure only because he is intrigued by the news bulletin which includes Martha's sister ('The Lazarus Experiment'). At the end of this episode, she is only invited along as companion because she refuses one more trip as a 'passenger' and the Doctor changes his mind about leaving her behind; she is only given her own key to the TARDIS at the end of '42'. Martha therefore only holds the formal status of full-time companion for four stories ('42', 'Human Nature/The Family of Blood', 'Blink', 'Utopia/The Sound of Drums/Last of the Time Lords') – although 'Blink' suggests that other adventures took place. Their relationship is also unbalanced: she feels more for him than he does for her. She is the rebound companion of a Doctor pining for Rose. He speaks affectionately of Rose on many occasions, and fails to notice or acknowledge Martha's hints of her feelings for him. When circumstances force them to share a bed in 'The Shakespeare Code' he is oblivious to her flirtation ('Us two here, same bed. Tongues will wag.'), instead pondering the mystery they have recently observed. Although face-to-face with Martha he does not see her: 'Something really close, staring me right in the face and I can't see it. Rose would know. A friend of mine, Rose. Right now, she'd say exactly the right thing.' He ends this with a put-down, 'Still, can't be helped. You're a novice, never mind. I'll take you back home tomorrow.' In 'Daleks in Manhattan', Tallulah assumes Martha and the Doctor are a couple because 'I've seen the way you look at him. It's obvious.' But it is not at all obvious to him – in 'Evolution of the Daleks', Martha says that 'sometimes I say something or do something and he looks at me, and I just sort of think that he's not seeing me. He's just remembering [Rose]'. Similarly, in 'The Sound of Drums', Martha is observing the Doctor as he tests the perception filter he has just built, he describes its actions: 'Doesn't make us invisible, just unnoticed. Oh, I know what it's like. It's like... it's like when you fancy someone and they don't even know you exist. That's what it's like.' Martha shares a look with Jack, who replies 'You too, huh?' And in 'Human Nature', Martha talks back at the recording of the Doctor: 'You had to, didn't you? Had to go and fall in love with a human. And it wasn't me.' The constant repetition (ritual) of this motif of being overlooked and having her emotions ignored renders Martha an in-between companion, drawing attention to her liminality. Yet, this apparently temporary and unnoticed companion's very liminality underpins her positioning with respect to the Doctor as messiah figure. Martha becomes his disciple and apostle, ending her time with the Doctor by evangelising. This raises interesting questions in considerations of Martha's position within the metanarrative of the messiah, particularly with respect to the disciples and apostles of Christ, not least because femininity and feminine agency are key areas of debate in relation to the Christian church.

Becoming a disciple

In 'Smith and Jones', the Doctor clearly sees something in Martha and chooses her out of all the people in the displaced hospital as possessing calmness and competence as he does habitually when finding a new companion. She has 'good thinking', deduces that something other than the closed window must be keeping the air in and is undaunted by the view of the moon from the balcony, finding it 'beautiful'.

But if Martha's journey with the Doctor is towards becoming an apostle, then she ought to begin as a disciple. The common conception of the followers of Jesus is that they were recognised and called to follow him (Matthew 4:18-22) and that those called left their families and gave up their possessions in order to do so (Matthew 19:27-30). The opening of the episode establishes that Martha has a normal hectic life with a demanding job and a close-knit family, before the Doctor calls her to something more. At the end, he comes to her outside a family celebration – 'I just thought since you saved my life and I've got a brand new sonic screwdriver which needs road testing, you might fancy a trip' – and she leaves with him without a word to her family. In 'Gridlock', she tells Milo and Cheen that 'I didn't really think. I just followed the Doctor, and they don't even know where I am, my Mum and Dad. If I died here, they'd never know.' However, Martha does not hesitate to go with him. She already recognises the Doctor as someone special, in a romantic sense ('That was nothing?' when he kisses her for the genetic transfer) and in the sense of his alienness ('What sort of species?'). Her first meeting with him is also accompanied by wonders and miracles – the rain going up, being transported to the moon, his immunity to radiation, his coming back to life, the demonstration with the tie that he can travel in time. To some extent, she is a receptive believer before she met him – she talks about the aliens that have visited Earth and that her cousin was lost at the battle of Canary Wharf. She also has faith even before she really knows who the Doctor is: 'I promise you, Mr Smith, we will find a way out. If we can travel to the moon, then we can travel back. There's got to be a way.' At first she still sees him as Mr Smith, a patient in the hospital; she has to become a witness to his miracles before she accepts him as someone who can save them. So when he tells her that he is called the Doctor, she states that as 'far as I'm concerned you gotta earn that title'; he earns it in her eyes when she recognises his non-human powers and starts calling him the Doctor after he survives the radiation that he used to kill the Slab. She is also witness to him as a saviour of the humans trapped in the hospital, after the Plasmavore has drained his blood: 'He gave his life so they'd find you' – and of course she is also witness to his resurrection.

Martha's role in 'Gridlock' also sees her ambiguously fluctuating between romantic love for the Doctor and her journey as a disciple. She fulfills the generic expectations of the companion who is in trouble (she is kidnapped and trapped at the bottom of the motorway being attacked by the Macra) and must be rescued, but her responses to her situation are more nuanced. During the broadcast of the 'daily contemplation' (a hymn), Brannigan says that 'we're not abandoned, not while we have each other.' This, perhaps, is another mood drug, similar to the patches the Doctor has already railed against – indeed he does not join in singing 'The Old Rugged Cross' and looks on with a mix of scrutiny and calculation. Martha on the other hand joins in, but her expression is far less beatific or lifted by religious ecstasy than those of Milo and Cheen. It is as though she is worried, perhaps for herself and perhaps for her relationship with the Doctor, or working these things out. It is not made clear at this point whether she realises the Doctor has lied to her, but a developing faith in the Doctor starts to emerge. With two minutes of air left she says 'there's always the Doctor', demonstrating her hope in salvation. Cheen thinks this is a false hope, but Martha bears witness: 'you haven't seen the things he can do. Honestly, just trust me, both of you. You've got your faith, you've got your songs and your hymns, and I've got the Doctor.' This equating of the Doctor as on the same level as Milo and Cheen's faith is notable, and Martha's belief in him is confirmed when he restores the power, opens the roof of the motorway and orders the cars to drive up. It is then that Martha has her moment of ecstasy, squealing 'He did it!' as she claps her hands and bounces in her seat. At the very end of the episode, Martha sits in the understreets of New New York while the cars still rise in the air and the people sing 'Abide With Me', demanding to be taught. The Gospels state that the disciples called Jesus 'teacher'; Luke 11:1 describes a disciple saying 'teach us to pray' and goes on to record the Lord's Prayer. The Doctor does not teach Martha to pray (although a form of prayer will become a significant ritual in 'Last of the Time Lords') but he does give her a description of Gallifrey that sounds like paradise or heaven: 'Oh, you should have seen it, that old planet. The second sun would rise in the south, and the mountains would shine. The leaves on the trees were silver, and when they caught the light every morning, it looked like a forest on fire. When the autumn came, the breeze would blow through the branches like a song.' This continues the account he began when she asked to visit his homeworld before they came to visit New New York. In the romance narrative, this casts his interactions with Martha as a rebound relationship; New New York was where the Doctor took Rose just after his regeneration in his tenth incarnation. It was also part of a lie, as he did not tell Martha that his home had been destroyed and that he was the last of his kind. In this final scene though, he confesses and tells her the truth: 'I lied to you, because I liked it. I could pretend. Just for a bit, I could imagine they were still alive.'[21] But in the tableau that ends the episode mid-scene this is more than a confession. The Doctor sitting and teaching Martha clearly suggests a turning point in Martha's journey.

The following story ('Daleks in Manhattan/Evolution of the Daleks') continues to see Martha growing in her role and belief in the Doctor. When the Doctor is taken from Hooverville by the Daleks he leaves her with a 'gift' – his psychic paper – and she must work out for herself what it is he needs her to do. Similarly, when they are at the top of the Empire State Building he must go to the top alone to remove the Dalekanium, telling her 'I'm sorry, Martha, but you've got to fight.' In these two instances she is already being entrusted with his mission. In '42', salvation is shown operating in both directions, building Martha's status alongside the Doctor. When she is in the jettisoning escape pod, he declares that he will save her, twice. In return, she has to save him when he is possessed by the solar life form. Just as significantly, the theme of faith is continued. Trapped with Riley in the escape capsule, Martha bears witness even more emphatically than she did in 'Gridlock': 'You don't know the Doctor. I *believe* in him' (my emphasis). She later proves that she is able to carry out the Doctor's instructions in freezing him to drive out the solar entity and venting the engines of solar material to free the life forms. All of these declarations of faith and belief build up to her apostolic role in 'Last of the Time Lords'.

Martha as Missionary

It is in 'Human Nature/The Family of Blood' that Martha's role as apostle comes into sharper focus. Significantly, these episodes tell the story of the Doctor taking human form and living as an ordinary human on 1913 Earth for two months – 'I have to stop being a Time Lord. I'm gonna become human.' – inviting the link with the concept of Jesus as God-made-flesh (John 1:14). In the pre-credits sequence and in flashback throughout the episodes, it is revealed that Martha has been given an explicit mission by the Doctor. 'It all depends on you', the Doctor tells her before taking on human form via the Chameleon Arch. She is thus entrusted with his secret and the secret of the fob watch on which his life also depends, as well as keeping the TARDIS hidden. She is also provided with information in the form of a list of numbered instructions (up to 23, though not all of them are revealed) and guidance on what to do should certain circumstances arise: 'Martha, before I change here's a list of instructions for when I'm human.' This is provided as a file in the TARDIS console that she consults like a catechism (if we extend the allusion) whenever the Doctor's human identity is threatened or he puts himself in danger of discovery. It could be said at this point that the watch is a testament in the sense of being a covenant between the Time Lord (the Doctor) and humanity (John Smith) and the instructions a set of commandments or religious principles (Martha fast forwards and backwards through these to listen to points at random as a Christian might do opening the Bible at random to find an answer or comfort). However, the allusion breaks down rather too easily. Just as the Bible cannot provide straightforward answers to explicit questions, the Doctor's instructions cannot give guidance on every unexpected danger – the arrival of the Family of Blood's craft that Martha sees as a meteor or falling star – but more importantly due to the human situations that John Smith gets himself into, primarily his falling in love with Joan Redfern: 'That's no good. What about the stuff you didn't tell me, what about women? Oh no, you didn't think of that. What in hell am I supposed to do then?' Despite the final instruction 'If anything goes wrong, [...] then you know what to do', Martha does not at this point have complete agency. Her love continues to be unrequited, but even more significantly she lacks power due to the socio-cultural conditions of the time (her ethnicity and apparent lower-class status as a maid) that place her in a position of subservience and powerlessness. Because she must take the role of John Smith's maidservant she must keep quiet about her knowledge as the Doctor's companion and as a trained medical doctor. She does not and cannot speak of the Doctor's true nature, even to him (his confidante at this point is Joan). Her liminality is thus emphasised. Even Joan is confused about Martha's role, right up to the point where the watch is opened: 'You're this Doctor's companion … What exactly do you do for him? Why does he need you?' In fact, Martha's place has been to bear witness and preserve memory, and if nothing else this serves to anticipate the role of apostle that Martha will take on in 'Last of the Time Lords'. In the later episode, the Master says of the Doctor that 'he trained you well', and it is as if Martha's journey through the whole season has been a training for her final mission.

The last story of the series, of which 'Last of the Time Lords' is the final episode, emphasises themes of apocalypse and salvation through the use of a dystopic narrative. The depictions of a dying world at the end of the universe with the last of humanity assailed by the savage Futurekind in 'Utopia' and of a decimated, scorched Earth in 'Last of the Time Lords' link to the apocalyptic imagination (inherited from Judaism) of early Christianity. The key influence according to Caesar Montevecchio in this respect is on interpretations of the crucifixion and the hope it offers of salvation.[22] Montevecchio's interpretation of dystopia in popular culture is that it parallels the evangelists' hope that Jesus will bring deliverance from various forces. It is significant that the theme of dystopia and salvation has been foreshadowed in the series already. In 'Gridlock', the dystopic vision is undercut by the unifying and comforting presence of the traditional Anglican hymn 'Abide With Me' and the gospel song 'The Old Rugged Cross'. Clearly this can be read as an ideological way of keeping the population passive, since, as Davies says, 'There is no

higher authority'.[23] But the use of these hymns is nevertheless telling.
'The Old Rugged Cross' can be read as symbolic of the crucifixion
and the hope of salvation it offers when the commuters are trapped
in the darkness of the smog within the enclosed motorway, whilst
'Abide With Me' sees that hope fulfilled as the cars rise up into the
sky after the roof of the motorway has been opened up. Again, this
is a portrayal of dystopia as in Montevecchio's account, and it is the
Christic figures of both the Doctor and the Face of Boe who bring
salvation (Novice Hame, appropriately a nun, calls Boe her Lord and
says he 'gave his life to save the city'). In fact, Novice Hame later
tells the Doctor that sealing the people off in the enclosed motorway
was to save them from the death that overtook the city when the
Bliss mood enhancer transmitted a mutated virus that could kill in
minutes.

In 'Last of the Time Lords' it is Martha who spreads the message
of that hope, a message in which the Doctor is most overtly a Christic
figure. As Montevecchio argues, 'dystopian film helps accentuate
specific patterns of contemporary experience from which salvation
is needed.'[24] In this episode, which not-coincidentally concludes
her time as companion, it is Martha who acts as the evangelist for
the salvation that the Doctor can bring. Her role here fits the literal
definition of an apostle, 'one sent on a mission', but she also bears
witness to what she has seen. The Pauline criteria for apostleship
include claiming to have seen the risen Christ and being engaged
in missionary work (1 Corinthians 9:1). Martha, of course, has
already seen the Doctor risen – seemingly returning from the dead
in 'Smith and Jones', giving a little bit of his Time Lord DNA (his
body and blood) to the Dalek human slaves in 'Evolution of the
Daleks', becoming human and then sacrificing his life to rise again as
the Doctor in 'Human Nature' and 'The Family of Blood' – and she
believes in him as declared in 'Gridlock' and '42'. In 'The Sound of
Drums', she is given a direct command by the Doctor as he whispers
in her ear before she teleports away from the Valiant. It is only later
revealed (in the next episode) what Martha has been tasked with,
but the exchange of looks and her determination are already clear
in 'The Sound of Drums', as is her statement of intent when she sets
off from London: 'I'm coming back.' A significant amount of time
passes between the end of 'The Sound of Drums' and 'Last of the
Time Lords' and it is during this gap (the 'year that never was') that
Martha carries out her mission. As summed up by the Master in his
broadcast ('Stories of a child, walking the Earth, giving you hope'),

this fulfils the criterion of hope in salvation within the dystopic text. Her year spent travelling around the world is of great significance. She is 'the famous Martha Jones' and 'a legend' who is 'gonna save the world'. 'The blessed saint Martha', the Master calls her ironically, but in this reading isn't this exactly what she has become? Her mission is revealed when she preaches to the people in the London house: 'It's all right, they want me to talk and I will.' In the speech that follows her message takes on the function of preaching. She is a missionary who has been 'told [...] to walk the Earth' by the Doctor, telling her congregation how she has travelled around the world 'from the ruins of New York, to the fusion mills of China, right across the radiation pits of Europe'. Though she offers hope to the remnants of humanity living as slaves, she says it is wrong for Martha Jones to become a legend because her name is not important. Rather she is an evangelist for the Doctor: 'He has saved your lives so many times, and you never even knew he was there. He never stops. He never stays. He never asks to be thanked. But I've seen him. I know him. I love him. And I know what he can do.'

Martha renders herself liminal here ('my name isn't important'), she is the delivery system for the Doctor's message, the words spoken in his name. On one level, this can be interpreted as communion, as defined by David Bakan as the opposite of agency.[25] Her missionary work requires contact, openness and union. In this respect, words have power. They become what J. L. Austin calls performatives.[26] In Austin's definition the utterance of a word or words is not simply the speaking of something, it is – in whole or part – the doing of it. Words as performative utterances are extremely significant in the Christian context. In Genesis 1, God speaks and the world comes into existence. Furthermore, the word Word itself signifies the Messiah: 'In the beginning was the Word, and the Word was with God, and the Word was God' (John 1:1) and 'The Word became flesh and made his dwelling among us' (John 1:14). In 'Last of the Time Lords', the word 'Doctor' becomes such a performative, as Martha explains 'I told them that if everyone thinks of one word, at one specific time … A telepathic field binding the whole human race together, with all of them, every single person on Earth, thinking the same thing at the same time. And that word…is Doctor.' Not simply a profession, a title or a name, as uttered by all the people Martha has preached to and all the people who have passed on her message, the word Doctor brings into being (makes flesh and restores his body to fullness) and brings back (resurrects in terms of his power) the Doctor himself.

'I told a story, no weapons, just words', she tells the Master, and 'I told them to pass it on, to spread the word.' The scientific rational explanation for these events is the Doctor's psychic integration with the matrices of the Archangel Network, but in this reading the Master's reference to prayer being the weapon that Martha sought becomes much more than an ironic put down. 'Faith and hope? Is that all?' the Master says, but in Montevecchio's account this is the function of the dystopic text. The word – Doctor – does signify faith, but more importantly it is a performative utterance, an 'instruction' as Martha calls it that through her mission she has brought into being.

Martha Who?

So what might be made in a larger context of this reading of Martha as disciple and apostle to the Doctor as Christic figure? As Amy-Chinn also points out with respect to readings of the Doctor as messiah, this negotiated reading of Martha as evangelist clearly illustrates the ways in which *Doctor Who* can be opened up as a polysemic text.[27] Nevertheless, this allows the character of Martha to be explored further in terms of ethnic identity and female agency. Throughout the series Martha has to not only confront her liminal relationship with the Doctor (unrequited love) but the liminality of her own identity as a time traveller. When she first travels with the Doctor out of her own time (multicultural Britain of the twenty-first century), it is to Elizabethan London and she is understandably worried about how she will be received. As the first ethnic companion of the Doctor (Rose's boyfriend Mickey was only an occasional fellow traveller), Martha's status and female agency are in question (see Robinson for a fuller discussion of the black female presence in the series).[28] 'Am I all right?', she asks, 'I'm not gonna get carted off as a slave, am I? ... Not exactly white, in case you haven't noticed.' The Doctor, perhaps because he is an alien himself despite looking ethnically 'white', is oblivious and suggests she 'just walk about like she owns the place'. In fact though, Shakespeare struggles to find a term that is acceptable to her, she cannot believe what she is hearing when he calls her 'delicious blackamoor lady', 'Ethiop girl', 'swarth' and 'queen of Afric'. On one level this is an ideological comment on political correctness, but more significantly – in one of *Doctor Who*'s frequent knowing references to the Doctor's many impacts on human history – it turns the whole question of 'race' around when Shakespeare later calls her 'my Dark Lady' and proposes writing a sonnet to her. Martha's liminal status as a modern black woman in a historical time where she is out of place is rejected in favour of her being the poet's muse (though of course this still positions her as without female agency).

Race is not raised as an issue again until the third historical story of the season. In 'Daleks In Manhattan/Evolution of the Daleks' Martha's ethnic identity is not called into question, not least because the leader of Hooverville is also black. Nor can it be in 'Gridlock' when there are people who are bright red and stark white (literally so, and not in the sense those terms have in denoting existing human skin colours and ethnicities in the present day), not to mention humanoid cats (Cheen's ethnicity is similarly unremarked, and there are also young Japanese women, elderly lesbians and nudists among the multi-ethnic population of New New Earth). So it is noteworthy then that race becomes an issue only in the story in which Martha begins to practice the role of apostle, 'Human Nature/The Family of Blood'. Set during 1913, racism is a casual and accepted part of the power relations between the upper-class schoolboys and masters, and the lower-class serving maids. Martha, in protecting John Smith and preserving the memory of the Doctor, thus has to endure the racist taunts of the schoolboys. There is a sense of cruelty in Hutchinson's 'With hands like those, how can you tell when something's clean?', but even the sympathetic Joan exhibits the prejudices of the era. Martha, in explaining her true self to Joan, states that she doesn't just follow the Doctor around (her place at the school has only been obtained because John Smith has brought her there from service with his family), 'I'm training to be a doctor. Not an alien doctor, a proper doctor. A doctor of medicine.' Joan dismisses this as nonsense (from her perspective): 'Women might train to be doctors, but hardly a skivvy and hardly one of your colour.' What is interesting here is the conflation of gender, class and race since this is one that also underlies the position of women in the New Testament and the Christian church. Martha's name, however coincidental this may be, brings to mind one of the female followers of Jesus, Martha, sister of Mary and Lazarus (another name referenced within the series in 'The Lazarus Experiment'). The biblical Martha is associated with ministry in the sense that she and her sister ministered to Jesus (that is, served him), but another aspect of such female ministry was financial support.[29] The Martha of *Doctor Who* similarly ministers to the Doctor, not only working for him as his maid in 'Human Nature/The Family of Blood' but also in 'Blink': 'I've got a job in a shop, I've got to support him!' This is interesting not least since the roles of women within Christian leadership continue to be debated today. The early church may have 'written out' female apostleship from the New Testament,[30] but Martha's role in 'Last of the Time Lords' clearly resembles that of Junia, the female apostle of Romans 16:7 whose name was masculinised by the early church. However, in one sense, Martha too has been written out, as her apostolic work took place during a year that no longer exists when the temporal paradox is healed, and no one outside of the TARDIS crew and her family remember it.

At the end of 'Last of the Time Lords' then, Martha's mission is complete but not unproblematically so, it having taken place during a year that never was (as well as within the temporal gap between episodes), rendering the journey she has taken and the word she has spread (her work as an apostle) in and of itself liminal. As the Christic-figure at the end of 'Last of the Time Lords' the Doctor seeks non-violent solutions – 'As if I would ask her to kill' – and offers forgiveness rather than retribution to the Master. For Martha, however, there is no redemption save by her own agency. The Doctor still does not and cannot return her love – he is like Sean in the story Martha tells him about her friend Vicky: 'He never looked at her twice. I mean, he liked her, but that was it. And she wasted years pining after him, years of her life, 'cause while he was around, she never looked at anyone else'. And here Martha takes her own advice, having always told Vicky to get out: 'So this is me, getting out.' Significantly, it is she that decides to leave him, even though he offers to take her with him again when he leaves. The re-enactment of the apostolic mission has been empowering for Martha on her own terms, it gives her the strength to reclaim her own life as a doctor – and as head of her own family. 'Spent all these years training to be a doctor. Now I've got people to look after.' She maintains the possibility of contacting the Doctor, giving him her phone, but when she does reunite with him it is not as his companion but in respect of her work as a doctor with UNIT. She is able to do this because she has found strength within herself. When the Doctor tells her that she saved the world, she says 'Yes, I did. I spent a lot of time with you thinking I was second best. But you know what? I am good.' The act of salvation restores her own agency to her, a not insignificant development for a black female character in popular culture.

Hills states that: 'Chief among [the] textual attributes is the programme's highly unusual conflation of ordinary, everyday elements and extraordinary, fantastical aspects.'[31] If all aspects of British history and culture are up for grabs, then religion, and popular perceptions of Christianity, are bound to be part of this 'wholesale making-strange of the familiar'. Martha's apostolic role makes strange the familiar story of unrequited love. Despite her liminal status in the text, she remains an important companion in terms of ethnic identity and female agency.

7.

'Humany-Wumany': Humanity vs. Human in *Doctor Who*

Laura Brekke

In 2010, more than 10.4 million viewers in the UK alone watched the fifth series finale of *Doctor Who*,[1] while fewer than one million people sat in Church of England pews each Sunday.[2] These are indicators of what Brits themselves already know: their country is becoming more and more secularised. Among its loyal following, the cult science-fiction classic *Doctor Who* has emerged as a 'social religion' – an ideological frame that imparts a particular ethic to its viewers. The internet is ablaze with discussion of 'What Would The Doctor Do?'[3] It is this ethic, this internal moral code, which will be examined in this chapter. In particular, we will examine what it means to be 'human'.

Whirling through space in a sexy blue box, the Doctor and his human companions encounter a universe of 'others'. Despite their aesthetic differences, the Doctor assumes that the 'others' he encounters possess a certain level of humanity, which he can engage for the good. This humanity is more than a biological disposition; it is an intangible quality beyond genetics. Focusing particularly on the Cybermen, we will examine what it means to possess humanity as articulated in *Doctor Who*.

The Cybermen are almost-but-not-quite human; they began as biologically human but had their humanity stripped away. By observing what human qualities are sacrificed in the 'upgrade' from human to Cyberman we can parse out concrete principles of what it means to possess humanness within *Doctor Who*. Humanness, in this context, is much more than biology and being a resident (or descendent of a resident) of planet Earth. Humanness is an intangible matrix of qualities that one cannot quite touch but are always evident.

Christian theologians have called this matrix of qualities the *Imago Dei* or the soul. Our objective is to map this quality, and to see how the Doctor engages it in others.

As we look at the Doctor's understanding of humanness, we will look also to how Christian theologians have grappled with this intangible matrix of qualities. The Doctor and Christian theologians alike have noticed that there is a 'double-reality' in being human. On the one hand the biology of bodies and chemistry of brains; and on the other hand, the experiences of feelings like love, longing and loss.[4] The Doctor identifies what Christian scholarship terms the *Imago Dei* not just in humans, but in the alien as well. Neither race nor species can exempt a being from the Doctor's high standards of ethical behaviour.

The Doctor always optimistically engages the 'other' on his misadventures across the universe, seeing this immaterial quality where his companions do not. In light of this profound ethic modelled by the Doctor, viewers themselves are challenged to question what it means to live in this 'humany-wumany' world.

Human v *Humanness*

When we begin to ask 'what is humanity?', or 'what does it mean to be human?', we have to separate the idea of 'humanity' from being *homo sapien*. If we can imagine that 'humanity' is a quality that non-*homo sapien* aliens (like Time Lords) can possess, then we can gain a better grasp on that intangible characteristic.

Humanness is a quality that is beyond mere biological disposition. It is not a factor of genetics or DNA. Instead there is an intangible quality, something you can't quite touch, that imbues us with humanity. Christian theologians have called this ineffable quality the soul or the *Imago Dei* – literally the image of God.[5] It is a quality that separates human beings from the rest of the created world, and endows them with special gifts (and arguably privileges). Just what the nature of the *Imago Dei* is, theologians have speculated and argued over the centuries.

The Doctor recognises this soul-quality, not limited to earth-dwelling *Homo sapiens*, but present in many of the aliens he encounters throughout time and space.

Humanness as Weakness: The Cybermen

The Cybermen begin as human beings, complete with human biology
and ineffable *humanness*. Men and women, born biologically human
but modified to the farthest degree, are left as only the human brain
'sustained indefinitely within a cradle of copyrighted chemicals
… and bonded onto a metal exoskeleton'.[6] What is left after these
extreme modifications is a metal humanoid, run by a human brain
with human memories, but without emotions or free will.

From the Cybermen we can draw a picture of humanness by
looking at what human characteristics they sought to eradicate.
Cybermen are undying, unfeeling, uniform in design and thought,
and made with one purpose: to 'upgrade' the whole of the human
race, and to 'delete' any persons (earthling or alien) which stand
in their way. What they lack – capacity for emotions, individuality,
freedom of thought and will, and finiteness – makes light of what is
contained within the characteristic of humanness.

Emotions

The Doctor, in a conversation with the newly 'upgraded' John Lumic,
creator of the Cybermen, says that when he restores emotions to the
Cybermen he is giving them back their souls. Seeing what they are –
a brain inside a metal body – drives the Cybermen to madness and
death.[7] Earlier in the episode, Mrs Moore, in a conversation with the
Doctor, comments on the emotional inhibitor they find inside a dying
Cyberman. He explains that it 'keeps them from feeling anything', a
necessary augmentation for a human brain to function inside a metal
body. A shocked Mrs Moore observes that the Cybermen have cut
out 'the one thing that makes them human'.

And why? In the first of the two episodes, 'Rise of the Cybermen',
the Doctor explains to Rose that the Cybermen were people who have
had their brains artificially preserved inside the machine bodies,
removing their emotions in the process. Rose herself is shocked and
confused by the information, asking why they would want to rid
themselves of emotions. The Doctor simply replies, 'because it hurts'.

Emotional intelligence, the capacity to feel – both joy and pain – are
wrapped up in what is means to be human, to possess 'humanness'.
The emotional inhibiter suppresses these human emotions, voids
those feelings which can potentially cause sorrow, but at the same
time voids the feelings which cause pleasure. It must be done,

declares the Doctor, for if the human brain was aware of itself inside the metal body – a body so different from the fragile flesh and blood body assumed at birth – it would go mad. Indeed, his analysis is correct as the return of their emotions through an override code to the inhibitor causes the Cybermen to go mad on a grand scale.

For Lumic human emotions are a form of vulnerability. It is seeking to stamp out this vulnerability – both to emotional and physical pain, suffering and weakness – that has led him to create the Cybermen. He is incapable of understanding the value that human emotions represent. This is brought into sharp relief in a conversation with the Doctor shortly after his capture.

Lumic questions the Doctor about his emotions in a bid to convince him of their uselessness. But the Doctor responds to each of Lumic's questions by emphasising how important it has been for him to embrace his emotions. He has felt grief and rage and pain, but from the Doctor's perspective, to live without emotions is not to live. To live devoid of the capacity to feel – even to feel grief and pain – is to lack something of the human essence.

Individuality, Creativity and Imagination

The Doctor also highlights another characteristic of humanness: individuality and the capacity for creativity and imagination.

In a speech made to Lumic in 'The Age of Steel' the Doctor chastises the upgraded businessman for limiting the human creative capacity. In a world of uniform Cybermen, Lumic is in effect killing human imagination and ingenuity. 'Everything you invented you did to fight your sickness, and that's brilliant, that's so human', the Doctor remarks, pointing out the irony of Lumic's desire to end the human creative capacity. The Cybermen won't have the need to advance, they'll simply stay as they are indefinitely; a 'metal earth, with metal men, and metal thoughts, lacking the one thing which makes this planet so alive – people! Ordinary, stupid, brilliant people!'.

This observation leads to a second, connected one – the importance of human individuality. If the Cybermen are 'upgraded' by becoming united and uniform – having the same appearance, thoughts and will – then the variety, individuality and the ability to make our own choices is fundamentality related to this understanding of 'humanity'. The capacity to choose, to be unique among all of our peers, and to act individually is a human quality.[8] That uniqueness is not simply a matter of distinct biology, but the capacity to imagine, to create, to reflect.

Lumic's 'children' as he refers to the newly minted Cybermen, have no free will. They respond to his questions on their new status by remarking that they 'feel nothing' and that they 'think the same. We are uniform'. From their synchronized mechanics, to their single-mindedness of thought, the Cybermen are corporatised, lacking originality. When Lumic asks them about non-upgraded people, they respond as one might expect a Cyberman to respond: 'We think of their difference and their pain. They suffer in their skin. *They must be upgraded.*' Human vulnerability is suffering, weakness, an obstacle to be overcome – or deleted entirely.

Cybermen think, act, even march with an eerie uniformity. They turn, stop and move with precisely calculated steps. They are unified, more like cogs in a machine than individual people. They have lost the ability to be compassionate, to think what it must be like to be human – they merely respond with cold uniformity: to be human is to have weakness, and that weakness must be eliminated through upgrading.

When Peter Tyler is stopped by a recently converted Cyberman inside the Cybus Industries factory, he learns that this Cyberman was previously his wife. *Was*, not is. The Cyberman acknowledges that those human qualities are gone, that the individual quirks of Jackie Tyler are in the past. All the attributes that made this Cyberman Jackie Tyler have been stripped away leaving in her place an unrecognisable machine.

To be an independent, creative being is also to live in relationship with other independent creative beings. Many scholars assert that the *Imago Dei* is the capacity to live relationally, both with God and the created world.[9] To be human, is to be created for relationships and reflecting God's own interrelatedness. However, Cybermen are incapable of freely relating to others. There is no freedom of will, no individuality. Not even the glimmers of memory in the Jackie Tyler Cyberman could change the programed response to her not-yet upgraded husband. In an effort to impose streamlined efficiency, the Cybermen have lost their creative capacities, individuality, and ability to live in mutual relationship with one another.

Vulnerability and Finiteness

A third observation about humanness is that it has something to do with vulnerability. Cybermen 'never sicken', they are part-machine and not susceptible to illness (or bullets as Mickey and the Preachers discovered). They lack all of the biological vulnerabilities that define human beings (and, consequently, all of the natural world). But, this lack of finiteness, this perceived inability to die speaks to the essence of what it means to be human.

Finiteness, in some measure, defines the human experience. Our susceptibility to death – at least of the body – is part of that elusive quality called the soul.[10] Indeed, finiteness could be *the* defining human characteristic, as our vulnerability makes us precisely what God is not. In the first creation story in Genesis 1:26-27, God creates human beings, male and female. They, like all of life which has come before, are creatures. They are finite beings, for that is how God has created them. And, this finiteness is not bad, but a condition of their creatureliness.[11] To seek to overcome finiteness – to literally live forever – is to cease being a creature and to anoint oneself a god.

Even knowing the merits of 'upgrading' – invulnerability to illness and death – no human being willingly chooses this path. The poor and hungry street men are taken against their will by Lumic's lieutenant Mr Crane. The people of London are coerced into upgrading by Cybus Industries earpods which directly send messages to their brains. Even Lumic, who is the creative genius behind the Cybermen, resists. After being attacked by Mr Crane, and even facing the threat of death as his life-support machines begin to fail, Lumic is adamant that he does not want to be upgraded 'until my final breath'. His Cybermen reply 'Then breathe no more'.

Even the creator of these unfeeling, undying humanoid beings wants to hold on to his humanity for as long as possible. Even a man who lives with the pain and discomfort of disease protests against the 'upgrade'. As much as we may hate our vulnerability to sickness, pain, emotional distress and death, we also instinctively seem to know they make us who we are.

Humanity and the *Imago Dei*: A Word on Being Made in God's Image

To look at what humanity is from the Christian context is to acknowledge the *Imago Dei* in every person. From Genesis 1, we are given a theological story which tells us that all human beings, unlike the rest of creation, are uniquely made in the *image of God*. This *Imago Dei* has been attributed to the human capacity for rationality, the 'soul' as a spiritual characteristic distinct from the body, and as human moral capacity.[12] However, theologically speaking, each of these falls short. To look at what is means to be human, to fully embrace 'humanity' in the most profound sense, is to look at the example of true humanity in Jesus Christ.

Theologian Karl Barth posits that we come to know true humanity in the person of Jesus Christ.[13] His point is this: we must discover what it means to be fully human in this miraculous man who is both fully God (and therefore fully 'Other') and fully man. In Barth's words, Jesus represents the 'ontological determination of humanity'.[14] That is, our very being, our essence is determined by Jesus being the human incarnation of God. Because Jesus is the truest, fullest human being, so we see what is means to be truly and fully human.

Looking at Jesus as the measure of humanity, then, reveals that emotions are not suppressed or denied. They are experienced to their fullest – in both joy and sorrow. Unlike the Cybermen, Jesus is moved. His emotions are embraced, and they impact his actions. His words and deeds are not stark utilitarianism or taciturn rationalism. One need not look any further than the death of Lazarus to see Jesus, moved by the grief of his friends, weeping.[15] When Jesus sees that the crowds, who have followed him to hear his teaching, are hungry and without food, he has compassion upon them and provides bread in abundance.[16] Emotions, and the capacity to be moved by those emotions, characterise the humanity of Jesus and are a profoundly human trait.

Jesus as the fullest embodiment of humanness illustrates relational living. To be human, then, means 'that humans find their true identity in coexistence with each other and other creatures'.[17] The travelling band of disciples marks as foundational the need and desire to live in relation with others. Jesus also lives in a mutual relationship with God, and, thus, emphasises this need to live relationally with God and with creation in the two-fold Great Commandment:

'You shall love the Lord your God with all your heart, and with all your soul, and with all your mind.' This is the greatest and first commandment. And a second is like it: 'You shall love your neighbor as yourself.'[18]

Loving the *Other* – God or the innumerable neighbourly others – is at the heart of humanness. Living relationally is an essential element in our humanity. Jesus embodies compassion, empathy, and loving respect for those with whom he is in relationship. He is uniquely himself, and coexists in relationship with others who are uniquely themselves.

If Jesus is the yardstick for humanity, his own death – his susceptibility and vulnerability – imply that to be fully, truly human is to also be vulnerable. He felt hunger,[19] he felt physical pain and humiliation,[20] and ultimately he succumbed to death.[21] If the incarnation of Jesus is the fullest representation of humanity, then vulnerability and finiteness are part of humanness. The Cybermen's frank determination to stamp out vulnerability of all kinds led them to kill or artificially inhibit those very aspects which made them human to begin with.

What we learn from looking at Jesus as the measure for humanness is 'that to be truly human in the image of God is not (merely) to possess some intellectual, moral, or spiritual capacity *within* ourselves; it is realized only in relatedness, community, or fellowship *outside* ourselves...'[22] Each of these aspects – emotional intelligence, creativity and imagination, relationality, and vulnerability are all qualities that the Doctor values in his companions, and honours in the countless examples of alien life he encounters.

Engaging the Other: *Doctor Who's* Principles of Humanity in Action

It is clear that *Doctor Who* has a concept of humanness – the human soul – which is not linked to biology but instead is possessed by most of the alien life that the Doctor and his companions meet in the course of their misadventures across the stars. The Doctor assumes that all alien life he encounters possesses this soul quality, regardless of their outer appearance. Often, his ethic of honouring that implicit humanness – especially if an explicit appearance of humanness is not readily perceivable – must be taught to his companions.

In the episode, 'Planet of the Ood' (2008) the Tenth Doctor and his companion Donna Noble come upon a dying Ood in the middle of a barren snowy landscape. When Donna persists in calling the Ood an 'it', the Doctor responds sharply, scolding her that 'He's a "he", not an "it"'.

The Doctor clearly sees what Donna cannot – that despite an extraordinary difference in outward appearance, this alien creature is still a creature possessing humanness. The Doctor seeks to honour that humanness with respect and empathy. It is an ethics of respect and empathy which leads the Doctor, with Donna in tow, to liberate the Ood from forced servitude at the hands of Ood Operations and the company's vicious CEO Klineman Halpen.

The Doctor expresses an ethic of respect and tolerance for the 'Other' – other races, other cultures, other alien beings who often look and act differently than himself (as a Time Lord) or his chosen companions (as human beings). Catherine Cornille identifies empathy as a fundamental trait for interreligious dialogue.[23] Dialogue of any kind is engagement with an 'Other' – another person of any background. In particularly difficult situations of dialogue, empathy can play a role in breaking down the barriers which separate 'us' from 'them'.

Empathy is the process by which one 'transposes oneself into the feelings, the thoughts, and the experiences of another'.[24] The Doctor's ability to look beyond the exterior differences and see something of the internal 'humanness' is rooted in empathy. The Ood, dying in the snow, is not an 'it'. He is not a distant creature devoid of the capacity to feel and know pain and suffering. The Doctor's tender care is an acknowledgement of the Ood's humanness and a desire to reach out to him.

Empathy is precisely what the Cybermen lack. They are incapable of empathy, for it involves the capacity for imagination, creativity and compassion. To 'transpose oneself into the feelings' of someone else requires an imagination. It involves emotional intelligence, and an awareness of difference. Cybermen, with their emotions artificially inhibited, and their minds so constructed that they see no value in diversity, cannot (as a matter of function) be empathetic.

The Doctor represents the best of empathy. He is unlike every other creature in the universe. He is the last of his kind. Very few alien beings he comes across know quite what it feels like to be so completely alone.[25] He is willing to engage these 'Others' – alien life in a variety of forms across galaxies near and far – and this makes him exceptional. He looks upon every encounter with an optimistic glee, often without regard to the apprehension his human companions feel at the same venture.

But where does the Doctor's empathy run out? It is no secret that the Doctor hates. The seemingly indefatigable Daleks plague the

Doctor and are among his bitterest enemies. In his dealing with the Daleks, the Doctor does not reach out with empathy. He does not look upon them with compassion, or with a hope of connecting to some common bond they may share. Why?

One could argue that a (very long) life-time of constant war and struggle against the Daleks would condition anyone to hate. But the Doctor does not hate the Sontarans – a warrior race of aliens who also have constantly instigated war throughout the universe. Even as he sees the Sontarans preparing for the invasion of Earth, the Doctor gives them the option to choose peace over destruction, all the while knowing they will not and cannot choose to avoid conflict.[26] What is the difference, then, between the equally destructive Sontarans and the Daleks?

Looking at the characteristics which the Cybermen divested themselves of, we discover clear similarities with the Daleks. The Daleks have bred out emotions over centuries of genetic mutation. They are coldly rational, and abhor any ripple of non-conformity. Their purpose is to conquer and subdue the universe, exterminating all non-Daleks in their quest for ethnic purity.

Daleks feel no emotion. In fact, when the Cult of Skaro (a secret Dalek sect) chose to experiment with human-Dalek mutations, it is Dalek Sec's emotions – his vulnerability to feeling – which made him an unwanted liability.[27] They have no use for free will, but move as a unified, single-minded force. It is no wonder then, for a Time Lord who prizes humanity with all of its flaws and virtues, that the Doctor should hate the Daleks. To the Doctor, Daleks have no humanity. There is no soul-quality. It has been long lost.

The occasions where the Doctor shows the inklings of empathy and compassion toward his virulent enemy are the few occasions where they have become precisely what they are not. When the Doctor and Rose encounter what they believe is the last remaining Dalek ('Dalek' (2005)), hidden in the underground museum-bunker of megalomaniac millionaire Henry Van Statten, the Doctor first responds with rage and violence. In an attempt to revive itself, this last surviving Dalek takes a scan of Rose's DNA into itself and is irrevocably changed.

As Rose's humanness invades and mingles with Dalek's genes, this Dalek begins to experience emotion, and desires to feel the sunlight against its wasted body. Ultimately, its own programmed design – to 'exterminate' any non-Dalek – leads to its own self-destruction. The last Dalek is mutating, and is no longer purely Dalek. The advent of emotions and individual ideas is overwhelming, and the Dalek chooses suicide over this new un-Dalek life. For the Dalek, a life with emotions, feelings, individual thoughts and ideas is 'not life, this is sickness'.

The Doctor confirms that the Dalek is changing into something new – a new life, a new creature. But this newness, this chance at a life with complex humanity, is abhorrent to the Dalek. Shortly before the Dalek self-annihilates, the Doctor gently says 'I'm sorry'. In watching the struggle of the new human qualities invading the old Dalek, the Doctor again reacts with empathy.

It is no surprise, then, that the Doctor's two greatest enemies lack humanity. For this Time Lord glorifies what makes us human. It is not rationalism that moves the Doctor, but the ability to live and wonder, to create and experience life as individuals, to feel – pain and joy – and to live at our fullest when we live in relation to others. These are exactly the attributes the Doctor's greatest enemies despise. And, perhaps we, like our favourite Time Lord, both hate and fear what we would become without our humanity.

Conclusion: Embodying Humanness and Teaching Humanity

The Doctor himself embodies this complex matrix of qualities which make up the *Imago Dei*. He is, himself, saturated with this soul-quality. He experiences the wide range of human emotions, from murderous rage,[28] to deepest sorrow,[29] to affection and love.[30] The Doctor is himself creative, looking for ways around the use of force and violence.[31] He values the ingenuity of human beings, remarking on their creative capacities. He desires to live in mutual relationship to others, and intentionally recruits companions to share in his adventures. The Doctor is even vulnerable to death (although he is marvellously good at cheating it), knowing that (although his risks may be less than his non-regenerating human companions) if he is incapable of regenerating, he will die.[32]

As a new kind of hero, the Doctor embodies a way of approaching humanness, which assumes its presence in the Other. As fewer and fewer people root themselves within religious (specifically Christian) communities,[33] the Doctor has emerged as a dynamic voice in demonstrating ethics.

His ethics are built on empathy and respect, and a heavy dose of curiosity. He is whimsical, and chooses to prize intellect over brute force. He believes in redemption, and second chances. In many ways the Doctor represents the best of humanness.

In the episodes 'Human Nature' and 'The Family of Blood' we see in the clearest sense that the Doctor embodies what it is to be human. He strips himself of his Time Lord knowledge, insight, even his Time Lord biology. Like Jesus, the Doctor literally 'empties himself'.[34] This is an explicit parallel to the Incarnation. This human Doctor – John Smith – loves, feels pain and sorrow, and the risk of his finiteness. He relies on his human companions – on Martha and Joan Redfern – to help him live fully. And, when John Smith chooses to open the pocket watch and return to being the Doctor, he selflessly chooses to die for the good of creation.

In this way, we are certain that the Doctor – like Jesus – embodies the best of humanity.[35] The qualities of Jesus which epitomise humanness are those same qualities which the Doctor most values in himself and others. His very life, whirling through time and space to intervene where there is trouble and to aid in loosening the bonds of injustice, embodies humanness to the fullest extent.

A generation of young people are growing up knowing less and less about the life of Jesus, and more and more about the wisdom of the Doctor. In the Doctor, the ever-broadening audience is seeing a lived example of empathy. The Doctor speaks through his actions, standing on the side of the vulnerable, challenging systems of injustice, and consistently looking for non-violent third ways. Despite his advanced years, he looks with child-like wonder at the stars and invites the audience to share that wonder.

The Doctor's model for embracing the humanness of others – however different – is one that stands as a lived example of ethics in action, a lived theological anthropology that is shown rather than explained. When Whovians ask 'What Would the Doctor Do?' they are asking 'What does it mean to be empathetic?' and 'What does it mean to value emotions, relationships, creativity and vulnerability?' For all the great distance between ourselves and our favourite Time Lord, at the end of the day, we are all humany-wumany.

8.

The Monstrous and the Divine in *Doctor Who*: The Role of Christian Imagery in Russell T. Davies's *Doctor Who* Revival

Jennifer L. Miller

Near the beginning of the fourth series of the rebooted *Doctor Who*, the Doctor and his companion Donna travel back to the city of Pompeii in the year 79 BCE, shortly before Mount Vesuvius erupts. In this episode, entitled 'The Fires of Pompeii'(2008), the Tenth Doctor (played by David Tennant) has to decide whether or not to save any citizens of Pompeii. He ultimately chooses to 'play God' and save a man named Caecilius and his family; the episode ends six months after the eruption of Vesuvius with a scene showing the successes of each of the family members. Caecilius himself is prospering financially; his daughter, Evelina, is fitting into the Roman social scene; and his son, Quintus, is studying to be a doctor, instead of throwing his life away as he was before. Metella, Caecilius' wife, tells Quintus to 'give thanks to the household gods' before he leaves for his studies, and in the final shot before the credits, we see the shrine to these household gods – a stone relief sculpture of the Doctor and Donna standing on either side of the TARDIS, which is positioned on top of a Roman-style staircase. This scene points to something noticed by many scholars of *Doctor Who*, both before and after its 2005 revival – namely, that 'the Doctor seems touched by divinity'.[1] Such a reading of the Doctor is reinforced by his ability to regenerate, his seemingly infinite knowledge of the universe, and the powerful technology that allows him to travel almost anywhere and access anything – a combination that renders him nearly omnipotent. Even the Doctor's very identity as a Time Lord contains a strong suggestion of divinity.

And yet, an examination of Christian imagery during the first four seasons and subsequent special episodes of the revival of *Doctor Who*, which originally aired between 2005 and 2010, demonstrates that during Russell T. Davies's tenure as producer of the show, the overall narrative arc of the show points to a very different interpretation of who the Doctor is in relation to humanity. In his *Politics*, Aristotle claims, 'He who is unable to live in society, or who has no need because he is sufficient for himself, must be either a beast or a god'.[2] While it is certainly possible to read the Doctor as a god-like figure, certain elements of the show from 2005 to 2010 call into question this reading, particularly the imagery seen in the Christmas specials and the failed moment of apotheosis in 'Journey's End' at the end of the fourth season. In fact, these moments suggest a need to consider the possibility that the Doctor falls on the *other* side of Aristotle's spectrum – that is, as something that is closer to a beast. And while the beast is someone or something that merely cannot live in society, an extension of this category is useful when considering the Doctor, given his continual active rejection of the rules of society. In other words, not only is the Doctor perhaps closer to being a beast than a god, but he might even be closest to being a monster, that is, someone who rejects the established rules of society, abiding only by his own laws. Viewing the Doctor in this way is vital to understanding the importance of his human companions in making him appealing and relatable to viewers.

Both the language and imagery of the show, as well as the work of scholars, makes it initially easy to interpret the Doctor as divine. Take, for example, the narration of Timothy Dalton's character during the Doctor and the Master's initial showdown during the episode 'The End of Time', the final *Doctor Who* special of Davies's tenure on the show. Dalton's narrator describes the Master as 'a madman', while he describes the Doctor as 'his saviour' who 'looked upon the wilderness in the hope of changing his inevitable fate'. Such language invokes the image of the Doctor as a god, and in particular, the figure of Jesus Christ in the gospel story of Jesus' temptation by the devil in the wilderness. Todd Comer is one scholar who makes a similar connection; he notes that the Doctor is not 'domestic', and argues that 'the writers of *Doctor Who* have connected the Doctor's non-domesticity explicitly to divinity'.[3] Comer also connects the fragmented nature of the Doctor's identity to divinity, arguing, 'While a typical notion of the Cartesian subject is that it is localised, focused around a centre of being, the Doctor seems to exist with no fixed centre. His various faces suggest a dynamic centre, and when, as eventually happens, we see two Doctors on the screen at the same time, it is difficult not to see him as complicating identity in much the same way as some Trinitarian notions of God.'[4] Such examples and analysis demonstrate that the Doctor as seen in the first four seasons of the rebooted version of the show is frequently interpreted as someone who is connected to divinity, as well as suggesting an understanding of this divinity that fits within the Western, and specifically Christian, understanding of the term.[5]

There is also great interest in reading the Doctor as a Christ figure, with parallels being drawn between him and Jesus both by Christian fans of the show and scholars analysing religious imagery throughout the series. In the spring of 2008, for example, a group associated with the Church of England held a conference on spirituality and *Doctor Who*. During this conference, themes of resurrection and redemption were analysed throughout the series, and the Doctor himself 'was likened to Christ in his willingness to sacrifice himself for others'.[6] Dee Amy-Chinn is one such scholar who analyses some of these connections to Christian imagery, identifying the season three finale 'The Last of the Time Lords' as containing particularly strong religious imagery. In this episode, the Tenth Doctor is imprisoned by another Time Lord called the Master, who has established himself as the dictator of Earth with the help of the Archangel network, a satellite system that subtly influences the thought patterns of everyone on the planet. Martha Jones, the Doctor's companion, escapes the Master's control and, as Amy-Chinn describes, 'spends a year in the wilderness preaching the gospel of the Doctor'. She ultimately coordinates the Doctor's return through 'what the Master terms "prayer", a worldwide telepathic plea to the Doctor at a single point in time'.[7] These examples are not provided to argue for *Doctor Who* as a show that promotes or embraces Christian ideals, but rather to demonstrate how it is common, for both fans and scholars, to read the Doctor as a divine figure. As Amy-Chinn says, 'no one disputes that the Doctor is both mythical and heroic'.[8]

There are some critics, however, who take issue with an understanding of the Doctor as divine, not because they disagree with this reading of the show, but because they are concerned with the implications of such a portrayal. John Paul Green, for example, argues, 'A worrying trend in the recent series has been to cast the Tenth Doctor (David Tennant) as messianic hero'.[9] Not only does Green examine the ways in which the Tenth Doctor emphasises characteristics such as wisdom, forgiveness, and healing, but he looks at the iconography of the show, noting, 'The Ninth Doctor's regeneration mimicked the Christ-like pose with arms splayed out cruciform'.[10] This alignment of the Doctor with a specific version of the divine – Christianity's Jesus – is problematic because it overwrites the Doctor's own mythology with a particular religious tradition. David Rafer describes how the Doctor is connected to both an original mythology as well as familiar myths and legends from Earth; he notes, 'The Doctor himself is a carrier and purveyor of his own myth but also encounters images and patterns drawn from ancient world mythology.'[11] Green's concern, then, comes with the possibility that the Doctor's own mythic significance will become overwhelmed by real-world theological concerns. He writes, 'part of the allure of the Doctor is his supposed apolitical, religiously ambiguous position. He should operate as the blank canvas upon which we the viewers ascribe meaning or significance, but with the Tenth Doctor, the iconography of Christianity comes to the fore, asserting the hero figure not only into the realm of the mythic, but also the theological.'[12] Here, too, while we see concern with the portrayal of the Doctor as divine, his divinity, and particularly, his Christ-like divinity, does not come into question.

However, the Christmas specials from 2005, 2006 and 2007 – 'The Christmas Invasion', 'The Runaway Bride' and 'Voyage of the Damned', respectively – *do* call the Doctor's divinity into question through the unsettling and uncanny use of Christian imagery throughout each episode. 'The Christmas Invasion' portrays the transition from the Ninth Doctor (Christopher Eccleston) to the Tenth Doctor, as well as the invasion of Earth by the Sycorax. In 'The Runaway Bride', Earth is threatened by the Empress of the Racnoss, a spider-like alien race that the Doctor had thought was extinct. And in 'Voyage of the Damned', Earth narrowly avoids nuclear catastrophe when a luxury spaceship named the *Titanic* is set on a collision course with it. Traditional images of Christmas feature prominently in each of these episodes, with elements such as Christmas trees, the Christmas star, snow, Santa, and angels playing a role in the plot development of each episode, rather than merely serving as background decorations. Yet in each of these cases, the image is actually a perverted version of the traditional Christian icon. In 'The Christmas Invasion', for example, the Doctor and his companion, Rose Tyler, sit down with Rose's mother and boyfriend Mickey for Christmas dinner after the Doctor completes his regeneration and saves the Earth from the threat of the Sycorax. While the dinner appears to be a traditionally joyous celebration, complete with roast turkey and crackers that contain paper crowns, this joy is marred by the announcement on the television that Harriet Jones, the Prime Minister, is going up against a vote of no confidence – an event instigated by the Doctor's suggestion to her assistant that she looks tired, which he made in response to her destruction of the fleeing Sycorax ship. Joy is temporarily restored when the group looks outside and sees snow falling amidst what appears to be a meteor shower, yet this, too, is disrupted. Rose looks up and says, 'It's beautiful! What are they? Meteors?' to which the Doctor replies, 'It's the spaceship breaking up in the atmosphere. This isn't snow – it's ash.' Rose's response – 'Ok, not so beautiful' – reflects the unsettling feeling created by this perversion of an image of wonder and beauty traditionally associated with Christmas. The fact that it is the Doctor's words that disrupt the beauty of this final scene of the episode is significant; his presence, rather than being in harmony with the Christmas celebration, is actually a disruptive one. Therefore, although Green describes how 'the Ninth Doctor's regeneration [to the Tenth Doctor] mimicked the Christ-like pose with arms splayed out cruciform',[13] this disquieting image from 'The Christmas Invasion' of snow that is not snow, along with the weaponised Christmas trees and disguised Santas from the same episode, challenge an understanding of the Doctor as an unequivocally divine figure.

The traditional imagery of Christmas functions much the same way in the second of these specials, 'The Runaway Bride' (2006), in which the Doctor meets Donna Noble, a bride whose groom has filled her full of huon particles so that he can feed her to the ancient Racnoss race and revive them from their slumber at the centre of the Earth. The huon particles in Donna attract scavengers, who, as in 'The Christmas Invasion', are disguised as Santas. They converge upon Donna's wedding reception and attack the guests using radio-controlled Christmas ornaments. A stylised version of 'Jingle Bells' plays during this scene over the sound of explosions and people screaming, creating an uneasy juxtaposition quite similar to Simon and Garfunkel's song '7 O'Clock News/Silent Night'. The most memorable visual image from the episode is that of the Christmas star, which is actually the ship of the Empress of the Racnoss, with the capability to destroy the Earth. A star-shaped figure appears above the streets of London, glowing and sparkling; people stare and point in wonder, and a little girl even says, 'It's Christmas!' The

Empress then uses this ship to attack the people of London, shooting beams of light at them and bringing fear and terror to Earth, rather than joy and wonder. Perhaps most interesting is the treatment of snow in this episode. Unlike the snow in 'The Christmas Invasion', this snow is actually real snow that the Doctor creates for Donna in an attempt to cheer her up. The appearance of snow is accompanied by a soaring musical score, and Donna's laughter and exclamation, 'I can't believe you did that!' But only a few moments later, when the Doctor asks Donna to come with him to see the universe, she refuses. When he tells her that the universe is beautiful, she replies, 'And it's terrible. That place was flooding, and burning, and they were dying, and you stood there like, I don't know, a stranger. And then you made it snow! I mean, you scare me to death!' Although the snow that appears in 'The Runaway Bride' is real snow, because of its association with the Doctor, it too becomes an instrument of fear and disquiet.

The appearance of masked Santas in both 'The Christmas Invasion' and 'The Runaway Bride' creates an unsettling feeling that is even more pervasive throughout 'Voyage of the Damned' (2007) because of the presence of robotic angels known as the Heavenly Host. The disruptive nature of these angels is made very clear from the opening scenes of the episode. The Doctor is startled when a ship crashes into the TARDIS; a life preserver that falls onto the deck of the TARDIS reads *Titanic*, leading the viewer as well as the Doctor to think that perhaps the Doctor has landed back in 1912. This perception continues when the Doctor boards the ship, as the elegant stemware, wood-panelled walls, and string quartet music correspond to viewers' expectations of how the *RMS Titanic* would look. It is not until the Doctor, and the viewers, see the robotic angels that these expectations are disrupted – an effect that foreshadows the disruptive and violent presence that the angels will maintain throughout the entire episode. The disruption created by the perverted image of the angels even continues in scenes where they are absent. In the scene immediately following the Doctor's arrival on the ship, for example, the captain of the *Titanic* stands on the bridge, looking down on Earth, and says, 'They don't even know we're here. Silent night, I believe they call it. A silent night.' With the beeping of instruments in the background and the uncertainty introduced by the angels, the captain's words seem to be a sinister threat, rather than the familiar, comforting carol: 'Silent night, holy night / All is calm, all is bright'. Such examples show how pervasive the disruption created by the robotic angels is throughout 'Voyage of the Damned', as well as an excellent demonstration of how, throughout these Christmas specials from 2005, 2006 and 2007, the familiar, comforting images of Christmas are distorted and turned into images of terror, destruction and death.

In this way, these Christmas images are excellent examples of what Freud described as 'the uncanny' – namely, that which is both familiar and unfamiliar, that which is both comforting and disquieting. In his essay on the uncanny, Freud examines the German word 'heimlich', noting that it has two standard meanings – the first being 'familiar, tame, intimate, comfortable',[14] and the second being 'concealed, kept from sight, so that others do not get to know about it, withheld from others'.[15] Freud then moves on to look at the word 'unheimlich', which means 'uneasy' or 'eerie',[16] and he is intrigued by the fact that this definition is very similar to the second definition for the word 'heimlich'. This all comes together when he says, 'What interests us most in this long extract is to find that among its different shades of meaning the word *heimlich* exhibits one which is identical with its opposite, *unheimlich*. What is *heimlich* thus comes to be *unheimlich*'.[17] This leads Freud to make the argument that the uncanny (that is, the *unheimlich*) is that which is simultaneously familiar and strange; that which is both comforting and eerie. All of these images seen in the Christmas episodes from the new *Who* fit this definition perfectly. On the one hand, they are the comforting images of Christmas, but on the other, they are perversions of those images that lead to death and destruction.

These uncanny images of Christmas provide a lens through which other uncanny elements of the show come to the fore. In particular, they are beneficial for highlighting the uncanny nature of the Doctor himself, emphasising how he is close to being divine, but ultimately falls short. As was seen above, the Doctor is often the one who draws attention to the uncanny nature of these Christmas imageries, either because he is the one who recognises the truth about them or, as in 'The Runaway Bride', because his association with these images actually makes them somehow uncomfortable.[18]   This uncanny nature is also emphasised by the interstitiality of these Christmas episodes – the Doctor is often in between companions, and in 'The Christmas Invasion', he is even transitioning into a new body. This interstitiality adds to the feeling of uncertainty and discomfort of the uncanny, resisting a reading of the Doctor that comfortably places him in the category of the divine. The fact that these uncanny images are associated with Christmas is also significant, as Christmas is the celebration of the birth of a divinity; placing the Doctor against the backdrop of an established divinity makes it easier to see how he falls short. This understanding of the Doctor as an uncanny figure, established by the perversion of traditional images of Christmas in these special episodes, can then be extended to other episodes of the show, and, in fact, the underlying idea behind the show in its entirety. The very title of the show – *Doctor Who* – pairs something that is comforting, familiar, and meant for healing together with something that represents the unknown and the unfamiliar. The whole concept of the Doctor, in other words, has its roots in the uncanny.

It is the Doctor's uncanny nature – his closeness to divinity but without the perfection – that pushes him beyond Aristotle's category of 'beast' into the realm of the monstrous. In fact, the Doctor's progression toward being a monster is one of the narrative arcs that gives cohesion to the first four seasons of the new *Who*, in spite of the different companions and even different incarnations of the Doctor himself. Key moments in this progression frequently appear in the Christmas episodes, structurally emphasising the interstitial and uncanny nature of the Doctor. One such moment occurs at the end of 'The Christmas Invasion', when the Doctor reacts with rage at Prime Minister Harriet Jones's decision to destroy the departing Sycorax ship, rather than let them go after their surrender; with fury in his voice, the Doctor tells her, 'That was murder ... I should have stopped you.' He then asks her assistant, 'Don't you think she looks tired?', thus planting the seed that starts the domino effect that leads to a vote of no confidence, whose announcement disrupts Rose's Christmas celebration with her family and friends, and ultimately, ends with Harriet Jones's removal from office. While the Doctor's response is based in his belief in non-violence, it also demonstrates his power to make unilateral decisions about the fate of humanity without regard for what the humans themselves want or think is best. Viewers might resonate with the logic of Harriet's response to the Doctor's accusation of murder: 'You said yourself, Doctor – they'd go back to the stars and tell others about the Earth. I'm sorry, Doctor, but you're not here all the time. You come and go ... We have to defend ourselves.' Because Harriet has been established as a sympathetic character in the show, viewers are more inclined to consider the validity of her argument. And when the Doctor says that he should have stopped her, Harriet's reply raises the possibility that the Doctor might be in the wrong: 'What does that make you,

Doctor? Another alien threat?' The appeal of Harriet Jones' character, coupled with the uncanniness of the Christmas imagery throughout this episode, introduces the idea that not only does the Doctor have the power to change the fate of humanity, but he also might use that power in the wrong way.

The uncanny nature of the perverted Christmas imagery also emphasises the potential of the Doctor to be a monster in the next Christmas episode – 'The Runaway Bride'. The Doctor offers the Empress of the Racnoss a choice to leave Earth alone and resettle with her children on another planet. When she refuses, the Doctor uses the water from the Thames to drown these children, but rather than leaving, he stays with the Empress, watching the destruction of her race. Although viewers will undoubtedly be in favour of the Doctor saving humanity, the Empress' plaintive cries of 'My children!' along with the image of the Doctor standing amidst flames with a hardened expression on his face introduces uncertainty into this moment of triumph. This uncertainty is underscored by Donna, who, looking troubled, says, 'Doctor! You can stop now!' This scene, along with Donna's later assessment that that Doctor was 'a stranger' in this moment, adds force to a reading of the Doctor as monstrous, rather than divine.

The monstrosity of the Doctor, however, is most clearly depicted in two key moments near the end of Davies' tenure on the show – the episode 'Journey's End', which appeared at the end of the fourth series, and 'The Waters of Mars', one of the special episodes in between the fourth and fifth series. For starters, in 'Journey's End', Earth has been stolen by the Doctor's nemesis, Davros, and his deadly creation, the Daleks, and moved to a new position in the universe; the Doctor, of course, saves the day, and in the climax of the episode, works together with companions past and present, as well as a duplicate version of himself, to take the Earth back home. This scene includes characters from other associated TV series as well, including Gwen Cooper and Ianto Jones from *Torchwood* and Sarah Jane Smith and K-9 from *The Sarah Jane Adventures*. The music playing in the background is 'Songs of Captivity and Freedom', which was first heard in an earlier episode in the fourth series – 'Planet of the Ood'. Furthermore, as the Doctor prepares to take Earth back home, he explains that with everyone together, 'Now we can fly this thing [the TARDIS]...like it's meant to be flown.' An attentive viewer of the episode will even notice that the viewer is brought into the scene through Martha's gaze – at one point, she breaks the fourth wall and looks directly at the viewer, smiling in a conspiratorial way that invites the viewer to be a participant too. All of these elements work together to function as an apotheosis, as a scene that establishes the divinity of the Doctor. Apotheosis scenes in visual art often involve bringing together a wide array of notable people to surround and pay homage to the person being deified, such as Constantino Brumidi's famous fresco, *The Apotheosis of Washington*, on the inside of the US Capitol Building. This work depicts a glorified George Washington, surrounded by figures from classical mythology, as well as by figures representing the thirteen United States colonies. In music, the apotheosis involves bringing back themes from earlier in the work and raising them to a new, more glorious level. Both of these techniques are used in 'Journey's End', which therefore seems to support the idea initially explored in this chapter of the Doctor as a divine figure.

But a closer examination of 'Journey's End' reveals that this episode does not end with this moment of glory. Rather, the last fifteen minutes of the episode show the Doctor returning all of his companions to their rightful places on Earth, which includes him saying a final farewell to Rose, the love of his life, and wiping the memory of his current companion Donna, whose absorption of some of the Doctor's essence was slowly killing her. At the end of the episode, the Doctor is left alone, without any faithful companion, without any adoring crowds. The apotheosis of the Doctor is ultimately a failed one. While this is perhaps in part due to the nature of television shows, where complete resolution is antithetical to the need for continued plot tension, this failed apotheosis also makes clear what the uncanny Christmas imagery in earlier episodes had alluded to – that the Doctor is not divine, and that his existence outside of society therefore needs to be accounted for in another way.

The culmination of the Doctor's progression toward monstrosity is found in 'The Waters of Mars', the penultimate special episode of Russell T. Davies's tenure on the show. During this episode, the Doctor decides to disregard the laws of the Time Lords to save three members of a human colony on Mars. He tells the colony's leader, Captain Adelaide Brooke, 'There are laws. There are laws of time. Once upon a time there were people in charge of those laws, but they died. They all died. Do you know who that leaves? Me. It's taken me all these years to realise that the laws of time are mine and they will obey me!' While it's possible to read these actions as the actions of a divinity, the reactions of those around the Doctor once again point to these moments as perversions of the divine – that is, the monstrous. When the Doctor saves Adelaide Brooke and the other two survivors of the Mars colony, for example, none of them thank him; in fact, one runs away from the Doctor after saying in fear, 'Who the hell are you?' The word 'hell' is key here, suggesting that while the Doctor is perhaps supernatural, his is a devilish power, rather than a divine one. Adelaide herself says, 'You should have left us there ... The Time Lord victorious is *wrong*.' Shortly after saying this, she kills herself, preventing the Doctor's triumph over the laws of time from being complete. Such actions are a far cry from the deification of the Doctor and Donna in 'The Fires of Pompeii', as not only is the Doctor unable to prevent the death of Adelaide Brooke, but he is in the position of being judged and found wanting, both by Adelaide and the viewer, rather than in the position of being the supreme judge.

Certainly, the questioning of a divinity is something that is seen in the Christian tradition, with figures ranging from Abraham and Moses to Job and even Jesus questioning the actions of God. But in the case of 'The Waters of Mars', the Doctor himself even recognises his shortfallings and that he has made a mistake; at the end of 'The Waters of Mars', he says to himself, 'I've gone too far.' In the next story, 'The End of Time', a similar theme arises during a discussion with Wilfred Mott, Donna's grandfather. Wilfred asks the Doctor, 'Who have you got now?' and the Doctor responds, 'No one. I'm travelling alone. I thought it'd be better ...' He trails off, and then continues: 'I did some things that went wrong. I need ...'[19] At that point, the Doctor breaks down, becoming too overwhelmed to continue. Wilfred jumps in, saying, 'Don't you see, Doctor? You need her. Wouldn't she make you laugh again, good old Donna?' These conversations guide the viewer's reaction to the Doctor's actions as well, showing us that we, too, should be uncomfortable with what he is doing. In these episodes at the end of Davies's tenure as executive producer of the show, the uncertainty about the Doctor's divinity, raised by the uncanny nature of the perverted Christmas imagery over the course of several Christmas specials, is brought to a climax. The nature of the Doctor's actions, along with the way characters, viewers, and even the Doctor himself question these actions, demonstrates that during the first four series of the revival of *Doctor Who*, the show is ultimately interested in exploring the Doctor's monstrous nature, rather than his divinity.

Even more than emphasising the Doctor's monstrous side, however, the Doctor's conversation with Wilfred also highlights another very important feature of the show – that it is the Doctor's companions who prevent him from fully becoming a monster. While Amy-Chinn argues that 'mercy and compassion are most fully embodied in the very human companions that accompany the Doctor on his travels',[20] the first four seasons of the *Doctor Who* revival demonstrate that this idea must be taken even further: the Doctor *needs* his companions to prevent him from becoming a monster. They are the embodiment of society and social norms, which in turn keeps the Doctor himself close to being human. For example, in the episode 'Journey's End', right after the Doctor's failed apotheosis, the real Doctor attempts to convince Rose to stay with the half-human copy of himself. He tells her, 'That's me, when we first met. And you made me better. Now you can do the same for him.' And in 'Voyage of the Damned', the 2007 Christmas special, it is not the Doctor's sacrifice that saves humanity; rather, it is Astrid, his human companion, who saves both the Doctor and the entire Earth by sacrificing herself. Although these same episodes challenge the idea of the Doctor as a divinity through the use of uncanny Christmas imagery and a failed apotheosis, they also provide a way for him to avoid being a monster – his human companions.[21] While this sentiment on its own is appealing and heart-warming, the true significance of these companions for the Doctor is clear only after his monstrous potential is revealed.

Ultimately, as an examination of the uncanny imagery in the Christmas episodes reveals, the Doctor is close to being divine, but he falls short, demonstrating monstrous tendencies that are problematic to both those within the show and those watching it. It is his human companions who, with their embodiment of social norms, pull the Doctor back from this brink. The image of the Doctor and Donna as household gods, seen in 'The Fires of Pompeii', is therefore perhaps not all that far off from the truth – but it is *Donna's* presence in the carving, rather than the Doctor's, that makes such an interpretation possible. As the Doctor tells Donna at the end of this episode, 'You were right. Sometimes I need someone. Welcome aboard.'

9.

'With proof, you don't have to believe': *Doctor Who* and the Celestials

John Vohlidka

'I don't know what to believe anymore', said Leela when she found her life turned upside down in 'The Face of Evil' (1977). Her quandary mirrored the confusion of a British television audience facing the challenges and doubts of their society. As the Doctor prepared Leela to face her new world, so too would he prepare the British people for what lay ahead. Faced with the uncertainties of the 1970s, they searched for something to believe in.

Although dressed up in the guise of adventures in time and space, the classic series of *Doctor Who* (1963-1989) actually reflected the issues confronting Britain during the time the stories were transmitted.[1] The Doctor represented science and sometimes scepticism. However, it can also be argued that he represented faith as well by taking on different roles against the variety of monsters, aliens, megalomaniacs and villains he encountered.[2] Some of these enemies were seen as gods, claimed to be gods, or aspired to become gods. These 'Celestials' represented a prevailing tension in Western civilization: the fear of false gods or idols.

This chapter looks specifically at the Doctor's relationship with the Celestials during the 1970s and early 1980s. By Celestials, I am referring essentially to 'space gods'; beings with cosmic origins, originating from outer space, or having some sort of special power or ability over average humans.[3] Sometimes, the Doctor acts as a sort of John the Baptist character, preparing the way for them as in 'The Mutants' (1972). In other stories, as in 'Planet of the Spiders' (1974) or 'Pyramids of Mars' (1975), he confronts the Celestials directly, putting a final stop to their dangerous activities. Often, the Doctor represents the fear of idolatry by acting as a modern day Elijah to demystify false gods as in the stories 'The Face of Evil' (1977), 'Four to Doomsday' (1982), 'The Green Death' (1973) and 'The Power of Kroll' (1978). In this last role, while the Doctor appears to be a scientific sceptic, many of his actions and attitudes are firmly grounded in the Judeo-Christian tradition suggesting the possibility of a blending between religion and science.

In the 1970s, Britain was in a state of social turmoil: tensions over Northern Ireland, economic recession and immigration resulted in a more jaded society. This led to some people 'dropping out' and an increase in experimental alternative lifestyles and the counter-reaction to such lifestyles.[4] The series reflected much of the tumultuousness of the time, with the Doctor serving as a beacon of calm, proper behaviour. He was first and foremost a British hero, the type many British people were waiting for to restore faith in the government and deal with the myriad of problems facing the country.[5]

British society in the 1970s and 1980s was not as secular as previously thought, and religion and religious ideals and forms continued to be understood by many citizens.[6] It is against this backdrop, a period when Britain was, as Stuart Clayton calls it, 'de-churching' but not necessarily secularising, that *Doctor Who* will be examined.[7] This is not to deny that the series in the seventies and eighties was not essentially pro-science or that it used science as a 'cover' for a series of coded religious messages.[8] In general, *Doctor Who* was clearly pro-science and there have been phases in its history where a serious attempt was made to ground those stories in accepted scientific theories and ideas. I am arguing that, at times, the show's attitude toward religion was varied and employed a specifically Judeo-Christian theistic 'language' at a time of 'believing without belonging' in British history when Church of England membership was down, but spirituality was being explored by the British public.[9] This is shown by the Doctor's actions toward these Celestials.

'You have shown the Way'

The Third Doctor (Jon Pertwee), was tall, dashing and arrayed with a variety of 'miraculous' gadgets such as his sonic screwdriver. His superior knowledge allowed him to understand what was happening before any of the other characters. His style of dress, frilled shirts and tuxedo jackets, made him very trendy for the Britain of the time.[10] He also displayed a strong moral sensibility which put him at odds with mad scientists, monsters and invaders from space; this usually placed him on the side of the oppressed versus the oppressors. Often, he acted as an agent of higher powers, the Time Lords, who sent him on various missions, as in 'The Mutants'.

In 'The Mutants', human Overlords, led by the Marshal, attempt to change the atmosphere of Solos to suit humans. This interferes with the natural life-cycle of the native Solonians, stalling it and mutating them into 'Mutts'. The Solonians have been under the rule of Earth for 500 years and tension had been mounting between the two parties. Just before an important conference, one of the Solonian leaders, Ky, makes an impassioned speech to his fellows on the evils of progress. He blames the Overlords for polluting their planet and enslaving his people.

Such a speech could be made by any rebel against any empire, but it is reminiscent of Judean discontent against the Roman peace. Such discontent was quasi-religious in nature, centring on a God-sent 'messiah'. The story sets Ky up as just this kind of messiah. His later transformation into a Celestial reinforces this position.

Into this mix steps the Doctor. In this story, he fulfils the role of John the Baptist with help from Professor Sondergaard, an Earthling who lives in a cave on Solos in a fashion not dissimilar to the desert hermits. Unlike the Overlords, Sondergaard has dropped out of his society. He dresses in long robes and spends his time researching the caves or helping cast-out Mutts. Sondergaard is like a 'voice of one crying out in the wilderness' (Luke 3:4) to prepare the way. The Doctor also prepares the way. He arrives with a message from the Time Lords. The box the message is in will only open for the intended recipient, so even the Doctor does not know who it is for. When Ky touches the box, it is revealed the Doctor has been sent to help him. The box contains stone tablets defining the seasons, or rather, the lifecycle of the native Solonians. These tablets had been lost to them and so was the knowledge of their own potential.[11] The Doctor then works to help the Solonians against the Marshal and solve the mystery of the Mutts.

The Doctor and Sondergaard share the John the Baptist role, working together to solve the mystery of the Time Lords' message, explain the mutations and 'baptise' Ky, helping him become aware of his status as a super-being. When the Doctor enters the radiation cave to retrieve the crystal, he describes it as beautiful, 'like a cathedral'. He takes the crystal from what appears to be a glowing statue or mummy. He later hands off the crystal to Sondergaard, also passing off the John the Baptist role at the same time. In the refuelling chamber, when Ky is wracked with pain, Sondergaard gives him the crystal, effectively baptising him (in radiation instead of water) allowing him to become his true self. The metamorphosed Ky, now ephemeral in glowing colours, thanks Sondergaard, 'You have shown the way'. The Doctor paves the way for Ky, who then saves his people by destroying the Marshal and leading them to freedom. 'I thank you Doctor, for all my people', he says at the climax of the story. Ky disappears at the end, almost ascending like Jesus.

Frequently, the Doctor fulfils the role of what Hugh Ruppersberg calls the 'alien messiah': a character from a culture so advanced he appears 'divine' or 'miraculous' to ordinary mortals.[12] This is particularly the case with the Doctor in his stories during the 1970s. Ruppersberg argues that science-fiction cinema in the 1970s and 1980s was, in fact, reactionary in its rejection of science in favour of the supernatural.[13] Although Ruppersberg was discussing cinema in particular, his critique holds up for television as well, particularly 'The Mutants'.[14] Although the Doctor's role in this story is less messianic, he fulfils many of the supernatural qualities Ruppersberg discusses. But, in the end, the story boils down to a supernatural theme: ancient tablets and the Doctor's wisdom about the seasons result in Ky becoming the messiah for his people.

'Your Evil is My Good'

While in some of these stories, the Doctor works to aid these Celestials, a more common role is to fight them. In 'Planet of the Spiders', the lead villain is the Great One, a gigantic 'eight leg' enlarged by radiation found in the hills of Metebelis 3. She uses a Buddhist monastery on Earth as a portal to retrieve a crystal the Doctor took years ago. At the climax of the story, the Doctor admits to his theft of the crystal and puts it down to his own greed: greed for knowledge. By acknowledging his greed and agreeing to return the crystal, the Doctor returns to the right path, one that leads to the defeat of the would-be Celestial, the Great One.

It is clear the Great One considers herself to be a god. The lesser spiders cry out fanatically and ritualistically: 'All hail to the Great One!' whenever her name is invoked. Her chamber in the mountains resembles a temple with a flight of stairs leading up to where she sits. Why spiders would need such a flight of stairs is not explained and no human could survive the radiation in her chamber. Clearly, the point of the design was to make the viewers think in terms of a temple. When she has the final crystal in the matrix and her powers are increased a thousand-fold, she cries out: 'Bow down before me planets! Bow down stars! Bow down o' galaxies! And worship the Great One! The Me! The great all-powerful Me!'[15]

The Doctor, who brought her the remaining crystal, tries to warn her but she refuses to listen. This would-be Celestial finds such power too much for her, and she dies as a result. The Great One is a false god. The radiation in the cave is too much for the Doctor as well, who gives his current life in this battle and regenerates.

The Fourth Doctor (Tom Baker), was less dashing, but just as physically imposing as his predecessor. His bohemian style of dress gave him a sort of credibility with a maturing audience.[16] His long scarf resembled those worn by Oxbridge students.[17] This look emphasised his Britishness. He too displayed a strong moral sense, particularly against the Celestial Sutekh.

In 'Pyramids of Mars', the Doctor tries to prevent the escape of Sutekh from his prison. Sutekh, and the other Osirians, were considered gods by the ancient Egyptians. Horus, another Osirian, imprisoned Sutekh beneath an Egyptian pyramid, with a signal on Mars holding him there. Sutekh takes over the body of archaeologist Marcus Scarman, who refers to himself as Sutekh's 'instrument'. Another servant, Namin, refers to Sutekh as 'noble god'. Sutekh, in his confrontation with the Doctor, sets the terms of the divisions between himself and all others: 'Your evil is my good. I am Sutekh the Destroyer. Where I tread I leave nothing but dust and darkness. I find that good.' This is an absolute division. Sutekh is the enemy of all life. As author Bernice Martin points out, when something shocks us morally, we prefer to identify the perpetrator as evil.[18] The Doctor responds by cursing Sutekh and referring to him as a 'twisted abhorrence'. When the Doctor defeats him by throwing him into the time vortex, he is defeating a being who claimed to have the right to destroy all life.

The moral of both these stories is clear: both Celestials, one a gigantic mutated spider and the other described as 'abhorent', are evil. Their goal is destructive: one will enslave humankind and the universe; the other will destroy it all. Despite their power, or perhaps because of it, they must be challenged and stopped. False gods can lead to ruination.

'He believes he ... is God'

In the history of monotheistic religion there has always been a fear of false gods. This is a basic tenet of monotheism: one god means only one god, any other god is and must be false. It is the first of the Ten Commandments: 'I am the Lord your God ... you shall have no other gods before me' (Exodus 20:23). There arises from this a certain jealousy of false gods; the idea that the worship of such draws away from the one true God.[19] Jealousy and concern about false gods thus permeates Judeo-Christian religion and also the history of Western civilisation.

In the 1970s and 1980s, a growing reliance on technology and the need for money to fuel the growing materialistic culture seemed to be replacing the traditional values once held dear by society and threatened to replace the need for God and religion. One major trend in the stories discussed below is the Doctor confronting a false god, a Celestial that claims to be or believes itself to be a divine entity. These false gods can take many forms: technology; seduction; greed; or even blind faith. These things became modern day idols. It is not enough simply to battle these Celestials, but to demonstrate that they are false gods.[20] In other words, the Doctor fights against idolatry, which is interrelated with the notion of worshipping false gods.[21] The Doctor's goal in these stories is not just to defeat them, but to demonstrate that they would lead others down a wrong path. The Doctor acts to debunk these false Celestials like the prophet Elijah, who challenged the priests of Ba'al and thus demonstrated that Ba'al was a false god. To combat these idols, the Doctor replaced these empty and false gods with faith in humanity and the freedom of the will.

In 'The Face of Evil', the computer god, Xoanon, represents a sort of Manichean dualist belief. Xoanon and the Evil One are both considered gods by the Sevateem, one light, the other dark, striving against each other. At the same time, they are part of a single godhead, as represented by Xoanon's split personality. Both are actually the result of the Doctor accidentally imprinting his personality on a spaceship's computer he thought he was repairing years earlier. His unintentional meddling resulted in the computer going mad, creating a split not only in the computer's mind, but in the population the computer served. The crew of the spaceship was divided into the Sevateem and the Tesh who became enemies. The Tesh ended

up servants of the computer and remained in the ship, while the
Sevateem went native and lived off the land.

By wiping his own personality from the computer core, the
Doctor reveals the truth: Xoanon is not a god after all. A new form
of life perhaps, and one with tremendous powers, but not a god. He
thus desacralises Xoanon. But does the Doctor desacralise Xoanon in
the name of science or faith? The answer lies in his relationship with
Leela. At the beginning of the story, Leela is cast out by the Sevateem
for the blasphemy of denying Xoanon. She then meets the Doctor,
who she mistakes for the Evil One (whose carved cliff image was that
of the Doctor). Even when he convinces her that he is not the Evil
One, he does not stop there. He is determined to cultivate a different
way of thinking and speaking in Leela. When she later says, 'I don't
know what to believe anymore', he responds, 'That sounds healthy
anyway, Leela'. Leela's confusion leads to questions about the belief
system she has inherited. After all, true inquiry is part of faith.[22] He
also insists that she not refer to objects in faith-based language, but
in science-based language. When she later refers to the chamber of
Xoanan as the 'sacred heart' she justifies herself by pointing out it
is the name used by others. 'And what do you call it?', the Doctor
insists. He is noticeably pleased when she now refers to it as the
'main computer complex'. In other words, he is trying to change the
way she thinks, but generally expects her to accept these changes on
faith – faith in him.[23]

As the story of 'The Face of Evil' nears its climax, Neeva and
Tomas stand inside a cave, looking out at the rocket ship that is both
reality and legend to them. Both of these characters were looking at
the physical existence of their religious beliefs, while at the same time
coming to the realisation that their 'god', Xoanon, had been lying to
them and using them. Neeva laments, 'we start getting proof and we
stop believing.' According to Daniel Migliore, blind faith is the same
as idolatry. Tomas's response, 'with proof, you don't have to believe',
is the rejection of blind faith. The Doctor's arrival had led to inquiry
and investigation, which in turn led to the truth. The 'proof' was that
their blind faith had led them to worshipping a false god (in this case
literally a machine or idol). Conflicting emotions in both characters
lead them to different fates: Neeva's desire for revenge leads to his
destruction while Tomas's scepticism towards Xoanon and his faith
in his friend Leela leads to his survival in a new society. Not having
to believe does not necessarily mean that you cannot believe.[24] In the
end, their future was theirs to choose.

We see a similar pattern in 'Four to Doomsday', featuring Fifth Doctor Peter Davison. The Fifth Doctor's style is the most conservative and most grounded in history. While the Third and Fourth Doctors' looks were inspired by contemporary culture, the Fifth dressed in an Edwardian cricket outfit, representing a sense of Britishness from a time that predated youth rebellion, social upheaval and the sexual revolution (in fact, a time predating all the social turbulence of the 1970s).[25] When the TARDIS lands on an alien ship, the Doctor and companions meet Monarch, a sort of collector of humans, headed to destroy Earth. According to the character Bigon, Monarch believes himself to be God. He seems proud that he has converted his entire race into micro-chips, transcending the 'flesh time'. He refers to his mission to Earth as a 'crusade'. Monarch's ultimate goal, according to Bigon, is to travel faster than light and go back to the creation of the universe. 'Monarch believes he will meet himself there. He believes he ... is God', says Bigon. Monarch is dangerous, not just because he believes he is God, but because he wishes to convert others to this way of thinking. This danger is highlighted when Adric is converted to Monarch's cause, seduced by his apparent power and wisdom.[26] The Doctor's response to this is also telling. First he humours Adric, then when he believes that they are not being overheard, he forces his companion to choose, referring to Monarch as 'evil' (a moral absolute). Adric sides with his friends in the end: choosing friendship over the seduction of evil.[27]

In the end, Monarch is defeated by the Doctor, who throws a virulent virus at him, revealing that Monarch himself is still in the flesh time.[28] His destruction demonstrates that he is a false god. The Doctor does not use rational discourse to defeat Monarch, but action. And like Elijah towards the Phoenician priests of Ba'al, he shows no leniency towards him.[29] The Doctor showed no remorse over the defeat of this foe. The Fifth Doctor has usually been described by his critics as fairly feckless and in this story he often appears indecisive. In retrospect, his behaviour is actually quite harsh. This is one of the few times he actively destroys an enemy, unlike his usual technique of tricking them into destroying themselves. The Doctor carries the virus 'for studying purposes' but shows no compunction towards using it to destroy Monarch.[30]

'The Green Death' deals with idolatry in the form of the worship of money. The Third Doctor investigates strange happenings at a chemical factory in Wales. Pollution from Global Chemicals, created in a rush for profit, results in giant mutated maggots. Lust for wealth can also be considered idolatry, as greed is considered a competitor to God.[31] Those who commit the sin of greed have set up their own idol in competition with God. This is the same in both the Jewish and Christian tradition where love of money is considered the same as setting up an idol. This rejection of idolatry is aimed not just at outsiders but also insiders of the faith.[32] Martin Luther argued that anyone who focuses on wealth 'has a god, called mammon, that is, money and riches – on which he fixes his whole heart'.[33] In this story, the enemy is not the giant maggots nor the computer BOSS, but greed and its consequences. Global Chemicals is willing to poison the Earth creating potential bio-hazards – all in pursuit of the pound. Stevens, the head of the company, submits to BOSS; essentially trading his soul for money.[34] He and others co-opted by BOSS even resemble automatons at times. They are portrayed as men who have sacrificed their souls, shown by an unwillingness to aid others who suffer. This is particularly true of the character of Fell, who spoke in a monotone and demonstrated no compassion for either the miners who were trapped (and died), or the Doctor and Jo, who were stuck in a waste pipe.

In contrast, the intellectuals at the Nut Hutch, the community set up by Professor Jones and his companions to explore an alternative lifestyle, represent a cleaner form of living that is closer to nature. They live near the mining site and oppose the environmental impact Global Chemicals is having on the area and search for new ways to better society. The seventies were not a confident decade and there was an increasing distrust of forms of authority. Although the inhabitants of the Nut Hutch cannot be said to be an overtly religious group, neither are they all scientists. Instead, their communal form of living where they have dropped out of society only to work for society's salvation (i.e. Professor Jones's experiments designed to end food shortages around the world) is reminiscent of a monastic community.[35] Historically, monks formed monasteries away from settled areas (although communities eventually rose up around them) for the purpose of denying themselves the evils of the physical world, but also to pray for humanity's salvation. This was the monastic paradox: a monastery was both apart from society, and yet an integral and active part of it.[36] The Nut Hutch fulfils a similar function in 'The Green Death'. Professor Jones and the others have set up their own community but are still part of society. This is seen when they protest outside Global Chemicals, and when 'Mum' hears important gossip about the company's plans. Both actions show the members of the Nut Hutch remained concerned for the society around them. Their community is in direct contrast to life at Global Chemicals, where everything is stark and lifeless. The Doctor's choice to remain at the Nut Hutch is telling. His remaining with them, working with them, and sharing communal meals with them is a deliberate endorsement of their lifestyle and a condemnation of the kind of society the pursuit of greed creates. This is reinforced in the climax, when the Doctor defeats BOSS (and greed too) by reawakening Stevens's humanity. Stevens's choice of self-sacrifice to destroy BOSS indicates the man's redemption.

The ultimate false god presented during this period of the show is Kroll in 'The Power of Kroll'. This story was part of a season long arc in which the White Guardian recruits the Fourth Doctor to retrieve and assemble the pieces of the Key to Time, an immensely powerful object that would restore the balance of the universe. This makes the Doctor a sort of divine instrument, but clearly not divine himself.[37] His behaviour in the story suggests failings in personality (but not in his intellect or ability), which has the purpose of humanising him as a character for the audience. The missing segments of the Key were all disguised as other objects, so the Doctor, accompanied by Romana, was given a 'tracer' which allowed them to find the segments and transform them back into their proper form at the touch of the tracer. In 'The Power of Kroll', one of those segments was hailed as a god.

This segment was on the moon of Delta Magna where native Swampies worshipped the giant squid Kroll. The appearances of Kroll are referred to as 'manifestations' in the Old Book, a sort of Swampie Bible the Doctor finds at the bottom of a well. The Swampies believe it necessary to sacrifice Romana to Kroll to gain his good will before they attack the methane miners intruding on their land. Both Romana and the Doctor are less than impressed with this holy aspect attributed to the giant squid. When Ranquin, the High Priest, declares, 'When the servants of Kroll appear in his guise they are part of him, doing as he bids them', Romana responds, 'That's simply keeping a myth alive'.

This mockery is reminiscent of the way Elijah taunted the priests of Ba'al. Patrica Berlyn has stated that Elijah's taunt:

> was at reliance on any god or gods who can be preoccupied, or absent, or dormant, or dependent on the antics of the clergy; a mockery of devotees who must not merely adore them but

shore them up with magical rituals, lest they lose the power to perform.[38]

In other words, the powers of these gods exist only in the minds of the worshippers, and priests must use rituals and tricks to convince worshippers of the gods' power and keep them essentially hoodwinked. Ranquin uses a priest made-up to look like Kroll to kill sacrifices and even makes false claims as to whether Kroll 'accepted' the sacrifice. According to Migliore, such false claims are akin to controlling 'revelation' which in essence replaces theology with idolatry.[39] The worship of Kroll is thus idolatry in two interrelated forms: first, the blind faith in a monstrous creature, and second, in the attempt to control and modulate that worship which creates the blind faith.

The mockery by the Doctor and Romana continues after Ranquin intones, 'Kroll is all wise, all-seeing ...' only to be interrupted by the Doctor, 'All baloney! Kroll couldn't tell the difference between you and me in half an acre of dandelion and burdock!' Angry, Ranquin responds, 'I tell you Kroll will not be denied!' Ranquin is soon eaten by his god. This is a final mockery of Ranquin's claims as to Kroll's godliness. The 'all-knowing' Celestial did not even recognise his High Priest.

Ruppersberg argues that such science-fiction stories are actually reactionary in that they reject science and advocate the supernatural.[40] This is certainly the case in 'Kroll'. On the surface, both the Doctor and Romana appear to doubt Kroll's divinity on rationalist grounds. But then the Doctor easily defeats Kroll by touching him with the tracer, removing the Key to Time from Kroll and reverting him to an ordinary squid. The Doctor uses the tracer, essentially his magic wand or miniature staff (shades of Moses) given to him by the White Guardian (again the Doctor is an agent of a higher power), to desacralise Kroll and free the Swampies from their idol worship.

Conclusion

In dealing with these false gods, the Doctor is not just battling monsters, but also combating a theistic rival. It is not enough to simply challenge and defeat these celestials; they must be exposed for what they really are: false gods. The Doctor generally acts as a beacon, guiding the other characters down the correct path and for the audience, shining a light on the dangers of idolatry in its many forms whether the corruption of money, ideas or ideologues.

Upon examination, the theistic language employed in numerous iconic episodes of *Doctor Who* and the fact that it clearly resonated with the audience demonstrates that Britain in the 1970s and early 1980s was not as secular as previously thought. As a science-fiction show, *Doctor Who* did not exclude religious ideas, language and metaphors. Clearly, in some of the stories, as those discussed above demonstrate, the show did not hesitate to use ideas firmly grounded in the Judeo-Christian tradition. This should not be surprising for a show which lasted twenty-six years and covered a variety of genres. Some stories were meant to be firmly grounded in science. In other stories, religious metaphors as a part of the common culture were used with the expectation they would be understood by the British audience and evoke a response. Dispensing with what Jeremy Morris refers to as the 'straightjacket of secularization', the secularisation theory championed recently by Callum Brown, such stories can be seen as part of a larger narrative of Christianity's internal criticism.[41] That is, that 'secular' criticism is a misleading concept, as much of the critique comes from Christianity itself.[42] The Doctor's encounters with these Celestials were mainly in the stories broadcast during the 1970s, a time when Britain was anxious concerning the myriad of challenges facing the nation (and political leaders lacking the will to find a way out). The Celestials, then, tended to represent different challenges. Sometimes, they needed the assistance of the Doctor ('The Mutants'); sometimes they needed to be stopped ('Planet of the Spiders', 'Pyramids of Mars'); mostly though, they symbolised the dangers of idolatry: the act of worshipping the wrong god or being led down the wrong path ('The Face of Evil', 'Four To Doomsday', 'The Green Death', 'The Power of Kroll') and needed to be exposed for the false gods they were.

This resonated with a fragmented society where so many were exploring new paths. The Doctor symbolised the correct way. His responses to the Celestials gave a hint to the audience on how to deal with temptations of various sorts. His credentials for doing this were twofold: in the context of the stories he was generally a representative of a higher power (Time Lords, White Guardian, etc.); and he was the hero. The brief of the series described the Doctor as '...searching for something as well as fleeing from something'.[43] This made him a kindred spirit to the British people who were trying to put the dark side of imperialism behind them, while wanting to restore the glory which was once theirs. The Doctor personified the 'keep calm and carry on' attitude that had gotten the previous generation through the Blitz and showed that the same resilience and resolve would get them through the present challenges. Despite being a Time Lord from Gallifrey, he was British. He was there to prepare the way and teach them to believe in themselves.

10.

'Her brain was full of superstitious nonsense': Modernism and the Failure of the Divine in *Doctor Who*

Kieran Tranter

As a vast narrative, *Doctor Who* presents numerous challenges to cultural scholars.[1] The production length, the changing actors, and producers, aesthetics, and genres, means it is difficult to discern consistent values and themes. Even the recent transition in 2009/2010 from Russell T. Davies to Steven Moffat has seen significant changes; from David Tennant's heroic Tenth Doctor to Matt Smith's more alien Eleventh Doctor, and a move towards a stronger horror emphasis.[2] With the show continually being reinvented, an 'unfolding text' as John Tulloch and Manuel Alvardo called it,[3] a tendency has been to focus on specific episodes or specific producer/Doctor eras.[4]

This chapter's focus encompasses the televised episodes of *Doctor Who* both in the 'classic series' (1963-1989) and the post-2005 BBC Wales regeneration, 'New Who' (2005-). It finds something to say in taking seriously the unfolding text of *Doctor Who*. The consistency in *Doctor Who* has been change. In this it reflects the Doctor's inter-text universe(s). The Doctor adventures within changing universe(s) of matter, energy and time. The divine is repeatedly shown as illusionary. This backdrop of a secular universe(s) suggests that the Doctor can be seen as adventuring in a universe described by two other doctors, Charles Darwin and Thomas Huxley.[5]

This chapter argues that the Doctor, regeneration after regeneration, endures because he continually tells an aspiring story of living well within secular universe(s) of matter, energy and time. This argument is in three stages. The first stage highlights the continual reoccurrences of the failure of the divine within *Doctor Who*.

The second stage connects this feature of the show to its presentation of secular universe(s) of matter, energy and time. This stage locates *Doctor Who* within H. G. Wells's 'scientific romances'. The Doctor's universe(s) change; there is evolution, entropy and chance. The third stage argues that the Doctor's actions in these universe(s) present an aspiring story that resonates with us moderns. For Wells, drawing on Huxley, a divine-free universe was an invitation to responsibility. It presents the dangerous opportunity of modernity: of creating futures; of fixing past injustice; and legislating for future (brave) new worlds. The Doctor, with his violent sovereignty safeguarding the potential of life, presents the power and possibilities of mere mortals, as gods, in a universe without divinity.

The Failure of the Divine

Religion and the divine are all over *Doctor Who*. Rarely is there an episode where religion is not on show. From the Christmas iconography in the recent festive specials, to the Christ-like sacrifice of the Tenth Doctor in 'The End of Time' and the Buddhist-inspired Fifth Doctor (Peter Davison) story 'Kinda', *Doctor Who*'s writers and producers have regularly drawn upon religious sources. Within its foundational season the First Doctor (William Hartnell) faced myth and religious rites in 'An Unearthly Child' and 'The Aztecs'. However, there is something particular about *Doctor Who*'s presentation of religion and the divine. In this it must be contrasted to another science-fiction television show regenerated in the 2000s, *Battlestar Galactica* (2003-2010).

In *Battlestar Galactica*, religion was a cynical space for politicking. From the Cylon's zealot monotheism in the early seasons to Baltar's (James Callis) evangelism in the final season, religion was politics under another name.[6] However, that show was not cynical about the divine.[7] As the seasons progressed, the plans of humans and machines became more understandable as in accord with a divinely-instigated grand design. The divine was represented seriously. With the discovery of 'New Earth' populated by primitive humans, the return of Starbuck (Katee Sackhoff) as the heraldic 'Angel of Doom', and the final scenes that have Inner-Six (Trica Helfer) and Inner-Baltar revealed as agents or manifestations of a 'God who doesn't like the name',[8] *Battlestar Galactica* presented an active divinity. The 'creator' moved in that universe in mysterious yet obvious ways;

and by the end of the final season faith, and plot credibility, was a matter of seeing rather than believing.

Religion and religious institutions get similar treatment in *Doctor Who* as in *Battlestar Galactica*. The Doctor has come across numerous cults, sects and churches that are revealed as morally bankrupt, corrupt or degenerate. The Fourth Doctor (Tom Baker)/ Sarah Jane (Elisabeth Sladen) story 'The Masque of Mandragora' (1976) presents the usual account of religion in *Doctor Who*. In that Philip Hinchcliffe/ Robert Holmes minor classic a doomsday cult, led by a megalomaniac, is infiltrated by an alien. The devotees of the 'Brethren of Demnos' are shown as faceless, violent pawns; the leader, warped from the beginning by ambition and greed, is consumed by the alien invader; and the Doctor saves Renaissance Italy with a combination of science, luck, toothy grins and companion pro-action. The cult with its superstitions and its otherworldliness is defeated by reason and faith in the material world. Befitting a 70s *Doctor Who* story a structural binary can be identified at play with 'The Masque of Mandragora'.[9]

Structural Account of 'The Masque of Mandragora'

Positive	Negative
Duke Giuliano (Gareth Armstrong), Rightful Duke of San Martino, devotee of reason	– Count Federico (Jon Laurimore), Uncle to Giuliano, would-be usurper to the Dukedom – Hieronymous (Norman Jones), corrupt astrologer, leader of the Brethren of Demnos
The Doctor, rightful alien influence	Mandragora Helix, would-be conquering alien
Light and colourful – Interiors of the Castle of San Martino – Giuliano's costumes – The Doctor's costume	Dark and monochromatic – Interior of the crypt of the Brethren – Purple robes of the Brethren and Hieronymous
Belief in the senses and the material world	Belief in supernatural
Reason	Superstition
Choice	Destiny / predetermined
Good	Evil
Life	Death

Religion and belief in the divine is aligned with destiny, evil and death; while belief in the senses and the material world with choice, the good and life. This orientation towards religions recurs throughout *Doctor Who*. The Third Doctor (Jon Pertwee) adventure 'The Dæmons' has the Master (Roger Delgado) impersonating a vicar; while the Tenth Doctor story 'Fires of Pompeii' has the 'Sibylline Sisterhood' possessed and twisted by an alien presence. In *Doctor Who* it seems that religious organisations and religiosity are not to be trusted. The Doctor rarely collaborates with religious leaders or organisations as opposed to his preferred partners, scientists and the military. The Eleventh Doctor works with a militarised future Church in the Weeping Angel epic 'The Time of Angels/Flesh and Stone'; but aside from some superficial titles (cleric, bishop, Papal mainframe) the Doctor's collaboration with them is as a military and not a religious organisation. Its closest precursors are Brigadier Lethbridge-Stewart (Nicholas Courtney) and UNIT in the Pertwee era. Further, the Church, complete with an order of wacky headless monks, reappears the following season – confirming 'The Masque of Mandragora' template – aligned in the dark (the dimly lit space station of Demons' Run) with forces against the Doctor.[10]

The reoccurrence of this structure presents *Doctor Who* as an anti-religious text. The humans and aliens that are coded as religious are presented as naïve and in that naïvety dangerous. They are manipulated to do evil. Religion appears as a wrong path; an ignorant path leading to death. Indeed, from 'An Unearthly Child' onwards, religion and cults seem particularly fixated on companion sacrifice.[11] But what of the divine itself? *Battlestar Galactica* presented a distinction between religious institutions that were subject to the vagrancies of becoming, and the divine itself which graced the later seasons with its being. *Doctor Who* does not make this distinction. Not only is religion presented as a failed form of knowing and doing, but the divine is also presented as failure. While the Doctor meets many a 'god', these claims to godhood are invariably illusionary.

A taxonomy of gods can be seen in *Doctor Who*. The first group of gods are the maniacal baddies drunk on power and triumph. Stranded Time Lord leader Omega (Stephen Thorne) in the tenth anniversary special 'The Three Doctors' tells the Second (Patrick Troughton) and the Third Doctors that he needs to be worshipped as a god. Fifty-first-century war criminal Magnus Greel (Michael Spice), hiding in late Victorian London, masquerades as the god Weng-Chiang.[12] The deranged computers in 'The Face of Evil' and

'Underworld' self-style themselves as gods. Mr Finch (Anthony Head) in 'School Reunion' tries to entice the Tenth Doctor to join the Krillitanes by promising him god-like powers. All these are gods by self-coronation. Their claim to divinity is based on their perceived predominance within the little world that they made. Omega has made an anti-matter world by sheer will, while Xoanon in 'The Face of Evil' has constructed Leela's (Louise Jameson) warring societies of Sevateem and Tesh. What is common is that these gods are mortal. Their godhead is illusory for they are defeated and dissipate. Their god-talk is presented as a symptom of delusion and the Doctor orchestrates events to bring them back to the reality of their finitude in time and space.

The second group of gods are the sad gods; the aliens whose technology meant that they had been worshipped as gods by primitives. In this *Doctor Who* plays out Arthur C. Clarke's 'Third Law' that, in a primitive society, advanced technology will be explained as magic.[13] In these stories 'gods' are explained as the cultural traces from alien exposure. 'Pyramids of Mars' (1975) is a good example of this sort of god. In that story the inspiration for Egyptian mythology is revealed as early human exposure to a war between alien Osirians. As such Sutekh, trapped in his prison pyramid, is presented as the fountainhead for the Egyptian deity Set. But he is no god, just an alien with mental powers and robotic servants that is defeated by a sabotaged space-time tunnel. The eponymous creature from 'The Dæmons' is presented as the template for medieval representations of Satan, precisely because it is explained inter-text that it last interacted with humans in that time period. This iconography and explanation is repeated in the Tenth Doctor and Rose Tyler double episodes 'The Impossible Planet/The Satan Pit'. It is also present in the Eleventh Doctor episode 'The God Complex' where the Minotaur-like alien, once treated as a god, has been exiled by its people within a holographic labyrinth. While these gods, unlike the delusional megalomaniacs, do not actively claim godhood, *Doctor Who* proposes that it is their past involvement with primitives that explains the latter's cultural heritage and shared memories of gods. However, like the delusional megalomaniacs they are mortal; beings in time whose power is limited and whose time runs short.

This brings us to the third group of gods in *Doctor Who*, the transcendents. Occasionally, the Doctor meets a being who is seemingly outside time. Some, like the Great Vampires from 'State of Decay' (1980) or the Racnoss from 'The Runaway Bride' (2006), are explained as creatures of great age from the early universe that the Time Lords had defeated. These are essentially the same as the sad gods; their seeming transcendence is explained as based on alien physiognomy that evolved in the early universe where the laws of matter behaved differently. As such the Doctor defeats them, thereby affirming their existence within time and proving their mortality. The Seventh Doctor's confrontation with the Gods of Ragnarok in 'The Greatest Show in the Galaxy' follows this template. So too does the Tenth Doctor's encounter with the Trickster in the 2009 *Sarah Jane Adventures* episode 'The Wedding of Sarah Jane Smith'. These 'gods' are just powerful aliens.

However, there do appear to be genuine transcendentals in *Doctor Who*. Several deserve mention. The Celestial Toymaker and the intelligence from 'The Mind Robber' seem transcendent. They reign over a no-space of mental projection, subjecting the First and Second Doctor to various games. This celestial testing is explained inter-text in physical terms as an alternative/parallel/other dimension/ universe, with the trickster/tester conceived as the indigenous life-form.[14] In this, these early adventures are better catalogued as alternative dimension/universe stories along with 'Inferno' (1970), 'Rise of the Cybermen/The Age of Steel' (2006) and 'The Doctor's Wife'(2011).

The White and Black Guardians from the sixteenth season's 'Key of Time' story arc are the most memorable transcendent beings that manifest in the Doctor's 'normal' universe. These initially present themselves as beyond time and matter, the embodiment of cosmogenical forces of light and dark, good and evil whose balance vouchsafes the order of the physical world. However, by the arc's climax in 'The Armageddon Factor' their transcendent divinity is called into question. They appear to have no capacity to act in the normal universe, just observe and talk, a characteristic reinforced in the Black Guardian's pathetic attempt to use Vislor Turlough (Mark Strickson) to destroy the Doctor in the twentieth season's mini-arc of 'Mawdryn Undead', 'Terminus' and 'Enlightenment'. The suggestion is that they are creatures from a parallel plane projecting into the Doctor's universe. In this, the Guardians seem to be the closest to representing the divine in *Doctor Who*. Yet they are not gods, merely shadows.

What these three categories of failed gods, along with the negative portrayal of religion, suggest is that *Doctor Who*, notwithstanding its changes over 50 years of broadcasting, has been profoundly consistent in presenting a secular account of the universe. Unlike in *Battlestar Galactica,* the divine fails in *Doctor Who.* The best that the metaphysical realm has achieved are the less-than-impressive Guardians. There is always a reason in *Doctor Who* and that reason connects to the physical world of matter, energy and time that can be observed. It is this character of the *Doctor Who* universe(s) that is explored in the next section.

Matter, Energy and Time

There is always a reason for the fantastic in *Doctor Who.* The show seemingly delights in explaining the supernatural. Werewolves,[15] ghosts[16] and vampires[17] turn out, like the various gods identified above, to be aliens. The recent episode 'The Rings of Akhaten' (2013) presents a culture of child sacrifice to appease an 'old god' that is actually a living planet. These are all wonderfully diverse, yet mortal, creatures of matter, energy and time. The horror genre's walking Mummies are really Osirian service robots,[18] the Siren and pirate lore of the 'black spot' is explained as a lost alien medical vessel.[19] All manner of the unexplained in human affairs becomes explained. The mystery of ghost ship *Mary Celeste* is solved; the crew abandoned ship when it was suddenly boarded by Daleks chasing the First Doctor.[20] Further, the stock novums associated with science fiction – time travel, parallel universes, alternative dimensions, creatures of pure energy, creatures of stone, instantaneous matter transfer, artificial intelligence, cyborgs, clones, nanotechnology, faster-than-light space travel – are present and readily and explained. This is not to say that the explanations are plausible or sensible. There are rare moments when *Doctor Who* does do hard science fiction, where its speculation has an orientation in contemporary physics or biology, but mostly the inter-text reasons are fantastic – like the Third Doctor's 'reverse the polarity of the neutron flow'. Notwithstanding the technobabble, the significance lies within the basic form of the reasons. There is a de-mystifying of the universe in *Doctor Who.* Phenomena can be comprehended as combinations of matter, energy and time. Ultimately, the Doctor's profession – although a point of conjecture in the fan literature[21] – is as a scientist, and his restless travelling is often explained as a compulsion to experience and understand the new.

Significantly, this knowledge of the physical universe is not esoteric. *Doctor Who* continually emphasises the use and value of reason. The universe is not only able to be comprehended, but it is malleable. TARDISes can be grown/constructed, life-forms can be engineered, and planets moved around. The Doctor is not just a scientist but also very much a technologist. From the sonic screwdriver, to his frantic tinkering, to the ingenious improvised machines, the Doctor represents not just a knowing of the world, but applied doing-in-the-world. His universe of matter, energy and time is a universe of resources that can be comprehensible, ordered and capable of being reordered.[22] It becomes standing-reserve.[23] *Doctor Who* is consistent in offering a pro-technological message. The Doctor does face many mad scientists of the Victor Frankenstein variety, from Solon (Philip Madoc) in 'The Brain of Morbius' to Lazarus (Mark Gatiss) from the 'The Lazarus Experiment'. The celebrated 'Genesis of the Daleks' can be seen as a *par excellence* retelling of the *Frankenstein* narrative of flawed creator/scientist (Davros, played by Michael Wisher) destroyed by his created life. However, the Doctor's defeat of mad scientists and the overcoming of the mad creation do not present an anti-technological message that is familiar within much of the 'Frankenstein archive'.[24] The Doctor leaves via his 'time machine' having been triumphant by being a better technologist. What amounts to being a 'better technologist' is taken up in part three of this chapter; however, before this can be done the precise nature of the Doctor's technologically amenable universe needs further clarification.

The failure of the divine means that the Doctor triumphs within universe(s) of matter, energy and time that are comprehensible. But the primal combinations of matter, energy and time are not absolute. They are raw resources that intelligence and will can fashion and change. Life, as a spontaneous accident of matter, energy and time, reorganises matter and energy in time. This does not present a limitless universe of absolute potential. The 'doing of life' is consistently presented in *Doctor Who* as transitory. Civilisations are shown to rise and fall.[25] For every society represented at the height of its success there is always another story of decline, the remnants lost amidst the detritus of a once materially sophisticated society.[26] There are many stories of evolution; of the present explained as matter changing over eons of time.[27] This evolution is presented in a form that is stripped bare of teleological connotations. There are episodes that show evolution resulting in complexity and diversity; the stories inspired by von Däniken suggest that humanity has evolved into its present form through a process which included alien unnatural selection.[28] There are episodes that show evolution in the other direction. Entropic stories of weary decline, devolution, and endings. The destruction of the Earth by the Sun's death throes is a recurring backdrop.[29] This universe of evolution and entropy has a distinct pedigree. It is H. G. Wells's *The Time Machine* (1895).[30]

That the *Doctor Who* mega-text is inspired by *The Time Machine* has been pointed out regularly.[31] The TARDIS, particularly with its tendencies towards elements of Victorian/Edwardian interior decor, along with its crystal oscillating central column, immediately suggests Wells's time travelling bejeweled chair.[32] Individual episodes continually reference core elements of Wells's seminal text. There are many stories, from 'The Daleks' (1963) onwards, about future life as the evolved descendants of past social divisions.[33] Even without needing to focus on the dreadful Sixth Doctor (Colin Baker) adventure 'Timelash', in which H. G. Wells (David Chandler) makes his appearance as an episode-specific companion, Wells and the *Time Machine* were clearly on Sydney Newman's and Verity Lambert's minds when the Doctor was conceived. Further, Wells's influence is seen throughout *Doctor Who*, with individual stories deriving ideas, concepts and structures from Wells's 'scientific romances' – from the alien invader and bacterial immunity deficiency of *The War of the Worlds* (1898)[34] to hybridity and the failure to artificially civilise beastly flesh of *The Island of Dr Moreau* (1896).[35]

However, Wells's influence runs deeper than a source for individual episodes. *The Time Machine* is *Doctor Who*'s ur-text; and in particular it prefigures the Doctor's universe(s) of matter, energy and time. The dominant and lasting image of *The Time Machine* is not the social commentary about class with the dim-witted Eloi and subterranean Morlocks,[36] but its vistas of evolution à la Charles Darwin via Thomas Huxley.[37] The Time Traveller sees the ebb and flow of the material world as he travels into the future,[38] he sees the decaying material culture of eons of humanity in the Place of Green Porcelain,[39] and he witnesses a dying planet and the devolved crustaceans that are humanity's descendants.[40] Unlike the messianic traditions of Wells's time, the Christian faith in the second coming[41] and the socialist belief in revolution,[42] the future in *The Time Machine* was a future agnostic to the faith and dialectics of present humanity.[43] *The Time Machine* presented a secular universe and anti-teleological future; the future will happen, there will be change – even the very being currently called human will change – but there is no meaning, and no transcendence, beyond the material fact of change.[44]

This reading of *The Time Machine*, with time as the ultimate manifestation of Social Darwinism's cruel and indifferent nature, has been criticised as presenting nihilistic tendencies.[45] Given its intellectual origin in Wells, this criticism could also be made of *Doctor Who*. It regularly presents the impermanence of values and the random fragility of life. Accidents happen in the *Doctor Who* universe. Many a crashed, lost, and confused alien needs to be rescued,[46] life on Earth is explained as triggered by the accidental explosion of a spaceship,[47] and the timely arrival of the Doctor is often presented as chance.[48] This is a bleak vista for doing-in-the-world; a material reality of animalistic competition within a universe agnostic to survival. The Dalek war against the universe, their rage and extermination, appears as a natural reaction of life to the universe's indifference. Within the Doctor's secular universe(s) genocide, mass extinctions and tyranny appear de jure; evidence of the struggle for survival by intelligent beings with no wider care or responsibility. *Doctor Who* with its Daleks, Cybermen, Sontarans and even the warring, corrupt Time Lords[49] can be seen as endorsing this way of responding to the nihilism of the secular universe of matter, energy and time; of might is right in the battle for survival.

The Doctor and 'Us' Moderns

But might as right in the battle for survival is not the enduring message of *Doctor Who*, nor of Wells's scientific romances. In *Evolution and Ethics* (1892), Huxley argued that the idea that 'natural selection' and 'survival of the fitness' should be seen as authorising an asocial 'fanatical individualism' was absurd.[50] For Huxley civilised humanity, as opposed to the prehistoric state of nature from which humanity emerged, was marked by collectivity and care.[51] For Huxley a secular universe of matter, energy and time presented humanity with the opportunity of not being a slave to natural inclinations, nor past prejudiced and social structures, but a freedom to imagine and strive towards a better future.[52] In Huxley there was a manifesto to be modern.

This modernism was projected, elaborated, and animated by Wells. While Wells affirmed reason, he did not advocate an untrammelled reason in the service of aggressive self-preservation at all costs. Balanced against the power of reason and will to change the world was a humanism; a tempering belief in the good of humanity.[53] Each of the narrators of Wells's scientific romances are not blind to the suffering of others; the Time Traveller has sympathy towards Weena, the Eloi, and the Morlocks,[54] and the recorder of *The War of the Worlds* does not gloat over the pitiful cries of the dying Martians.[55] This is not a rejection of rationalism but its sublimation: the Traveller, armed with devices to measure and record the future, sets off once more.[56] Rationalism goes hand-in-hand with a civilising will. John Huntington conceived Wells in the scientific romances as postulating the challenge of 'ethics', for humans to be reflective in their dealings with each other and the cosmos.[57] In the conclusion of *The Island of Doctor Moreau*, the narrator finds peace in the rational explorations of chemistry and astronomy, and in the '… glittering hosts of heaven. There it must be … that whatever is more than animal within us must find its solace and its hope.'[58] This conclusion encapsulates Wells's modernism. There is an acceptance of the secular inhumanness of the universe and the endless march of time, but not to succumb to an aggressive survivalism.[59] Rather to use reason and will – science and technology – to be responsible for the future.

In Wells the present connects with the future. Actions in the present determine the future – the class divisions of Victorian England give rise to the evolutionary division of humanity into two distinct species in the year 802,701.[60] Importantly, this future that will evolve from the present was inhuman; there can be no guarantees of civilisation enduring, no teleological unfolding towards the good. This places responsibility onto the present: a preferred human future can only be achieved through rational activity in the present to mould and guide. However, this was not a complete surrender to technology, to pure manipulation whatever the consequences as manifested by the Martians or Moreau. Reason was the tool, not the end; the end, for Wells, lay in what was 'not animal', but in the human potential to care for other members of the species.[61] In Wells the secular universe of matter, energy, and time presented the dangerous opportunity of modernity: of creating futures, of fixing past injustice and legislating for future (to borrow from Huxley's grandson) 'brave new worlds'.

Wells's image of finding solace in the stars has been a repeated image within *Doctor Who*; often the Doctor looks star-wards with longing and hope.[62] The Doctor as 'ethical' has been well dissected within Who-studies. His politics,[63] masculinity,[64] his 'war ethics',[65] and his cosmopolitan-ness[66] have all been focused upon. So too Wells' modernism, his upper-middle-class paternalism, his skirting of Social Darwinism, and the proto-fascist elements of centralisation and techno-management from his speculative 'future histories' have attracted critical attention.[67] The Doctor's decisions within individual stories are sometimes controversial; most recently the Eleventh Doctor's murdering of Solomon (David Bradley) in 'Dinosaurs on a Spaceship' and weapon-brandishing aggression in 'A Town Called Mercy'. Indeed, if there is a god in the Doctor's universe(s), it is the Doctor himself. As Lynette Porter observes, the Doctor stands god-like outside of space and time, passing and executing judgement.[68] He is often a harsh, vengeful god; murderous, genocidal and seemingly random in his punishment. The 'innocent' Racnoss children are drowned to punish their mother;[69] while the Master is given chance after chance.[70] The Doctor is a locus of 'terrible decision', a point that Russell T. Davies made in the 2005 rebooting episode 'Rose', where the comment was made that if the Doctor is about, people are going to die. In wielding this power of life and death, the Doctor appears as sovereign within his universe of matter, energy and time.[71] The Doctor's technical manipulation of matter, energy and time is different to that of the survival by conquest of the Daleks and Cybermen. Self-preservation never seems that high on his order of priorities, especially some of the high-camp, devil-may-care escapades of the Fourth Doctor or the post-traumatic Ninth Doctor (Christopher Eccleston). In Thomas Hobbes's definitional account of sovereignty, Leviathan – total, authoritarian and capable of exterminating – has these powers for a purpose: the safeguarding of human existence from its own wolfish dark side.[72] So too the Doctor lords over his universe to safeguard life.

What *Doctor Who* shows more clearly than Wells or Huxley is that, in a secular universe, the accidents of life and intelligence are precious. That matter and energy can become more complex and organised over time, can become aware of itself, and then can be conscious and proactive in its dealings with matter and energy, reintroduces value into an ostensibly valueless, divine-free space. The key is potential. The Doctor intervenes or holds off, depending on whether the circumstance into which he has materialised has potential for life. This can be seen in the many narratives involving repulsion of an alien invasion, from 'The Dalek Invasion of Earth' (1964–65) to 'The Sontaran Stratagem/The Poison Sky' (2008). In these narratives, the Doctor chooses to protect the diversity of the status quo against the destruction and uniformity that the invader brings. This does not mean that the Doctor is just a conservative figure. Where the 'invasion' brings promises of greater potential, the Doctor goes from defender to advocate. This is the attraction of the Silurian stories which end with an angry/despondent Doctor pleading for peace and cooperation between humans and Silurians with the promise of a better future for both species.[73] Then there are the innumerable stories where the arrival of the TARDIS in a space and a time often spells the end for a nefarious overlord and the freeing of the servile.[74] The Doctor can be seen as both conserver and revolutionary depending on the possibilities for life. In the words of the Eleventh Doctor, humans are to be valued: 'Because that's what they are. Not pests or plague, creatures of hope. Forever building and reaching. Making mistakes of course. Every life form does. But— they learn. And they strive for greater.'[75]

And this is what *Doctor Who* teaches 'us' moderns. It teaches us how to be modern, to accept the divine-free universe but not to retreat into shells of bumpy armour, angrily waggling protuberances. Through adventuring within universe(s) of matter, energy and time prefigured by Wells, the Doctor shows not only the amenability of such universe(s) to science and technology, but that doing within this secular space can be ethical. The Doctor uses his terrible powers over matter, energy, and time to safeguard the potential of life. He is not just a passive observer, the scientist capturing and archiving the universe as standing-reserve. Nor is he a base technologist who manipulates matter, energy and time with the goal of survival of the technological-mediated fittest. He is a better technologist because his meddling with matter, energy and time has a purpose: the safeguarding of the potential of life.

But he is no god, infallible and on high. The Doctor's safeguarding of the potential of life is not without its mistakes.[76] Anger, sadness or enthusiasm clouds his judgement, explaining his need for companions to keep him focused and grounded. The overconfidence of the 'Time Lord Victorious' of the Tenth Doctor[77] was brought back into check by the Eleventh.[78] Notwithstanding regeneration, the freedom of time travel, and the Eleventh Doctor's own faked death, the Doctor is ultimately mortal, living out his lifespan as a being within an individual timeline. He teaches us moderns that through our knowledge and technologies we are creatures of great power able to master and manipulate matter, energy and time. He also shows that this can be done ethically, notwithstanding the absence of the transcendent or divine. For what there is in our secular universe is life and its potential. The Doctor, echoing early calls from Wells and Huxley, entreats that our doing-in-the-world should work towards safeguarding the potentiality of life. But he does not just charge us with these god-like powers and responsibilities. His failings and mortality reflect that we moderns remain fallible and within time; that our doing in the world will not always go according to plan. He exhorts us to engage and embrace our mistakes. We have 'to learn' so as to 'strive for greater'.[79] He shows how we mortal gods can live well in our divine-less universe.

11.

Religion in *Doctor Who*: Cult Ethics

Karma Waltonen

'Have you ever heard,' he said, 'of Ethics?'

'Somewhere in Howondaland, isn't it?'

'The Ephebians were very interested in it.'

'Probably thinking about invading.'[1]

Travelling across time and space, the Doctor and his companions encounter a variety of religions and cults. The treatment of these faiths is similar to the treatment of the governments, corporations and colonisers who rule alien races across the universe in the Moffat/Davies series: they are dangerous if they involve physical or mental enslavement. This enslavement can be literal or figurative, as the Doctor attempts to save those enslaved through destructive dogma, wanting individuals to be able to choose, even if their choice is potentially wrong.

Depictions of religion in the new series are always linked to issues of ethics – what is the role of agency when faith demands unquestioning obedience? If religion preaches that one species or group is superior to another, does it sanction hierarchal power relationships? To what extent is evil an acceptable method to achieve good? When can one use war and weapons to achieve peace?

The Daleks

While the iconic image of the Dalek is a creature of metal, one must remember that Daleks and Cybermen have more in common than they would like to believe. Both are actually cyborgs, combinations of flesh and machine. The Daleks, however, still largely capable of emotion, have a larger capacity for religious thought, fascist/eugenist ideas about 'purity', the capability to turn on their own kind, and other cultish behaviours.[2] One such cult is the cult of Davros, lord and creator ('The Stolen Earth/Journey's End' (2008)). The language used to describe Davros is religious in connotation, as are his circumstances: with his small following growing to larger numbers, with splinter groups, with attacks from non-believers, even with Caan, the 'mad' Dalek who resembles a seer, spouting prophecy and nonsense from a damaged body. Caan ultimately betrays his cult, having seen pure time and the soul of the Daleks. His madness in this case is to be admired, as he, like the Doctor (and basically all non-Daleks) is able to see the ethics of Dalek behaviour and finds them lacking.

Davros's DNA causes problems for a few surviving Daleks who find their 'progenitor' in 'Victory of the Daleks' (2010). The progenitor is programmed to prioritise 'purity' and '[cleansing] the unclean', so it does not recognise the Daleks that have been created from Davros's DNA without testimony from the Doctor that they are indeed Dalek. The ability to rebuild with the progenitor is a chance at 'the resurrection of the master race'. The 'tainted' Daleks willingly allow themselves to be destroyed once 'pure' new paradigms are created by the progenitor.

Although such concerns about 'purity' might usually be considered secular, we know from the 'Bad Wolf' arc that the impurity of the Daleks is a religious problem. It is not just forbidden to discuss how the Emperor has mixed human DNA into the Daleks – doing so is 'blasphemy'. The Emperor has also declared himself their God. The Doctor is a heathen (or worse – their Devil; in 'The Wedding of River Song' (2011), he says to a Dalek that he's 'the Devil himself'); Rose must protect him from 'the false god'. Upon taking the time vortex into herself, she echoes the biblical God: 'I can see the whole of time and space, every single atom of your existence, and I divide them. Everything must come to dust'.[3]

The Daleks' denial about what they have become in this arc is evidence, according to the Doctor, of madness. This kind of thinking closely resembles the mind/body dualism that exists in so many human religions, which theorise that it is the impure failures of the body that cause our downfalls, and are that which must be denied.

This denial of all that is non-Dalek becomes problematic when the Emperor creates the Cult of Skaro, an organisation of Daleks who can think like their enemies, and thus who can think individually. When the Cult attempts to rebuild their Dalek empire in 1930s New York, Dalek Sec becomes convinced that purity will equal their extinction ('Daleks in Manhattan/Evolution of the Daleks' (2007)). Thus, these Daleks create hybrids. Sec goes so far as to merge himself with a human. Unlike the Emperor, however, the Cult of Skaro does not attempt to deny the basic fact of what human DNA and traits might mean. Dalek Sec, once completely integrated with a human, does not deny his human side, including human emotions. This alienates him from the rest of the Cult; while they desire survival, they abhor the thought that human emotions might change their ultimate goal to exterminate all other life in the universe.

The images of blasphemy and madness allow us to think through the relativism inherent in cults. Blasphemy does not have to be a lie – it is only a statement or idea that leaders do not want repeated. Madness from inside the cult is seen as deviating from the dogma, while those outside the cult see people as mad when dogma overrides logic. While 'Asylum of the Daleks' (2012) illustrates that any model of Dalek can go mad, it is the Cult of Skaro that most consistently shows madness in some form or another. This is because the defining characteristic of the Cult is a better capacity for critical thinking. The Cult breaks apart when members turn against their leader, Sec. Although they are 'created to follow him', they 'have doubts'. As Thay explains to Sec, 'You told us to imagine, and we imagined your irrelevance'.

The Sisters of Plentitude

In 'New Earth' (2006), we are introduced to the order of Cat Nurses that keeps the Face of Boe alive. This religious order is devoted to health care, but, finding themselves overwhelmed by humanity's illnesses, they devise a dubious plan to keep people healthy. They keep 'a human farm' to experiment on 'for the greater cause'. The Matron is callous in the face of evidence that her livestock are conscious and in pain. When the Doctor discovers how the hospital really works, the sisterhood's justifications sound pathetic: clichéd excuses about good intentions. The nurses are not shown to have developed empathy for their livestock in the way they do with their patients. Instead, their beliefs have allowed them to de-humanise the humans under their control. However, the episode places most of the blame on the Matron, allowing many of those nurses with poor judgement to escape from punishment once the Doctor (and the escape of highly infectious people) has demonstrated the error of their ways.

The Sibylline Sisterhood

The prophet Sibyl is recognised in various histories and literatures, so the appearance of her followers in 'The Fires of Pompeii' (2008) adds to the feeling of accuracy in depicting an actual historical group. These sisters, however, have been perverted from their original soothsaying and other religious duties by the awakening of an alien race in the volcano – the Pyrovile. As the Pyrovile and temporal rifts cause the women's prophecies to come true, they follow their new leader, even when she declares that the prophecies of the original Sibylline Sisterhood are false, challenging their history, their founder, their truth. When the women start to change into stone, they believe the change and the pain associated with it are proof of the gods' favour. It is only when the volcano erupts that one of the order's women realises that the original prophecy about the arrival of 'the blue box' coinciding with a betrayal has come true.

The Sisterhood and a similar group in Pompeii, the Cult of Vulcan, are both inclined to believe that the Pyrovile aliens are gods not only because of prophecies, but because of the aliens' promises, which concern Pompeii's empire spreading. It is thus a desire for power and a belief in colonialism that pushes the cults into false belief. Their faith is so unwavering that they are willing to contradict their older beliefs and to kill without hesitation upon command.

The Cult of Saxon

In 'The End of Time' (2009/10) we discover a cult we might name the cult of Saxon, a group of human women who 'never lost faith' in the Master and who work to bring him back. They refer to his secret books, work as a secret society, and use the power of relics to work their magic. Saxon's wife belongs to a counter-cult, one designed to prevent the Master's rise. How exactly these cults came to be and how they operate is not explained, but the cult of Saxon resembles imagined satanic cults on Earth, raising the same question: why devote yourself to a god who will attempt to destroy you? Saxon/the Master ultimately does rise again, fulfilling all negative expectations of his behaviour. Most astonishingly, he takes over humanity by transforming them all into a version of himself, thus leaving no one with his or her own mind. The horror of this moment emphasises agency as an essential aspect of both humanity and freedom.

In this arc, we also meet the council of the Time Lords. On the day of their destruction, they locked themselves in time and altered the Master so that he would be able to unlock them and bring them to Earth. It is quickly apparent that the council is yet another cult. In fact, through the idea of the initiation children must endure, one may categorise the entire species as cultic. As we're told, the children don't have childhoods – but instead 'a life of duty'. The look of the council, with its ceremonial robes, echoes various religious traditions. As with some other cults on the show, there is a seer: 'the visionary'. One minister is murdered for disagreeing with the equivalent of the high priest, making this less a council than a theocracy.

The council has manipulated more than time in this instance. The Master has been tortured ever since his initiation so that they might live. His madness is a product of their desire for survival. Sympathy for the Master is almost inevitable – he has been tortured throughout his life by the constant sound of drums in his head, which the council has used to prepare him for their resurrection. His realisation of their callous use for him pushes the fallen angel to redeem himself. Death is his atonement.

The Headless Monks, the Church and the Silence

> There are two silences. One when no word is spoken. The other when perhaps a torrent of language is being employed. This speech is speaking of a language locked beneath it. That is its continual reference. The speech we hear is an indication of that which we don't hear. It is a necessary avoidance, a violent, sly, anguished or mocking smoke screen which keeps the other in its place. When true silence falls we are still left with echo but are nearer nakedness.[4]

Three religious orders, the Headless Monks, the Church and the Silence, come together to fight the Doctor in the 2011 series. The Silence appear to be in control. The motivation for the other orders joining them is unclear.

As with any religious order, the Headless Monks inspire a quiet awe in those who encounter them – part of this may be from the religious cachet – people hold an admiration for those who would devote themselves to an order, who would presumably always be silent. As with other orders, there are rules for engaging with them and rumours about them. For example, it is a level-one 'heresy' to remove a monk's hood. Another odd aspect of the order is the forced conversion of some of the military personnel who live on the asteroid with them. We see one young man leave for his ordered religious training, only to discover that training means that his head will be forcibly removed. Once this is done, he is a full member. The symbolic implications are clear. There is no capability for individual thought in the order – no choices – no heresies.

Heresy comes from the Greek word for choice. To be a heretic means that one has been educated about a religious dogma, yet chooses not to believe it. Thus, it would be impossible for a member of the Headless Monks to also be a heretic. This lack of agency, represented by the lack of a head, is frightening. Without agency, they are walking weapons for whatever god or power is controlling them.

The military personnel on the base are a contrast – they are members of the Church (Anglican). In the fifty-first century, we see members of this Church led by Father Octavian – they work with the Doctor to fight the Weeping Angels;[5] by the fifty-second century, the Church has allied with the Silence against the Doctor. Most of the faithful probably do not know the religious dogma surrounding their mission (though they've been told that the Doctor is bad), nor would they choose to belong to the Silence. They are, as most armies ultimately are, mercenaries – weapons without convictions. In fact, the soldiers often speak admiringly of the Doctor and note, 'We're being paid to fight him'. While the Church was problematic to the Doctor a century before, as he was disturbed by their militarism, one wonders if this order has any moral code left. Although their commander says they are men of God, he has sacrificed at least one to the Headless Monks and has allied with dark powers, it seems, only for the money.[6]

Lorna Bucket stands out from the rest of the Church not only because she has met the Doctor before, but because she is kind – to Melody/River, to her mother, and ultimately to the Doctor. Her sacrifice is not in the name of ignorant following of orders, but a choice to go against the orders/dogma of her leaders.

This foreshadows River Song's ability to do the same decades later. In 'Let's Kill Hitler' (2011), River meets the Doctor for the first time (in her timeline). River is the product of perhaps the most egregious violation of ethics in the universe. Stolen from her mother, raised by brainwashing, turned into a psychopath, River is bred to be an assassin – an assassin of one man. Although she is smart, sexy and vivacious, her life is not her own at the start of this episode. River may work for the Silence, but it is clear that her attempt to fulfil her mandate is not born of any conviction – she does not know why the Doctor may deserve to die. While she knows who her parents are, her knowledge is superficial – she feels no connection to them. Her brilliance at first seems stunted, as she is incapable of being self-aware enough to turn her anti-authority feelings against those who have programmed her.

However, in this episode, River reclaims her agency after she is able to watch the Doctor in action. It helps, of course, that he tries, literally with his dying breath, to save her from being punished for his murder. River's choice to defy her masters changes the trajectory of her life, pushing her toward scholarship (mixed with a healthy dose of kicking ass) and a life-long devotion to her 'sweetie'.

The Silence's programming failed the first time because of River's ability to think for herself and to make decisions. This second attempt succeeds because choice is taken away.[7] River is a heretic because she actively rejects the dogma, but the brainwashing and the astronaut suit used by the Silence make her heresy a moot point. Her will is essentially taken. She becomes once again what she was always meant to be – merely a weapon: a weapon with great significance – a weapon the Doctor has reason to love and to protect – and the more powerful and terrible a weapon for it.

River becomes a romantic heroine in this moment, as we see her suffering begin, understanding that she spends years believing she killed her love, spends years out of sync with him, spends years in a cell for a crime she was led to believe she committed. The romantic heroine is always a suffering one in literature. Yet as with any romance, the suffering ends with a marriage – in 'The Wedding of River Song' (2011), River is relieved of (some of) her guilt.

'The Wedding of River Song' also restores River's agency. Although the astronaut suit is in control of her actions, she is able to discharge the weapon before it kills the Doctor, rewriting history. This puts the whole of the universe and time at risk. She is convinced she will suffer more than every living thing if she has to kill the Doctor. His plan to use a 'Doctor suit' allows River to fulfil her destiny without killing him, so she agrees to return time to its normal flow, to allow the Silence to 'win'.

The nature of the Silence (the Sentinels of History) is unclear. We are told they are not a species, but a religious order. And while their envoys, all marked with an eye drive, are from different species, the Silence who take over the Earth (and control the envoys) all appear, in fact, to be members of the same species. Perhaps because we never see their homeworld, we are not privy to the sane members of their species, who think this eschatological cult is made up of crazy people. Maybe the rest of their species talks over tea about how glad they are that the cult members are off on Earth causing trouble there.

The immediate goal of the cult is to prevent a prophecy from being fulfilled. The Pandorica will open. A question hidden in plain sight ('Doctor Who?') will be asked. When this oldest question is answered, the Silence will/must fall. The Silence are therefore willing to take over the Earth, to murder the Doctor, to sacrifice their allies on the base, and to kidnap and brainwash a baby to prevent the fall of their religious order.

Although people like Madame Kovarian seem to want the Doctor dead (the Doctor's enemies routinely see him as 'the bad guy', in this case, the ultimate weapon), the Silence appear to have no personal grudge against him. His death is merely required as a form of self-defence.

Yet self-defence, at least in some laws, requires that the threat be a clear and present danger. To commit so much murder, to attempt to murder the Doctor, all so that he will be silent when the question is asked, is not necessarily morally sound. If one believes in a religion, should one resist a prophecy about that religion's end? Might that just be part of the higher power's plan? Does your higher power condone the murder and torture of innocents in its name? If self-defence is defendable in these ways, wouldn't your own actions completely justify the behaviour of your enemies as they sought to protect themselves from you? After all, the second you start to plan, you become the clear and present danger to the other side.

The Cult of the Doctor

'This is how they do things in Ethics, is it?' said Om sarcastically.

'I don't know. It's how I'm doing it.'[8]

With so many examples of questionable religious cults or authorities, the viewer may conclude that the show takes an inherently secular position. Of course, this would be an overly-simplistic interpretation, as secular governments and individuals (both alien and human) with no religious affiliation come under similar scrutiny. In fact, one of the aspects of the show that belies over-simplistic interpretation is the idea of the Doctor as a god – creating the cult of the Doctor.

Although it is possible for the Doctor to die (permanently), his powers of regeneration and rebirth cast him as a familiar icon – the god with many avatars. Before the internet and James Cameron, 'avatar' was a word with a specific religious connotation. Gods have avatars – various forms (faces) with which they appear to mortals. In some cases, as with Krishna, avatars are (re)incarnations of a timeless soul, an eternal god who might appear multiple times in multiple bodies. In other cases, as cultures came into contact with each other and discussed their gods, one representation of a particular god in one culture might be understood as merely one aspect of a larger god the two cultures shared.

While the Doctor has a personal timeline, this may also be seen as a consequence of embodiment. His regenerations are not merely movements between two bodies. As Tennant's Tenth Doctor states in 'The End of Time' (2010), 'Even if I change, it still feels like dying. Everything I am dies. Some new man goes sauntering away . . . and I'm dead'. When Smith's Doctor takes over where Tennant leaves off, he expresses a temporary confusion about aspects of his identity. While he knows who he is in general, he is uncertain about what *kind* of man he is.[9] His wardrobe choices, appetites and mannerisms emphasise that with each change he is an aspect, an avatar, of himself. There are also, of course, two avatars currently in existence – one in Rose's universe and one in ours.

Personal timelines aside, the very fact that the Doctor is a Time Lord invites comparison with a deity. While many modern followers of the Abrahamic God can only imagine an omnipotent and omniscient deity, religions throughout history and throughout the world are full of pantheons. These pantheons exist in another realm, have powers/talents we don't, may be considered our protectors, visit us frequently, and are usually capable of breeding with us. Pantheon gods are rarely all-powerful or all-knowing (how could they fight each other, otherwise?). Instead, they are created clearly in our image, representing our dreams and our basest qualities (jealousy, pride, etc.).[10] Even though some of the pantheon gods can die (Dionysus, for example), they are still considered eternal – timeless. Their death never completely erases them – it might move them instead to a more celestial plane or allow them to take their place among the stars – (Osiris/Orion, for example) as constellations (along with a few lucky humans who have been admired or who have been their companions).[11]

Comparisons with the Doctor are obvious. There are/were other Time Lords, Time Lords interfere with the humans of Earth (both as protectors and as antagonists, and sometimes unintentionally as both), Time Lords are associated with stars, they are 'timeless' given their powers to manipulate the time vortex, and they are 'lords'.

It is no surprise, then, that humans throughout history (in the world of the show) have worshipped the Doctor. In 'The Impossible Astronaut' (2011), River Song and the Doctor reminisce about a trip to Easter Island, with River noting how the inhabitants worshipped him. This is partly a joke at Matt Smith's jawline's expense, but is also indicative of the power of the Doctor – the cult of the Doctor engenders one of the wonders of the world with evidence outlasting the original inhabitants of the island.[12] The Minotaur describes the Doctor as a lonely god in an endless maze ('The God Complex' (2011)); The Face of Boe speaks to 'the lonely god' ('New Earth' (2006)); River complains about being married to a god ('The Angels Take Manhattan' (2012)) – the direct references that deify the Doctor are numerous.

After Donna convinces the Doctor to save a family from Pompeii, the grateful family makes them their personal household gods. The composite figure of The Doctor/Donna is also arguably deified by the Ood after the two save the Ood from slavery ('Planet of the Ood' (2008)). Although the Ood may not overtly pray to this deity, they do what civilisations have done for thousands of years of recorded history with their gods and heroes/demigods – pass down an oral tradition of songs (or lyric/epic poetry) about them.

Despite comparisons to pantheon gods, other episodes make clear comparisons between the Doctor and the Abrahamic God.[13] In 'The Last of the Time Lords' (2007), Martha acts as a disciple of the Doctor, venturing out into a world to spread his word – a word that will be able to save all of humanity. She is the apostle who takes the word to the gentiles, the believer who draws the fish in the sand despite the penalties for her religious belief. The Lord and Master cannot stop the spread of belief about this saviour.[14] Nor can he make himself humanity's god, no matter what religious language he uses about himself. Although Martha explains her actions as relatively secular ('I told a story; that's all'), the implications are clear ('Is that your weapon? Prayer?'). Here, our Time Lord can glow and fly angelically. The power of his word frightens the Master, even though the words are absolution: 'I forgive you'.

'The Next Doctor' (2008) emphasises these ideas by introducing the Doctor to a 'new' Doctor. At first, the Doctor believes that the man in Victorian garb is a future avatar. Yet the man is revealed to be just a man, an unintentional false prophet (with a small following) – a man suffering from a data-induced Messiah syndrome.

In 'Voyage of the Damned' (2007), the Doctor ascends, literally held by two glowing angels. As Martha explains in 'Gridlock' (2007), 'You've got your faith. You've got your songs and your hymns. And I've got the Doctor.' While the Doctor never calls himself a god, it is notable that he doesn't deny the title when it is bestowed upon him.

One of the most obvious ways in which the Doctor is paralleled to a god is in his embodiment of the Fisher King archetype. Simply put, the Fisher King myth is the myth system to which both King Arthur and Christ belong. The rough outlines of the myth are that a hero/king saves his people and ultimately dies. His followers remain loyal, knowing that this hero/king will return to save them again. The Doctor has died many times, but his death at the end of the 2011 series is believed by almost the entire universe to be final. True to the archetype, the following season's 'Asylum of the Daleks' (2012) starts with the recitation of a legend about his return – those who believe it are members of a cult – they believe in a rumour, based solely on faith, that their undying god is still watching over them: 'in time, he died. There are a few, of course, who believe this man somehow survived and that one day, he will return'.[15]

Thus, the Doctor embodies the same issue that all religious cults on the show do – ethics.

We are constantly asked to evaluate the ethics of the Doctor and of his followers – are they following him because he's right or because he's him? Should their lives be devoted to him or should they find their way without him? If his ethics change, must his companions change with him? In 'A Town Called Mercy' (2012), Jex claims, 'We all carry our prisons with us. . . . Yours is your morality', but given that the Doctor's ethics shift over avatars and time, the prison analogy may be flawed.

In fact, the Doctor's ethics are questionable in Jex's presence. Upon arrival in the Old West, the Doctor discovers a town besieged by an assassin. Upon discovering that the assassin was once a person turned into a weapon and that his intended victim is the war criminal who made him into a 'monster', the Doctor alternates between a desire to aid the assassin and to protect the war criminal from this relatively unlawful prosecution. Following a moment of anger, the town's sheriff is gunned down, and he passes the badge to the Doctor. Now, as a literal (clichéd) symbol of law and order,[16] he must do the 'right' thing. Luckily, the war criminal ultimately commits suicide, leaving a sad, lonely monster-weapon. The episode ends with the weapon becoming the law enforcement arm of the town, a role it fulfils for decades at least. The narrative voice explains that this is why her town has no judges or police officers – how things just get taken care of by the town's 'angel'.

The line is creepy. Decades after an incident in which the creature attempts extra-legal justice, it is now still the unelected, undemocratic law in a Western town in the USA. One might wonder which laws it enforces, how it enforces them, and whether there are civil liberties as such in the town.

While the Doctor initially has so much anger towards the war criminal Jex inviting comparisons between them (the anger underlines such associations), the end of the episode makes a different kind of comparison – between two aliens protecting humans, between two lonely creatures, between two weapons, between two powerful cultish figures. The voice of the old woman narrating the events, however, puts a sepia-toned patina over how disturbing these implications really are, especially considering that this episode is the first in which the Doctor picks up a gun willingly, carrying it without hesitation or complaint.

Every viewer I talked to about this episode was disquieted by the Doctor's sudden affinity for guns, after so many years of criticising those who carried them and forbidding his companions to do so. Of course, there have been extraordinary circumstances (such as the resurrection of the Master) in which the Doctor has handled handguns, but these moments have always been marked as difficult for him.

However, astute viewers are aware that the Doctor doesn't need a gun to kill. And while the Doctor is technically against killing, he has done it. A lot. Most often, the show justifies these deaths. The Doctor gives his opponents a chance to run away, a chance to relocate first. Deaths occur because the Doctor chooses his companions' lives or the lives of humans in general over whatever force is threatening them.

There are some moments, though, when the Doctor's choices are more problematic. Donna is enraged that the Doctor will not evacuate Pompeii, although he explains that the tragedy there is fixed in time. When he discovers that he must be the one to *cause* the Pompeii deaths, to save the rest of the planet, his conscience is more troubled.[17] Later, when confronted with another dilemma of a fixed point in time on Mars, the Doctor decides to save a few 'important' people – to alter time in a way that was forbidden by Time Lord law ('The Waters of Mars' (2009)). His impulse may seem a good one – the audience is also rooting for these characters to survive. Yet when pressed, we realise it is a moment of hubris: he is 'the Time Lord Victorious'; his actions prompt the commander he has saved to end her own life to maintain the correct course of history.

Other aspects of morality are similarly questioned. While enslaving others is always seen as wrong, the Doctor does not always interfere with slavery (in the first instance with the Ood; when visiting the ancient Roman Empire, etc). The Doctor relies on his friends, who always have the choice to follow him – to participate in what is an inherently hierarchal relationship, but there is also a moment when he presses people into service. In 'A Good Man Goes to War', the Doctor must raise an army. As he collects on some of his recent debts, many ally with him more or less willingly, but we see Dorium begging to be left out of the fight. The Doctor, it seems, gives him no choice. This particular episode, of course, is constructed to be an example of the Doctor falling low by his own standards. River upbraids him for not being himself – for raising an army in the first place. Notably, this episode begins with the Doctor blowing up almost a whole squadron of Cybermen, not because they posed an immediate threat, but because he wanted information about Amy's whereabouts. However, the Doctor's torture of (and presumably murder of) a Dalek at the beginning of 'The Wedding of River Song' for information about the Silence illustrates that his morality has gotten very slippery indeed.

This is perhaps because the Doctor's power precludes being overseen by outside law. Although the universe has 'The Shadow Proclamation' and at least two agencies policing intergalactic criminals, the Doctor usually finds himself obstructing law enforcement. This certainly satisfies viewers who mistrust bureaucracy, government or organised law enforcement, but it turns the Doctor into a vigilante. While the viewer may ultimately agree with his decisions, and while the Doctor sometimes works in concert with human governments (serving several queens and a few prime ministers), this particular way of protecting the Earth raises concerns. The results are usually relatively good – the Earth is protected, humans are given priority (even over species that sometimes have prior claims), etc. But the Doctor is an unelected saviour – often an unknown god (witness the surprise when he's actually thanked by Victorian London in 'The Next Doctor'). And in these moments, he acts as a god, as judge, jury, and occasional executioner. Violators of the Doctor's morality are usually given a chance at repentance, but if they refuse this moment of grace, consequences range from life imprisonment to death.

The Doctor's 'laws' are also complicated by the many rules about him. Rule 1: The Doctor Lies. While there usually seems to be a justifiable motivation, there are many moments when he's merely protecting his privacy or lying to himself. A lie to spare someone else pain is, after all, also a lie to protect us from witnessing or causing that pain in the first place.

Even when the Doctor's actions are justified, he causes chaos in the lives of those around him. His reluctance to take on new companions is caused by what has become of those who have travelled with him. It is worth noting that his most frequent advice is 'Run!'. Even when his companions aren't lost or mentally destroyed, they are changed by their encounters with him. Martha now routinely takes up the weapons in military actions. Amy kills Madame Kovarian 'in cold blood' as revenge for what was done to her child. Davros is arguably correct when he chides the Doctor: 'The man who abhors violence, never carrying a gun. But this is the truth, Doctor: you take ordinary people and you fashion them into weapons . . . behold your Children of Time, transformed into murderers. I made the Daleks, Doctor, you made this.' At the very least, the Doctor leaves a trail of unrequited love in his wake.

Yet one of the main themes throughout the show is that the Doctor should not be alone. Each companion, no matter how short lived, argues it, as do many of their family members (this seems to be even more true at Christmas). Ultimately, he gives in, both because of loneliness and because it may be more dangerous to travel alone. When giving the 'mortal' doctor to Rose, 'our' Doctor explains that Rose will need to 'fix' him, as he is in a new, dangerous state. The 2013 half-series (7b) opens with a genius girl becoming the Doctor's companion. However, after her appearance in 'The Snowmen' (2012), they seem fated to lose each other regularly.

The imperfections of our hero remind us of the folly of those who follow him unquestioningly. Faith in the Doctor (perfect faith) is what the minotaur feeds on from Amy in 'The God Complex'. The Doctor has to disabuse her of this faith. Amy's faith in the Doctor seems to be tempered afterwards with faith in her Centurion. Ultimately, Amy chooses her faith in Rory, dying with him (twice) in 'The Angels Take Manhattan' so that she may be reborn with him, against the Doctor's wishes.

Conclusion

Morality in *Doctor Who* is complex. There are hints at universal morality – right and wrong that every species should grasp, but every species needs rules to guide it to even these basic truths, which questions whether they are in fact true. In one small example, the Doctor claims that Captain Jack Harkness's very existence is outside the realm of right: 'That's why I left you behind. It's not easy, even just ... just looking at you, Jack, 'cause you're wrong ... I can't help it. I'm a Time Lord. It's instinct; it's in my guts. You're a fixed point in time and space; you're a fact. That's never meant to happen.' But Jack is able to get the Doctor to reconsider his appraisal: 'So what you're saying is ... you're prejudiced?' ('Utopia' (2007)).

The treatment of religious cults on the show illustrates a few basic principles in regards to ethics, however. First, agency and choice are paramount. No follower should follow blindly. Everyone should be allowed to make his or her own way. When the Doctor gives his adversaries a choice between change and their destruction, it is still vital that they make the choice themselves rather than having him defeat them via manipulation of the time vortex or via manipulation of their will. The opportunity to question the actions and motivations of one's leaders, even of the Doctor, is tied to this important ethical consideration.

Weapons as a whole are discouraged; turning others into weapons against their will is an abomination. If resisting the latter, one is able to use the former. Lethal force can be used in self-defence, in defence of a species, or in defence of one's loved ones. Yet even this simple rule can be interpreted quite differently depending on the point of view. If one species *believes* another is a threat, it might be tempted to commit genocide. If someone is a threat, but not an immediate one, should he or she be destroyed?

The show questions the morality of our characters – *all* of our characters – so that we might question our own in turn. The Master uses the rhetorical question 'What would the Doctor do?' to persuade Martha to give herself for others. This question is posed to viewers throughout the series, though the answers aren't always as clear. Would the Doctor actually spare Madame Kovarian when she begs Amy for her life, as she believes, or would his rage at what has been done to his wife be as overpowering as a mother's fury?

The question is not so much 'What *would* the Doctor do?' but 'What *should* the Doctor do?' In our worship of the Doctor, we Whovians should attempt to be the very best of humanity: 'Come on. Be extraordinary.'[18] And we should remember that maintaining ethics will always be tricky – that even the best of us are not inherently good: 'Good men don't need rules. Today is not the day to find out why I have so many.'[19]

12.

Mediating Between the Scientific and the Spiritual in *Doctor Who*

David Johnson

With a sound recognisable to millions of fans around the world, the familiar blue police-box shape of the TARDIS vworp-vworps into existence and the eccentric figure of the Doctor tumbles into some exotic adventure week after week in the television programme *Doctor Who*. While *Doctor Who* is generally considered to be in the genre of science fiction, complete with its own set of techno-babble ('Reverse the polarity of the neutron flow!'), what is most striking about the show is the frequency in which the character of the Doctor transgresses the typical boundaries of science fiction to instead explore ideas of belief and faith. From masquerading as an Aztec god to battling vampires and confronting the Guardians of good and evil in the Universe, time and again the Doctor can be seen exploring the complex relationship between science and religion, typically seen as separate realms. In most of these adventures, the Doctor serves as a sort of mediator, sometimes relying more heavily on science to resolve that week's problem, while at other times the Doctor must use distinctly supernatural or spiritual means to thwart the plans of whatever malignant force threatens the Universe. Implicit in that idea is an interesting question, though: why is there a need for a mediator in the first place?

By definition, the need for a mediator suggests there is an inherent conflict between two sides or forces, and that the issue between those two sides cannot be resolved without the assistance of a neutral third party. Superficially, it appears modern society views science and religion as completely incompatible with each other. Some see the two ideas as so diametrically opposed that they act almost like matter and antimatter, behaving fine in their own fields but highly explosive when mixed. A crucial point to consider for the Doctor serving as a mediator between these two ideas must be whether or not this apparent conflict between science and religion really exists, and if it does, what the nature of that conflict is. As the Doctor is a time traveller, an examination of the history of science and religion and their interactions seems an appropriate place to start.

The ancient Greeks were the first to really advance ideas that today we might consider scientific. Hippocrates, for example, suggested that diseases could be the direct result of natural causes rather than supernatural ones, and that natural remedies could cure them.[1] The idea that there could be observable, natural phenomenon at work instead of exclusively supernatural forces leads to what we call science. That is not to say that there wasn't conflict over this new way of thinking. The Greek philosopher Anaxagoras suggested that the Moon did not give off any light of its own, but instead reflected sunlight, and that the light from the Sun was a result of its being made of some fiery material. Instead of being given accolades for his ideas, Anaxagoras was put on trial for not respecting the spiritual traditions of Athens.[2] Despite missteps such as these, the Greeks laid the foundations for a new way of thinking that allowed for naturalistic rather than spiritual causes. It was not that the Greek world was without spiritual forces, but that those spiritual forces operated within the limits of natural laws. Plato himself proposed a cosmos which involved various deific components, but suggested those deities did not disrupt the course of the natural world.[3]

It is critical to recognise that both during antiquity and the medieval period that followed it, the word science was not as distinct a term as it is today. Instead, philosophy, theology and natural science were all different aspects of the same field of study.[4] Given the popular perceptions of the Middle Ages as a time distinctly lacking in science, it might be surprising that the medieval Church was in fact one of the greatest patrons of science of the age.[5] While this science was selective and limited, it was still a means of evaluating the world around us using the power of reason and even the power of doubt.[6] The medieval scholar Abelard suggested, 'by doubting we come to inquiry, and by inquiry we seek the truth.'[7] The truth was still to be found in a God-centric world, but there was no inherent problem with trying to understand the methods by which God's world worked. Perhaps most strikingly, medieval interpretation of the Bible allowed for a degree of flexibility as opposed to a strictly literal reading. For a medieval theologian, if the Bible seemed to conflict with common sense, a figurative interpretation was perfectly acceptable.[8] Not only was there no conflict in the medieval period between the methods of thinking we could consider scientific and the system of beliefs we call religion, but the Church and the sciences actually worked together quite effectively.

After the Renaissance in Europe, though, there were some rumblings of trouble. The trial of Galileo for heresy might appear to be a high-water mark for a conflict between religion and science, but a deeper evaluation suggests otherwise. The Copernican (sun-centred) model had been around for some time before Galileo wrote his book *The Starry Messenger*, and while the Church agreed Copernicus's system made the mathematics of predicting planetary motion simpler, it also violated common sense, and so could be dismissed as little more than an intellectual exercise. Thus the empirical evidence Galileo's telescopic experiments provided was the source of the problem

With his research, Galileo was not attempting to disprove God, nor was he attempting to violate the sanctity of Church doctrine. In fact, a close contemporary of Galileo's, Johannes Kepler, developed his rules of planetary motion specifically because he believed strongly enough in God's elegant design for the universe that he pursued the mathematics until he found an equally elegant solution to explain how planets moved.[9] Galileo was simply following his medieval precursors in trying to understand God's universe. The conflict that drove the trial arose because the same common-sense analysis of the Bible which allowed for figurative interpretations also allowed for a figurative interpretation of the Copernican model and Kepler's mathematics, which acknowledged that the numbers made sense, but only as a thought experiment, not as anything applicable to physical reality. So long as there was no direct evidence to support the Copernican theory, common sense prevailed, and both common sense and the Bible asserted that the Earth was unmoving, and therefore the centre of the universe. Yet Galileo's observations clearly showed otherwise. This violated the notion of common sense of the time, which suggested that if the Earth was moving, everyone would fly off into space like drops of water on a whirligig. The pivotal point is that the common sense at work in Galileo's trial was based on an incomplete understanding of the scientific laws that govern the Universe. Had the citizens and courts of early seventeenth-century Europe had access to the knowledge Newton would develop decades later, the common-sense problem at the heart of Galileo's run-in with the Church might not have been an issue at all. The shift in knowledge and perspective is absolutely crucial in considering the way the Doctor serves his role as a mediator between science and belief.

While Galileo's trial certainly represents a difficult encounter between science and religion, such encounters were actually quite rare. Great advances were made in all the sciences through the seventeenth, eighteenth and early nineteenth centuries, and yet no one was put on trial for discovering microbes with a microscope, inventing a steam engine by using an understanding of gasses and pressure, or developing artificial dyes with the application of chemical science. The origins of the current perceptions of conflict can be found in the second half of the nineteenth century. As with Galileo, the struggle was between common sense understanding and empirical evidence that contradicted it. For most people in the western world in the late 1800s, God made the Earth and all the creatures on it as they now appear on 23 October 4004 BC, based on Archbishop Ussher's seventeenth-century study of the genealogies in the Bible.[10] But geological evidence was rapidly emerging that the world was much older than that, and there were fossils for a host of creatures that had previously existed but somehow didn't make it onto Noah's Ark. Then there was Charles Darwin, whose research into a variety of species suggested that not only did existing species adapt or evolve, but given enough time and change, whole new species of animals could evolve. Darwin's ideas, coupled with the geological evidence for extinct species, suggested that humans must have evolved as well, rather than being divinely created in their present form. Given the potential conflicts with Biblical interpretation all this new information offered, it's no wonder that John William Draper felt the need to write the *History of the Conflict Between Religion and Science* in 1896, a landmark work in the modern conflict between science and religion.

The works of Charles Darwin are still central to a large part of the debate between science and belief that continues to this day. At the heart of the matter is what role God or some other spiritual force plays in the universe. For the purpose of this discussion, it is necessary to exclude the various direct-creation theories, including the often-mentioned Intelligent Design theory, as discussion of those theories frequently requires a willful ignorance of vast amounts of widely-accepted scientific data. It is more instructive instead to consider the debate centred around the idea of naturalism versus a concept that is generally represented as theistic or divinely-guided evolution. In the debate between these two positions, the issue is not whether or not evolution happens; both sides explicitly agree the evidence for evolution is overwhelming. Instead the crux of the matter is the driving force behind the evolutionary process. Naturalists posit that the process is entirely driven by natural forces, such as natural selection and random genetic mutation. Those in the theistic evolution camp posit that for various reasons the natural forces are not enough, and that a divine being, usually God, has instead directed the evolutionary process to achieve a desired end.[11]

There is an amazing amount of effort and rhetoric that goes into both sides of this debate, and so it is perhaps fair to say this is a source of genuine conflict between science and belief, if not directly with religion. That point is instructive; there are virtually no doctrinal arguments offered by those positing guided evolution. Instead of invoking any church-specific ideology, they prefer to discuss matters in terms of a designer or other generic spiritual force. The conflict is one between a scientific position and a position based on faith, not religion. An analysis of the issue will demonstrate the unresolvable nature of this debate, and by extension suggest why a mediator between faith and science, such as the Doctor, has such a significant role in society today.

Within the debate over the role of God in evolution, the naturalist position is perhaps better known, inasmuch as it has not shifted significantly since it was proposed. More commonly labelled by its opponents than by its proponents as 'Darwinism', the premise simply is that change both within a species and from species to species happens because a mutation in some way increases an organism's ability to reproduce or its chances to do so, thereby passing on that mutation. A classic case study in this is the English peppered moth, which has two colourations: a light one and a dark one. After the Industrial Revolution, the dark coloured variant rapidly superseded the previously dominant light-coloured one, as against the soot-covered bark, the lighter coloured was easy prey for bird and other animals that fed on insects.[12] While the environmental change was caused by humankind in this case, the actual process of natural selection was the same as if a natural environmental change had occurred. The central issue that the naturalists assert is that there is no need to invoke spiritual causes to explain the process at work, as a simple and observable environmental change can explain the differences in the moth population.

The simple answer is a fine scientific tradition that traces its way back to the late medieval period and the origin of the idea that today is known as Ockham's Razor. While today Ockham's Razor is usually summarised as 'the simplest explanation is the correct one', the original principle was 'Multiple entities should never be invoked unnecessarily'.[13] In the case of the peppered moth, the naturalists claim that natural forces are enough to explain the biologic conditions seen today, and so it is unnecessary to invoke a spiritual force. For guided evolutionists, though, that argument is not proof of the absence of a guiding spiritual force, inasmuch as there is no evidence a spiritual power did not produce the change.

How far apart the two camps are can be seen in a recent articles in which a famous anthropologist suggested the debate over intelligent design would soon be history as the growing body of evidence was overwhelming.[14] The scientific evidence supporting a natural, as opposed to a guided, supernatural evolutionary process is substantial, to be sure. But no matter how compelling or conclusive the evidence of a natural process is, it will never constitute definitive proof that there was not a supernatural force at work. For those who support a God-driven evolutionary process, there simply cannot be proof that God was not the reason for the particular set of mutations or events that led to a microbe, a panda, or a human. The comedic science-fiction programme *Futurama* put this point of view succinctly when a God-like being discusses intervention in the lives of others: 'When you do things right, people won't be sure you've done anything at all.'[15] From the guided evolutionists also comes a wide range of scientifically-framed proofs that God must be involved in the evolutionary process, usually invoking some degree of statistical probability that a particular element is so unlikely it would take longer than the lifespan of the planet for it to have evolved by chance. By extension then, the guided evolution argument asserts an empirical proof for God.[16] As with the naturalists' inability to comprehend the nature of a faith-based perspective, the guided evolutionists completely fail to understand the critical element of the opposing point of view.

Essentially, the naturalists are insistent that natural forces are a sufficient explanation for the reason things are the way they are, and that supernatural forces need not be invoked to explain anything, because the hand of God cannot be replicated in a laboratory. The guided evolutionists insist that evolution does not preclude God no matter what other forces might be at work. They further assert that evolution itself serves as a sort empirical proof for God, not realising an actual scientific proof for God is impossible for the very reason that the naturalists insist on excluding God in the first place. Is it any wonder that there is a perception of conflict between science and religion, and a great many people wish someone would step in and mediate between the two camps?

Enter the Doctor with his vast, well-travelled experiences and open mind to bridge the gap. A programme like *Doctor Who*, or indeed a host of other genre television programmes like *Star Trek* or even the comedic *Red Dwarf*, offers to viewers a safe way to consider difficult social issues by virtue of placing them in exotic or futuristic locales that distance the viewer from an otherwise threatening discussion.[17] Among its myriad stories, *Doctor Who* has offered several discussions on what role science and religion are to play in a society over its fifty year run, and the Doctor repeatedly serves in the role of mediator. In some stories he demonstrates the value of tangible science in place of faith, while in other stories he advocates for tolerance of apparently non-scientific beliefs and even actively engages in actions that result in a supernatural resolution to the plot. The stories 'The Dæmons' (1971), featuring Jon Pertwee as the Doctor, and the Mara duet of 'Kinda' (1982) and 'Snakedance' (1983), featuring Peter Davison as the Doctor, illustrate just how the Doctor serves the vital role of mediating between science and belief.

In 'The Dæmons' there is an interaction between the forces of science and religion from the very start. As soon as the Doctor hears of an archaeological expedition at the ominously-named Devil's End, he rushes off to stop it, despite previously dismissing companion Jo Grant's assertions about spirituality and the Age of Aquarius out of hand. At the archaeological site, local witch Miss Hawthorne asserts 'Man is tampering with forces he does not understand', a sentiment the Doctor seems to echo as he frantically tries to stop the opening of the barrow. Has the Doctor embraced the supernatural here? No. 'Everything has a scientific explanation for it, if you just know where to look for it', he asserts early in the story.

Therein lies the position of the Doctor's mediation for this episode. The Doctor comes down very firmly in the realm of science for the story of 'The Dæmons' even though the story is loaded with supernatural iconography, such as the near-clichéd devilish appearance of Azal, the principal alien, complete with cloven hooves and horns on his head. The supposedly supernatural manifestations, such as blasts of intense wind, impenetrable heat barriers and stone tiles that can nearly obliterate anything that passes over them, are all explained through the usual techno-babble of *Doctor Who*, such as the stand-by science-fiction convention of the force field, or the ability of Azal to change his size at will through an application of Einstein's theories equating mass and energy. Even when the Doctor appears to use actual magic to escape from a mob of angry villagers by summoning his yellow roadster, Bessie, to drive over to him despite an empty driver's seat, he is instead using a remote control previously fitted to the car, stating to Miss Hawthorne, 'Not magic. Science.'

There is however an interesting subtext in this story that further showcases how the Doctor can serve as a mediator between science and religion, and a closer examination of this suggests the scientific bias may not be as clear. Several elements through the story appear to give religion a very negative slant. Certainly, to knowledgeable viewers the appearance of Roger Delgado as redoubtable villain the Master, in the guise of the local vicar, suggests religion has been corrupted. The Master's plan to control Azal and dominate the world heightens this, as does a particularly poignant speech to villagers in which he asserts 'You can get whatever you want in this world, if you just listen to me ... All I need are your obedience and submission to my will.'

This, coupled with the reminder from Miss Hawthorne that the last witchcraft laws in the UK were only repealed in 1951, would seem to be further bolstering the position that religion is for fearful and mind-numbed plebeians unable to think for themselves. But there is a suggestive counterpoint. At the end of the story, when Miss Hawthorne recognises there are non-supernatural explanations for everything she asks if the rituals are all just nonsense. The Doctor replies that the Master was directing psychokinetic energy, and the rituals are 'a means of creating and directing those forces'. This is a significant assertion for such a 'scientific' story – the rituals are not window-dressing but a vital part of the process, albeit one that relies on explainable forces rather than mysterious and supernatural ones.[18]

The Mara stories 'Kinda' and 'Snakedance' from the early 1980s demonstrate a different approach to science and belief than that taken in 'The Dæmons'. In 'Kinda' the Doctor and his companions, Tegan, Nyssa and Adric, arrive on an Eden-like world inhabited by a very human-looking race known as the Kinda. This planet, Deva Loka, is being surveyed by humans from Earth for possible colonisation or exploitation, which sets up the principal conflict, inasmuch as the Kinda don't want the humans there, but are apparently unable or unwilling to fight them off. On a superficial level, this story is laced with Judaeo-Christian imagery, such as the humans eating a native fruit that resembles an apple, even though consuming native plants is forbidden, and the pseudo-resurrection of the elder Kinda priestess Panna into the body of Kaluna. There is also an inherent undercurrent of British colonialism in the attitudes of the surviving military figures towards the natives and the importance of Earth's needs at whatever cost to the natives. However, the story 'Kinda' more vitally serves to introduce a supernatural-esque being known as the Mara, and it is in this aspect of the story that the character of the Doctor is most sharply able to bridge the apparent gap between the religious beliefs of the Kinda, and the scientific system of the humans.

The Mara exists in 'the dark places of the inside', the nature of which is never suitably defined in this story or in its sequel, 'Snakedance'. The Doctor's companion Tegan spends a fair amount of time in whatever this realm is as she falls asleep under the influence of a set of chimes which the Kinda refer to as the 'place of the dreaming'. Viewers may speculate on whether this is some psychic realm, a parallel dimension or some other aspect usually employed within the standard science-fiction canon. The crucial aspect for the Doctor as mediator is that this realm exists within the belief system of the Kinda, and that they are well aware of the very real negative force within it, while the humans, including the most open-minded, the scientist Todd, generally dismiss the Kinda and their beliefs as harmless superstition.

That relationship between Todd and the Kinda highlights a fundamental shift from the position established in 'The Dæmons'. Here, the Earth scientist is made to seem the one who is unthinking, a blind servant to science rather than faith, only now instead of being subservient to supernatural forces, she appears to be bound by the idea of naturalism, which precludes forces outside the normal order of nature. This allows the Doctor to serve as mediator again, only this time advocating that there are forces beyond the limits of Earth science that need to be reckoned with, and that an apparently non-scientific resolution may be necessary. In the climax of the story 'Kinda' the Doctor references an aspect he is familiar with from the Mara legend, asserting 'What is the one thing evil cannot face, not ever? Itself!' This harkens back to vampire legends, wherein vampires cast no reflection in a mirror, an assertion which science would refute not only on the basis of a lack of evidence for vampires, but also on basic principles of optics. It is possible, though, to consider this apparently non-scientific plan in light of the position the Galileo trial exposed. The common sense of the humans on Deva Loka said the Doctor's plan was silly, but from the more advanced and experienced position the Doctor was in, it was an extension of science with which he was familiar. In this story, though, there is hope for humankind as the scientist Todd, after having experienced a distinctly non-scientific vision ritual, said 'I'm trying to understand', even though she freely admits what she has been through is far beyond her scientific experience. But perhaps her new experiences will eventually open the door to empirical understanding of ideas that now seem like superstition.

As in 'The Dæmons' where there was a subtext subtly validating certain aspects of religion despite a strong presentation of science, so too in 'Kinda' is there a subtle subtext validating science despite a strong presentation of supernatural forces. Much of the story rests on psychic phenomenon, a field which the Doctor has obviously encountered before, and which for him, as the experienced mediator, does fall into a realm of science rather than the supernatural. It is also technology that indirectly defeats the Mara, inasmuch as the mirrors the Doctor uses to force the Mara back into its own dimension are actually large solar panels. Most tellingly, though, is the Box of Jhana, apparently a sort of supernatural reliquary of the Kinda which has great power to affect the mind, usually in a negative way. The Doctor is not only able to face the box without having it alter his mind, but is able to casually explain at the end of the story that the box probably uses sound waves 'beyond our hearing' as a means of scientifically explaining what appeared to be a magical device.

As striking as the interplay between science and religion is in 'Kinda', there is an even more intriguing interaction in its sequel story, 'Snakedance'. Again the Doctor is called upon to serve a mediating role between the forces of science and belief, but more than in either of the previous stories, he must call upon a distinctly supernatural remedy to defeat the Mara again. In the story, the TARDIS lands on the former home world of the Sumaran Empire, now a protectorate of a generic human Federation. The Federation is preparing to celebrate the 500th anniversary of the defeat of the Mara, and the ceremony is being overseen by Ambril, a strictly factual figure that insists on 'not allowing our imaginations to run away with us'. Thus the polarisation between science and belief is at its most developed in this story, only now in sharp contrast to 'The Dæmons' the Doctor must advocate by, any means possible, the taking of actions with a decidedly supernatural bent to them.

A notable feature of 'Snakedance' is the group of figures known as the Snake Dancers, a mystic cult on the fringes of society that are regarded by the Federation as near-savages, living on roots and berries, covered in ash, and some of them 'almost naked'. The former director for the Federation, Dojjen, gave up his position to join them, convinced the Mara legends were real, and that the mystics knew the only way to protect the planet, leaving him frequently scorned by the very factual Ambril. In the climax of the story, the Doctor finds Dojjen and undergoes the snake dance ritual with him to 'find the still point' as the only means of defeating the Mara. The still point is not clearly defined in the story, but appears to be akin to a Zen-like nirvana. Significant to his role as a mediator, even as the Mara threatens imminent doom, the Doctor takes the necessary moment to honour Dojjen with a bow, showing a respect for the spiritual as well as the scientific. Equipped with the knowledge of how to use the still point, the Doctor is able to confront the Mara, and prevent its manifestation, although with a curious twist. He urges those in the Mara ritual 'Do not believe what you see!' because the belief itself, the fear the ritual was generating, was the force necessary to create a physical Mara.

The concept of the power of belief is a key similarity between the two stories: the rituals being used play a key part. In 'The Dæmons' the Doctor asserts that the rituals the Master uses focus psychic energy to awaken Azal, while in 'Snakedance' the Doctor asserts that the ritual the Federation is about to undertake as part of the celebration of the defeat of the Mara is the very thing necessary to focus the negative energy the Mara needs to manifest itself. In both stories, the invocation of faith and ritual play a vital role in creating power that can be used for good or evil, even though science can on some level explain why such rituals or beliefs are effective or important.

This set of three *Doctor Who* stories demonstrates the Doctor's role as a mediator between science and belief. In 'The Dæmons' the Doctor explains away apparently supernatural forces because of his superior experience in the field of science, beyond human sciences at the time. From his perspective, all the events of the story, even including the climactic moment when Jo's willingness to sacrifice herself befuddles Azal so profoundly he effectively destroys himself, can be explained through empirical, rational, scientific means. However, in the Mara stories, the Doctor employs distinctly non-scientific methods to counter the threat, invoking what seems to be superstition in one case, and a profoundly metaphysical approach in the other. There is still a rational principle at work in the Mara stories, rather than an absolutely magical one, inasmuch as the results can be assumed to be replicable, which is a key scientific requirement (i.e. focusing this kind of mental energy through this particular crystal will produce this result every time). The science at work, however, is far beyond the earthly, human science the Doctor so frequently interacts with. This provides the ultimate key to the Doctor as a mediator between science and religion, both within the programme's stories, and also in the world outside the television.

Our world (and Western society in particular) is a scientific world. Ever since the first Greek and medieval forays into scientific thinking began, the reach of science in daily life has been increasing. Civilisation has come to depend on science to find the answers to the problems it faces, even if at times those problems are created by that same science. For the most part, our society is comfortable with that. People don't utter prayers to the gods to ensure the water will boil when they put the kettle on. Civilisation has learned that a sufficient amount of heat applied to water will make it boil, every time. It is predictable; based on empirical evidence. There are, however, a great many things people still believe in, or wish to believe in, that defy empirical evidence, such as ghosts, psychic powers or even vampires. As yet, there is no empirical data to demonstrate any of these things, but the beliefs persist. A recent study suggests humans need to believe in something larger than themselves, and that some people are getting increasingly creative about what they put their faith in.[19] Adherents to these unproven beliefs take exactly the same approach the Doctor has done in many of his adventures: they argue that our science just hasn't found the proof *yet*.

Scientists will be the first to admit science has not found the answers to every question yet. That is what drives discovery – the human curiosity to seek out answers to why something is the way it is. This is what drove early medieval philosophers to consider how the natural world God created worked, understanding that using human reason as a gift from God was not a sin. The concern in today's world regarding whether or not science will explain away

God is really at the heart of the current struggle between naturalists and advocates of theistic evolution. The naturalist asserts that God is not necessary for evolution to have turned out the way it did, while the other side asserts that a lack of requirement does not constitute actual evidence of non-existence. Both sides are looking for a figure like the Doctor, a wise, experienced and well-travelled individual who can come in and bridge the gap, perhaps ultimately providing scientific, empirical proof for God. As yet, the Doctor has not come by with God's email address, so humans will keep asking questions and exploring new ideas. And humans will keep using television programmes like *Doctor Who* as a venue to safely discuss new ideas, including questioning the role of (and relationship between) science and faith in the modern world. That we, like the scientist Todd on Deva Loka, continue trying to understand is very hopeful for us indeed.

13.

Karma, Conditionality and Clinging to the Self: The Tennant Years as Seen Through a Tibetan Buddhist Lens

Kristine Larsen

One of the most beloved of all Tibetan Buddhist texts is *The Great Treatise on the Stages to the Path of Enlightenment* (*Byang chub lam rim chen mo*), composed by the Tibetan scholar Tsong-kha-pa in 1402CE. This work, said to be a summary of all the Buddha's teachings, is a lengthy commentary on the 68-verse poem *A Lamp of the Path for Enlightenment*, composed circa 1040CE by the Indian pandit Atisha specifically to spread the Buddha's teachings throughout Tibet.[1] Both Atisha's original work and Tsong-kha-pa's commentary are considered seminal works of the *lam rim* or graded path tradition in which teachings are given for the benefit of three classes of sentient beings: those of small capacity (who aspire for a better rebirth in their immediate next life), medium capacity (those who wish to leave the constant cycle of death and rebirth known as *samsara* and achieve enlightenment or *nirvana*), and those of great capacity (those who aspire to buddhahood in order to aid all sentient beings in becoming enlightened).[2] Among the small capacity teachings are lessons on suffering, karma, and the need to be mindful of the death and resulting rebirths that will be caused by one's accumulated karma.

Buddhist concepts have appeared in *Doctor Who* since the very first incarnation of the Doctor, for example in the First Doctor episode 'Marco Polo' (1964) and the Peter Davison era's 'Kinda' (1982) and 'Snakedance' (1983).[3] Specific references to Tibet also thread the classic series of *Doctor Who*, from the Troughton era's 'The Abominable Snowmen' (1967) to Pertwee's 'Planet of the Spiders' (1974) and Tom Baker's 'Terror of the Zygons' (1975). Indeed, given the Doctor's ability to regenerate (a form of reincarnation) as well as the Doctor's nearly constant battle against evil and suffering throughout time and space, such a Buddhist connection is fairly obvious. However, in the David Tennant years of the new series certain aspects of the Tibetan *lam rim* tradition take centre stage, such as the suffering of change and separation, and the general conditional suffering of existence within time and space (the suffering of samsara). This chapter will examine the Tennant years through the lens of Tsong-kha-pa's stages of the path for beings of small capacity, with the goal of demonstrating how such a reading ties together many important events throughout Tennant's forty-seven episodes as the Doctor.

Emptiness, Karma and Rebirth

Central to Buddhist doctrine is the concept of emptiness, the idea that all things arise in dependence on causes and conditions (a concept sometimes termed *dependent arising*). Even the self is considered dependent (or empty of inherent, independent existence) because it, too, arises in dependence on (but is not identical to) the five aggregates (or *skandhas*) – form, feeling, perception, mental habits and consciousness. Because all things arise, they have an ending, and are, by their very nature, impermanent. Nothing is its own cause, and no cause can create a result that is not concordant with that cause. This leads to the concept of reincarnation, as one moment of consciousness gives rise to the next moment of consciousness, and so forth from beginningless time.[4] Someone who has realised emptiness sees all of reality (including the self) as it truly is – dependently arising. A buddha is not only fully enlightened, but has achieved ultimate compassion for all sentient beings, or *bodhicitta*.

While the Doctor is certainly not portrayed as a buddha (being neither fully enlightened nor possessing ultimate compassion), he is wiser than most characters in the series, and, on occasion, displays greater compassion. As a Time Lord he certainly sees the interconnectedness between events throughout space and time, and occasionally admonishes his companions when they fight to change what cannot (or must not) be changed (for example in 'The Fires of Pompeii' (2008)). The entire episode 'Turn Left' (2008) focuses on dependent origination; the Trickster's Brigade beetle causes Donna to change a seemingly simple decision in her life, resulting in a complex chain of repercussions, chief of which is that she never met the Doctor, leading to his death at the hands of the Racnoss (referring to the events of 'The Runaway Bride' (2006)). Because the Doctor dies, he is not able to save Martha Jones when her hospital is transported to the moon ('Smith and Jones' (2007)) and all the passengers and crew of the spaceship Titanic (not to mention the Royal Family and countless other earthlings) die because he does not stop the crippled spaceship from crashing ('Voyage of the Damned' (2007)). These and other deaths are caused (in this alternate reality) simply because Donna Noble did not turn left at a fork in the road, a powerful lesson in dependent origination.

Compassion towards his enemies is also one of his strengths. For example, in 'The Sound of Drums' (2007) the Doctor explains to Martha that he does not intend to kill the Master, but rather he intends to attempt to save his long-time nemesis from his own self-destructive actions. Even after the Master attempts to destroy the entire human species, and temporarily strips the Doctor of his regenerative powers (aging him into a tiny, withered, 900-year-old creature), the Doctor forgives him, and prevents Martha's mother, Maxine, from killing the renegade Time Lord. The Doctor also extends compassion towards his other great enemies, Davros and the Daleks, on numerous occasions. When the Cult of Skaro turns on itself in 'Evolution of the Daleks' (2007) the Time Lord offers to help Dalek Caan, whom he believes to be the last of its species. Instead, Caan teleports away, ending up in the centre of the Time War where he manages to save Davros and the Dalek army (but at the price of his own sanity). When we next see Caan in 'The Stolen Earth/ Journey's End' (2008) the Doctor 2.0 (Doctor-Donna metacrisis) destroys Davros and his genetically engineered creatures. The Doctor pleads for Davros to come with him, promising that he can be saved.

However, the Doctor's compassion has its limits. In 'The Family of Blood' (2007) the Family discovers too late that the Doctor hid from them in order to save them from their own greed for immortality – 'He was being kind'. When they caused not only the deaths of innocent humans, but separated the Doctor from the chance for a happy life with Joan Redfern, his anger took over, and he devised cruel punishments for the members of the Family (such as binding the father in unbreakable chains).

In Buddhism, the mistaken view of the world as having inherent existence (denying emptiness) leads the unenlightened to fall prey to karma and harmful afflictions, and because of this cause suffering, not only to others, and not only to themselves in this life, but in all future lives as well. *Karma* is a Sanskrit word meaning action; all actions not only have their own causes, but themselves are, in turn, the cause for some future event. Therefore the so-called law of karma is the Buddhist version of the law of cause and effect.[5] Non-virtuous actions of the body, speech and mind, such as killing, stealing, lying and covetousness, lead to the accumulation of negative karma. This negative karma will become the cause for suffering in the future. Conversely, the accumulation of positive or virtuous karma (the effect of virtuous actions such as refraining from murdering or lying, or performing acts of kindness and compassion) lead to happiness in this or future lives.

But murder is not always a non-virtuous act. According to the *Upaya-kaushalya Sutra*, in a past life Buddha was a ship captain who was faced with a seemingly impossible choice. Deities informed him in a dream that 500 of his passengers – wealthy merchants – were going to be robbed and killed by another passenger. The captain could not allow the robber to kill the other passengers and accumulate the negative karma it would entail. He could also not simply tell the merchants, because they would take out retribution upon the robber, and also accumulate negative karma. Out of a sense of compassion, the captain killed the would-be robber, knowing that he himself risked spending 'a thousand aeons' in the hell realms.[6] The Doctor similarly makes impossible choices, weighing the lives of many against the lives of the few, as in the case of 'The Fires of Pompeii'. Here the Doctor makes the decision to allow the 20,000 citizens of Pompeii to die in the destruction of the Pyroviles (in the eruption of Vesuvius) in order to save millions of other humans. The destruction of his own species and home planet (as well as the Daleks) in the Time War is also an attempt to save numerous other lives. Dalek Caan likewise understands the destructive potential of his own species, and in 'Journey's End' helps in bringing together Donna and the Doctor's timelines (manipulating dependent origination as it were) in order to assure the final destruction of his kind.

Unenlightened beings are trapped in samsara because they keep accumulating negative karma through the powers of the ten afflictions (also called the ten delusions). As explained in Tsong-kha-pa's *Great Treatise*, the top four are attachment, hostility or anger, pride, and ignorance of the true nature of reality.[7] Attachment is not only an unhealthy clinging to objects that we own, but, because we see our individual self as being a permanent, independent, intrinsically existing entity, we grasp at things as being 'mine'.

Because everything we own is transient, and even our health and lives are transient, this leads to suffering. For this reason, attachment, anger and ignorance are often termed the three poisons.[8] In the case of the Doctor, much of his suffering clearly comes from his attachment to his companions, not only when they leave him or die, but when they are used against him (for example, as prisoners of his enemies). The Doctor (especially the new series incarnations) is also portrayed as having deep-rooted anger, in part because of the Time War. While he can demonstrate great compassion, as the Family of Blood discovered, his anger can be quite terrifying. In 'Journey's End' the Doctor becomes furious, thinking that Dalek Caan is responsible for the disappearance of the TARDIS and (he assumes) the death of Donna. Davros relishes the fulfillment of Caan's prophecy that the Doctor's soul will be revealed: 'The anger! The fire! The rage of a Time Lord who butchered millions!'. After the destruction of Davros and the Daleks, the Doctor banishes the Doctor/Donna metacrisis to the alternate reality with Rose. As he explains, his alter ego – the 'soul' that Dalek Caan decreed would be revealed – was 'born in battle. Full of blood and anger and revenge'. He asks Rose to rehabilitate his alter ego, as she had done for his ninth incarnation. The viewer does not know how successful Rose ultimately becomes at this task, but it is clear that both the tenth and eleventh incarnations continue to be slaves to their afflictions of anger, attachment, ignorance and pride. By the law of karma, this leads to suffering.

Suffering and Samsara

In the novel *Ghosts of India*, Gopal notes of the Doctor 'I have never seen a man look so angry and so sad before.' The Time Lord explains 'I've seen more suffering in my life than you can possibly imagine. But that doesn't mean it ever gets any easier.'[9] Suffering comes from the afflictions, from not understanding the emptiness of reality, and from the accumulation and ripening of negative karma. One cannot be liberated from suffering while one is chained to cyclic existence in samsara – while one is continually dying and being reborn.

While there are a number of different classifications of suffering found in Tsong-kha-pa's *Great Treatise*, the most fundamental delineation is into the three types: the suffering of suffering, the suffering of change, and the compounded or pervasive suffering that is inherent in cyclic existence. The suffering of suffering is self-explanatory. An example would be the Doctor feeling the pain of having his hand sliced off in 'The Christmas Invasion' (2005). The suffering of change can be as simple as an initially delicious meal causing stomach pains. In the case of the Doctor, this manifests in the aging of his friends and companions, and their eventual separation from him (as in the case of Reinette in 'The Girl in the Fireplace' (2006)). Pervasive suffering is more subtle. In the commentary to Tsong-kha-pa's brief work 'The Source of All My Good' pervasive suffering is described as 'the subtle condition of change, the fact that the physical, mental, and other parts of ourselves which we have taken on cannot remain, but begin to change from the moment after they came into existence … [It] is the kind of pain that pervades each and every thing produced by karma and mental afflictions.'[10] In 'The Fires of Pompeii' we catch a glimpse of the specific type of pervasive suffering of the Time Lord: 'That's how I see the universe. Every waking second I can see what is, what was, what could be, what must not. That's the burden of the Time Lord, Donna. I'm the only one left.'

Another classification of suffering described in *The Great Treatise* is the eight types. They are the suffering of birth, old age, illness and death, encountering the unpleasant, separation from the pleasant, not getting what one wants, and the suffering of being housed within the five aggregates.[11] As Time Lords, the Doctor and the Master both have to face the suffering of birth each time they regenerate. The Master's rebirth as a Time Lord at the end of 'Utopia' (2007) illustrates this quite explicitly, as does the Doctor's rebirth as a human via the chameleon arch in 'Human Nature' (2007). They also have to face the suffering of death (in terms of the pain of regeneration and being forced to end one's old life) and the loss of a body they have become used to (and regard as attractive). For example, witness Matt Smith's first dialogue as the Doctor in the second part of 'The End of Time' (2010) where he is concerned about the changes in his appearance after regeneration. While he normally does not feel the suffering of illness and old age (except in rare cases such as 'Last of the Time Lords' and 'The Family of Blood'), the Doctor does have to face these as well as death in terms of his companions. Encountering the unpleasant certainly includes Daleks, Cybermen, and all manner of monsters, and separation from the pleasant accurately describes the loss of Rose, Martha, Donna, and all other beloved companions. The suffering of not getting what one wants occurs whenever the Doctor is unable to save someone despite his best actions and intentions. As for the suffering of the five aggregates (a general weariness of being trapped in samsara), we see this in *Ghosts of India* when the Doctor explains to Gopal, 'I can't help thinking I've lived too long.'[12]

A number of episodes from the Tennant era clearly illustrate these myriad types of suffering. In Rose's first full adventure with the Tenth Doctor, 'New Earth' (2006), we are faced with the suffering of sickness on a grand scale. Here millions of humans are used as laboratory rats in a plague farm, held against their wishes and infected with every known illness in order to find cures for patrons of the Sisters of Plenitude. We are also reacquainted with Lady Cassandra, and witness the depth of her obsessive attachment to both beauty and her life. Living in the basement of the hospital with her assistant Chip, Cassandra abandons her dying body and takes over Rose's using a psychograph. A similar attachment to youth and seemingly eternal life, as well as illustrations of the suffering of illness and old age, is seen in 'The Lazarus Experiment' (2007). The professor experiments on himself in a desperate attempt to cheat both old age and death, leading to physical suffering on his and others' part, as well as numerous deaths. John Lumic also uses science in an attempt to overcome the sufferings of illness, old age and death in 'Rise of the Cybermen/The Age of Steel' (2006). Faced with his own suffering and imminent death, Lumic creates a cybernetic skeleton to house a human brain. Unfortunately, being housed inside a metal casing leads to excruciating mental, emotional and physical suffering, necessitating the use of an emotional inhibitor. As the Doctor explains to Rose, 'it hurts'.[13] On the other side, the Cybermen explain to their creator 'We think of the humans. We think of their difference and their pain; they suffer in the skin, they must be upgraded.' When Lumic is attacked by Crane and asks the Cybermen for help, they note that Lumic is 'in pain. We can remove pain forever … We will give you immortality'.[14] Not only does Lumic resist the 'upgrade' but it is obvious that the Cybermen's claim is a lie. There is pain (as demonstrated when the emotional inhibitors of all the Cybermen are disabled), and there is not true immortality (as seen when the Cybermen self-destruct).

Immortality is clearly unnatural, and, as numerous episodes demonstrate, not truly possible. Even the Time Lords are not immortal, but are rather serially mortal (in terms of their regenerations). All attempts at immortality are therefore doomed to failure, or are arguably not real lives.[15] An example can be found in 'Silence in the Library/Forest of the Dead' (2008). Here the intelligence and experiences of Charlotte Abigail Lux – CAL – are housed within the vast computer system of The Library. As the system malfunctions, Charlotte's consciousness malfunctions – it suffers – and even her well-intentioned relatives acknowledge that she is 'dreaming a normal life … This is only half a life of course, but it is forever' ('Forest of the Dead').[16]

But this artificial half-life cannot last forever. As Martha and Jack discover in 'Utopia' even the universe has an end, in the far distant future. Everything dies, quite literally in this case. As the Doctor explains to Martha, it is time itself that killed the abandoned structures: 'Time. Just time. Everything's dying now.' This is not only an excellent example of the suffering of change, but the suffering of death.[17] In 'Utopia' we learn that Rose had not only resurrected Jack Harkness in the Ninth Doctor's final episode 'The Parting of the Ways' (2005), but she had made him the 'man who can never die'. The Doctor realises the problem with this, noting 'it's not easy even just looking at you, Jack, 'cause you're wrong'.[18] But Jack, like the Doctor, is not exactly immortal, for he is now put into situations where he dies (often painfully) only to revive in the same body. For example, in 'Utopia' Jack is exposed to lethal and painful doses of electricity and radioactivity, and has to repeatedly endure the sufferings of suffering and death.

Another episode that clearly reflects various types of suffering is 'School Reunion' (2006). Here Sarah Jane Smith reunites briefly with the Doctor, and explains to Rose the suffering inherent in travelling with the Time Lord: 'We get a taste of that splendour, then we have to go back' to a mundane life. She admits to Rose that nothing could ever compare to travelling with the Time Lord. Sarah Jane clearly suffered because of her attachment to the Doctor and their time together, as well as the suffering of change and the suffering of being separated from pleasant things (no longer being able to travel with him). She also has to face her own mortality, and the suffering of old age and death. After Sarah Jane is returned to Earth, Rose asks the Doctor why he had never spoken about her. The Doctor explains the pain he suffers because of his attachment to his companions: 'You wither and you die. Imagine watching that happen to someone that you – I have to live on, alone. That's the curse of a Time Lord.' Similarly in 'The Next Doctor' (2008) when asked by Jackson why he is now travelling alone, the Doctor admits that eventually all his companions leave him; in the end, they all break his heart and he is alone once more. He is all the more alone because he is the last of his kind, having sacrificed his own planet – more than once, it turns out – in order to save the universe. Not much is said about the Time War until the end of Tennant's term, but the viewer is given a taste of the Doctor's suffering at the end of 'Gridlock' (2007): 'They're all gone now. My family, my friends, even that sky.'

But of all the suffering that the Doctor has undergone during his tenth incarnation, nothing can compare to losing Rose. Despite numerous examples of foreshadowing that they would be separated in a violent manner (e.g. 'The Satan Pit' (2006) and 'Fear Her' (2006)), both Rose and the Doctor refuse to acknowledge that their relationship would have an end until the end comes. The suffering of change is not only felt by Rose and the Doctor in 'Army of Ghosts/ Doomsday' (2006), but by Rose's mother Jackie, who sadly notes how Rose has changed. While Rose claims it is for the better, Jackie isn't convinced. She is concerned that Rose will change so much that she will stop being Rose Tyler, and even 'stop being human' ('Army of Ghosts'). Although Rose chooses to stay on one side of the reality breach with the Doctor (and therefore be separated from her mother forever), she instead becomes separated from her beloved Doctor. When they are temporarily reunited in 'The Stolen Earth/Journey's End' the suffering caused by their separation is even more keenly felt. The Doctor attempts to assuage Rose's suffering by entrusting her with the care of the human metacrisis, who will age and grow old with Rose – something he can never do. He can never end Rose's suffering; instead, he merely replaces the suffering of separation with the suffering of change, illness, old age and death.[19]

Mindfulness of Death and Future Lives

The reality is that all sentient beings caught in samsara die. That is a law of nature, not merely a tenet of Buddhism. However, according to Buddhist teachings, we die because we have been reborn – it is the cycle of existence, a merry-go-round that cannot be stopped unless one becomes enlightened. Therefore, Tsong-kha-pa's *Great Treatise* devotes many pages to the topic of being mindful of death by meditating upon it. This is not to instil fear in death by having one obsess about the things and people one will lose when they die. To do that would be to fall victim to further attachment. According to Tsong-kha-pa, a proper mindfulness of death is cultivated through three contemplations: the certainty of death, the uncertainty of the time of death, and the reality that at the time of death nothing – including our friends and family – will help except religious practice.[20] Among the reasons given for the certainty of death is that 'the Lord of Death will definitely come, and therefore cannot be avoided' and 'our lifetime cannot be extended and constantly diminishes'.[21] Here the Lord of Death is not an external demon, but rather our own personal accumulated karma and afflictions. Since no one can accumulate karma for us, in the end we are responsible for our future births and deaths.[22] Throughout Tennant's tenure, the Doctor is bombarded with reminders of the eventual death of this incarnation, including references to his impending death in 'The Shakespeare Code' (2007), 'Planet of the Ood' (2008), and 'Planet of the Dead' (2009). As Ood Sigma explains, 'Every song must end'[23] ('Planet of the Ood'). Tsong-kha-pa stresses that it is most important to reflect on the fact that the time of our death is uncertain, because there is no fixed lifespan, there are many conditions that can bring about death, and our bodies are relatively fragile.[24] As the previous nine incarnations of the Doctor have demonstrated, these limitations are shared by Time Lords as well as humans.

While the regeneration of Time Lords has a number of similarities with the Buddhist concept of reincarnation, there are important differences that must be acknowledged. For example, the average sentient being does not recall its previous lives, while a Time Lord apparently retains all memories of its previous regenerations. In Buddhism only special beings (such as the Dalai Lama) retain some memory of previous lives. Another difference is that Time Lords are apparently always reborn into humanoid forms rather than as other kinds of sentient beings (such as animals). In contrast, there are six realms of cyclic existence in Buddhism: the higher realms of the gods, demigods and humans, and the lower realms of the animals, hungry ghosts and hell beings. The realm into which one is reborn is completely governed by one's accumulated karma. Virtuous karma leads to higher rebirths, while negative karma leads to lower rebirths.

But while the Doctor might always be reborn into a high realm, according to Buddhism even these have suffering and afflictions. For example, the gods and demigods fight amongst themselves, and must deal with the knowledge that they have finite lifespans. Others around the Doctor have suffered as humans/humanoids, and even animals (such as the pig-men of 'Daleks in Manhattan/Evolution of the Daleks' [2007]). Tsong-kha-pa describes a variety of hell realms, such as the Eight Great Hot Hells. In the Reviving Hell, beings attack each other with various weapons until they fall to the ground, only to be revived and fight anew, therefore experiencing 'measureless suffering'.[25] This bears some similarity to the fate of Jack Harkness in 'Utopia'. In the Unrelenting Hell, beings are incinerated by engulfing flames, similar to Dalek Caan's experience in the Time War: 'I flew into the wild and fire. I danced and died a thousand times' ('The Stolen Earth'). The Master's painful and unstable regeneration in 'The End of Time, Part 1' (2009) is reminiscent of the Hungry Ghosts realm, where beings are tortured with constant hunger and thirst. Echoes of many of the Buddhist cyclical realms of existence can be seen in the Tennant years.

'The Waters of Mars' and 'The End of Time' as Buddhist Texts

David Tennant's last three episodes – 'The Waters of Mars' (2009) and 'The End of Time (Parts 1 and 2)' (2009/10) – continue to illustrate the Doctor's vain fight against the laws of karma and the inexorable role of suffering in samsara. In 'The Waters of Mars', the Doctor is unnerved to discover that he has arrived at 'Bowie Base One' on Mars, on the day that it is to be destroyed. He apologises to mission leader Adelaide Brooke that he cannot save them, because of the important part their deaths play in the future of human space exploration. As the Doctor explains, 'Your death creates the future'. This is clearly an illustration of dependent origination, of the interconnectedness of all events. Later in the episode, the Doctor falls victim to the affliction of pride, and declares that he has power over the laws of time (over the laws of karma, as it were), and safely transports three members of the crew, including Adelaide, to Earth. Adelaide is concerned that the resulting changes in history will lead to changes in the future of humanity. She therefore takes matters into her own hands, committing suicide and returning the timeline to normal. The Doctor realises the error of his pride, later admitting to Wilf that without travelling companions to be his voice of reason he had become reckless and arrogant, leading to actions with dire consequences ('The End of Time, Part 1'). 'The Waters of Mars' ends with a vision of Ood Sigma. 'Is this it? My death? Is it time?' the Doctor asks. He enters the TARDIS and ignores the cloister bell, firmly stating to the universe (and himself) 'No' before leaving.

The lesson of Adelaide's death is similar to the Buddhist story of the Shakya clan. When Prince Virudhaka threatens to slaughter all of Buddha's clan, Mugiputra appeals to Buddha to save them, but Buddha notes that it is their karma to die, so nothing can stop their deaths. Undaunted, Mugiputra attempts to hide the Shakyas in various places (such as in the Buddha's begging bowl) but in the end they are all killed.[26] The Doctor fails to learn this lesson from Adelaide's death, and instead of answering the Ood's summons embarks on an undetermined number of adventures before finally arriving on the Ood planet, explaining 'Last time I was here you said my song would be ending soon and I'm in no hurry for that'.[27]

If he knows he will regenerate, why does the Doctor fear death? In a conversation with Wilf, the Doctor explains the specific suffering of a Time Lord: 'I can still die. If I'm killed before regenerating, then I'm dead. Even then, even if I change, it feels like dying. Everything I am dies. Some new man goes sauntering away, and I'm dead' ('The End of Time, Part 1'). This reflects Rose's relief in 'Journey's End' when the Doctor is shot by a Dalek and redirects his regeneration energy into his severed hand: 'You're still you?' Wilf later tries giving a gun to the Doctor, begging him to use it on the Master. The Doctor refuses, explaining that such violence is what set the Master on the negative path. 'It's not like I'm an innocent', the Doctor admits. 'I've taken lives. I got worse – I got clever ... Sometimes I think the Time Lord lives too long' ('The End of Time, Part 2'). Here the Doctor acknowledges his karma as well as the pervasive suffering in his cycle of regeneration.

In the Gallifrey scenes we observe the depths of the Time Lords' suffering and slavery to their afflictions (especially attachment and pride). The seer declares that their species is 'Ending, ending, ending', to which a female council member sagely declares 'Perhaps it is time'. She notes that in the heart of the Time War 'millions die every second, lost in blood lust and insanity, with time itself resurrecting them, to find new ways of dying over and over and over again. A travesty of life.' While this seems to parallel the Resurrecting Hell referenced earlier, it can also parallel what is called the Occasional Hells, special realms of untold suffering created by the individual karma of one or more beings.[28] Rather than responding with compassion for these suffering beings (and acknowledging the inescapable nature of death), Lord Rassilon kills the council member and declares 'I will not die! Do you hear me? A billion years of Time Lord history riding on our backs. I will not let this perish. I will not!' ('The End of Time, Part 2'). Instead, he and the council doom the Master to uncounted years of physical and mental torment as they implant the drumbeat signal in his mind and set into motion their plan to escape the Time War by destroying all of reality: 'We will ascend to become creatures of consciousness alone. Free of these bodies. Free of time, and cause and effect, while creation itself ceases to be' ('The End of Time, Part 2'). While Lord Rassilon might believe he can outwit the law of cause and effect, he is dead wrong, because he cannot escape his karma. His torture of the Master has led to a chain of dependent origination that gives birth to a specific event, and in the end the Master and the Doctor send the Time Lords back to their hell realm inside the locked Time War. It is also made clear why the Doctor had brought about the end of his home planet – it was a compassionate decision made in order to save not only the universe, but to save the Time Lords from their own delusions and propensity for accumulating negative karma.

But again, we are reminded that the Doctor, despite his wisdom and compassion, is not a buddha. After defeating the Time Lords, he falsely feels that he has cheated death, only to hear the prophesied four knocks from the Lord of Death. In reality, it is Wilf, who has locked himself in the Immortality Gate in an attempt to save an innocent technician. In order to save Wilf from a lethal dose of radiation, the Doctor must sacrifice his own life (his current incarnation), which he does not initially do without first succumbing to his afflictions. Wilf is willing to die in order to save the Doctor, noting that he is an old man who has lived a long life. The Doctor agrees, pridefully proclaiming that he is capable of doing so much more than he has been able to do in the time he has been allotted. Releasing his anger in a scream, he finally admits that he has lived too long, and calmly meets his fate. But even in this final action, the Doctor still clings to his body and his life until the very last second, travelling across the universe to see some of his companions one last time and affecting their lives in some final way (for example, saving Martha and Mickey from a Sontaran warrior and Sarah Jane's son from a speeding car). After seeing Rose one last time, the pain overtakes him – the suffering of suffering, the suffering of death – and Ood Sigma appears. 'This song is ending, but the story never ends', he sagely explains, as the Doctor walks back to the TARDIS, alone. This life ends, but the cycle of samsara continues, and the Doctor begins to regenerate. However, he is still a slave to his afflictions, and with his final breath as the tenth incarnation cries 'I don't want to go' before screaming in the pain of birth. Thus in these last three episodes we not only witness many examples of the three types of suffering and the eight types of suffering, but also the six types of suffering: the faults of uncertainty, insatiability, repeatedly casting off bodies, being reborn, moving between the realms of existence and of having no companions.[29]

Conclusion

In his commentary to Tsong-kha-pa's 'The Source of All My Good' Pabongka Rinpoche explains:

> The nature of all pleasant things in the circle of life is that, no matter how much we get, and no matter how much we enjoy what we get, we never feel as though we've had enough. It only makes us want more, it only increases our desire. And this then delivers to us a whole variety of unbearable pain.[30]

Our bodies, our experiences, our loves, all arise from causes and conditions and are therefore temporary. Death comes whether we want it to or not, when we have exhausted all the projecting karma from our previous lives (be it positive or negative), or when we have exhausted all the positive karma that allows us to have the necessities of life (such as food and shelter). In the case of the Tenth Doctor it is these plus the third cause of death – a 'failure to avoid danger' – that leads to his regeneration.[31] The Tennant years not only illustrate the inevitability of death, and the suffering that comes with rejecting this truth, but also give the Doctor – in his very first adventure – examples of the peace that comes with an acceptance of death. In 'New Earth', Cassandra comes to accept her fate, after taking over the dying body of Chip, her devoted assistant: 'It is indeed time to die.' Similarly in the same episode, the Face of Boe tells the Doctor that he is dying of the incurable disease of death, and in 'Gridlock' old age is finally taking him after millions of years of life. If, as has been suggested, the Face of Boe is really Jack Harkness, then the 'man who can't die' finally found peace in the release from cyclical death and rebirth – he found nirvana.

When warned by the Doctor that his improperly resurrected body is unstable, the Master sagely notes 'This body was born out of death. All it can do is die' ('The End of Time, Part 2'). River Song echoes this sentiment in her ending narration to 'Forest of the Dead': 'When you run with the Doctor it feels like it will never end. But however hard you try you can't run forever. Everybody knows that everybody dies, and nobody knows it like the Doctor'. Indeed, this is central to the

lessons of Tsong-kha-pa's *Great Treatise on the Path of Enlightenment*.
It is as Tsong-kha-pa quotes from the *Extensive Sport Sutra*:

You die and pass on to another life, and in so doing

You are forever separated from people who are beautiful and
beloved.

Like a leaf fallen from a tree, or the current of a river,

You will never return and meet them again ...

People go alone, unaccompanied, with no companion –

Powerless because their karma has its effects.[32]

14.

'There never was a Golden Age': *Doctor Who* and the Apocalypse

Andrew Crome

The 'end of the world as we know it' has been a consistent preoccupation in *Doctor Who*. Anyone viewing the constant invasion and destruction of the Home Counties of the Jon Pertwee era or the repeated invasions of Earth during Russell T. Davies's tenure as showrunner in the 2000s would have little difficulty in substantiating the pattern of averted apocalyptic destruction visible in the show. These repeated portrayals of apocalyptic events are fascinating from two points of view. For the religious historian, they present an opportunity to explore the social and political concerns that worked their way out in representations of destruction on the screen. On a more general level, fictional apocalypse offers writers and directors the opportunity to probe the ambiguities and challenges of the apocalyptic form. Science fiction is a particularly fruitful genre for this form of exploration, precisely because it allows programme makers to imagine scenarios in which the world faces the potential of catastrophic destruction, and even to move beyond those points to present a post-apocalyptic landscape in which either utopias or dystopias can be projected.[1]

The mention of utopias should highlight the fact that the apocalypse need not be destructive. 'Apocalypse' simply means a revelation or unveiling, and in Christian thought has been linked with the coming of the Kingdom of God on Earth as often as it has been married to visions of catastrophic destruction. Taken from Revelation 20:1-6, which predicts a thousand year reign of the Saints on Earth, this form of millennialism (named for the Latin 'mille' – thousand) has been controversial throughout Christian history. Despite the passivism of most millennial groups, at times the hope for the coming Kingdom of God has led to violent action to attempt to bring it about.[2] The tension between the implied radicalism of apocalyptic speculation, married to the fact that such speculation can be encouraged by scripture, has led writers, artists and filmmakers to explore the apocalypse themselves – whether the ambiguities of its form, or by using it as a lens through which to view contemporary society. Here I will consider the ways in which *Doctor Who* can be used to explore the contemporary apocalyptic concerns of the time in which it was produced, as well as looking at how it has worked to deconstruct apocalyptic thought, particularly in the Russell T. Davies era.

Apocalypse as Judgement

It is no surprise that the destructive element of apocalyptic thought has been portrayed most often in *Doctor Who*, given its opportunity to quickly communicate ideas of universal danger while also (special effects budget permitting) providing opportunities to portray spectacular scenes of large-scale destruction. The depiction of apocalypse on television presents different challenges to portraying the end of the world on the big screen. Apocalyptic narrative can often be seen to be based around a need for closure, with the apocalypse itself (whether destructive or revelatory) bringing a sense of clearly-defined ending to proceedings. As Frank Kermode argued, in this way all narrative has an inbuilt 'apocalyptic' structure.[3]

This concept works well when applied to the standalone feature film and is well articulated in blockbuster 'mass disaster' movies. These films develop their narratives both through the destruction they depict, and the character/societal development they portray. For example, *Armageddon* (1998) sees a range of dysfunctional characters work together to avert an imminent asteroid collision and subsequently overcome their own neuroses and petty rivalries to experience new hope on an Earth spared from a fiery trial. The same scenario is evident in *Deep Impact* (1998), *The Day After Tomorrow* (2004), and *2012* (2010) as small numbers of human survivors regroup to begin a new and improved version of their now destroyed civilisation. While these films offer some hope for the future, their narratives work as self-contained units that offer a clear sense of resolution. Compared to this, the seriality of television shows such as *Doctor Who* serves to resist closure. When Matt Smith's Eleventh Doctor rips out the final pages of a novel so that 'it doesn't have to end', his actions are perhaps representative of the televisual form as a whole.[4] Indeed, the concept of time travel undermines the potential for each of the Doctor's adventures to offer the final word on the worlds he visits. Even if the Doctor visits a society at the point of catastrophic (and potentially final) judgement, as viewers we remain aware that he can return at any point in its past or future to encounter similarly apocalyptic events. The story is never fully told – so, for example, the seeming closure of 1972's 'The Curse of Peladon' is undermined by the problems highlighted in 1974's 'The Monster of Peladon'. Perhaps because of this, even at natural moments of ending, *Doctor Who* has sought to embrace its lack of narrative closure. The final episode of the 'classic' era of the show, 1989's 'Survival', was thus inherently open: 'There are worlds out there where the sky is burning, where the sea's asleep and the rivers dream ... Come on, Ace, we've got work to do'. The ending of regeneration is therefore immediately followed by the sudden imposition of the openness proclaimed by the emergence of the new incarnation – whether in the cry of 'Geronimo!' in the regeneration from David Tennant's Tenth to Matt Smith's Eleventh Doctor, or in Colin Baker's Sixth Doctor introducing his jarring change from Peter Davison's Fifth – 'Change, my dear. And it seems not a moment too soon!'[5] Even the show's title, posed as a question (Doctor Who?), can be seen to open up the text as an 'endlessly deferred narrative',[6] with the show's transmedia presence (in print and audio) meaning that even the tenures of past Doctors are still, technically, on-going and ever expanding. The constant opening of the narrative might therefore seem to be anti-apocalyptic. However, the form taken by television series as a medium (and *Doctor Who* especially) matches the apocalyptic archetype in a different manner. As Jacques Derrida argued, apocalyptic texts proclaim the possibility of closure while constantly deferring their own ends. The Book of Revelation, for example, can be marked by a number of repeating calls for Christ to 'Come!' a promise which is ultimately unfulfilled at the book's end.[7]

As well as possessing this Derridean apocalyptic structure, many of the stories told within *Doctor Who* have explicitly engaged with scenarios of apocalyptic destruction, toying with the potential of a 'final end'. In biblical apocalypse, this end is often portrayed as a judgement which serves as a theodicy. The sinful are punished while the righteous enjoy God's presence and the perfect justice that was denied to them in their earthly lives. Whereas in the Bible the parousia and final judgement are eagerly anticipated, within cinema the apocalypse is usually seen as a terrible event which requires averting. As John Walliss has pointed out, movies such as *Armageddon, End of Days* (1999) and *Deep Impact* imagine 'endings' that are very different from biblical visions of final judgement, which see a complete transformation of society from a world of injustice and material power to creation restored to the image of God. Such films see the apocalyptic threat (be it aliens, foreign invaders, or asteroids) overcome by the strength of human ingenuity and a restoration of the pre-apocalyptic status quo.[8] Indeed, Conrad Ostwalt has recently pointed to the differences between these secular 'catastrophe' films and the revelatory content of biblical apocalypse to argue that they should not be labelled as 'apocalyptic' at all.[9] Yet while this is an important point, it also tends to overlook the way in which popular film and television can not only reveal the mutation of apocalyptic narrative in popular culture, but can also offer some kind of limited revelatory function – even if, as Walliss has noted, they reveal only the valorisation of the status quo.[10] But popular apocalyptic film and television can also move beyond this template. This is clearest when it comes to environmental catastrophe, recalling the judgement of biblical apocalypse through an explicit moral condemnation of human 'sins' against nature. This is made explicit in *The Day the Earth Stood Still* (2008) when the alien Klaatu arrives from the stars to proclaim humanity's abuse of nature and begins wiping humankind from the planet before relenting when witnessing human love. The abrogation of judgement comes at a cost, as he renders all electrical devices obsolete before returning to space.[11] Environmental apocalypse is a category that can offer up the kind of hope, then, that Walliss finds lacking in modern film. Yet it is the very similarity of environmental warnings to traditional Christian apocalypse (Destruction is coming! Repent before it is too late!) that can potentially mark environmental apocalyptic movements as being as radical, driven, and possibly as dangerous as religiously motivated millenarian groups.[12]

It is exactly these kinds of ambiguities which are explored when *Doctor Who* has come to face environmental apocalypse. Such concerns were high on the agenda during the late 1960s and early 1970s. Books such as Rachel Carson's *Silent Spring* (1962), on the dangers of pesticide use, had been followed by works like Paul Ehlrich's *The Population Bomb* (1968) which posited that human life and the continued high birth rate were unsustainable.[13] The influence of Carson's book was evident in 1964's serial 'Planet of Giants', in which the Doctor and his travelling companions are shrunk to a fraction of their normal size and discover attempts to license a new fertiliser that will prove fatal to all insect life. Similarly, the 1973 story 'The Green Death' has Jon Pertwee's Doctor name-checking three of the four horsemen of the apocalypse as he attempts to deal with giant maggots, the unfortunate by-product of toxic waste: 'You've seen where this efficiency of yours leads. Wholesale pollution of the countryside. Devilish creatures spawned by the filthy by-products of your technology. Men ... men walking around like brainless vegetables. Death! Disease! Destruction!'

The most nuanced examination of the rhetoric of environmental apocalypse is found in Pertwee's 1974 adventure 'Invasion of the Dinosaurs'. The Doctor and Sarah Jane arrive in London to discover an evacuated city plagued by looters (in shots which recall images of nuclear apocalypse)[14] and menaced by the prehistoric reptiles. Their source is revealed to be time experiments conducted by a radical environmental movement, the 'Save Earth' group, who aim to restore the planet to an Edenic purity through the reversal of history.[15] Most members of the group remain unaware of the plan, living out their lives in a capsule they believe to be a spacecraft taking them to a 'new planet' – actually, a prehistoric Earth. Although not the series' finest hour for special effects, the story is a fascinating study of the way in which environmental apocalypse and apocalyptic dynamics work in crisis situations. Sir Charles Grovesnor, the leader of the 'Save Earth' movement, is portrayed as a man whose hopes for humanity have been disappointed. Author of a book entitled *Last Chance for Man*, he has abandoned a belief in progressive change and adopted the concept of apocalyptic cleansing followed by millennial peace: the planet will 'be swept clean and returned to its early innocence'. As the theorist of millennial movements Richard Landes has noted, when apocalyptically-minded reform groups find their hopes for a fundamental change in the world dashed, they can respond in a number of ways. This can include moving from a fundamentally passive, transformative apocalyptic scenario to an active cataclysmic position in which judgement (and the millennium) is brought about by the groups themselves.[16] 'Save Earth' takes exactly this step, as their focus shifts from converting others to their position, to destroying them. 'People on earth were allowed to choose', notes one group member, 'And see what kind of a world they made! Moral degradation, permissiveness, usury, cheating, lying, cruelty!' Destruction is the only option. As they anticipate the cataclysmic judgement that will lead to their millennium, all ties outside of the group become unimportant. Apocalyptic time – the moment of *kairos* – has arrived. Even a series regular, the UNIT Captain Mike Yates, submits to the power of this apocalyptic moment. Holding the Doctor and the Brigadier hostage, Yates reveals that the group's goal of millennial renovation trumps any concern for personal safety. When an incredulous Brigadier asks why Yates seems unconcerned for his own life, he can only reaffirm the importance of the coming, millennial goal: 'I'm not important. The others will get there'.

This same pattern was demonstrated within an explicitly Christian apocalyptic context in 2013's 'The Crimson Horror'. Here the Victorian scientist/preacher Mrs Gillyflower warned her audiences about imminent judgement: 'Will you be found wanting when the End of Days is come, when judgement rains down on us all? Or will you be preserved against the coming apocalypse?' She aimed to destroy the majority of imperfect humanity so as to establish 'the shining city on the hill'; the 'New Jerusalem' in which true perfection was to be achieved: 'My new Adam and Eves will sleep, but for a few months, before stepping out into a golden dawn.' When the Doctor attempts to thwart her, like the 'Save Earth' group, she enters apocalyptic time and accelerates her plan: 'You have forced me to advance the Great Work somewhat, Doctor. But my colossal scheme remains as it was'.

Yet the Doctor does not hold to this sort of apocalyptic logic. His reply to Yates's fervour in 'Invasion of the Dinosaurs' can be taken as representative for the series as a whole. 'There never was a Golden Age', he tells the radicalised UNIT man, a message which echoes throughout the series into its latest episodes, as his slightly less sympathetic reply to Gillyflower in 'The Crimson Horror' shows: 'I'm the Doctor, you're nuts, and I'm going to stop you'.

There is, therefore, always hope for humanity to change. The Doctor thus consistently rejects attempts by outside forces to judge humanity. When Matt Smith's Eleventh Doctor condemned the Shakri for their attempt to wipe out humanity for their transgressions ('Before the closure, there is the tally!'), he therefore declared that human achievements would outweigh sins: 'I will', he claims, 'back humanity against the Shakri every day.'[17] The moment of judgement is always postponed and the possibility of change embraced.

Apocalypse as Destruction

The form of apocalyptic 'judgement' advocated by 'Save Earth' sees an individual or group try to impose their views onto the wider world in an attempt to bring about a utopian vision. This plays into one of the most common apocalyptic scenarios seen in film and television: the attempts of pseudo-messianic figures to dominate the world. Although these individuals are often drawn as little more than cartoon sketches of real dictators, their regular appearance on screen builds on established archetypes of evil. In particular their popularity in the public imagination develops medieval and early modern ideas of the Antichrist as a last world dictator – a construction which also impacted upon portrayals of Louis XIV, Napoleon and Kaiser Wilhelm in popular propaganda. In a more contemporary vein, these figures also play into popular fears of the power of charisma to mislead followers – from the mysticism of George de Maurier's Svengali to the political magnetism displayed by Hitler.

Although often portrayed as 'larger than life' on screen, the actions of these figures have direct comparisons with those of individuals within the real world. In particular, their megalomania corresponds well with that displayed in a range of apocalyptic new religious movements, which seek to bring about a radical change to the world that will be manifested by the revelation and acceptance of their leader as messiah. This is where apocalyptic speculation blends with distinctly millenarian patterns of thought.[18] Plans for 'world domination', which at first glance may appear generic and lacking in motivation, can therefore been seen as a kind of politicised millennial hope.[19] In fiction, figures who pursue world domination therefore demonstrate a kind of catastrophic apocalyptic millennialism, which seeks to purge the world of alterity and restore it in their own image. Even if such plans are motivated by financial gain or political power, they nonetheless represent a powerful form of secularised apocalyptic thinking invested in the logic of millennial thought.[20]

Of course, as a quick glance at the 'super villains' found in graphic novels suggests, such figures also make for highly entertaining adversaries. In this sense, it is no surprise that *Doctor Who* has made explicit use of them. The Daleks' creator Davros is notable in this regard, as is the Doctor's nemesis the Master, who could be relied upon to try and bring about the apocalyptic transformation of the world every six to eight weeks in the early 1970s. In *Doctor Who*, such characters tend to display the kind of zero-sum thinking which serves as an essential part of millenarian logic. As Catherine Wessinger has pointed out in her examinations of millennial movements led by charismatic figures, when such groups face a combination of internal and external challenges they can respond by resorting to destructive violence.[21] Such thinking is found in 1975's 'Genesis of the Daleks', with Davros portrayed as a zealot who initiates the apocalyptic destruction of his own Kaled race in the hope of creating a millennial reign: 'Today, the Kaled race is ended, consumed in a fire of war. But, from its ashes will rise a new race. The supreme creature. The ultimate conqueror of the universe. The Dalek!' Similarly, the plant-obsessed Harrison Chase in 'The Seeds of Doom' (1976) imagines a planet reclaimed by vegetation as producing a nature-based millennium. 'We shall have perfection. The world will be as it should have been from the beginning, a green paradise', he comments, noting that such a world will of course necessitate the destruction of humanity: 'The time has come. Animals have ruled this planet for millions of years. Now it is our turn'. Chase is noteworthy for the liturgical language he employs in describing his love of flora and fauna. His greenhouse becomes 'my green Cathedral', where his flowers are treated to 'the hymn of the plants'.

Alternatively, we could think of the seemingly messianic 'Monarch' who confronts Peter Davison's Fifth Doctor in 'Four to Doomsday' (1982) with a slate of false millennial hopes, only to reveal that he plans to destroy humanity and populate the Earth with his own race, now perfected as machines elevated above the 'flesh time'. The human androids aboard Monarch's ship are convinced they are going to 'Heaven', while Monarch (who believes that he is God and creator of the Universe), specifically codes his mission of destruction as a kind of apocalyptic coming: 'I come to the aid of the Earthlings, to save them from themselves. They're not as intelligent as you. They war amongst themselves. They make more weapons than food and two-thirds of them are starving. It is all a problem of the flesh time. We come to rid them of it'. This sort of millennial thinking, dubbed by Robert J. Lifton 'destroying the world in order to save it', has been all too common in the history of apocalyptic movements, and centres upon the belief that it is only through the flames of destruction that the true millennium (and the chosen ones who will inhabit it) will emerge.[22]

Yet while apocalyptic destruction on film can be seen as the result of megalomania, it can also serve as a way of imagining human responses to the possibility of destruction beyond our control. In this way, apocalyptic films work as a sense-making tool through which the audience comes to terms with the danger of sudden, meaningless destruction. As James Chapman has noted, a number of 1960s episodes of *Doctor Who* dealt with contemporary concerns in sometimes quite obvious allegorical forms.[23] The show's first visit to an alien planet, in 1963's 'The Daleks', examined a society coming to terms with the aftermath of nuclear warfare. The apocalyptic concerns found in 'The Daleks' were expressed in two ways; simultaneously looking backwards to a secure historical past and forwards to an imagined dystopian future. As Nicholas Cull has suggested, much of *Doctor Who*'s classic period recalled the certainties of the Second World War, a trope which served to remind viewers of a united nation and a clearly defined 'evil' against which to fight. In their first episodes, the Daleks are clearly coded in terms which recall Nazi xenophobia and uniformity.[24] At the same time, however, the episodes warn of a society paralysed by the effects of nuclear warfare, and of the potential dangers of ignoring engagement with the enemy.[25] The peaceful Thals, refusing to fight the Daleks, need to be goaded into action by Ian and the Doctor who convince them of the necessity of engaging a totalitarian enemy.

The 1964 story, 'The Dalek Invasion of Earth', neatly reiterates this idea by focusing upon a twenty-second-century Earth under the control of Daleks. Here the Daleks as Nazis allegory is played out at its clearest. The shots of human slaves pulling large carts into tunnels are almost shot-for-shot recreations of the V2 slave labour complex at Mittelwerk. Similarly, the image of Daleks, sucker arms raised, rolling past landmarks of British democracy (including the Houses of Parliament and Cenotaph) invoke the 'what-if' scenario of Nazi invasion.[26] Perhaps most obviously, one of the final scenes of the serial finds a Dalek 'commandant' calling for the 'extermination of all humans'; a plan another Dalek describes as the 'final solution' while a third chants 'Kill! Kill! Kill!' repeatedly. Yet there is more subtlety in the portrayal of the Daleks than might be imagined. Although often seen in later stories as instituting an all-conquering blitzkrieg against their enemies, here they employ subtlety and subterfuge to overcome Earth, using meteorites infused with plague bacteria to wipe out humanity. 'Daleks were up in the sky just waiting for the Earth to get weaker', recalls the human resistance fighter Craddock. 'Whole continents were wiped out. Asia, Africa, South America. They used to say the Earth had a smell of death about it.' Unlike the Thals in the first story, humanity was not reluctant to fight for the planet. Yet 'Dalek Invasion' plays on fears that this will to fight might be undermined by enemy conspiracies – whether through warfare from a distance, or brainwashing. The zombie-like Robomen who serve the Daleks are human beings with their humanity removed – an operation which leaves them as the proxy agents of the invaders. They are eventually driven insane by their inability to reconcile their human and Dalek identities. This fear of infiltration and undermining of the self is a key part of conspiratorial apocalyptic scenarios, and played an important role in both popular Cold War propaganda and general concerns over the possibility of 'turning'. The early Dalek stories therefore serve as a window into the apocalyptic fears of the sixties, in which concerns about the nation's past merged with contemporary worries about the loss of identity and threat of infiltration to provide a terrifying post-apocalyptic vision.

Later Dalek stories emphasise the importance of negotiation and the avoidance of violence as ways in which to escape the dystopian apocalypse. 'Day of the Daleks' (1972) sees Jon Pertwee's Doctor face a band of rebels from a Dalek-occupied future, attempting to stop humanity's descent into war by travelling back in time and assassinating Sir Reginald Styles, the diplomat they hold responsible for bombing a UNIT peace conference. The realisation that the group themselves were responsible for the bombing leads them to break the temporal paradox, and thus prevents the Dalek invasion from ever happening. 'Genesis of the Daleks', meanwhile, highlights the regressive and futile nature of nuclear war, as both Kaleds and Thals are reduced to using more and more basic technology as resources are consumed. Similarly, 1978's 'Destiny of the Daleks' dealt with the zero-sum game of computerised total war, as both the Daleks and the Movelleans found themselves locked into a logical stalemate in a long-running war.

The destructive apocalyptic thinking of the Daleks therefore provides a way in which *Doctor Who* was able to deal with contemporary apocalyptic concerns, albeit in allegorised forms. Such destruction also opens up opportunities to think about the possibility of escape from apocalypse. In 1965's 'The Ark', the TARDIS arrives on a ship travelling to the planet Refusis after the Earth had been devastated by solar flares. The Ark contains the entire human population in miniaturised form, overseen by a select number of human 'Guardians'. They travel along with the Monoids, one-eyed alien 'servants' who are dismissed as primitives. The first two episodes of the serial play out in a fairly unsurprising fashion as the travellers overcome the suspicion of the Guardians, particularly security chief Zentos who believes them to be 'agents of the intelligences that inhabit Refusis'. While these suspicions are overcome, in the serial's final two episodes they are shown not to have been unfounded. Here the TARDIS travels 700 years to a future in which the Monoids have staged a revolt and enslaved the Guardians – whom they plan to destroy before they can land on Refusis, claiming the planet as a new Monoid home world. Aired in the same year as the passing of the Race Relations Act, 'The Ark' can be viewed as an allegory for British racial concerns, with the Doctor imploring different groups to get along. The humans are thus criticised for their intolerance. The Monoids 'were treated like slaves. Is it any wonder that when they got the chance, they repaid you in kind?' The story's resolution might therefore be read through an optimistic lens in which the post-apocalyptic exodus allows for the construction of a new, egalitarian society on Refusis. Yet elements of the story undermine the neatness of this resolution, suggesting the difficulty of integration of different groups within society. While the Doctor supports the mixing of cultures, the Monoids scornfully note that their rebellion was facilitated by the overly-trusting nature of the Guardians: 'They were a simple people. They actually encouraged the research that led to our voice box and heat rod. They were totally unprepared for the conflict when it came.' Refusis is revealed to be populated by invisible creatures who have lost physical form – allowing them to move unseen amongst the populace. The ending of 'The Ark' suggests that it is this secret presence that will be required to keep Humans and Monoids from attacking one another. The invisible creatures, passing unnoticed among both groups, will keep watch, and neither Humans nor Monoids will have 'any future on Refusis' should they show signs of intolerance. The peace will therefore be kept not by genuine understanding, but by threats of retribution – a rather disturbing implication in terms of British race relations.

Like 'The Ark', stories which focus on escaping apocalyptic destruction contain an inherent tension between the Doctor's approval of the human race's ability to survive and the likelihood of such survivor societies to be strictly hierarchical and discriminatory.[27] It is often forgotten that when Tom Baker's Fourth Doctor praises humanity's ability to survive in 'The Ark in Space' (*'Homo sapiens. What an inventive, invincible species ... All colours, all creeds, all differences finally forgotten'*), the society he discovers is far from being either inclusive or inventive. Instead, it is based on hierarchy, with scorn expressed for those seen as 'genetically inferior' (who had, it is revealed, been left to perish on Earth). Post-apocalyptic survival therefore raises questions which can destabilise the Doctor's position as a champion of humanity. By revealing tensions within the post-apocalyptic scenarios portrayed in *Doctor Who*, such stories also hint at concerns within their societies as a whole. Indeed, these tensions have been fruitfully explored and exploited in the revived series to undermine the very idea of apocalypse – either as a revelation, or as a destructive force.

The Russell T. Davies Years: Apocalyptic Inversion?

The revival of *Doctor Who* in 2005 represented an important shift in the way in which the series was made. As Matt Hills has noted, the show's identity was heavily tied into Russell T. Davies's role as showrunner, a fact which identified *Doctor Who*, for the first time, as *auteur* television.[28] As a result of this, the 2005-2010 'Russell T. Davies era' should not be viewed in isolation from Davies's other works, which include a recurring fascination with issues of sexual identity and religion.[29] In contrast to his successor Steven Moffat, Davies actively focused his scripts on apocalyptic scenarios which presented threats to contemporary Earth.[30] It is perhaps unsurprising, then, to find that Davies used his time on *Doctor Who* to explore and actively critique the structures of apocalyptic thought. His interest in the subject is betrayed not only by his episode titles ('The End of the World', 'Doomsday', 'The End of Time') but through the thematic unity of his series as a whole. As Elizabeth Rosen has noted, contemporary 'popular' cinema has used postmodern thought to 'deconstruct the simplistically binary traditional narrative to show that the world, even one which seems near some catastrophic ending, is a far more morally complex one than traditional apocalypse makes it out to be'.[31] The same kind of deconstruction of apocalypse is visible in Davies's *Who*, although his work goes beyond merely highlighting the ambiguities present in apocalypse to serve as a bleak critique of all apocalyptic visions.

At times, this can be straightforward. In 'The End of the World' (2005), Christopher Eccleston's Ninth Doctor ponders the human obsession with catastrophic endings: 'You lot, you spend all your time thinking about dying, like you're gonna get killed by eggs, or beef, or global warming, or asteroids. But you never take the time to imagine the impossible – like maybe you survive.' At other times, however, the deconstruction is more subtle. The villains the Doctor confronted during Davies's tenure were often motivated by distinctly apocalyptic desires. The Dalek Emperor faced by the Ninth Doctor at the end of the 2005 series therefore spoke in explicitly millennial language: 'Purify the Earth with fire. The planet will become my temple and we shall rise. This will be our paradise ... This is perfection. I have created heaven on earth!' Similarly, the Master's plan to forge an Empire lasting 'a hundred trillion years' in 2007's 'The Sound of Drums/Last of the Time Lords' parodies apocalyptic language and millennial hopes. The Master's own apocalyptic destruction is partly motivated by his fascination with the Doctor's role in destroying Gallifrey ('What did it feel like though? Two almighty civilisations, burning ... You must have been like God'). The Master therefore appropriates biblical language of creation for his own vision, reversing its meaning to show that apocalypse brings not hope, but only destruction: 'So it came to pass that the human race fell and the Earth was no more. And I looked down on my new dominion as master of all, and I thought it good.'

When the Doctor faces the Daleks again in the finale to the 2008 series, he discovers even clearer apocalyptic thinking. The returning Davros is portrayed as a millenarian radical: creating a reality bomb that will destroy all non-Dalek life. This is seen as the prophetic vindication of the Dalek race. Davros, describing himself as 'Lord and Creator' of the Daleks, is accompanied by his prophet, Dalek Caan: a Dalek that has been granted the ability to think as an individual, driven mad after rescuing Davros from the Time War. For other Daleks, Caan serves as a literal representation of Rudolf Otto's 'mysterium tremendum et fascinans' – the idea that the divine terrifies us as something wholly 'other', while simultaneously holding an inherent fascination and attraction to us. While Daleks describe Caan as the 'abomination' (a term with its own apocalyptic resonance),[32] at the same time they reveal a latent faith in his prophecies – rather than destroying the potentially destabilising presence that Caan represents, they revere him, placing him on a separate, backlit platform from which he prophesies.[33] Davros, in accepting Caan's prophecy of the Doctor's arrival on the Dalek mothership, believes that all history is coalescing around a crucial apocalyptic moment in which the Dalek race will be vindicated. When he learns that the Doctor's former companion Sarah Jane Smith is also present, just as she was in 'Genesis of the Daleks', he uses it to affirm his belief that history is dealing with its narrative loose ends. The historical process is characterised as being, at one and the same time, linear and circular – a narrative that must be completed before the millennial reign can begin; a dualistic battle between good and evil in which the apocalypse must mirror the creation myth. 'This was meant to be' he extols, 'You were there, on Skaro, at the very beginning of my creation ... The prophecy unfolds'. Finally, in Davies's last episodes, the 2009-10 'The End of Time', the returning Time Lords are found seeking an apocalyptic dissolution of all materiality to find spiritual fulfilment: 'The End of Time will come ... [and] we will ascend! To become creatures of consciousness alone. Free from these bodies, free from time and cause and effect.'

By linking the Doctor's enemies to millenarian hopes and explicitly biblical language, Davies serves to undermine the hope of apocalypse for change.[34] Peter Y. Paik has recently criticised postmodern portrayals of the apocalypse in science fiction for a fascination with destruction combined with an 'inability to imagine change on the more modest scale of history'.[35] For Davies, however, this appears to be precisely the point. It is only the Doctor's enemies who can imagine fundamental change to the status quo on a world historical level. Such change, however, is inherently counter-productive – its attempts to create the millennial dream inevitably descend into dystopian nightmares. This is a resoundingly bleak vision of the future, and the potential for human change and improvement. Indeed, beneath the celebration of humanity which often appears on the surface of Davies's scripts lies a dark vision of the human race which serves to constantly undermine the Doctor's positive assessment. In 2007's 'Utopia', for example, the Tenth Doctor, can praise 'The fundamental human. End of the universe, here you are!' Yet such assumptions are undermined in the next episodes, in which the Master unleashes his apocalyptic vision through the vicious Toclafane – those same humans, reduced from their 'fundamental shape' to shrivelled heads in spheres, killing for sport. The human race, the Master notes sardonically, are the 'greatest monsters of 'em all'. The journey to 'Utopia' revealed only a world of 'Furnaces burning. The last of humanity screaming at the dark'. When the Master's wife reveals her impressions of Utopia, we find the abandonment of all millennial hope: 'Dying, everything dying. The whole of creation was falling apart and I thought ... there's no point, no point to anything ... not ever ... There was no solution. Just the dark and the cold.' One wonders if, in Davies's tenure, the Doctor would have been as confident as he was in the Moffat-era 'Power of Three', when telling the Shakri that humanity's achievements outweighed their sins.[36]

This idea is constantly reinforced in Davies's work. In 2008's 'Turn Left', which imagines the Earth without the Doctor's protection, we find that Britain's response to apocalyptic events is not to transform for the better, but to embrace military rule and send immigrants to concentration camps. As apocalyptic events pile up without the Doctor to prevent them (the draining of the Thames; nuclear destruction of London; toxic smog) Britain's population is shown to have 'apocalypse fatigue'. The appearance of alien spacecraft over America, seen in a news report, generates only disinterested resignation: 'Aliens...'; 'Yeah'. When the final apocalyptic events unfold and the stars begin to vanish from the sky, we realise that the end will not be (indeed, cannot be) averted without the Doctor.

Of course, the bleak world of 'Turn Left' is precisely our world – the world without the Doctor. We therefore face apocalypse without the prospect of positive transformation or salvation. Other than the descent into dystopia, there is only one option. This, as the voiceover informs us in the pre-credits sequence to 'The End of Time', is simple: 'It is said in the final days of planet Earth, everybody had bad dreams ... Every single one of those people had dreamt of the terrible things to come, but they had forgotten. Because they must. They forgot their nightmares of fire and war and insanity. They forgot.' For Davies, the dreams of those who believe in a coming apocalypse are little more than nightmares of 'fire, war and insanity'. If these events actually do come to pass, it is likely they will lead not to change but our destruction. The only answer is, even as we are on the edge of destruction, to turn away, to change our focus – to forget.

Conclusion

This chapter has traced some of the ways in which apocalyptic thought can be examined through a long-running science-fiction show such as *Doctor Who*. Obviously, as the product of a large number of writers, directors and producers over a long period of time, it is impossible to claim that *Doctor Who* presents any one image of apocalypse. Yet from the limited analysis presented here, we have seen some ways in which the show serves as a useful tool for examining the contemporary concerns of the time when it was produced. It also provides examples of distinct types of apocalyptic thinking which can have practical applications. Such examples can be particularly useful when teaching British religious history, as well as serving to highlight some of the essential ambiguities and contradictions which drive apocalyptic thought. Thus the uneven societies imagined by those who escape the final end, the contradictions in visions of environmental apocalypse, or even the ironies and parodies of post-modern apocalypse in more recent episodes all find expression in the show. In its structure and focus on universal threats, *Doctor Who* will always return to the pressing danger of apocalyptic annihilation. It remains to be seen what form this will take in the future. Even if, one day, *Doctor Who* on television again faces its own cancellation, like the Doctor ripping the final page from the novel so that 'it doesn't have to end', we can be sure that in print, audio and online, the Doctor will continue to face (and defer) the apocalypse. The Doctor's refrain thus echoes through *Doctor Who*'s serial and expanding transmedia form: 'I hate endings!'

15.

'Qui Quae Quod': *Doctor Who* and the History of Magic

Alexander Cummins

The Doctor is a mercurial figure, a trickster, a protector, a guide and a keeper of secrets. He is a scientist, an explorer, a *bon vivant* and a psychopomp leading us through hell. He is a self-identifying future Merlin and Space Gandalf. He is an old wise man, a resurrected king, a lord of time. The Doctor brings transformation, both for events and people. He nurtures the best and challenges the worst in us. He wields a magic wand that opens doors, fixes things and casts his spells. Recent arcs of the rebooted series have even directly addressed the mythic dimensions of the Doctor's reputation within the multiverse of the series. He is identified as an archetypal Great Wizard in countless stories and legends of various cultures across his cosmos. It has even been hinted he may be the very reason we have wizard myths in the first place ….

But what of the Doctor's encounters with magic? What is even meant by the term 'magic'? This chapter will explore the depiction of occult philosophy and magical practice in *Doctor Who*, analysing how magic has been understood throughout the series, and approaching some of the occult themes of its stories in terms of their magical and historical contexts. In showing us portrayals of magic across time, the Doctor rends the veils between worlds. He summons encounters with historical constructions of realities very different from our own, with wholly differing perspectives on nature, time and our place in the universe. These are the realities of astrologers and wizards, of demons and night-hags. This chapter will offer a whistle-stop tour of the historical magics that make up the sorceries and witchcrafts of the Doctor's cosmos, in order to better understand those of our own history.

Magic has always been a matter of practical religion. In recognising the existence and agency of non-human intelligences and energetic principles, magical activity has concerned itself with the best ways to attract, propitiate, question, command and collaborate with monotheist and polytheist gods, as well as hosts of demons, angels and various spirits; including fairies, elementals and the ghosts of the dead. In considering the reality and affective power of these agents – not to mention the human soul – conceptions of nature and the natural can be considered rather more broadly in these pre-modern times than in the current secular materialist West. There is also a function of othering to be considered in relation to the theology of magic. The word 'magic' comes to us from the Greek adoption of *magos* from the Old Persian *maguŝ* or *magush*, referring originally to a member of a priestly caste. It has therefore always had connections with both religious rites and the work of foreigners, that which is exotic: the Other. To speak broadly, many societies frequently tend towards the attitude that '*we* practice religion, *they* do magic'. A further othering occurs in more modern positivist dismissals of the 'primitive' belief in magic, deliberately contrasted to the 'enlightened' practice of science.

This chapter focuses on operative magical activity in *Doctor Who* to introduce and analyse applications of occult philosophy and ritual magic. It will use a few depictions of magic as windows and doorways into our history, scrying mirrors and interstitial vortices allowing us to step into our own past and engage with the wonders and terrors of historical magic.

Don't wander off.

The End of Devils

Our investigation begins with one of the earliest *Doctor Who* stories to directly address occult themes: 'The Dæmons' (1971). The first idea associated with magic is one of the magical properties of time itself: the Age of Aquarius. This New Age re-popularisation of far older ideas refers to an astrological phenomenon known as the precession of the equinoxes, and an accompanying notion of the astrological zeitgeist of a period. Precession is the result of the way the band of the zodiac that encompasses the earth falls slightly short of a full revolution each year, meaning that eventually the year should start and end in a different zodiacal sign. So the Aquarian part of the age refers to the 'slipping back' of the end of the year from the sign of

Pisces to Aquarius. The human significance of this comes from the notion that the sign governing a period of time imparts some special qualities to the character and experience of that time. Just as the wax and wane of the planets through the sky was (and, in many circles, still is) thought to herald particular influences on earth or encourage proclivities to particular personality traits at birth, so too did the zodiacal sign of the current Age affect the characters of us all. There was a certain destiny, a particular feel, to a period of time.

Beyond associations with the occult, magic itself is treated by the Third Doctor as the non-scientific, the unnatural, the freakish, the *inexplicable*. This is the prevalent modern description, even definition, of magic – as a thing beyond or in direct contradiction with the established laws of physics – a definition present in the very turn of phrase 'as if by magic'. And yet the magic in this story – waves of cold and heat, shrinking and growing, howling winds, mind control, invisible walls of protection, even the summoning of horned otherworldly beings capable of destroying the planet – is merely the advanced technology of the Dæmons, alien visitors from the planet Dæmos. It is a *psychic* technology but, sticking to his definition of magic as the absence of science, the Third Doctor is very clear: psychokinetic energy is not magic.

So what does magic in 'The Dæmons' look like? We see some evidence of the Master's magic ritual, yet clearly this is more entertaining than historical. There are no chalked circles of divine names, popular in the medieval and early modern grimoires (that is, magical handbooks) often attributed to semi-mythical wise men, such as King Solomon or (particularly in Spanish-speaking regions) St Cyprian. There are no astrological forces drawn down for their particular influence, as studied and developed by Italian magician Marsilio Ficino or German occult philosopher Heinrich Cornelius Agrippa. There is no Renaissance Christian Cabala, such as that of Giovanni Pico della Mirandola, for climbing the cosmological ladder of Jacob up the Great Chain of Being to become empowered by Almighty God. Instead, hooded figures in black robes swear obedience to a cultic leader and collectively chant. However, there are a few features that can be picked out from a fictional dramatisation which reflect genuine occult heritages.

The text on the Master's robe (reading, rather unimaginatively, 'MASTER') is in the magical alphabet known as Theban, named after Honorius of Thebes. This sometimes argued to be the same Honorius who is said to have written the *Sworn Book of Honorius* (a popular

grimoire appearing in the early thirteenth century) and to have been
the son of the fourth-century CE Greek mathematician, Euclid.[1] The
general use of special and specifically magical letters and words has
an established occult importance. Agrippa explains in his *Three Books
of Occult Philosophy* (originally published in Latin in Antwerp in 1531;
with the first English version appearing in 1651) that such characters
are considered 'nothing else than certain unknowable letters and
writings, preserving the secrets of the Gods, and names of spirits
from the use and reading of prophane men, which the Ancients
called Hyeroglyphicall [sic], or sacred letters, because devoted to the
secrets of the Gods only'.[2] The older the letters, the more powerful
the magic.

The use of nonsense or 'barbarous' words results from a similarly
established tradition in ritual magic. Usually considered the ancient
and venerable names of God, such untranslated and untranslatable
occult words and phrases have formed a central feature of the practice
of magic throughout the ages. Significantly, in the case of barbarous
words, the semantic meaning is not the important part. As Agrippa
puts it, 'sacred words have not their power in magical operations,
from themselves, as they are words, but from the occult divine
powers working by them in the minds of those who by faith adhere
to them'.[3] In other words, using old words that were considered
magical was enough for early modern magicians: the force of belief
was more important than accurate translations. In this case, one of
the Master's ritual incantations is merely 'Mary had a little lamb'
backwards. It is tempting to see this as a pun on the etymological
roots of the term 'barbarous' itself.

The ritual magic of the Master contains fragments of genuine
occult paraphernalia – a magical alphabet, barbarous words, mottos[4]
and statements of intent – as well as some ritual activity, such as the
consecration of his altar with water and salt. Overall, however, it can
be said to owe rather more to the works of pulp horror writer Dennis
Wheatley than the Hermetic Order of the Golden Dawn or any other
established magical tradition. We are not expecting the story itself to
privilege historical accuracy over dramatic plotting.

One of the main characterisations of magic in 'The Dæmons' is
that of deceit, of fraudulent tricks: from a remote-controlled vehicle
to the Master's promises to the villagers of their hearts' desires. The
Doctor must even pose as the Great Wizard Qui Quae Quod in order
to win over the villagers poised to burn him at the stake, perhaps
reflecting a notion that it takes a magician to catch a magician. Such

trickery for noble ends is far from unusual behaviour for the Doctor (we may recall River Song's Rule One: 'The Doctor lies'), but as a man of science and lover of truth the Third Doctor immediately discards this ruse to come clean with the people of Devil's End. Truth triumphs over lies, as honest science and compassion overcomes deceitful magic and the desire for power.

Nevertheless, we also have the figure of Miss Hawthorne, arguing for a slightly more nuanced approach to magic. Not only is she an effective magician – countering attacks by aerial spirits and breaking the mind control over a police constable – she also makes accurate predictions of potential doom from her runes and talisman of Mercury. Her magic is truthful as it relates to her worldview and understanding of events. Miss Hawthorne also presents a real challenge to the Third Doctor's division of science and magic. While he initially describes what has occurred as the focused raising and direction of 'a tremendous charge of psychokinetic energy' created by a group of humans and channelled for the nefarious purposes of the Master, Hawthorne points out that, by her standards, 'that *is* magic – that's precisely what black magic is.' There is no fundamental distinction between the Doctor's 'scientific' description of such psychic phenomena and Miss Hawthorne's operative magic. The Doctor however remains adamant that this does not count as magic. Hawthorne attempts to clarify: 'Are you trying to tell me that the invocations, the rituals, even the sabbat itself are just so much window dressing?' The Doctor is forced to admit that such ritual techniques and observances are indeed 'essential to generate and control the psionic forces, and to control the Daemon himself'.

Something Miss Hawthorne calls magic and the Doctor calls a 'secret science' can affect tangible change in the material world, bring forth an alien agent of destruction, and harness the psychic energy of groups of people focusing on a common effect. The issue begins to appear to be one of nomenclature rather than ontology.

Old Gods, New Blood

The conflict between honest science and dishonest magic is also played out in 'The Masque of Mandragora' (1976). In this story, a usurped young prince fights an evil astrologer and secret priest of an old pagan deity, Demnos. The astrologer Hieronymous predicts deaths and, for good measure, engages in a courtly bit of poisoning, while the good prince Giuliano speaks hopefully of the new science.

Not only is this a struggle between a benevolent new rationalism and an older bloodthirsty paganism, but there is an additional issue of fraudulence when it is taken into account that the being Hieronymous worships as 'Demnos' is in fact the sentient energy-form, the Mandragora Helix. In contrast, in 'The Stones of Blood' (1978), we have an ancient alien who is actually the Celtic deity, the Cailleach: she has existed for the past five thousand years and come to be known as the goddess, rather than assuming the identity of an already formed deity. This alien is still in a disguise of sorts, however, pretending to be human as a fugitive from an alien justice system. This story is also a return to the theme of twentieth-century occultism begun in 'The Dæmons', this time moving away from the summoning of demons (or, more accurately, a Dæmon), and instead focusing on blood sacrifice and modern druidry.

The rites performed by the druids of 'Stones' offer an interesting example of a principle of imperative compulsion used to distinguish between religion and magic, between prayer and spell. The blood sacrifices are offerings to a goddess, a devotional form of worship of an aspect of the divine, rather than a magical compelling of divine forces to affect and achieve the magic-users' intent. Indeed, chief druid de Vries insists the Cailleach has demanded this sacrifice of them – the congregation are serving, the goddess is the one giving the orders. As in 'The Masque of Mandragora', the bloodthirsty pagan magic is in fact powered by alien science, in this case the globulin-hungry physiology of silicon-based life forms, the Ogri.

The Fourth Doctor also expresses doubts about magic, but makes appeals to historical rather than scientific truth. Rather than attack a magical worldview that includes the ability to summon and direct occult forces, the attack is made on the purported history of 'Druidic lore': 'Well, I mean there's so little of it that's historically reliable, is there? The odd mention in Julius Caesar, Tacitus, no great detail. I always thought that Druidism was founded by John Aubrey in the seventeenth century as a joke. He had a great sense of humour, John Aubrey'.

John Aubrey (1626-1697) is mostly known as a seventeenth-century English antiquarian and biographer, although he also carried out extensive work finding and cataloguing features of English natural history and archaeology. Along with writing about the days and ways of such people as famed astrologer William Lilly, Aubrey was instrumental in conducting studies of Stonehenge and several other megalithic monument sites, eventually collected into the *Monumenta Britannica*. It has been judged that 'in its descriptions and surveys of ancient sites across Britain, many of which have since disappeared or been significantly altered, the *Monumenta Britannica* remains the foundation text of modern archaeology.'[5] In particular, one of his studies, *Templa Druidum* – commissioned by Charles II and contained in *Monumenta* – was a work documenting various ancient archaeological sites as ancient places of druidic worship and magic. It is from this source, written thousands of years after the supposed fact, that the rites and beliefs of the ancient druids began to be revived. Describing this revival as a 'renaissance', Philip Carr-Gomm, the current Chief of the Order of Bards, Ovates and Druids, considers that 'in many ways John Aubrey can be seen as the real founder of the modern Druid movement'.[6]

Aubrey was also very interested in documenting folk-lore, ceremony and traditional beliefs. This involvement was more than antiquarian interest in bygone practices. Aubrey possessed a version of the popular grimoire of ritual magic *Claviculae Salmonis*[7] which he had copied (and expanded) in 1674. He was also very engaged in astrology, with the analysis of horoscopes forming a central part of his biographies. Finally, Aubrey was also very engaged in collecting a wide variety of accounts of what we might nowadays call paranormal (even downright Fortean) phenomena: ghostly hauntings, conversations with angels and sprits, and various forms of 'psychic' episodes such as visions, dreams and prophecies. It should be noted that as well as a considerable interest in occult matters, Aubrey was a member of the Royal Society and close friends with a number of the most well-regarded scientists of his day, considered (both then and now) men of substantial learning, discernment, and rationality. He is typical of his time, in that his interests in archaeology, natural history and science were not seen as incompatible with his engagement with magic, in both its high ceremonial and more popular folk forms.[8]

Like the Devil's Hump in 'The Dæmons', the source of magical power in 'The Stones of Blood' centres around the site of an ancient alien ship. Again, the strangeness and danger of the English landscape is revealed, shown to be hiding anomalous secrets of physical and experiential space. Rather than shrunk to occupy some inverted proportion like the barrow site at Devil's End however, a crashed vessel in this case is suspended in a 'hyperspace', a liminal zone of inter- or non-dimensionality. Such is the weirdness of the very concept of hyperspace that even the Doctor claims a cheerful inability to fully understand it. What is clear is that the stone circle forms a liminal gateway space between worlds. There is an essential locative aspect to the magic of 'The Stones of Blood', a sorcery of place.

In filming the story, the part of the Nine Travellers was played by the Rollright Stones, an ancient stone circle on the border of Oxfordshire and Warwickshire. Not only does this site have a significance in local faerie lore, but has an origin story typical of standing stones: they are knights petrified by a witch. Indeed, there are even reports that this witch was the legendary English prophetess Mother Shipton. A 'stock character' in much early modern English literature, portrayals of Shipton (whose historicity as an actual person is unclear) went from ancient visionary to wicked witch to daughter of the Devil across the seventeenth century.[9] Yet prophecies attributed to Shipton grew in popularity during this period, eventually amassing into a large and amorphous body of various oracular pronouncements and dream-books attributed to her.[10] As for her connections with the Rollright Stones, it is less likely a semi-mythical Yorkshire witch would have travelled this far down the country; and far more likely that such connections emerge from the simple geographic proximity of the site to a village called Shipton-under-Wychwood.

The Time of Restitution

'The Stones of Blood' introduces the notion of a hyperspatial or transdimensional nature (or at least origin) of magic. However, the story that most directly explores and analyses this notion of magic – as the physics of another dimension – is the Seventh Doctor story, 'Battlefield' (1989). The action of this adventure involves visitors travelling to Earth not backwards or forwards in time but actually 'sideways in time, across the boundaries that divide one universe from another'. The English countryside, this time Lake Vortigern, is once more invaded by otherworldly forces. The 'curtain of night' is parted to permit warriors from another dimension, perhaps even another *kind* of dimensionality, to fight their final battle.

Although we see the thinning and piercing of boundaries between worlds as gateways for travel between them, rather than simply sources from which to draw out evil forces, the later summoning of the Destroyer (an alien being so powerful it cannot even be controlled by Morgaine, its summoner) does mirror more archetypical conjurations of a demonic agent. As in 'The Dæmons', a somewhat diabolic horned alien threatens Earth with annihilation.

The main convocation however is not the summoning of a Dæmon from across space or even from under a barrow. Nor is it the sending forth of alien henchmen as familiar spirits or *fetches* to do a magician-goddess's bidding. Instead, it is transdimensional travel 'beyond the confines of this universe' from a universe of swords and sorcery.

There is a certain continuation of the exclusivist division between technology and magic, with the Arthurian denizens of the magical dimension criticising this world for its obsession with machines and the 'limitations of their technology'. Yet this story also marks a point in *Doctor Who* in which this issue is addressed directly. Exploring the submerged bio-ship, Ace and the Doctor discuss 'magic'. Ace is sceptical – asking him to be 'feasible' – until the Doctor reminds her of Clarke's Third Law, that advanced technology would be seen as indistinguishable from magic. The Doctor addends that 'the reverse is true', prompting Ace to consider that 'any advanced form of magic is indistinguishable ... from technology'.

There is also a certain subtle continuance and development of the theme of magic as fraud found in 'The Dæmons'. Along with various other references to Arthurian legend, the Doctor is identified as Merlin who is called a 'prince of deceit'. As Merlin, the Seventh Doctor does indeed lie, defraud and trick: even hypnotising the landlord and archaeologist to evacuate the village. As at the unorthodox maypole-cum-witchburning at Devil's End, the Doctor's lies serve a greater purpose than his own power: those deceived are deceived for their own good.

We also see the power of magic in the rallying and motivating power of prophecy, of myth; of story. These are not lies as malicious deceitful manipulation to benefit the liar, but stories composed of affective words to motivate and preserve. The Arthur legend, spread by the Doctor, acts as 'propaganda', and also treats magic as a form of history; albeit one of facts misunderstood and made legendary. The exact details of the historical truth are mystified, becoming myth. Furthermore there is a modelling of magic as concepts, characters and stories which have accrued mythic significance over time, not unlike Agrippa's 'Hyeroglyphicall' letters and barbarous words.

There is one aspect in 'Battlefield''s portrayal of magic that we have not yet encountered, one that underlies a great deal of occult philosophy and magical action: that of *similitude*. Similitude is a magical premise about the operation of the cosmos that maintains that things considered similar have a unified and unifying meaning or effect. This premise is demonstrated most obviously in an idea popularised by the German theologian and mystic Jakob Böhme (1575-1624) known as the *doctrine of signatures*. This doctrine holds that, for example, lungwort is a good medicine for the maladies of the lungs because it resembles their shape. It is in this way that 'life calls to life, biomass to biomass, energy to energy'. Mordred's very words are echoed in Agrippa's judgement that 'everything moves, and turns itself to its like, and inclines that to itself with all its might.'[11] So it is that the brother-sword of Excalibur can be used to convoke into this dimension.

The principle of similitude is also present in the theories utilised in image magic. Broadly speaking, this held that the representation of a thing held some of the power, effect or influence of that thing. So images were cast in metals and other materials, which were often placed in specific locations or acted upon in some relevant manner, to affect a desired result. Agrippa cites the example of 'Nectanabus the magician' who 'made images of ships in wax after that manner and art, that when he drowned those images in water, that the ships of his enemies were in like manner drowned in the sea, and hazarded.'[12]

Similitude covered not just the morphologically similar, but the functionally alike or operationally identical. A chalk circle is a boundary, being *like* a wall in two dimensions means it *is* a wall in three. It offers the protection of a wall, in this case from evil sorcery. We also here have a repeat of that idea that only magic can comprehend, address and defeat magic.

One can say that the TARDIS *is* a 'ship of time' that does indeed 'deceive the senses being larger within than out'. The failsafe release code *is* an incantation: a specific formula to be pronounced at a certain time to create a particular effect. From similitude itself the notion resurfaces that what one dimension calls science the other may call magic, and that these may not in actuality be different things. At the very least in fact, they are indistinguishable.

The Play is the Thing

The most recent of the Doctor's adventures to directly address magic has been 'The Shakespeare Code' (2007), which also happens to be one of the best suited of the recent stories to evoke and introduce not simply the magic of a past historical age, but the very world, worldviews and practices of that age. From a cursory reading of this story, much is familiar. Again, magic is depicted as psychic energy used to bring forth destructive alien forces. Yet this fairly standard *Doctor Who* model of magic belies details that contribute to a particularly human feel to the London of 1599, a time with 'one foot in the Dark Ages' and another in modernity.

As the city is introduced, similarities to our modern urban living are initially emphasised. The comparison between projections of the current global warming crisis and millenarianism is a particularly interesting one. While there are still plenty of popular religious millenarian apocalyptic scenarios in modern times – for example, ideas centred around 2012 and Mayan-inspired mystical calendrical eschatology[13] – comparing the preacher's projections to global warming offers us an insight into the mainstream authority such millenarian claims could and did exert in early modern England.[14] Like global warming, debates over millenarian teleology were matters of respected men and women[15] disputing methodology, rather than simply fringe mystical radicalism or counter-culture. The threats of an end to the early modern world concerned everyone, from politicians and scientists to street preachers and magicians.

Along with links between early modern religion, environment and politics, 'The Shakespeare Code' also offers us a glimpse of early modern English magical biology and medicine. The humoural theory, by which the Tenth Doctor publicly explains the death-by-sorcery of the censor Lynley, plays a central part of the history of magic. Humoural theory was *the* main diagnostic and explanatory model for European medicine for at least 1500 years. It began with the second-century Greek physician Galen, and expanded into a whole body of ideas explaining cases of ill health and means by which to remedy them. The ideological roots of humoural theory rest on three foundations. Firstly, that the human body contains humours or moistures, whose excess or deficiency has an effect on that body. Secondly, that these humours correspond to the four classical elements, whose admixture is considered in magical ontology to make up everything in the cosmos. Thirdly, that the humours were in constant flux, and that good health was therefore a matter of proper equilibrium. So choler, the fiery humour, brought on heat and expansive activity in the body, whereas the watery phlegmatic humour cooled and moistened various parts and processes of the patient's anatomy.

The elementist model of the magical universe used qualitative rather than quantitative description to discuss the nature and activity of things. It considered the elements in terms of manifest or elementary qualities of heat, cold, moisture and dryness: the transfer of these qualities (themselves unchangeable), was used to explain how one element could transform into another. Thus fire (which is hot and dry) could lend its heat to water (which is cold and moist) and thus produce steamy air (which was considered hot and moist) as well as sooty earth (which was cold and dry) on the container. All things were considered to possess fiery, watery, airy and earthy properties based off their elementary qualities. These qualities were not necessarily the same as the actual tangible phenomena of fire, water, air or earth, but they could certainly transfer and combine to create them.

Any number of factors could influence a person's humoural composition from one moment to the next. Most of these factors were grouped together as the 'non-naturals', factors of human choice and effect, such as diet, sleep, exercise, as well as the astrological influence of the heavens, with the signs of the zodiac each afforded an elemental influence. The humoural constitution was neither fixed nor certain. It is a sudden and excessive imbalance of water in the lungs (along with an attack on the heart)[16] that kills Lynley, drowning him on dry land. By the rationale of humoural explanation, the notion of the body spontaneously generating water would not have seemed quite so bizarre to early moderns: it could indeed be considered 'regrettable but natural'.[17]

The means by which the Carrionites carry out their magical assassinations further demonstrate the principle of similitude we encountered in Mordred's convocation. The Carrionite poppets are an excellent example of representational magic and the use of other kinds of items linked to the target, of the bond between a person and their personal effects, such as hair clippings. Exactly the nature of this sympathetic link is used as another illustrative example of the distinction between magic and science. As she binds a lock of his hair around her curse-doll of the Doctor, Lilith gloats that 'Men to Carrionites are nothing but puppets'. Here, the Doctor does not merely proclaim magic as inadequately understood science as he has in previous adventures. Instead the two explanations, the scientific and the magical, are presented as different attempts at understanding the same phenomena. While the Carrionites 'might call that magic', the Doctor describes the link as 'a DNA replication module'. Lilith pragmatically reinforces the point – calling it something different makes her weapon no less effective. 'What use', she asks, 'is your science now?' By whatever means the poppet is conceived to work, by whatever model of reality one uses to understand a phenomena, or its operative mechanics and observable effects, it is still (at least potentially) deadly. Such a case seems an appropriate re-articulation of the concept that 'a rose / By any other name would smell as sweet'.

Elsewhere, the Carrionites' magic, their technology, is described by the Doctor himself as merely another approach to investigating and manipulating nature: 'Well, it's just a different sort of science. You lot, you chose mathematics. Given the right string of numbers, the right equation, you can split the atom. Carrionites use words instead.' Here magic is merely an alternative choice in technological specialisation, no less rational or effective. I would argue that this statement marks the single most historically and anthropologically sensitive contribution to the 'magic vs science' discourse in *Doctor Who*.

This emphasis given to the power of words in the story is also important to consider. There are spoken components to a magical action such as hexing, just as many early modern medicines were prescribed with an accompanying Psalm or charm to incant.[18] There is a further time-travelling take on barbarous words in the form of 'Expelliarmus' – a fictional magical word from a twentieth-century children's novel brought back and used as effective banishment in the late-sixteenth century.[19] There are puns of slippery semantics with real effect: the 'witch/which' homonym literally opens a door; the assassin's 'poppet' becomes the more generally controlling 'puppet' used to create the play-cum-energy converter. There is also the 'old magic' of the power of a name.

It is a long established magical tradition that a name could be magically used to affect, summon or constrain the named. This tradition emerges from a conception of names as being literally essential parts of the signified phenomena. They were not simply arbitrary signifiers made of culturally constructed and randomly accrued phonemes or letter-markings – they were a handle with which to grasp, to *apprehend*, some part of the fundamental essence of the named thing or being. Calling or writing the name of a spirit or an energetic principle of cosmos could put that being or force at the disposal of a magician. Most obviously, this was found in the frequent magical use of various names of God in early modern European ritual magic. In short, the signifier was part of the signified. This idea, of the essential (rather than arbitrary) nature of names, has even been suggested to be at the very core of magical thinking.[20] It is in this light that the Doctor's obfuscation or even complete absence of his own name can be considered a profoundly magical act.

A play, rather than an explicitly occult ritual, acts as an energy converter. This raises a question pertinent to considerations of both religion and magic: what shared and distinguishing features are present in both theatre and ritual, in drama and psychodrama? After all, storytelling itself is afforded a power, demonstrated in poor Peter Street the architect being able to disassociate from his past traumas through considering it a mere 'winter's tale'.

However it is in analysis of drama in terms of technology – both scientific and mystical – that we come to a particular magic of theatrical performance and experience. The play, indeed drama as a whole, may be eventually described as a psychic energy conversion, but it is explained and analysed as spell-work. At his most hopeless, when Shakespeare despairs that a theatre is 'just a theatre', the Doctor engages – indeed, enthuses – in the very discourse of 'magic': 'Stand on this stage, say the right words with the right emphasis at the right time? Oh, you can make men weep, or cry with joy. Change them. You can change people's minds just with words in this place'.

In considering theatre as magical, we can also examine magic in terms of its dramatic effect. The late twentieth century saw the emergence of a new kind of approach to occultism, known as Chaos magic.[21] Chaos magic, *inter alia*, continued and expanded upon a trend present in Western occultism often referred to as the 'psychologising of magic'. This trend is usually exemplified by the pronouncement of infamous occultist Aleister Crowley (1875-1947) that the 'Goetic' demons of *The Lesser Key of Solomon* were merely 'portions of the human brain'.[22] As Phil Hine, one of the occultists central to the emergence of Chaos magic, puts it:

> The Psychological Model grew out of the rise of Psychoanalysis, particularly the work of Carl Gustav Jung, and has come to be the dominant model for explaining magical phenomena. In the Psychological Model, the Gods, Elementals, Demons, etc., have no existence beyond the human mind – they are merely symbols or archetypes of deep parts of the human psyche.[23]

Even in this psychologised magical view, ritual is at the very least a psychodrama: action staged with appropriate 'set and setting',[24] designed to affect and direct particular feelings, experiences and realisations. It is transformative, affective and effective.

Conclusion

Throughout *Doctor Who*, magic is depicted thoroughly negatively. It is a means to control, compel, and destroy, to bolster the power of oppressors, fool the trusting and keep the weak or subjugated subservient. There are however also themes of illicit travel, border-crossing and portal-opening that extend out into wider science- and weird-fictional contexts.

We should bear in mind that depictions of magic in a time-travelling series such as *Doctor Who* also raise wider and deeper issues concerning both commonalities and distinguishing features of fantasy and science-fiction literature. It is far more common to find antagonistic depiction of magic in 'hard' science-fiction stories than in those of softer science fantasy: indeed, characterisation of the magical is often a defining separator of these subgenres.

As a final concluding meditation, it is perhaps most suitable we should consider (if only briefly) the magic of time itself. *Doctor Who* is very much about the occult nature of time – its hidden qualities and the magical actions that utilise them. It addresses huge philosophical issues of determinism, fatalism, providence and free will in a variety of ways. One of the more recent trends in the writing of *Doctor Who* has been to emphasise 'fixed points' in time, those nexuses of place, event and action where time cannot be re-written, not one line. One of the alien (literally, super-human) sensory faculties of the Doctor as a Time Lord is the ability to be aware of such fixed points, to sense the interconnectivity and flux of time itself – to both know and dare to take advantage of the hidden mechanisms of the temporal world.

I would like to end our magical tour with two relevant examples of such sorcery. One of the most popular questions put to pre-modern astrologers by their clients was 'When is the *best* time?' Such questions would be asked of the timing of business trips, marriage proposals, declarations of war, coronations and many other projects. These astrologers would determine the moment most likely to merit the success of such ventures. They would do this by setting an 'election', a chart of the motions of the stars through the heavens that could be analysed to discover the time when influences sympathetic to one's intent would be present: for instance, when Venus was well-aspected with the prominent zodiacal signs in the horoscopes of yourself and your lover.[25]

The second example comes in the form of a more recent definition of magic, from writer, poet and occultist, Andrew D. Chumbley

(1967-2004). In a February 2002 interview with pagan magazine, *The Cauldron*, Chumbley was asked what he understood by the term 'magick' and what it meant to him in a practical sense:

> I would like to give two successive understandings. Firstly, I would propose the following definition: 'Magick is the transmutability of the Quintessence of all Nature'. This is to say that 'magick' is the all-potential power of change characterising the root-nature of all that has existence. Secondly, I would suggest a distinction between 'magick' as 'power' and 'sorcery' as the means of manipulating that power through knowledge: 'Sorcery is the knowledge of the universal points of transmutation'.[26]

Turning from immutable fixed points we might instead consider our relationship with the transmutability of time as part of the ultimate underlying nature of the cosmos. By such standards, by his capacity to evaluate propitious moments for intervention and change in time's eddying whorl and weft, the Doctor should indeed be considered a powerful sorcerer. After all, sometimes magic really is all a matter of timing.

16.

The Church Militant? The Church of England, humanity and the future in *Doctor Who*

Marcus Harmes

Among the extensive critical commentary offered on *Doctor Who* since its revival in 2005, analysis of the presentation of religion in the programme has featured prominently. The influence of executive producer Russell T. Davies, showrunner from its 2005 revival until 2010, seems *auteur*-like in terms of the range and scope of his impact on the themes, tone and values of the programme. Davies has offered frequent commentary on his own atheism;[1] given the extent of his creative impact on all aspects of the programme, it is reasonable to suggest that Davies's atheism has informed the way Christian religion is presented in the programme. Certainly both popular and academic commentary has suggested that under Davies's influence the programme became not just anti-religious, but overtly anti-Christian.[2] In 2010 Stephen Moffat succeeded Davies as executive producer. Moffat has proven far more reticent than Davies in proclaiming either belief or unbelief, and he certainly has not made this aspect of his life a part of the public discourse surrounding *Doctor Who* as did Davies. Nevertheless his public comments on religion and *Doctor Who* do again tend to the derogation of religion.[3] However, I suggest that it is illuminating to compare the treatment which organised religion receives in serials overseen by Davies and by Moffat. To do so significantly clarifies the way in which Christianity, but more specifically the Anglican Church, has appeared in the revived *Doctor Who*.

On first analysis, a survey of particular episodes of the revived series suggests that Moffat's treatment of the Church is significantly more constructive than Davies's, who seems to have produced an overtly anti-Christian programme and who found this to be one of the creative potentials of the programme. I suggest that Moffat has in fact presented a vision of organised religion – especially the Church of England – which is more dynamic and indicates a more enduring institutional identity than is found in Davies's era of the programme. This is not to say that, as John Milton was allegedly of the Devil's party without knowing it, Moffat is of the Anglican party without realising it. But three key episodes from his period, 'The Time of Angels' and 'Flesh and Stone' (2010) and 'A Good Man Goes to War' (2011) show the Church as a dynamic and integral part of future human society, a point of comparison to Davies-era stories such as 'New Earth' (2006) where it has clearly been obliterated by the passage of time. But the terms upon which this future Church functions and upon which it has survived into the future are nuanced and striking. The Church is a de-sacralised, militarised institution, mostly shorn of its religious character or functions. It still has clergy or officials with the traditional titles, such as bishop, cleric and verger, but is no longer principally a religious institution. Thus the argument of this paper is that Moffat's vision of the dynamic Church in the far future shows that it survives, but does so at the cost of being a religious institution.

The episode title 'The Time of Angels' immediately points to both a book and a metaphysical condition that draw out this point. The book is *The Time of the Angels*, a 1966 novel by the Anglo-Irish philosopher and novelist Iris Murdoch (d.1999). The condition relates to the novel's characters: an atheist Anglican vicar and his strange family who are living through the 'time of the angels', a metaphysical period when God is dead, the angels, which had been God's dreams, are set free, and yet paradoxically the Church still exists and there is still need for its priesthood. The ideas of this novel intersect with Moffat's episodes and clarify the terms upon which he delineates the Church of the far future. Murdoch's novel suggested that in the 'time of the angels', there was more need than ever for a priesthood, an idea immediately salient to understanding the epistemological underpinning of the Church out in space and in the far future

Religion, Science and the Future

Science-fiction writers have imagined a number of different futures for Christianity, and these are rarely positive. Many projections of future society simply do not include Christianity or organised religion at all. Some science-fiction writers have however imagined the Church in space and in the future. To put futuristic religion in *Doctor Who* fully into context, it is worthwhile briefly exploring major examples of science fiction that project into the future of Christianity. The Church of England appears as a part of human society in stories set in the near and far futures. In Alan Moore's graphic novel *V for Vendetta* (and the point is also true of the 2006 film adaptation), the Church remains a part of English society, but Bishop Lilliman its leader is a paedophile and a creature of a fascistic government that conducts horrifying and unethical biological experiments on humans.[4] Moore here toys with the establishment status of the Church, extrapolating this status to a point where the state church of the future is part of an overtly Christian and moral regime but is a covertly corrupt institution. But this story is set in a recognisably close future; projections of the Church in the further future move beyond the institutional and moral implications of establishment status to consider the challenges to Christianity as an epistemological foundation for existence. Harry Harrison's *The Streets of Ashkelon* (1962) is an extrapolation of the missionary activities of the nineteenth-century churches; rather than African natives, Father Mark the missionary in Harrison's story sets out to convert an alien species, the Weskers, but in doing so he causes his own death. The Weskers demand a practical demonstration of the doctrines he is teaching and crucify the missionary. Harrison depicts a clash between the metaphysics of faith and the practical empiricism of the aliens. In fact the missionary is a victim of his own success; the Weskers had been prepared to believe Christian dogma, if only the missionary had risen from the dead. Harrison's story ends on a note of ironic tragedy, with the alien creatures apprehending that far from being saved through the grace imparted by the resurrection, they have simply become murderers.[5]

Religion, particularly organised religion, is an aspect of other science-fiction futures. John Wyndham's 1955 novel *The Chrysalids* describes a post-apocalyptic and post-technological future dominated by religious fundamentalism. In an indeterminate future period, human society has survived a nuclear holocaust, a holocaust that did nonetheless destroy all human writings except the Bible.[6] The type of religious ethos that Wyndham narrates is fundamentalist Protestantism based on the literal interpretation of the Bible. The implication of this religiosity is that any organic or natural deviations from a supposed image of human normalcy are ruthlessly destroyed, whether manifesting in crops, livestock or even in humans.[7]

Like Harrison, Wyndham's assessment of Christianity in the future is based on the interpretation and application of dogma and doctrine; both show religion in the future as faith-based. Wyndham's post-apocalypse is interestingly in tension with the 2010 film *The Book of Eli*, where the King James Bible has survived an apocalypse and has become a precious artefact, totemic of lost culture and civilisation.[8] It does however resonate with Margaret Atwood's 1985 novel *The Handmaid's Tale* (filmed in 1990) in its account of a future society gripped by biblical fundamentalism.[9] In Wyndham's story the Bible has survived to become an agent of bigotry and persecution. Both Wyndham and Harrison pinpoint religious weakness as coming from the metaphysics of faith and the understanding of sacred texts. In *The Streets of Ashkelon* the missionary is killed because the aliens have heard the Gospel narratives of the crucifixion and carry out a scrupulously detailed reconstruction of that event, even creating their own Golgotha. In the society of *The Chrysalids*, the Bible is the determining agent of morality and human conduct. But in both instances the science fiction takes issue with not simply religious faith, but the approach to understanding faith that these societies and individual Christians possess. In fact, Wyndham's novel strongly brings out the irony of the religious beliefs of the fundamentalist community in *The Chrysalids*, as he implies that their insistence that the human form is the ultimate expression of normalcy is almost blasphemous in the way it presupposes what the 'true image' of God may be.

But common to both these stories is that they show faith as the animating factor behind institutional religious activity in humanity's future. The missionary in space or the post-apocalyptic Protestants are believers in the reality of God and the Resurrection and religious dogma remains the driving force in religious practices and institutions. These thoughts bring us to considering religion in the revived *Doctor Who*. The programme has dealt with religion – especially Christianity and more particularly the Church of England – in a variety of ways, but most recently it has done so in stories that insist on the Church as surviving as a de-sacralised institution.

This is an emphasis at odds with, but thrown into relief by, earlier science-fiction projections of the future, notably Wyndham or Harrison's portrayal of a future version of Christianity that is still dogmatic and doctrinal.

The Place of Religion in *Doctor Who*

As overseen by Davies, the revived series of *Doctor Who* is saturated with references to institutional English religion. These appear in stories with widely divergent settings and time periods. In stories set in the present day, the Church is a familiar backdrop to sacraments and rites of passage, such as marriage, but it is confounded by alien intervention. In 'Father's Day' (2005) an Anglican church is the setting for a wedding attended by companion Rose's mother and father; but it is also the locus of alien attack and the vicar is gobbled up by a time eating monster who eradicates the clergyman's entire existence from history. The church building itself is only a place of sanctuary because, so the Doctor explains, the older walls of the building can temporarily resist the time-eating creatures threatening those inside, not because of its inherent sanctity.

Stories overseen by both Davies and Moffat further show church buildings in contemporary Britain as locations of alien menace, or depict their sacrality as compromised by alien attack. In 'The Runaway Bride' (2006) the wedding is taking place in a traditional English parish church. The service is permanently disrupted when alien science snatches the bride out of the church, leaving an indignant vicar at a loss to explain the phenomena. In 'The Hungry Earth' (2010) things are even worse; a church building, boarded up and disused, is the site of ominous activity by subterranean monsters.

Davies is an outspoken atheist and it is tempting to quantify the extent to which this has informed the creation of stories under his direction. There is indeed internal evidence from the programme's narratives which might suggest the impact of his outlook on *Doctor Who*. In the 2005 episode 'The End of the World', an announcement at the beginning was heard to remind the inhabitants of the space station where the story was set that 'the practice of religion' was forbidden, along with other clearly unsavoury and anti-social practices such as smoking. A later story, 'The Stolen Earth' (2008) showcased a cameo appearance from the evolutionary biologist Professor Richard Dawkins, who in reality is a vocal and vociferous opponent of organised religion. In another 2008 story 'The Unicorn and the

Wasp' the character of a quintessential Church of England vicar, the Reverend Golightly, turns out to be an alien entity, the Vespiform. At the moment of the narrative which reveals the Vicar's alien nature a number of semiotic and cultural codes all come into conflict. 'The Unicorn and the Wasp' is a pastiche of various story-telling tropes from Agatha Christie's detective fiction and the character of the Vicar is one of many in the story which deliberately play upon traditional story-telling types. Others are the butler, an eccentric Colonel and the vampish jewel thief. It is thus especially jarring when the Vicar not only turns into a wasp, but before doing so derides humans for their primitive belief in a 'tribal' sky god. The sight of the Vicar, in dog collar, castigating the narrowness of human belief is a strong image from the Davies era and leaves little room for any suggestion that the story presents an affectionate pastiche of classic English characters. In Davies's era depictions of the Church in the present day show it as beleaguered; its clergy and its sacred sites under attack from alien menace. In the future, as 'The End of the World' indicates, what was beleaguered in the twentieth century has simply ceased to be.[10]

The Moffat Era and Religion

So far, stories produced under Moffat have not offered any sustained consideration of the Church in the present day; they have, however, presented striking visions of religious institutions in the far future. The future societies depicted in *Doctor Who* make a number of points about religion. In stories set in humanity's future, institutional religion (and especially its religious orders) is still an aspect of life and thought. The trappings of institutional religion appear in future-set stories, the antiquity of these being sharply juxtaposed against the futuristic settings. In 'A Good Man Goes to War' the order of headless monks appears, clad in the traditional and clearly by then millennia-old brown robes of Christian mendicants. The same story shows the Doctor in a museum associated with the headless monks, and it is an overtly church-like building.[11]

Moffat's most striking future depiction of the Church is in the 2010 two-part story 'The Time of Angels' and 'Flesh and Stone', which is set in the fifty-first century. The Church of England still exists as an institution, including its clergy. However the version of Anglicanism which appears is strongly at odds with how the Church functions in the current era. In these stories this is truly the Church militant. The bishops, clerics and vergers of this Church are military personnel.

Of course there need not be anything necessarily incongruous about combatant churchmen. Ecclesiastical history abounds with reference to militant clergy, from the 'Chapter of the North', a body of medieval bishops and churchmen riding out against Scottish border incursions, to the canons of Hexham Abbey preparing artillery against Henry VIII's monastic commissioners, to perhaps most famously Bishop Henry Compton, the last English prelate to have worn armour, leading Princess Anne to safety with an armed troop during the Glorious Revolution of 1688.[12] Yet churchmen in armour from earlier centuries were on the whole fighting for some religious or godly cause, in Compton's case the defence of Protestantism itself. The militant churchmen of the future fight ambiguous battles. The vision of the future Church in fact encompasses a range of complex semiotic, linguistic and historical codes. The appearance of the churchmen takes us far from the customary garb of the clergy. These churchmen of the future wear unambiguously military uniforms. But the language they use cuts across this impression. Their leader, Octavian (Iain Glen), carries the name 'Father', a traditional priestly honorific. Casual language is in fact tossed about in these two episodes as well as in 'A Good Man Goes to War' that is redolent of ecclesiastical usage. Thus spaceships have 'transepts', traditionally an architectural term for parts of a church building, and some of the names of the churchmen under Octavian's command have strongly Christian resonances, including Angelo, Philip and Crispin. Even the name of the spaceship they are attempting to penetrate is the 'Byzantium', a name recalling the ancient city of the Bosporus, the capital of Constantine, the first Christian emperor.

However other equally casual language consistently undercuts the religious ambience created by this terminology. Thus one of the 'sacred names' is the exceptionally prosaic 'Bob'. Moffat's script constantly juxtaposes the ecclesiastical with the military to incongruous effect. 'Verger, how are we doing with those explosives?' bellows Father Octavian. Octavian carries the traditional title of an ecclesiastical dignitary – he is a bishop – but even this familiar title is undercut by a military nomenclature, for Octavian is a bishop, second class.

An important clue to the status and functions of the Church of England in these two episodes is given by the first episode's title. This is clearly a play on *The Time of the Angels*, the 1966 novel by Murdoch. Barring the similarity of titles, and therefore the fact that both talk about angels, there may seem to be little to link Murdoch's novel and Moffat's television story. The novel is set in post-war London and the television story in space in the fifty-first century. The novel is about a range of issues, including multi-racial identity and incest, that have no place in Moffat's story. Yet it is illuminating to compare them. Both engage with similar ideas, relating to the receding of faith but the continued necessity of clergy, and both of course are concerned with the untrammelled and dangerous release of angels to feast on humanity.

Moffat's own story is very much a 'time of the angels' in the manner of Murdoch's novel. *The Time of the Angels* narrates the loss of faith of a Church of England priest, the Reverend Carel Fisher. In the book, Fisher is almost an ontological absurdity, a priest without faith but also a priest without a church in which to officiate. *The Time of the Angels* is set in post-war London where Fisher has been appointed Rector of a church which no longer exists, as the Wren church was destroyed in the Blitz and only the tower was left standing.[13] As one character comments on the almost sinister unreality of this situation: 'it isn't a real parish. There aren't any people'.[14] Murdoch also makes great play with the dense fog surrounding the rectory in 1950s London; it isolates the rectory from the view of the towers, spires and domes of the London skyline that point to the churches that proliferate in the streets. Metaphorically, the fog encases and isolates the rectory's inhabitants; denying them the view of the city's religious architecture; it also signifies their isolation from faith.[15] By the end of the novel, even the relic of the church tower is being demolished to make way for modern housing developments. The atheist Fisher is also dead by the end of the story, and while his faith has departed, so too has the physical evidence of the church effaced. On a microcosmic level, Fisher's loss of faith and the destruction of the sacred site of his church stand in for a broader retreat of faith; what philosopher-novelist Murdoch meant by the 'time of the Angels' was an intermediate period, where God has died and only the angels, which had been God's dreams, remain but have been let loose. The book speaks to the disappearance of faith from English cultural identity.

The Church in Moffat's two episodes is having its own 'time of the angels'. Moffat plays with the title in a punningly literal sense, for in this story angels do indeed appear. On a less literal level, the Church is in the midst of a 'time of the angels', as it is an institution from which God has disappeared and where faith has departed. What then is its role? 'The Time of Angels' and 'Flesh and Stone' are set in outer space in the fifty-first century. In this time and place, the Church's role is to offer military support to an investigation into the crashed Byzantium. They are equipped with heavy firepower and their role is defensive. In fulfilling this role, the Church plays a more dynamic part than the passive victim role in Davies-era stories such as 'Father's Day' and 'The Runaway Bride', where church buildings come under alien attack or clergy are attacked and killed. The Church in Moffat's episodes by contrast is dynamic and organised. It is also, however, part of a setting where traditional Christian iconography has undergone a radical re-imagining.

Angels Unleashed: Religion without God

In suggesting that there will still be a Church of England in the very far future, Moffat could almost be accused of optimism. Current commentary on the future of the Church is overwhelmingly pessimistic. Church leaders, secularists, bloggers of different persuasions and others who take an interest in the Church all concur in seeing an institution experiencing crisis on various levels. The global communion of Anglicans is split on the questions of gender and sexuality; in England and other parts of the western world the basic fact of numerical decline suggests extinction within one to two generations;[16] and overall the Church seems to be experiencing a crisis of identity and faith. Most current commentary on the Church, especially in the British press, carries this emphasis, especially as relates to the politics of gender and sexuality within the Church. Papers such as the *Daily Mail* report crises over plans to marry or ordain gay people or consecrate women bishops.[17] 'Will the last person to leave the Church of England please turn out the lights?' asks the *Independent* journalist Adrian Hamilton provocatively but perhaps presciently, commenting that 'I can't help feeling … that the Church of England will not survive my children's lifetime and quite possibly not even my own.'[18]

Commentary on the decline of the Church of England invariably relates this decline back to faith, or rather its absence. The Church's decline has been concomitant with the rise of secularism in society, a line of argument suggesting that, as belief vanishes, the institution of the Church is squeezed out. But both Murdoch and – following her lead – Moffat, suggest an alternative understanding of the loss of belief. Murdoch's novel was written in the light of her extensive philosophical commentary on belief, including her account of why we can no longer believe in God.[19] In particular Murdoch suggested humankind in the later-twentieth century was emerging from a 'mythological childhood'.[20] But the implications, epistemological and doctrinal, of this awakening to maturity did not necessarily come at the expense of the Church. Instead Murdoch proposed that 'Christianity can continue without a personal God or a risen Christ, without beliefs in supernatural places and happenings'. While the novel's insistence that 'God is dead' seems very Nietzschean, it is in fact more helpfully thought of in terms of 'Death of God' theologians such as the American William Hamilton, whose writings from 1966 onwards proposed the idea that God is dead. However Hamilton did not entirely write off the Church in the light of God's demise, suggesting that the institution surviving without God was a possibility and he speculated at length on the possibility that 'Christianity continues to be important long after it has ceased to be true.'[21] In this vein Murdoch further suggested the dynamic regenerative potential of the Church, arguing that 'It has always changed itself into something that can be generally believed.'[22] Indeed it is the Bishop, a church leader, in *The Time of the Angels* who also says that 'mankind is growing up'.[23]

A number of Murdoch's writings iterate this theme, including the *Metaphysics* and her critical essay 'On "God" and "Good"', which spoke dismissively of 'a small number of mystically minded people who, being reluctant to surrender "God", fake up "Good" in his image, so as to preserve some kind of hope'.[24] In *The Time of the Angels* Murdoch is even more blunt, one character asking 'You don't believe in God and all that crap, do you?'[25] Murdoch's philosophical writings, as we have seen, suggested an altogether more dynamic alternative to actual belief within a Christian institutional framework, ideas that receive yet fuller development in *The Time of the Angels*.

Murdoch places in Father Carel's mouth a set of fully thought through speculations on the death of God, but the paradoxical but seemingly concomitant continued need for the priesthood. The novel includes several extended discussions of secularism and what one scholar of Murdoch, Elizabeth Dipple, refers to as 'secularized religious thought'.[26] Another clerical character, Fisher's Bishop, himself proclaims his understanding that the Church was living through an 'interregnum', in which traditional faith must be replaced by new systems of thought. The Bishop comments that 'The Church will have to endure a very painful transformation'.[27] Yet Father

Fisher suggests that, even through a process of transformation, the priesthood is still necessary. 'If there is no God there is all the more need for a priest' he argues.[28] These are the words of an atheist priest obsessed with God's dreams of angels, and the release of these angels after God's death. For Carel Fisher, God's death meant that the priesthood was necessary to defend against the existential horrors of the time of the angels. Although there was no longer a God to worship (an idea reinforced by the fact Fisher does not have a church in which to conduct the rites and sacraments of the Church) the priesthood is necessary to combat the angels.

These observations irresistibly bring to mind the Church of England in Moffat's 'The Time of Angels' and 'Flesh and Blood'. His two-part story can be read as showing the end result of this metamorphosis of which the Bishop spoke. Even more so, Moffat's story builds on what Father Fisher understood was the 'time of the angels': Fisher says 'The disappearance of God does not simply leave a void into which human reason can move. The death of God has set the angels free. And they are terrible'.[29] Moffat's story is indeed preoccupied with angels. They are terrible creatures, and are loose upon creation. But yet there is no void; the Church is still there.

While proclaiming the disappearance of God, Father Fisher does not necessarily see his own redundancy. Speaking further of the angels whom he believes have been set free by the death of God, he ominously comments 'We are the prey of the Angels'.[30] Father Fisher of course was speaking in theologically speculative terms, and as the novel indicates, the prey at stake is more the happiness and sanity of people than anything else. The weeping angels of *Doctor Who* prey on humans in a different way, as contact with them can remove a person from their own time and abruptly move them backwards in history; the angels also kill by snapping the necks of their victims. Father Fisher proposes a remorselessly bleak and empty universe; Murdoch's novel established the irony that it is Fisher's brother Marcus, who is a fashionably agnostic intellectual, who is most affronted by the Bishop's modish theology and most tormented by Carel's insistence on the death of God. He wishes for there to be a Church to comfort and protect and despairs that his brother seems so 'unchristian'.[31]

He may have been comforted that, according to Moffat, the Church of England does survive. As the Doctor himself comments, in the fifty-first century 'The Church has moved on'. The army of clerics commanded by Bishop Octavian suggests a complex engagement with faith in the fifty-first century. None of them, from the Bishop downwards, refers to God, except once. Bishop Octavian does refer to praying and insists to the Doctor that 'we have faith', but this is an ambiguous statement, as a moment before the Doctor was asking the clerics to have faith in him. It certainly does not indicate orthodox Anglican belief. Octavian does however recognise the nature of the deadly angels pursuing him and his army of clerics, for they are 'dreams', but ominously, their 'dreams no longer needed us'. His observation resonates with Murdoch's conception of the time of the angels, when God is gone, but his dreams in the form of the terrible angels remain.

In the Future the Church is Gay

The army of clerics returns to confront the Doctor in 'A Good Man Goes to War'. Again, the Church of the future is anchored to the past, while incongruously expressing its futuristic militaristic identity. They are part of a world where religious concepts still seem to prevail. Accordingly there is a spaceship with a transept, a 'papal mainframe', which dialogue establishes is a source of authority, and dire penalties apply for a 'heresy class one'. But the language of the Church from the past does not obscure the very clear distinctions between the Church of the future and the Church of England of the twentieth-first century or earlier. One of these differences relates to sexuality. Across the late-twentieth and early-twenty-first centuries, the Church of England has been convulsed by schism and disorder relating to homosexuality, one issue that has led so many observers to predict its ultimate demise. The consecration of a gay bishop in New Hampshire, the attempted but frustrated consecration of a gay bishop in the diocese of Oxford, and major international tensions between liberal and conservative factions within the Church have dominated the institution in recent years.[32] Yet two characters in 'A Good Man Goes to War' are the 'thin fat gay married Anglican marines'. The concatenation of names and epithets given to this couple, which indeed comprises one thin man and one fat man, encapsulates both the tensions of the modern Church and Moffat's striking imagining of its future incarnation.

Again, it is hard to escape some degree of optimism about the institution's future in Moffat's story, even if it is rather facetious optimism. Moffat's trio of stories shows a Church than has endured, but at a cost. The army of clerics who confront the angels in the fifty-first century retain many historical names and trappings, but these clerics are militarised. They may speak obscurely of faith and prayer, but they are known by their actions, and these are violent and based on military strategy and the use of hardware. Thus the Church still exists, but if understood in Murdochian terms, this is because its clergy still meet a need, but in a universe without traditional understandings of God. 'A Good Man Goes to War' enriches this impression of the future Church. The cheerful casualness with which the fat and thin Anglicans proclaim not only their role as marines but their homosexual coupling and their Anglicanism seems centuries away from the anxious and acrimonious tensions which beset the Church and its teachings on homosexuality in the early-twenty-first century. Admittedly the impression is not entirely consistent. 'The Time of Angels' does contain a brief but expressive exchange between the Bishop and the Doctor relating to 'self-marrying' among the two-headed alien species the Aplan. The fact that, as the Doctor points out, the Church tried to ban the practice suggests that even the Church far in the future still drew some lines in the sand relating to dogma and practice. Nonetheless the practice referred to – of two-headed alien creatures marrying themselves – is far removed from the topicality of the clearly human gay Anglican clerics. If these clerics have perhaps transcended the need for God, the Church also seems to have transcended the dogma which is at present dividing the institution and imperilling its authority.

Conclusion

Steven Moffat's delineation of the Church in *Doctor Who* differs markedly not only from Russell T. Davies's account of the institution in the same programme, but even from a longer history of the portrayal of the Church in science fiction. In particular serials written and produced by Moffat, the Church is a forceful, dynamic agent of action. It assists the Doctor in his exploration of the Byzantium, although in 'A Good Man Goes to War', it is allied with forces ranged against the Doctor. A number of differences are apparent between how Davies and Moffat dealt with religion. Davies treated the Church in the modern period (that is, early-twenty-first century) as under attack both physically (such as assaults on church buildings) and epistemologically (as alien intervention in humanity assailed Christian teachings on creation and the ordering of the universe). In stories set in the future, Davies explicitly indicates that the practice of religion is forbidden. So far, Moffat's stories set in the present day have not offered a depiction of the Church, but stories set in the future do portray a future in which the Church has survived but also been transformed. The Bishop in Murdoch's *Time of the Angels* spoke of a 'very painful transformation'.[33] The Church in Moffat's 'The Time of Angels' is indeed an institution transformed. Part of the transformation of which Murdoch's Bishop spoke was the decline of belief and the void this would leave. His comments were prompted by the atheist yet angel-obsessed rector Carel Fisher. Carel Fisher is dead by the end of Murdoch's novel; the Church of the fifty-first century is however one he may have recognised; it fills a void left by the death of God, and remains ready to deal with the angels let loose on humanity.

17.

Bigger on the Inside? Doctoring the Concept of 'Religion or Belief' under English Law

Russell Sandberg

Part One

The beginning of the twenty-first century witnessed a rather unexpected comeback. It was thought that modern British society had moved on. Although it was fondly remembered, for most of the population it was a relic of the past, which now only attracted the attention of a small number of increasingly obsessed followers. Yet, against all the odds and the predictions of many, it had not only come back but became more significant than before, often making headline news. The beginning of the twenty-first century witnessed the return of religion.

From 11 September 2001 onwards, long held expectations about the decline of religion have come to be questioned by talk of religious resurgence and religious fundamentalism. Greater levels of immigration and lingering doubts about 'otherness' have pushed questions concerning religious identities in the public sphere to the top of the political, social and media agendas. Although there remains ample evidence to support aspects of the predicted secularisation thesis, recent years have clearly witnessed the rebuttal of the Post-War 'assumption that religion had become a purely private matter with no public or political significance'.[1]

This has been reflected in the continuing 'unfolding text' of *Doctor Who*.[2] While several Tom Baker adventures (such as 'The Brain of Morbius' (1976) and 'The Face of Evil' (1977)) portrayed religion as the preserve of primitive groups, several Matt Smith stories have shown how 'the Church has moved on' and the power of numerous military religious orders such as the Order of the Headless Monks, the Clerics and the Order of the Silence (as represented in 'The Time of Angels/Flesh and Stone' (2010) and 'A Good Man Goes to War' (2011)).[3]

The opening years of the twenty-first century has also witnessed the 'juridification of religion'.[4] In the United Kingdom, there have been a number of new laws protecting religious freedom and these have led to a number of high profile court cases. Religious freedom is increasingly seen as an individual right and the language of religious rights has become commonplace. One legal development has been legislation to outlaw discrimination on grounds of religion or belief.[5] Since 2003, it has been unlawful to discriminate against people on grounds of their 'religion, religious belief, or similar philosophical belief'.[6]

These new laws have provoked several Employment Tribunal claims concerning the width of the definition of 'philosophical belief'. At first, the use of the word 'similar' was used to exclude certain non-religious beliefs. In *Williams v South Central Limited*,[7] it was held that a belief that a national flag should be worn was not 'similar' to a religious belief and so was not protected. And in *Baggs v Fudge*[8] a claimant who was rejected for a job because of his membership of a far-right political party was told that he could not bring a successful claim since political beliefs fell outside the definition of 'similar philosophical belief'.

However, since 2006, the definition of belief has changed and the word 'similar' has been deleted.[9] The reason for this was to appease those who professed non-religious beliefs such as atheism and humanism; and who objected to their beliefs being regarded as being religion-like. However, this new definition has resulted in a number of contradictory Employment Tribunal decisions which have interpreted the definition of 'philosophical belief' in a number of novel and surprising ways. This contradicts the statement given by the then Government Minister, Baroness Scotland, who claimed that the deletion of the word 'similar' would make no difference because:

> The term 'philosophical belief' will take its meaning from the context in which it appears; that is, as part of the legislation relating to discrimination on the grounds of religion or belief. Given that context, philosophical beliefs must always be of a

> similar nature to religious beliefs. [...] It will be for the courts to
> decide what constitutes a belief [...] but case law suggests that
> any philosophical belief must attain a certain level of cogency,
> seriousness, cohesion and importance, must be worthy of
> respect in a democratic society and must not be incompatible
> with human dignity. Therefore an example of a belief that might
> meet this description is humanism, and examples of something
> that might not [...] would be support of a political party or a
> belief in the supreme nature of the Jedi Knights.[10]

The subsequent Employment Tribunal decisions suggest that the
Baroness was incorrect. The removal of the word 'similar' has made
a difference. And, ironically, it was the Baroness's explanation of
why the law has not changed that has itself prompted a change in
approach. Her summary of the case law requirements has been used
to provide a series of tests which Employment Tribunals apply to
determine whether a belief is capable of being protected. This has led
to an increasingly uncertain interpretation of the term 'philosophical
belief'.

This change in interpretation has also questioned the two
examples Baroness Scotland gave of beliefs that 'might not' meet
the definition. The uncertainty expressed in the word 'might' and
her explicit reference to 'support of a political party' rather than to
holding political beliefs have led Tribunal chairs to speculate that
some political beliefs may now be protected.[11] Moreover, as this
chapter will argue, the Employment Tribunal case law now suggests
that there is no reason why beliefs derived from science fiction could
not be protected. While the Baroness gave the example of the Jedi
Knights from *Star Wars*, this chapter will question whether beliefs
concerning *Doctor Who* could, and should, be regarded as falling
within the definition of religion or belief found within the UK's
Equality Act 2010. In short, could *Doctor Who* be regarded as a
religion under English law?

Part Two

The claim that *Doctor Who* could constitute a 'religion or belief' is
not as outlandish as it might first appear.[12] The Australian sociologist
of religion Adam Possamai has produced a large body of work on
what he terms 'hyper-real religions'.[13] This describes 'how some
science-fiction, horror, and fantasy narratives can be understood

as cultural reservoirs for the construction of religion by spiritual consumers'.[14] These 'subjective myths' are brought together in 'a simulacrum of a religion partly created out of popular culture which provides inspiration for believers / consumers at a metaphorical level'.[15] Similarly the Australian Religious Studies academic Carole M. Cusack has concluded that:

> Invented religions, rather than being exceptional and best classified as 'fake' religions, are properly understood as the inevitable outcome of a society that values novelty, and in which individuals institute their identity through the consumption of products, experiences, cultures and spiritualities.[16]

Hyper-real[17] religions inspired by science fiction include neo-Pagan groups such as Church of All Worlds[18] and largely Internet-based movements such as Jediism (based on George Lucas' *Star Wars* films) and Matrixism (based on The Matrix film trilogy by Larry and Andy Wachowski).[19] Possamai uses the term to cover the way in which science-fiction narratives are 'idiosyncratically borrowed by individuals to support their spirituality'.[20] Although there is little research as to the volume of such beliefs, there is no doubt that hyper-real religiosity is a real and growing phenomenon.   In the UK 2001 census, 390,000 people declared themselves to be 'Jedis', a figure that is equivalent to 0.7% of the population. And research by Beth Singler has indicated that, although this figure was exaggerated due to a 'viral' email campaign, there remains a minority of 'genuine' believers who regard Jediism as a spiritual path for self development using the Internet to construct their spiritual identities.[21]

Although the academic research to date has not included *Doctor Who* as a potential hyper-real religion, a number of journalists have included the programme in reports that arrive at similar to conclusions to Possamai *et al*.[22]   Writing in the *Guardian* in 2009, Cole Moreton listed *Doctor Who* as an example of BBC television programmes inspired by ideas drawn from alternative spiritualities which supported the conclusion that 'at its loosest, Paganism is beginning to look like our new national faith',[23] while in 2011 Stephen Kelly argued that *Doctor Who* features 'a god for our times' as part of a 'wider social shift' whereby 'heroes of popular culture [are] becoming modern figures of worship'.[24] The programme itself has also toyed with the idea of the Doctor as a God-like figure; most notably in 'The Curse of Fenric' (1989) and 'The God Complex' (2011) in which the respective companion has been forced to lose their faith in the Doctor.[25]

The claim that *Doctor Who* could constitute a 'religion or belief' for the purpose of the Equality Act 2010 is supported by a number of recent Employment Tribunal decisions which have taken a wider interpretation of 'philosophical belief'. The turning point was the decision of the Employment Appeal Tribunal in *Grainger PLC v Nicholson*,[26] which concluded that a belief in man-made climate change was capable of constituting a 'philosophical belief' because it met the criteria laid out by the case law of the European Court of Human Rights which was directly relevant. Although this European case law has not reached a watertight definition of belief, the approach has been to consider all claims determining their success on their merits. The Court has considered claims concerning Scientology,[27] Nazism,[28] Druidism,[29] Pacifism,[30] Communism,[31] Atheism,[32] pro-life,[33] Divine Light Zentrum,[34] and the Moon Sect.[35] And the only line which has been drawn is to exclude beliefs that are mere opinions rather than a worldview.[36]

Grainger PLC v Nicholson has been followed in a series of Employment Tribunal decisions. In many of these claims, it was held that the definition of 'philosophical belief' had been met.

In *Greater Manchester Police Authority v Power*[37] it was held that a belief in Spiritualism and life after death and psychic powers was protected. In *Hashman v Milton Park (Dorset) Ltd*[38] it was found that a belief in the sanctity of life, comprising in particular of anti-foxhunting beliefs constituted a philosophical belief. In *Maistry v The BBC*[39] it was held that a belief 'that public service broadcasting has the higher purpose of promoting cultural interchange and social cohesion' was included. And in *Streatfield v London Philharmonic Orchestra* Ltd[40] it was held that Humanism was protected.

However, in some cases it has been held that the definition of 'philosophical belief' had not been met. In *Kelly v Unison*[41] it was held that Marxist/Trotskyite beliefs held by trade union members of the Socialist Party did not constitute a 'philosophical belief'. In *Farrell v South Yorkshire Police Authority*[42] a belief that 9/11 and 7/7 were 'false flag operations' which were authorised by the respective national governments in order to give material with which they could persuade their respective populations to support foreign wars was excluded. And in *Lisk v Shield Guardian Co Ltd & Others*[43] a belief that a poppy should be worn during the week prior to Remembrance Sunday was not protected.[44]

It is worth noting that the finding that a belief is protected as a philosophical belief does not mean that the Claimant automatically wins their claim. As Employment Judge Hughes noted in *Maistry v The BBC*, recognising that something may be a philosophical belief simply means that the claim does not fail at the first hurdle. All other aspects of the claim still need to be proved: 'the real battleground is whether there has been less favourable treatment and, if so, whether it was on grounds of the belief relied on'.[45] It can therefore be argued that a wide definition of 'religion or belief' ought to be taken: rather than dismissing claims by saying that they are not 'beliefs', claims should be considered properly and fully.[46]

With this in mind, the next section will ask whether *Doctor Who* should be capable of being a 'religion or belief' for the purpose of the Equality Act 2010. Do the tests derived from the European Court of Human Rights as elucidated by *Grainger PLC v Nicholson*[47] and subsequent cases allow for this possibility?

Part Three

In *Grainger PLC v Nicholson*, Employment Judge Burton drew upon the case law of the European Court of Human Rights to summarise the meaning of 'philosophical belief' as having five requirements:

(i)   The belief must be genuinely held.

(ii)   It must be a belief and not ... an opinion or viewpoint based on the present state of information available.

(iii)   It must be a belief as to a weighty and substantial aspect of human life and behaviour.

(iv)   It must attain a certain level of cogency, seriousness, cohesion and importance.

(v)   It must be worthy of respect in a democratic society, be not incompatible with human dignity and not conflict with the fundamental rights of others.[48]

Returning to Baroness Scotland's statement, Burton observed that one example she had given of a belief that would not be included was 'a belief in the supreme nature of the Jedi Knights, and this would fail on the basis of non-compliance with at least four of the limitations'.[49] However, by reference to the case law that has followed *Grainger*

PLC v Nicholson, it can be argued that there is no reason why beliefs deriving from science fiction should be automatically excluded, whether they concern Jedi Knights or Time Lords.

The first test is that the belief must be genuinely held. The leading case on this is the House of Lords decision in *Williamson*[50] concerning the interpretation of human rights laws protecting 'religion or belief'. As Lord Nicholls noted, the question of genuineness is a 'question of fact' and a 'limited inquiry'. While courts may be concerned with whether the claim was made *in* good faith, they are not concerned whether it is *a* good faith in terms of judging the validity of that faith:

> it is not for the court to embark on an inquiry into the asserted belief and judge its 'validity' by some objective standard such as the source material upon which the claimant founds his belief or the orthodox teaching of the religion in question or the extent to which the claimant's belief conforms to or differs from the views of others professing the same religion. Freedom of religion protects the subjective belief of an individual.[51]

There is no reason why a belief derived from or relating to *Doctor Who* could not meet this requirement. In *Streatfield v London Philharmonic Orchestra Ltd* it was held that the Claimant's humanist beliefs were genuinely held because there was evidence she had held these beliefs from an early age and had 'lived her life adopting a general adherence to those principles'.[52] This is the case for many *Doctor Who* fans who have been enthusiasts for a long time and whose fandom shapes their lives even when the programme is not on air.[53] Even the most cursory visit of internet forums shows the way in which fans discuss and creatively contribute though the maintenance of blogs, the writing of fan fiction and through arts and crafts. Moreover, as *Streatfield v London Philharmonic Orchestra Ltd* confirmed, this requirement would still be met even if the Claimant did not manifest their beliefs at all times. Courts would still treat such claim as being genuine.

The second requirement is that a belief must not be merely an opinion or viewpoint based on the present state of information available. The leading case on this is *McClintock v Department of Constitutional Affairs*[54] concerning a Justice of the Peace who resigned since he could not in conscience agree to place children with same-sex couples on the basis that he felt further research was needed on the effect this would have upon the children. Both the Employment Tribunal and the Employment Appeal Tribunal held that the

Claimant's objection did not constitute a belief because he had not as a matter of principle rejected the possibility that single sex parents could ever be in the child's best interest. In *Farrell v South Yorkshire Police Authority* it was held that this requirement was met since, unlike in *McClintock*, the Claimant had come to a conclusion that the evidence pointed one way and not another. The crucial factor was that whilst he was prepared to admit that he might be wrong, he did not believe himself to be wrong.[55]

Again, beliefs concerning *Doctor Who* are capable of meeting this requirement. Fandom goes further than merely having an opinion on the merits of a television programme. Moreover, in order to meet this threshold, a belief concerning *Doctor Who* would not need to constitute or allude to a fully-fledged system of thought: as stated in *Grainger PLC v Nicholson*, a 'philosophical belief does not need to amount to an "-ism"'.[56] Yet, it is striking that many of the debates and divisions found in fandom are similar to those which are found in religious traditions. This would include debates as to the mythology found within and deriving from the programme as well as debates as to structure such as the division between the 'classic' and 'new' series; the debate as to whether non-televised stories are canonical and controversies as to the dating of particular events and stories (such as the dating of the Doctor's interactions with UNIT). Fan dialogue on such matters could be seen as constituting a form of theological debate.

The decision in *Hashman v Milton Park (Dorset) Ltd*[57] indicates how beliefs regarding specific matters can meet the definition of philosophical belief of being more than an opinion where they form part of a larger philosophy. It was held that beliefs concerning hunting met this requirement because the Claimant's beliefs were to be 'considered within the parameters of his general beliefs ... in the sanctity of life'.[58] This could easily apply in relation to beliefs concerning *Doctor Who* which could be regarded as being part of the Claimant's wider beliefs. For example, *Doctor Who* beliefs could be regarded as part of wider beliefs concerning the values of individualism and human endeavour. Such beliefs are regularly espoused in the programme, most famously in the speech by Tom Baker's Doctor in 'The Ark in Space' (1974) on the 'indomitable' nature of *Homo sapiens*.[59] Moreover, beliefs concerning the value of *Doctor Who* may be considered to be inseparable with beliefs concerning the value of public service broadcasting. *Maistry v The BBC* confirms that such beliefs can meet this threshold.[60]

The third requirement is that the belief needs to relate to a weighty and substantial aspect of human life and behaviour. In *Grainger PLC v Nicholson* it was confirmed that this is not a bar on beliefs which are not shared with others or 'one-off' beliefs such as pacifism and vegetarianism which do not govern the entirety of a person's life.[61] And in *Maistry v The BBC* it was held that:

> A belief in the importance of providing a non-commercial, non-Governmental, independent public space in which a cultural, social and political tensions can be debated and explored and in which tolerance of other viewpoints is fostered, clearly relates to weighty and substantial aspects of human life and behaviour.[62]

It may be pointed out that many *Doctor Who* stories relate to 'weighty and substantial aspects of human life and behaviour'. As incoming executive producer Steven Moffat was keen to stress in the initial publicity for the 2010 series, *Doctor Who* is a fairytale. Many stories boil down to a good versus evil conflict with monsters representing social and political evils. Most notoriously, this is shown by the Daleks and their Nazi-like beliefs about racial purity.[63] And these are contrasted with the virtues of other characters, not least the protagonist and his companions. Episodes of the series have dealt with such weighty and substantial matters as environmentalism,[64] colonialism,[65] slavery,[66] the role of the media,[67] drugs,[68] taxation,[69] justice,[70] mental illness[71] and the European Union.[72] And several episodes are inspired by religious themes such as the appropriation of Buddhist philosophies in various Jon Pertwee adventures such as 'Planet of the Spiders' (1974) and the Peter Davison stories 'Kinda' (1982) and 'Snakedance' (1984).[73] Indeed, in most episodes cultural, social and political tensions are debated and explored and tolerance of other viewpoints is fostered. Fan discussion and analysis of these themes can be used as a means of fostering spiritual development and to shape a world view.

The fourth requirement is that the belief needs to attain a certain level of cogency, seriousness, cohesion and importance. As Lord Nicholls noted in *Williamson*, this means that the belief must 'be coherent in the sense of being intelligible and capable of being understood'.[74] A non-religious belief 'must relate to an aspect of human life or behaviour of comparable importance to that normally found with religious beliefs'.[75] However, his Lordship stressed that these 'threshold requirements should not be set at a level which would deprive minority beliefs of the protection they are intended to have':

> Typically, religion involves belief in the supernatural. It is not always susceptible to lucid exposition or, still less, rational justification. The language used is often the language of allegory, symbol and metaphor. Depending on the subject matter, individuals cannot always be expected to express themselves with cogency or precision. Nor are an individual's beliefs fixed and static. The beliefs of every individual are prone to change over his lifetime.[76]

However, some Employment Tribunal decisions seem to have taken a different approach.[77] In *Farrell v South Yorkshire Police Authority* Employment Judge Rostant held that this requirement had not been met in the case of the Claimant's belief in conspiracy theories regarding 9/11. He held that 'some sort of objective assessment of the cogency and cohesion of the philosophical belief is expected of the Tribunal'.[78] This meant that the test would be more difficult to meet where 'beliefs are about matters where there is a substantial amount of evidence in the public domain, as opposed to where beliefs relate to the unknowable, for example the existence of the deity'. This was because 'the assessment of cogency and coherence must take into account the broadly accepted body of knowledge in the public domain'.[79] The difficulty for the claimant was 'that the conspiracy theory he advances remains in the light of subsequent events and the weight of evidence, wildly improbable. There is no body of respected academic commentary in peer reviewed journals that supports the theory'.[80] This, coupled with the numerous 'internal contradictions inherent in Mr Farrell's position',[81] meant that the philosophical beliefs failed to meet any minimum standard of cogency or coherence. They did not attract the protection of the Regulations since 'applying an objective test they are absurd beliefs albeit sincerely held'. [82]

It is submitted, however, that the decision of the Employment Tribunal in *Farrell v South Yorkshire Police Authority* is incompatible with the House of Lords judgement in *Williamson* and so should not be followed. As Lord Nicholls stated in *Williamson*, 'Freedom of religion protects the subjective belief of an individual'.[83] The fourth requirement is met where the Claimant considers their beliefs to be important and where those beliefs are capable of being explained to another. The fact that, objectively, such beliefs are unlikely to be true is irrelevant. Atheists would maintain that all religions would fail to meet this test. This cannot have been the intention of Parliament in enacting the law. The type of claim which the fourth test seeks to exclude is the deliberate sham religion. An example of such a claim can be found in the US case of *Kuch*,[84] where the Claimant contended that she had a constitutional right to take drugs because it was part of her religion, the Neo-American Church. The court reached the 'inescapable conclusion' that the purpose of the church was their desire to use and take drugs regardless of religious experience. The sole 'duty' of the faithful was 'to partake of the sacraments' consisting of marijuana and LSD which were described as the 'Host of the Church, not drugs'. And each of the 20,000 members of the Church carried a 'martyrdom record' to reflect their arrests. The District Court determined that Kuch had 'totally failed' in her effort to establish that the group was a religion since the membership was 'mocking established institutions, playing with words and [was] totally irrelevant in any sense of the term'.[85] Beliefs concerning *Doctor Who* would be capable of meeting the fourth criterion if such beliefs are cogently held and can be expressed with some coherence.[86]

The fifth and final requirement is that the belief must be 'worthy of respect in a democratic society, be compatible with human dignity and not in conflict with the fundamental rights of others.'[87] Beliefs will meet this threshold unless they abuse the rights of others. As Baroness Hale noted in *Williamson*, 'A free and plural society must expect to tolerate all sorts of views which many, even most, find completely unacceptable'.[88] The case law has provided some hypothetical examples of the type of beliefs that would be excluded. Lord Nicholls in *Williamson* gave the example of beliefs 'involving subjecting others to torture or inhuman punishment would not qualify for protection',[89] while in *Grainger PLC v Nicholson* it was suggested 'a racist or homophobic political philosophy' would be excluded.[90] In the Parliamentary debate, Baroness Thornton suggested that 'any cult involving illegal activities would not satisfy the criteria'.[91] In short, it is likely that most beliefs concerning *Doctor Who* would meet this criterion, unless such beliefs were based on the philosophies espoused by the Doctor's enemies.[92] As with the other four tests, there is no reason in principle why beliefs derived from or concerning science fiction cannot be regarded as philosophical beliefs for the purpose of the Equality Act 2010. This raises the question: was Baroness Scotland incorrect to automatically rule out beliefs derived from science fiction?

Part Four

One rare point of consensus that seems to have emerged from parliamentary debates and judicial decisions concerning the definition of 'religion or belief' is that allegiances towards or deriving from works of science fiction are not protected. A belief in the Jedi Knights is the example readily given of what falls outside the scope of the definition.[93] For example, in the parliamentary debate concerning the Equality Bill, Baroness Thornton stated that it would ultimately be for the courts or tribunals to determine whether something met the definition of 'religion or belief' according to the criteria established by case law.[94] However, it was striking that she was willing to give one example of something that would not meet the definition:

> The Government do not think that views or opinions based on science fiction can be considered akin to religious or philosophical beliefs. It was not the underlying principle behind drafting the definition of 'religion or belief' to cover such views.

And, as noted above, in *Grainger PLC v Nicholson* it was observed that 'a belief in the supreme nature of the Jedi Knights ... would fail on the basis of non-compliance with at least four of the limitations'.[95] Yet, discussion of those five tests shows that science-fiction derived beliefs are capable of meeting the requirements. It is clear that the five requirements overlap with one another and have a rather elastic nature. With the exception of beliefs that are deliberately insincere and/or harmful to others, it is possible to argue that most beliefs could meet the criterion. And it is also possible in many cases to easily argue that they do not. Two people may reach directly opposing conclusions as to whether the same belief was 'weighty and substantial', for example.

Given this, a generous approach should be taken. There are two reasons for this. The first is that this is consistent with the judgement of the House of Lords in *Williamson* and in particular with Lord Nicholls's insistence that, 'Freedom of religion protects the subjective belief of an individual'.[96] As Lord Walker noted in that case, for 'the Court to adjudicate on the seriousness, cogency and coherence of theological beliefs is ... to take the Court beyond its legitimate role'.[97] The second reason is that holding that the Claimant's belief is capable of being a philosophical belief does not mean that the Claimant wins their claim. It simply means that the first threshold is met. As a point of principle, the first threshold should not be set too high so that the full merits of the claim can be assessed.

The case law to date has suggested that a largely generous approach is being taken (with the exception of cases concerning political beliefs). This undermines Baroness Scotland's assertion that the deletion of the word 'similar' would make no difference. Given the developing case law, the examples the Baroness gave are now also questionable. Although judges have followed the Baroness in referring to beliefs in Jedi Knights as an example of a belief that is definitely outside the Equality Act 2010, there is nothing to support this claim either in the Act itself or in the burgeoning case law. The application of tests derived from the human rights jurisprudence suggests that an inclusive approach will continue to be taken, though the vagueness of the tests afford a great deal of discretion to the judiciary in terms of deciding whether the tests have been met. It is possible to argue that all of the tests can be met in relation to beliefs deriving from science fiction. The conclusion that flows from this analysis of beliefs concerning *Doctor Who* is that, under the new case law, the definition of religion or belief under the Equality Act 2010 is now bigger on the inside.

18.

'Something woolly and fuzzy': The Representation of Religion in the Big Finish *Doctor Who* Audio Adventures

Noel Brown

To fans acquainted only with the series's BBC television incarnations (1963-89; 2005-), the independently-produced *Doctor Who* 'audio plays' featuring past Doctors and companions produced by Big Finish and released monthly since 1999 may seem little more than a minor footnote in the illustrious history of the franchise. Certainly, it would be foolish to suggest that these adventures, produced largely for a pre-existing audience of *Doctor Who* aficionados, possess cultural significance commensurate with that of the television shows. Nevertheless, emerging as they did during the so-called 'wilderness years' between the cancellation of the original series in 1989 and its high-profile resurrection in 2005, there was a perception in fandom that these BBC-licensed releases – which constituted the first substantively performed *Doctor Who* in a decade and featured many of its former stars – were somehow more 'real' than the vast array of original novels, comics and spin-offs that had previously kept the flame alight in the series's absence from the screens. Their proficiency served to reinforce this attitude, as did the profile of many of the contributing writers, some of whom had written for the original series (Marc Platt, Andrew Cartmel, Philip Martin), while others (Mark Gatiss, Paul Cornell, Gareth Roberts) would become scriptwriters on the revived BBC Wales series.

Several Big Finish *Doctor Who* releases are direct meditations on religion; many more explore religious themes or foreground religious (most often Christian) iconography. Of course, as a science-fiction show, the original series dealt with such issues as religious mythology, faith and their intersection with science and rationalism, often in ways which were codedly – but rarely explicitly – critical of its position within contemporary culture and society. As David Layton has argued:

> Because of the Enlightenment and humanist intellectual ground on which it stands, *Doctor Who* usually discounts the concept of supernatural entities that guide humanity and intrude on human affairs [...] In *Doctor Who*, what might be called 'Gods' come from the early times, even the origin of the universe, characterised as a dark, chaotic period. These 'gods' derive whatever powers they have from the universe itself, not from outside it, and these gods are not creators of the universe. These gods are aloof, capricious, warmongering, and unsympathetic. In short, 'gods' are not to be trusted, and humanity is better off without them.[1]

This liberal-humanist, secularist perspective is largely reflected in and shared by *Doctor Who* fandom (particularly in its British iterations).[2]

As fans and fan-producers assumed artistic control of *Doctor Who* in the 1990s in its absence from the screens, these values became even more tightly inscribed, initially in Virgin's *New Adventures* novel range (1991-96) and *Doctor Who Magazine*'s comic strips (1979-), then in the BBC-produced novels (1997-2005) and finally in the initial wave of Big Finish productions. What distinguishes the representation of religion in certain Big Finish productions from their television counterparts are their particular directness (taking advantage of the additional creative freedom availed by the medium), counterpointed by clearly relativistic emphases. In this chapter, I will focus largely on two relatively early releases: Rob Shearman's *The Holy Terror* (2000) and Jonathan Morris's *Bloodtide* (2001). I will argue that they reflect a core assumption among British *Doctor Who* fandom that religion is no longer socially or spiritually relevant. At the same time, they can be located within a countervailing liberal tradition of relativism, which emphasises subjective (rather than objective) conceptions of reality and thereby supports the validity of a range of ideologies and belief systems. With close analysis of these texts, I will show how the Big Finish releases relate to broader debates within *Doctor Who* fandom concerning the positioning of religion within the series, situating them within the wider moral and ideological dimensions of the franchise.

Big Finish

Big Finish Productions was formed by businessman Jason Haigh-Ellery in 1996. In 1997, Haigh-Ellery and Gary Russell, the former editor of *Doctor Who Magazine*, approached the BBC with a bid to obtain a license to produce *Doctor Who* on audio, but the BBC – still hopeful that a full series may yet emerge from the *Doctor Who* television movie starring Paul McGann (1996) – rejected the bid. Russell and Haigh-Ellery elected to concentrate on audio dramas featuring Professor Bernice Summerfield, one of the Seventh Doctor's companions (and latterly a stand-alone character) from Virgin's *New Adventures* range. By 1998, it had become clear that there would be no swift return to the television screens for *Doctor Who*, and Big Finish's bid for an audio license was reconsidered. The company approached all the surviving Doctors from the original series (Tom Baker, Peter Davison, Colin Baker, Sylvester McCoy and, slightly later, Paul McGann) and all but Tom Baker agreed to reprise their roles, as did most of their respective 'companions'. The first production, *The Sirens of Time*, a multi-Doctor story starring Davison, Colin Baker and McCoy, was released on double cassette and CD during the summer of 1999, and, from January 2000, these plays were being released on a monthly basis.[3] As of spring 2013, over 170 stories have been produced. According to Haigh-Ellery, Big Finish:

> sell[s] to established fans of the series, although there are always new fans to be had. By using actors such as Anthony Stewart Head, we've been able to attract back fans that have moved away from *Doctor Who* to other series. Big Finish's listeners tend to be male, but vary in age between ten and 100.[4]

This cross-demographic address is reflected in Haigh-Ellery's admission that 'we don't go as far in pushing the envelope out as, say, the novels or novellas. Nor would we want to. No sex. No gratuitous swearing. No gross violence. Our market is different to the books – more traditional, I think'.[5] Big Finish's avowedly 'traditional' approach has prompted Matt Hills to argue that the Big Finish *Doctor Who* stories are a form of 'textual conservationism', offering 'authentic', 'traditional' and 'televisual' *Doctor Who* – albeit in the aural medium – for their 'target market of fan-consumers'.[6] I believe that this interpretation has merit, but tends to overlook the comparatively radical intent of some of the early Big Finish releases.

Like Virgin's *New Adventures* novels, various Big Finish stories venture into entirely new territory.

Patterns of Representation

Religious themes in Big Finish's *Doctor Who* oeuvre can be loosely divided between five basic story types:

i) The historical, in which the protagonists visit a period in Earth's history and interact with its culture. Examples include *The Land of the Dead* (2000), *The Marian Conspiracy* (2000), *The Church and the Crown* (2002), *The Council of Nicaea* (2005), *Son of the Dragon* (2007) and *The Witch in the Well* (2011).

ii) The sinister religious cult narrative. This genre requires little explication, and will be familiar to viewers of both the classic and revived television series. Examples include *The Stones of Venice* (2001), *Primeval* (2001), *The Rapture* (2002), *The Dark Flame* (2003), and the Eighth Doctor/C'Rizz 'Foundation' story arc (2004-07), which spans multiple adventures.

iii) The mock supernatural narrative. In this genre, largely determined by sci-fi conventions, what superficially appears to be a supernaturally-themed narrative (involving ghosts, demons and suchlike) is ultimately explained through some rational, scientific means. Examples include *Phantasmagoria* (1999), *Winter for the Adept* (2000), *Minuet in Hell* (2001) and *The Haunting of Thomas Brewster* (2008)

iv) The satire. Unlike the original series, which avoided this potentially taboo mode, Big Finish have produced two notable satires of religion: *The Holy Terror* and *Faith Stealer* (2004).

v) The evolutionary narrative. Although there are several references to evolution in the original series, its relationship with religion is only really explored in the notoriously complex 'Ghost Light' (1989). Big Finish have been similarly cautious: while *Loups-Garoux* (2001) explores the primal link between humans and werewolves, only *Bloodtide* dramatises the conflict between evolutionary theory and creationism.

The first three genres are staples of a series which explores time and space from an explicitly rationalistic perspective. Although outwardly secular, there is nothing in these genres which criticises 'legitimate' (i.e. real-world, chiefly Western) religions. It is *The Holy Terror* and *Bloodtide*, productions which memorably and controversially embody the satire and the evolutionary narrative respectively – and which are among the most secularist *Doctor Who* stories in *any* media – which interest me here.

The Holy Terror and the Religious Satire

Perhaps one of the most efficacious ways of communicating a contentious message is through satire. Described by author Rob Shearman in his initial story proposal as 'a skit on religion', *The Holy Terror*, although it was Big Finish's poorest-selling *Doctor Who* release for some time, received rave reviews in the cult sci-fi publications and among fanzines and online forums, ultimately winning *Doctor Who Magazine*'s annual readers' poll in 2000.[7]

The plot is rather complex. The TARDIS apparently takes the Sixth Doctor (Colin Baker) and his shape-shifting companion, Frobisher (Robert Jezek) – currently in the shape of a penguin – to a medieval castle where the ruling emperor is also worshipped as a living god. Chronicling every event is an elderly scribe, Eugene Tacitus (Sam Kelly). The Doctor and Frobisher arrive to discover that the living god, emperor Pepin VI, has died, and his son, emperor Pepin VII (Stefan Atkinson), is about to be anointed as the new god. Hailed as messengers from heaven, they inadvertently foil an attempted coup by Pepin's bastard half-brother, Childeric (Peter Guinness). Childeric is joined in his planned rebellion by the treacherous high priest, Clovis (Peter Sowerbutts), who kidnaps the Doctor and Eugene, taking them to the castle vaults, where Childeric reveals that his plans to seize the throne rest on the assumed powers of his young son, who has been kept in complete isolation since his birth in an attempt to preserve him from man's corruption and imbue him with god-like powers. Meanwhile, Pepin, unable to maintain the masquerade that he truly is a god, abdicates and nominates Frobisher as his successor. When word reaches Childeric that 'the bird-god' has taken over the throne, he decides to release his son immediately.

A terrified Eugene seems to recognise the child, and warns that he will kill everyone. The experiment appears to have been successful: possessed of godlike powers, the child promises to destroy the castle, at which point he will be alone with his father, and they will rule forever. The Doctor and Eugene flee, but when Eugene expresses bewilderment that the homicidal child – which he claims to have killed repeatedly – keeps returning, the Doctor returns to the vaults.

Attempting to enter the mind of Childeric so that they will become a single entity, the child is enraged to discover that Childeric is, in fact, *not* his father, and vengefully tears him apart. The child demands that the Doctor reveal the true identity of his father. The Doctor instructs the child to lower his voice and speak as the adults do; his voice is that of Eugene. The Doctor deduces that the child is, in fact, a device designed to torture its one prisoner, Eugene, whose captive mind has created this entire world. By the time the Doctor rejoins Frobisher and Eugene (who have taken refuge in the throne room), the child has destroyed the fictional world and all its inhabitants. Eugene's memory begins to return, and with horror he remembers his crime – he murdered his son. The child asks Eugene why he killed him; Eugene explains, simply, that he is insane. Unable to endure the guilt, Eugene asks the child to kill him, whereupon both of them disappear, leaving only empty void, and the TARDIS. The Doctor and Frobisher depart, sadly.

Of course, this synopsis scarcely does justice to the comedic aspects of the play. Its playfully ironic tone is established in the opening scene, where Eugene is brought to the castle dungeons to be interrogated by the guard captain, Sejanus (Dan Hogarth):

SEJANUS: You have been brought here to answer one question.

EUGENE: Oh, well, fire away.

SEJANUS: Whom do you worship, Eugene Tacitus?

EUGENE: Well, I'd say the living God, Emperor Pepin VI. Doesn't everyone?

[*Gasps*]

SEJANUS: Easy, men. Don't be shocked by the blasphemy.

EUGENE: Do I take it that's the wrong answer, then?

SEJANUS: The living God, Emperor Pepin VI, is dead.

EUGENE:	Oh, whoops.
SEJANUS:	He fell asleep in his bathtub, and drowned.
EUGENE:	Not a very dignified way to go.
SEJANUS:	The new living God is Emperor Pepin VII, and all those who worship Emperor Pepin VI commit heresy, and must be executed forthwith.
	[Sound of swords being unsheathed.]
EUGENE:	Oh, dear. Forthwith, you say.
SEJANUS:	According to holy rituals, the condemned will have one eye gouged out, the other left intact to watch the flames rise, as he is burned at the stake.
EUGENE:	Not a terribly dignified way to go, either.
SEJANUS:	You are to be taken from this place, to a cell, awaiting execution. You will be allowed no contact with your family, and your remains will not be placed in holy ground. And your name will be reviled for ever more, and held as a byword for apostasy – unless you are prepared to recant, immediately, and pledge allegiance to the living God, Emperor Pepin VII!
EUGENE:	Oh, well, I think I'll recant then.
SEJANUS:	Is that your final decision, Eugene Tacitus?
EUGENE:	Absolutely.

SEJANUS:	[tone lightening] Oh, well, that's fine, then. Swords back, then – we've got another one who wants to recant!

In this exchange, one is reminded of the similarly comic exchange in the BBC's *Blackadder* (1982-89) in which Thomas More's baffling failure to think of saying 'I recant my Catholicism' as a means of averting his imminent execution is recounted. Such ironic subversion doubtlessly bespeaks increasing freedom of expression. But it also reflects, on a more pervasive level, the decline of religion in modern Britain and, simultaneously, its liberalisation.

In *The Holy Terror*, almost every participant in this religion is aware that it is a sham, but they are unable or unwilling to break free of its constraints. Pepin's decision to abdicate is precipitated by the knowledge that:

PEPIN:	One of my first commandments will be to execute one-tenth of the population for heresy.
FROBISHER:	What?
PEPIN:	Tradition. Fair's fair: they are all guilty. Last week they worshipped my father. They'll have to be punished, somehow.
FROBISHER:	*Why*? You're the god, aren't you? Tell them you forgive them. Tell them you just won't do it.
PEPIN:	But the people *demand* it. They won't let me stand against tradition. There's no point in having a god if he isn't a little vengeful, now and again. Either their god kills them, or they will kill their god. That's what religion is all about.

The conversation takes a darker turn when Pepin reveals that, by now, an angry mob will have torn apart his father's corpse in retribution against his perceived betrayal. On the surface there is a palpable fear of mob mentality, but there are also echoes here of

Marxist perspectives on the relationship between organised religion and 'the masses' as an unthinking, homogenous entity, willingly controlled by highly ritualistic religious doctrine (which in turn protects the ruling elite from the threat of violent uprising).

An even more direct exchange occurs shortly afterwards. On this occasion, it is the Doctor who offers his thoughts on organised religion:

CHILDERIC: No-one really believes in God, any more. That's what makes Pepin's honesty at the coronation all the more pathetic. No one *expects* him to become immortal and rule forever. Oh, they'd kill him for saying so, of course. The laws against heresy are without mercy. But there is no true faith, any more. The people commit heresy secretly every day in their hearts. The laws by which their ancestors feared for their lives have become empty rituals, without number, and without meaning.

THE DOCTOR: Childeric, it's inevitable. No matter how fundamentalist a religion may be at its root, it gets compromised sooner or later. It happens to every belief in every nation, on every planet. The extremists die out, and what's left is something woolly and fuzzy.

Later in the same scene, the Doctor refers to the institutional decline of organised religion as 'a fact of life which must be accepted – a consequence of civilisation'.

By the start of the second half of the story, the sly leg-pulling, playful intertextuality and religious satire of the first two episodes have largely given way to a far darker, more disturbing and, in places, truly horrific narrative of fanaticism, murder and infanticide. The story appears to be have been informed by fear of religious extremism. One idea which seems to have particularly appalled Shearman – and which is reconstituted in the play – is the theological belief, inherited from the story of the tower of Babel from the Book of Genesis, that humankind is separated by God by its corrupt language, and that a child isolated from the rest of humanity at birth would, in its purity, inherit the language of God.[8] The moral message communicated at the end of the story, in which the Doctor and Frobisher both assert the importance of free will, and mourn for the deaths of the fictional population of this universe, is expressly humanistic. It refers back to their opening exchanges, where the Doctor objects to Frobisher's using the TARDIS's systems to create fish to hunt, on the grounds that the fish – although Frobisher's creations – are able to feel fear and pain. Thus, the ethical integrity of the secularist worldview is reaffirmed.

Perhaps the most prominent influence behind this story is the secularisation thesis itself, which held sway in (Western) sociological explications of religion for several decades. The argument has varied between a 'strong' form, which proposes that ultimately, secularisation is an inevitable function of organised religion (the perspective assumed by *The Holy Terror*), and a comparatively 'weak' form which has documented the decline of organised religion in Western Europe but is more cautious in its conclusions. However, by the turn of the century, the secularisation thesis was becoming challenged by an increasingly organised counter-movement. In the early-1990s, Grace Davie (in)famously proposed that religion in modern Britain is characterised by 'believing without belonging'.[9] In 1999, Peter Berger – formerly a well-known proponent of secularisation – 'recanted' by asserting that, contrary to his prior belief, there is, in fact, little evidence that religion is declining globally.[10] And in 2001, Callum Brown offered a very different account of secularisation, which rejected the conclusions of earlier proponents of this thesis that religion has been gradually declining in Britain for two centuries. Instead, he proposed that a far more sudden and precipitous downward spiral has been taking place since the 1960s.[11] In retrospect, *The Holy Terror* may have been premature in its secularist predictions. The debate rages on, but the arguments for and against secularisation no longer appear quite as clear-cut as they once did. This is especially true in the United States, which continues to be far more religious than most countries in Europe.[12] Indeed, this is borne out in the criticisms of the portrayal of religion in *Bloodtide* from US-based fans.

Bloodtide and the Evolutionary Narrative

Bloodtide opens during the prehistoric era, where the Silurians – a race of intelligent, bipedal reptiles who ruled the Earth millions of years ago and first appeared in the serial 'Doctor Who and the Silurians' (1970) – are preparing to enter deep hibernation, hoping to survive a catastrophe which they believe will ravage the surface of the planet. S'rel Tulok (Dan Hogarth), one of the Silurians' greatest scientists, is being tried on charges of 'perverting the course of nature' by genetically engineering a lesser species (as yet unidentified) in order to improve their flavour, while raising their intelligence so that they can cultivate themselves. It is revealed that such experimentation runs contrary to 'the most sacred tenets of Silurian law', and despite his protestations, Tulok is sentenced to be banished to the Earth's surface. Tulok is escorted to the surface by his friend, Sh'vak (Helen Goldwyn), who seemingly ignores his pleading and expels him from the protective shelter.

Millions of years later, the TARDIS brings the Sixth Doctor and his companion, Evelyn (Maggie Stables), to Baquerizo Moreno, one of the Galapagos Islands, during the mid-nineteenth century. They encounter young naturalist Charles Darwin (Miles Richardson), who is conducting research that will subsequently provide the basis for his theory of evolution through natural selection as part of the survey expedition of the *HMS Beagle*, under the command of Captain Fitzroy (George Telfer). They discover that many of the inhabitants of Baquerizo Moreno – which is being used as a penal colony by the British, under the jurisdiction of Governor Lawson (Julian Harries) – have been mysteriously disappearing. It transpires that a colony of Silurians – led by Tulok with the assistance of scientist Sh'vak – have awoken from their hibernation, and, with Lawson's assistance, have been feeding on the human population of the island. Making contact, the Doctor tries to persuade the Silurians that coexistence is possible, but Tulok is adamant that humans are vermin that have overrun the planet, and determines to eradicate them with the aid of a lethal airborne virus developed by Sh'vak.

Meanwhile, Darwin's religious faith is shaken by the Silurians, the existence of which refutes the creationist model of world history and also denies the Bible's teaching that God created man in his own image. The Doctor, Evelyn, Fitzroy and Darwin are all captured by the Silurians and held prisoner in their underground bunker. By this point, Tulok has released the virus on the surface of the island, wiping out its human population. Darwin's theory of 'descent with modification' as the origin of all species is by now concretising, and he angrily denies the existence of God, but Tulok reveals to the group that it was *he* who created humanity by genetically modifying the apelike hominid *Australopithecus* to make *Homo sapiens*. The Doctor manages to convince Sh'vak that Tulok deliberately sabotaged the hibernation mechanisms of many of the Silurians, killing them. With Sh'vak's help, the Doctor, Fitzroy and Darwin are able to resist Tulok's telepathic attack, while Evelyn plants an explosive in the Silurian submersible (with which Tulok intends to release the virus globally), and he and the rest of the Silurians are destroyed when it detonates. With the indigenous population of the island decimated, Darwin and Fitzroy depart on the *Beagle*.

Unlike *The Holy Terror*, *Bloodtide* is founded more on heated philosophical debate than satirical humour. Morris 'wanted to write something with a point to it, something with a subtext that I could run with, a theme that I could explore and develop' and hit upon 'the conflict between creationism and evolutionary theory'.[13] The ongoing theme of Darwin's loss of faith is an allegory for the far more ambiguous process of secularisation in Western Europe. Fitzroy is the voice of the prevailing orthodoxy in Victorian Britain in relation to God and to man's exalted position in the natural order; he is an embodiment – albeit a benevolent one – of the counter-argument against Darwin's new and dangerous idea. We hear Darwin's and Fitzroy's opposing beliefs articulated during the climactic scene, in which Tulok attempts telepathically to induce them to kill the Doctor. Instructed by the Doctor to resist Tulok by concentrating on something in which they believe totally, Darwin vocalises his belief in his theory of descent with modification, while Fitzroy recites the Lord's Prayer. As with two televised *Doctor Who* stories, Ian Briggs's 'The Curse of Fenric' (1989) and Toby Whithouse's 'The God Complex' (2011), both religious and non-religious faith is shown to be a powerful instrument, capable of galvanising, motivating and protecting, but its pluralism is consistently reaffirmed; and by concentrating on the properties of faith as an abstraction, rather than the ideas and beliefs in which it is invested, each writer attempts to avoid implications of hierarchy.[14]

In this scene, the two sides in the ideological battleground are unified by their resistance to the false god figure, Tulok, and their friendship appears as strong as ever during the play's closing moments. Nonetheless, the Doctor is very much on Darwin's side of the debate, reasserting the dubiousness of the distinction between humanity and animal kind, and attacking the hypocrisy of Fitzroy's claim to morality and civilisation with reference to humankind's apparently insatiable appetite for persecution and self-annihilation. Furthermore, in accordance with Darwin's position, nature is not subject to processes of glorification, sanitisation or pastoralisation. It is made explicit throughout that all animals, except those fortunate enough to be at the top of the food chain, are subject to predation, and that the need to adapt to the environment leads to the process of 'descent with modification' (later popularly vulgarised as 'survival of the fittest') that Darwin identifies. Darwin acknowledges that the Silurians' natural inclination will be to master or destroy humanity, asking rhetorically, 'what does *any* species do to its inferiors'?

A significant passage of dialogue can be found in the dialogue leading up to the third cliffhanger:

DARWIN: *That* is the origin of our species. We are
                           just these lizard-men's cattle.

FITZROY: Charles, what you're saying, it's ... it's
                           beyond blasphemy.

DARWIN: What? That man is the result not of divine
                           providence but the struggle for survival?
                           Oh, we assume that the abundance of
                           nature is proof of the Lord's existence,
                           but what if that is not so? What if our
                           existence is just the result of blind chance?

FITZROY: What do you mean?

DARWIN: A God that did not create the world, the
                           oceans, and animals and plants; a God
                           that did not make man; a God responsible
                           for nothing may as well be no God at all.
                           Do you not agree, Doctor?

                           [*Pause*]

EVELYN: Doctor?

THE DOCTOR:	I ... don't know. But I'll tell you one thing. In the skies above us are a million suns, each circled by their own worlds, and on those worlds, wherever there is the *opportunity* for life, you will find it. *That* is the miracle. Life endures; it thrives; it defeats every adversity. It creates order out of chaos.

Although Tulok's revelation immediately afterwards that humanity is the result of his genetic experimentation, and that *he* is their god, provides a sting in the tail – and a memorable cliffhanger – the essence of the story, surely, is contained in the exchanges above. There are two parallel threads in this dialogue. The first is Darwin's rationalisation of what has been happening; his epiphany that what he has been working towards – the theory of natural selection – actively disproves the creationist account of the origins of species.[15] The second thread is the Doctor's response to the long-unarticulated question: whether *he* believes in a God. Inevitably, he demurs; the Doctor is a character imbued with such moral and intellectual authority that to answer such a question directly would betray his egalitarian principles.

Nonetheless, on numerous occasions the Doctor explicitly states that, contrary to the teachings of the Bible, humankind possesses no dominion in the natural order. Even today, this is a controversial statement. In one notable speech, he attempts to explain the presence of the Silurians to islander Greta (Jane Goddard):

Years passed, and the Earth not only healed itself; it blossomed. Nature covered the globe once more, filling every corner with new species of plants and animals. While the Silurians remained dormant, the world above was reborn. The lifeless planet they abandoned was transformed into the world you live in today.

What is interesting here is the almost biblical language the Doctor uses to describe the 'rebirth' of the planet. It is the Creation myth reconfigured as a secular narrative in which Nature – and not God – is the omnipotent instigator. This is mirrored by the Silurians' conviction that 'life exists only as nature's servant', and the similarly biblical cadences of the Doctor's later assertion that it is nature that 'creates order out of chaos', and that it is *that* (note the emphasis, suggesting an alternative) which is 'the miracle'. While the sentiment may be very different, the lyricism is consciously retained from the passages in Genesis dealing with the Creation, possibly as a rebuttal to the oft-repeated accusation that evolutionary theory, whatever its empirical foundations, lacks the poetry of the Biblical account. Morris claims that:

> One thing that was incredibly important to me [...] was to make sure that the story was not a polemic, and that the Doctor – or, indeed, the story itself – should not take sides on the issue. I was careful to make sure that the story didn't categorically state that creationism is wrong.[16]

One particularly provocative scene – which was omitted from the final version of the script after the BBC's Jacqueline Raynor expressed concerns that it was too partisan – is worth reproducing, as it seems to deny this claim to impartiality:

DARWIN: I cannot see a day when men will be prepared to accept that particular heresy.

THE DOCTOR: One day, they will, Charles. Give it time.

DARWIN: Not whilst there is religion in men's hearts and they are confirmed to prejudice. Not whilst they choose what to believe based on faith rather than facts. We assume that the abundance and grandeur of nature is validation enough of the Lord's existence. But to refute that firm conviction, to deny God's hand, would bring about such condemnation...I would not dare to voice such an idea.

THE DOCTOR: One day. Maybe not for many decades, but one day the world will be ready for your ideas. And you will win the argument, Charles. Because rationalism will always defeat ignorance. All you need do is present proof of your case and let the clear truth speak.

DARWIN: Perhaps, Doctor. I will mark your words. Perhaps, when I have collected enough evidence, I may be able to convince them.

THE DOCTOR: That sounds like an excellent plan.

This decision to cut this dialogue was prudent, as its polemical tone would have undercut the more relativistic aspects of the script. Morris insists that 'I tried not to cause offence. But I didn't do that very well, presumably, because people were offended – some of them quite a lot'.[17]

Subsequent Developments

Having courted controversy with *The Holy Terror* and *Bloodtide*, Big Finish henceforth adopted a more cautious and conciliatory approach in relation to contentious material – particularly religion. As Nick Briggs recalls, his initial script for *Creatures of Beauty* (2003) carried a religious subtext:

> There'd been some criticism from our US-based listeners about the presentation of religion in plays – *The Holy Terror* and *Bloodtide* spring to mind – so Gary [Russell] was anxious not to inflame the Bible belt in any way. I assured him that the religion thing wouldn't be significant. As it turned out, I found I didn't need it at all.[18]

Overtly religious-themed productions have since constituted a relatively small proportion of Big Finish's output, and those that have emerged are, in the main, historicals, sinister cult or mock-supernatural narratives.

Whatever allegorical meaning such stories may possess, their religious commentaries are, no doubt purposely, too displaced to offend. A similar point may be made concerning *Faith Stealer*, which is a religious satire, but of a far more benign ilk than *The Holy Terror*. It is set in another universe (which further serves to distance its reality from our own) in a city called the Multihaven, where numerous religions coexist peacefully, with adherents shifting allegiance in accordance with their whims. *Faith Stealer* alludes to the 'free-market', supply-side theory of contemporary belief, with characters (including the regulars) invited to 'try out' different religions.[19]

There is considerable scope for comedy – many of the faiths alluded to are blatantly frivolous. The subtext here is double-voiced. On the one hand, what we see in this play is religion losing its behavioural distinctiveness – arguably one of the characteristics of secularisation. As Steve Bruce observes in relation to religion in North America, 'religion is no longer a set of rules which must be obeyed because God says so. It is a personal therapy which can be adopted. Its key terms no longer have any referents beyond the psyche'.[20] Because 'this basic change involves replacing the other-worldly with the mundane', he continues, 'there seems no obvious reason not to regard it as secularisation'.[21] A more sinister edge emerges when one religion violently attempts to eradicate its competitors and establish itself as the one true faith.

Yet, on the other hand, *Faith Stealer* carefully avoids the implication that religion has become irrelevant; indeed, purged of the dangerously fundamentalist religion which attempts to impose a tyrannical monotheism, the polytheistic community (the leader of which is urged to have 'faith' by the Doctor in the closing moments) continues much as before. There is clear progression from *The Holy Terror* and *Bloodtide*, which had both attempted to position secularism as a viable alternative to religion. *The Holy Terror* can be interpreted as an affirmation of the ethical viability of secularism, contrary to assertions that it lacks a moral dimension, while *Bloodtide* attempts to imbue evolutionary theory with the lyricism of the Creation myth. In comparison, the overall themes of *Faith Stealer* are neatly relativistic in their implications: the fatuousness of these 'religions', and their valorisation of the individual at the expense of the divine, may suggest the banality of modern forms of worship in Western societies, but they are seen to be capable of inspiring acts of goodness in individuals while fostering social stability.

Emerging at the end of a decade in which Doctor Who was sustained and developed by a new generation of fan-producers, it is not surprising that Big Finish's early releases seem to have been imbued with a similar spirit of freedom of expression. In a sense, the boldness of productions such as *The Holy Terror* and *Bloodtide* reflected Big Finish's aspiration to transcend their prospective identity as purveyors of nostalgia for the die-hard fans. For several years before the premiere of the new television series in early-2005, their releases were arguably the primary vehicle for 'new' *Doctor Who*. Until Eccleston's unveiling, Paul McGann was widely construed as the 'current' Doctor, and his stories (unlike those of his predecessors) were released in monthly instalments packaged as 'seasons'. This first 'season' of stories was marketed as 'season 27', implying that it was continuing where the classic series left off. Given the uncertainty over whether *Doctor Who* would *ever* return to television, it appeared that it may have found a permanent home with these ongoing audio adventures. *Doctor Who's* return to the screens has inevitably reconfigured their identity.

With its current status as the BBC's flagship drama series and its command of mass audiences both nationally and internationally, television *Doctor Who* is the primary arena in which the 'big issues' are tackled. Everything else – books, comic strips, audio stories included – necessarily play second fiddle. Big Finish are prohibited from using any of the new series' Doctors (i.e. Eccleston, Tennant, and Smith), and the most notable recent development in Big Finish's *Doctor Who* series has been Tom Baker's belated return to the role after a 30-year absence; nostalgia would seem to be the order of the day. This is not to denigrate these spin-offs; merely to suggest that they are no longer the primary media through which contemporary ideologies and belief systems are negotiated and integrated into *Doctor Who*. Their mandate is not to push boundaries, but simply to entertain. And it must be remembered that Big Finish is a relatively small company that can ill afford to alienate its prospective audience-base. The position of religion in modern Britain is subject to continual negotiation in all levels of public and private life; compromise is the eternal watchword. Perhaps *Doctor Who* – so long tacitly if not expressly secular in orientation – has reached a similarly relativistic compromise.

19.

Doctoring the Doctor: Midrashic Adventures in Text and Space

Joel Dark

By the time *Doctor Who* left television in 1989, it had long since taught its viewers how to say goodbye. As he walked into the distance, the Doctor's final lines reflected on the infinite expanse of the universe in perhaps the most romantic poetry of the programme's long history before concluding that the tea somewhere was getting cold and that there was work to do. These last words of *Doctor Who* followed over two decades of similarly hopeful farewells, as audiences had taken their leave of departing companions and even departing Doctors. The first such scene in 1964, rebroadcast as the introduction to the programme's twentieth anniversary episode in 1983, already exemplified this tradition. 'Just go forward in all your beliefs', the Doctor had said, 'and prove to me that I am not mistaken in mine.'[1]

What happened next paradoxically proved the sentiments of *Doctor Who*'s final farewell both correct and very much mistaken. Some fans moved on, reconciling themselves to the loss of *Doctor Who* and remembering it over the years with various levels of fondness and embarrassment. Others hoped eccentrically that it might somehow come back. Many did both. To the extent that they continued to draw on the best of the programme's fictional world, their post-*Doctor Who* stories would certainly have interesting things to say about *Doctor Who* and religion. The subject of this chapter, however, is a group of fans who devised a different response. Writers, actors, artists, composers and directors – professionals and amateurs, accomplished and aspiring – they would apply the imaginative bequest of *Doctor Who* to the problem of its own demise. For themselves, for other fans, and for another generation, they would achieve something surprising and extraordinary. They would bring back the Doctor.

They would eventually bring back all of them. At the time of writing, Tom Baker, Peter Davison, Colin Baker, Sylvester McCoy and Paul McGann all continue to star as the Doctor in new, full-cast audio episodes, and the first three Doctors – played by actors now deceased – feature regularly in audio productions narrated by the actors who played their companions on television. Preceding and then continuing alongside these plays from the studios of Big Finish Productions are hundreds of original *Doctor Who* novels, which began publication in 1991 and have continued to the present. The phenomenon has surpassed even the most hopeful dreams of *Doctor Who* fans, as new episodes and even new seasons have inserted themselves throughout the history of the programme. On audio and in print, speculative fan creations like 'Season 6B' and 'Season 19B' have become reality; the Doctor has carried on undeterred through the show's 'hiatus' in 1986; the cancelled 1990 season of the programme has been produced; and the failed 1996 television movie has become a success, launching its new Doctor on a long career. Witnessing these developments, fans of a time-travel programme could be forgiven for wondering if someone has been tampering with the past.

When *Doctor Who* made its celebrated return to television in 2005, the new series drew profoundly on the books and audio dramas of what then became known as the programme's 'wilderness years'. Both head writers of the new series, Russell T. Davies and later Steven Moffat, were attentive followers of the creative work of this period. '*Doctor Who* has finally become what it was created to be', Davies had written of Big Finish in 2003, adding that two of its stories – *Spare Parts* and *The Holy Terror* – were 'some of the best drama ever written for any genre, in any medium, anywhere'.[2] During the 1990s, Davies and Moffat had even made their own contributions to non-televised *Doctor Who*, writing one novel and one short story, respectively. Their new seasons of *Doctor Who* would reference and develop motifs from the books and audios, enlist their authors as scriptwriters, and even adapt whole stories for television, bringing to the programme a vast wealth of fan imagination that continues to contribute enormously to its quality.

These achievements of *Doctor Who* books and audio stories are arguably without parallel in the history of television, and they reveal a great deal about its religious dimensions. Writing for the journal *Religion & Literature*, Rachel Barenblat has recently argued that works of fan fiction are a kind of midrash, sharing some of the textual insights and practices of Judaism as a 'read/write tradition'.[3] Making analogies with both classical rabbinic and modern midrash, she writes that fan fiction similarly expresses love for shared texts, frustration with their silences, and a determination to expand and continue their stories.[4] Although *Doctor Who* novels, audios and short stories are licensed by the BBC and considered, strictly speaking, to be 'tie-in' or 'spin-off' media rather than fan fiction, these works compellingly exemplify the approach to narrative texts that Barenblat and others have associated with midrash. By keeping *Doctor Who* alive in the wilderness years, winning recognition and acclaim among the creative talents of the original series, and then infusing the revival of the programme, they have also challenged simple understandings of the relationship between television stories and the imaginative work of their audiences.

Although Barenblat's essay follows a significant body of scholarship that has explored connections between midrash and literature, reflections about midrash do not enjoy widespread currency in conversations about creative responses to television and popular fiction.[5] The status of midrash in this regard contrasts remarkably with the more established career of the concept, also religious, of canon. Since its beginnings in Sherlock Holmes fandom, the idea of canon in serialised narratives, and particularly science fiction and fantasy, has become so commonplace that one can easily take its logic for granted. Unlike the Holmes canon, generally understood to comprise the original stories of Conan Doyle, canon in *Doctor Who* is largely a question of medium – i.e., television – rather than authorship, copyright, precedence, or even plot continuity.[6] For strict adherents to canon, non-televised stories by regular television writers, audio productions with full casts of television actors, books published by the BBC, and even works later 'spun off' into television episodes all fall short of this single criterion. Critiquing his own earlier commitment to this understanding of canonicity, Russell T. Davies has described it as 'that idiot equation, the dull $e=mc^2$ of fandom: canon=telly'.[7]

In fact, the origins and inner workings of canon equations are fascinating and complex. Like Barenblat's exploration of fan fiction as midrash, the idea of canon in *Doctor Who* and other modern myths belongs to a discourse that blurs distinctions between sacred texts and popular fiction. Writing extensively about this phenomenon among early Holmes fans, the historian Michael Saler has termed it 'modern, ironic belief', in which followers of sustained fictional narratives intentionally 'become immersed but not submerged' in imaginary worlds.[8] Although Saler allows for the possibility of 'escapism', he generally views this practice as positive and purposeful – an escape *for* rather than merely an escape *from*. Through ironic belief, he argues, modern fan audiences free their imaginations to engage critically, and in community, with the more serious, venerated narratives that construct and constrain their social realities.[9]

The emergence of canonicity as a significant question for Saler's ironic believers and its remarkable persistence are largely attributable to the religious context within which modern fandom developed. Although the concept of canon is hardly unique to British and North American Protestantism, the version of canon that became a reference point for modern fandom owed significantly to this religious culture. Broadly speaking, this has involved the understanding of a canonical text as bounded, coherent, unambiguous and authoritative. For distinctive but not entirely dissimilar reasons, modern Protestantism and modern entertainment have sought to provide for mass audiences reliable, readily comprehensible, and commonly understood texts. With the continuing evolution of protections for intellectual property, these values have also acquired legal implications. Unlike Conan Doyle, who claimed that he had authorised the writer of a licensed Holmes play to 'marry him or murder him or do whatever you like with him',[10] individual and corporate producers of more recent myths have even adopted their own official positions on canon.[11]

To the extent that *Doctor Who* has managed to free itself from this particular construction of canon, it has done so, like the Doctor himself, through a combination of genius, failure, and well-timed coincidences – not necessarily in that order. In retrospect, one of the happiest accidents of the programme's history may well have been its abandonment by the BBC at a critical juncture in the transformation of fan culture, soon to be reinforced by a revolution in communications technology. In the 'hiatus' year of 1986, as some viewers organised to protest the programme's first suspension, future Big Finish producer Nicholas Briggs was already playing his own version of the Doctor in whole seasons of stories produced by fans on audiocassette.[12] By the mid-1990s, Steven Moffat would be adding his two cents to a Usenet fan discussion of *Doctor Who* canon – arguing against – from his CompuServe account.[13] During the

1980s and 1990s, in a development still underway today, the reading public of Saler's Holmesians was becoming the writing public of Barenblat's midrashic fan communities. One can almost imagine the Doctor imploring the BBC not to banish him into this blue box.

A second happy accident for *Doctor Who*'s midrashic future was the almost impossible contradictory complexity of its twenty-six year narrative. This was actually a long series of accidents. If 'surface irregularities of the text', in the words of the biblical scholar James Kugel, are 'the grain of sand which so irritates the midrashic oyster that he constructs a pearl around it',[14] the original *Doctor Who* series was a beach. Leaving aside peripheral problems such as the three destructions of Atlantis,[15] television *Doctor Who* was inconsistent even in basic facts about its main characters. The Doctor's most famous antagonists had two origin stories – 'The Daleks' in 1963 and 'Genesis of the Daleks' in 1975 – both written by Terry Nation and belonging to the best-known episodes of the series. After revealing that the Doctor was about 450 years old in 1967, the series had moved the decimal point (by at least one place) to 'several thousand years' in the following decade before then moving it back again.[16] Perhaps most remarkably, the 1976 story 'The Brain of Morbius' had briefly showed viewers the faces of eight pre-William Hartnell Doctors, never seen before or since. If *Doctor Who* had actually been trying to resemble an ancient composite text preserved in fragments over centuries, one could hardly imagine a more convincing performance. To the extent that canon, in the sense of a continuous story, could even be said to exist under these circumstances, it was already the midrashic work of fan imagination.

It was largely two more prominent and celebrated features of *Doctor Who*, however, that allowed fans to turn these doubtful virtues of the programme into extraordinary creative achievements. The first of these was time travel. Although arguably underdeveloped in much of the television series, where it served as a device for locating more conventional stories, the premise of traversable time was foundational to *Doctor Who*. Likely speaking for more doubtful members of the programme's first audience in 1963, the character Ian Chesterton had protested that time 'just happens and then it's finished',[17] but he was already alone in a fictional world that would eventually introduce time loops, scoops, streams, eddies and of course the web of time. While sometimes posing problems for the Doctor to solve, the nonlinear, or multi-linear, complexity of time expressed in these metaphors was more often an opportunity for the exploration of delightful narrative possibilities. On three memorable occasions, the series had even brought the Doctor together with earlier, relatively speaking, versions of himself.[18] For fan writers eager to develop this element of *Doctor Who* further, the programme ended in 1989 with the entire series, at least potentially, in the present and the future.

Perhaps equally important for the midrashic potential of classic *Doctor Who* was the fact that its main character was a personified question mark. As with time travel, one could argue that this second foundational concept had also receded into the background of most television adventures, where the Doctor appeared as a familiar character with an increasingly established backstory. Even when the Doctor was at his least alien, however, the question of the programme's title was there with the strange music at the beginning of every episode. The tune had no words, but when the BBC did release a single with spoken lyrics – Rupert Hine's 'Who is the Doctor' in 1972 – they began, 'I cross the void beyond the mind …'[19] It was ironically Jon Pertwee's avuncular, Earth-bound Doctor who performed this strange text, but such incongruity was a part of the mystery. The Doctor was a frail grandfather and an action hero, a tired exile and a bright-eyed explorer, a distracted tinkerer and a burdened citizen of the cosmos, a more or less human scientist-inventor and an alien Time Lord. Remarkably, he was an almost accidental participant in most of his own television stories and yet also, the programme suggested, an intentional actor in an unfathomably larger narrative.

These four features, among others, of classic *Doctor Who* allowed the books and audio stories that followed it to develop its narrative profoundly without, to borrow the memorable language of the programme, rewriting even one line of its history. Conservatives, whether canon devotees or just attentive custodians of loved stories, could enjoy the books and audios as the exegesis of texts that already, potentially, contained everything. For progressives, they could be brave departures in new directions. In the early years of the *Doctor Who* novels, as a generation of maturing young writers puzzled over the difference between serious new fiction and the indulgence of nostalgia, there was even briefly an attempt to map this distinction onto two separate series of books. The Doctor's intrepid *New Adventures* would explore the former, and his cosier *Missing Adventures*, featuring past Doctors, would accommodate the latter. Perhaps needless to say, this did not work. An elusive or even imperceptible distinction in practice, it collapsed completely when time travel inevitably brought the two ranges together, introducing the adult characters and themes of the *New Adventures* into a *Missing Adventure* with the innocent TARDIS crew of Peter Davison's 1982 season.[20]

Although books and audios both preserved and transformed *Doctor Who*, the sum achievement of these stories was to make the programme more itself. It has often been noted that the imagination of viewers enhanced the subjective visual experience of classic *Doctor Who* far beyond the limitations of its budget, but this was also true for the programme's implied narrative, which its television format could only begin to explore. While not laconic in the same sense as biblical stories, with their remarkable economy of language, televised *Doctor Who* implied a narrative vastly larger than its weekly episodes could contain. And as with midrash, albeit for different reasons, filling in lines and connecting the dots were allowed. In print and on audio, one could insert a new episode between lines of a television script, fill larger gaps with whole new seasons, explore the significance of a seemingly incidental line of dialogue, and link an episode from the 1960s to a story from the 1980s – or vice versa.[21] For fan writers, classic *Doctor Who* became a television text where everything could matter. And in a seemingly endless series of unfolding connections, elucidations and extrapolations, they proved that it did.

One of the most important achievements of this work – broadly comparable with the ethical interrogation of religious myths associated with modern midrash – was the retelling of stories with attention to neglected or missing voices. Perhaps inevitably for *Doctor Who*, these included the perspectives of the monsters and villains who had contributed so much to the programme's success. Widely known through its later adaptation for television, Robert Shearman's audio story *Jubilee* presented a single, isolated Dalek as a complex and tragic character. Shearman's gift of voice to a famously unsubtle television icon radically challenged the received interpretation of the Daleks while, in his exploration of their identity as damaged soldiers, remaining entirely faithful to a central theme of their television stories.[22] In David McIntee's novel *The Dark Path*, which recounted the Master's turn to the dark side, the television source text – 'I've wasted all my lives because of you, Doctor' – was specific and, appearing at the beginning of the book, explicit.[23] Still more masterfully midrashic was Marc Platt's audio drama *Spare Parts*, which constructed a profoundly tragic origins story for the Cybermen around its title, borrowed from the first words of the characters in the television series. Reinterpreted through Platt's audio story, the strangely homespun appearance of the 1966 Cybermen and their incongruously ordinary description of themselves as creatures of 'spare parts' were no accident but revealed instead a remnant of their humanity, wrapped and buried for protection from the dark, the cold, and finally from knowledge of itself.[24]

Happily, most of the voices waiting to be discovered in *Doctor Who* belonged to more positive characters. The Doctor's companions – approximately thirty in total, depending on the criteria – had been one of the greatest strengths of the programme, which had nevertheless only begun to realise their potential. The limitations of their development in the original series were attributable in part to gender stereotypes and other storytelling conventions of the period, such as the role of the 'assistant' or 'sidekick', that more recent television writing has at least attempted to challenge. Then as now, however, other narrative constraints for the Doctor's companion were more intrinsic to television. Although these characters were, in one sense, literally made for television, both the short, episodic format of television storytelling and the regular replacement of supporting cast members clashed awkwardly with their central importance in an epic spanning vast reaches of space and time. By suggesting unexplored depths in the Doctor's companions, moreover, the programme's skilful writers and actors had made this contradiction between their medium and their characters even more striking, further magnifying the midrashic spaces in their stories.

The creative development of *Doctor Who* companions in books and audio stories has been especially meaningful because of their celebrated role as identification figures for the programme's audiences. In a short essay for the recent collection *Chicks Dig Time Lords*, the literary scholar Francesca Coppa reflects on this phenomenon in the case of Nyssa of Traken, one of the most compelling of the Doctor's companions and, for Coppa, a personal role model.[25] Coppa's essay is organised around three positive elements of Nyssa's character, the first two of which – her substantive interaction with another female character (i.e., the Bechdel test)[26] and the validation of her genius by intelligent peers – refer to her portrayal on the television. Building on these observations, however, Coppa's third argument is that the 'structure of Nyssa's time with the Fifth Doctor', with its potential 'other stories and what-ifs', has permitted even further exploration of her character in books, audios, and fan fiction.[27] For Coppa, these media have both preserved Nyssa as a teenage inspiration and, in their continuation of her story, allowed her to grow up with the author.

Admittedly, Nyssa is an especially strong *Doctor Who* character, and the narrative space to which Coppa refers between her two main television seasons is especially pronounced. Remarkably, however, Coppa's reflections about 'other stories and what-ifs' now apply to every companion in the original television series, from the most ephemeral to the most fully realised. As noted above with reference to *Doctor Who* monsters, even subtle hints of character development in the television text have drawn the midrashic attention of fan writers, and this has clearly benefited both well-drawn characters like Nyssa and many of their otherwise worthy counterparts whose television episodes, one may unfortunately assume, fail the Bechdel test by a wide margin. Like Nyssa, most of these companions have featured in 'missing' stories set in their own television period as well as stories that give at least some sense of their later lives. On audio, Big Finish has produced entire ranges of stories focused on *Doctor Who* companions, including *Sarah Jane Smith* (which preceded television's *The Sarah Jane Adventures* by several years), *Jago and Lightfoot* and the ongoing *Companion Chronicles*. Writing for *The Companion Chronicles*, Marc Platt even provided the beginning of a continuing backstory for the Doctor's granddaughter Susan Foreman, the eponymous 'unearthly child' of the programme's first episode. As with *Spare Parts*, Platt's audio story *Quinnis* drew in minute detail on a relatively obscure moment of dialogue from the early years of the television series. 'The planet Quinnis in the fourth universe', the Doctor and Susan had explained in the programme's third story, was 'where we nearly lost the TARDIS, four or five journeys back'.[28] Inventively locating the near loss of the TARDIS (before it was a blue police box) as the traditional cliffhanger for his drama, Platt's script opened a whole world of pre-television *Doctor Who*, including the still-unfolding mystery of the Doctor's first companion.[29]

The further development of the Doctor's companions in print and audio has been primarily an exploration of their complexity as individuals rather than an extension of their representative diversity as a group. The *New Adventures* novels did introduce, in Rozz Forrester from the thirtieth century, the first *Doctor Who* companion of African ancestry, and her space police partner and fellow companion Chris Cwej challenged heterosexism in Russell T. Davies's 1996 novel *Damaged Goods*, explaining that categories of sexuality were rarely an issue in his own time.[30] In the audio stories, the character of Evelyn

Smythe, created by Jacqueline Rayner, also finally gave the Doctor an older companion, the importance of which was appreciatively recognised by the Doctor himself.[31] Although these examples and others – new male companions, an Egyptian pharaoh, and (as a follow-up, at last, on the Doctor's name dropping) Mary Shelley – attest to significant diversity gains over the television series, *Doctor Who* books and audios have broadly followed the television convention of pairing a centuries-old white male Time Lord with young, single, white women, frequently from modern Britain. Their achievement has been instead to give greater prominence to the perspectives of companions and, free from television casting constraints, to allow their stories, like the Doctor's, to continue. Anticipating both Rose and River Song in the new television series, the Edwardian Charley Pollard came to love the Eighth Doctor, travelling with him longer than any television companion, only to then continue her journey as the new companion of the Sixth Doctor, who was oblivious to her identity although perceptively suspicious. Essentially impossible to realise on television, overlapping story arcs of this kind have allowed *Doctor Who* companions to escape from their more or less linear succession as temporary characters into print and audio media that more fully allow them, and their companionship with a Time Lord, to matter.

One of the most fascinating aspects of this storytelling ethic has been its grounding in real-world relationships among different generations of *Doctor Who* writers, actors, and fans. The alchemy of fan devotion, professionalism, and hard work that allowed these relationships to develop certainly merits a study in itself, but it is clear that they represent something extraordinary, if not indeed unique, in the history of television. The *New Adventures* and *Missing Adventures* novels of the 1990s, and the BBC ranges that continued these stories through 2005, had already brought contributions from writers in their twenties together with books by Terrance Dicks and Barry Letts, who had written and produced *Doctor Who* in the early 1970s. It was largely the work of Big Finish, however, building on earlier professional relationships with actors from the programme, that brought television generations separated by decades together in producing new stories. For reflections on fan works as midrash, the company's spectacularly successful commitment to original-cast dramas is significant not only as an expression of attention to textual detail but also because it involves participation in an intergenerational storytelling community.[32] Recently returning after more than three decades to her role as Leela alongside Tom Baker's Doctor, Louise Jameson charmingly pitched her first line to provide a seamless transition from a 1977 episode into its new sequel, matching or even surpassing her fans' devotion to continuity.[33] The reciprocal miracle of Big Finish is that *Doctor Who* actors, invited into an unanticipated reverence for the stories they created, have proved themselves and their stories more than worthy of this devotion.

It would be fanciful, as well as a discredit to countless creative talents, to attribute these achievements to the mysterious Doctor himself. The fact that one can even plausibly joke about such a possibility, however, speaks to an underlying truth in this suspicion. Superficially, of course, the title character of *Doctor Who* is anything but a careful custodian of his own stories, let alone their finer details. This is indeed commonly regarded as a strength of the programme. Bounding boldly across time and space from one blank canvas to the next, the Doctor represents the love of the programme's audience for stories that are always new, exciting, and original. Viewing the Doctor in these terms alone, one might expect fans inspired by his character to create a new series, or perhaps to attempt the now-familiar 'reboot', rather than imaginatively curating characters, stories, and narrative possibilities dating back to the 1960s.

This, however, is a very limited understanding of the Doctor. Already in the classic television series, he was an affectionate steward and imaginative engineer of things old, broken, ordinary, and obsolete, including his own time machine. And he was interested in – was indeed, when asked, a doctor of – 'practically everything',[34] perhaps looking forward but always, just as importantly, looking closer. Scholar and healer, reverent explorer and inventive repairer, the Doctor of the television programme was, in many ways, a doctor of midrash, and the books and audio stories that he inspired would make him even more so.

Building on themes intimated in the television series, one approach to this characterisation of the Doctor in print and audio has been to imagine time and space as a kind of text through which he travels, in multiple directions, appreciatively and redemptively. *Doctor Who* stories are famously inconsistent about the 'laws of time' and how much of this text can, or should, be changed, but it is clear that the Doctor does not regard it entirely as a closed canon. Rejecting the dual temptations of his Time Lord heritage – passivity and power – he refuses either to view the text from the detached complacency of privilege or to do it injury through the assumption of mastery. Instead, as with midrashic approaches to religious texts, he engages in the history of the universe from below and from within – sometimes minutely, sometimes audaciously, sometimes clumsily, sometimes confidently, but almost always compassionately, imaginatively, and in collaboration with companions.

These attributes of the Doctor are not unfamiliar, but it is largely in the books and audio stories that they have been explicitly applied to thinking about the preservation and transformation of texts. Some instances of this are transparent and lighthearted. In the first of the BBC novels that succeeded the *New Adventures*, Terrance Dicks took the new Eighth Doctor on time travels through the original television series, sorting out several of its more superficial continuity problems along the way.[35] And for the programme's fortieth anniversary, Big Finish sent the same Doctor back in time with former companions to recover a Douglas Adams episode lost to a BBC strike in 1978.[36] Other *Doctor Who* novels and audio stories, however, have placed the character in more profoundly complex relationships with the text, meaningfully exploring the remarkable narrative possibilities of *Doctor Who* and the nature and character of the Doctor. Three brief examples of this approach include Paul Cornell's 1995 novel *Human Nature*, Steven Moffat's 1996 short story 'Continuity Errors' and Steven Hall's 2010 audio drama *A Death in the Family*.

As indicated in its title, Cornell's novel is best known for presenting readers with a human Doctor, allowing the character, in the form of the 1914 history teacher John Smith, a rare and beautifully written love story. Equally compelling, however, is Cornell's achievement in turning 'the Doctor' himself into a story. Distinct from Smith for much of the novel, the Doctor is split into two texts. The deepest part of the Doctor resides as a story in Smith himself, who experiences him in his dreams and his attempts at amateur fiction. The second part has been stored in a 'biodata pod' – a science-fiction metaphor for a book – discovered and protected by a bullied pupil named Tim Dean. In the course of Cornell's novel, 'the Doctor' frees both Smith and Dean from the dangerous narratives and certainties of their pre-war military school and its wider culture, allowing them to think imaginatively in a world that does not encourage them to think. In much of *Human Nature*, the Doctor is not a character but rather, in Smith's words, 'a useful mental model'.[37] He is an idea, a story, and a way of questioning stories. He is 'a word on a page in a book that he also was' or words 'both read and invented'.[38] He appears in songs still to be written, in the question-mark handle of Smith's umbrella,

and in the white poppy, a future symbol of peace worn by both Smith
and Dean. In the final scene of the novel, set in 1995, a white poppy
falls from Dean's wheelchair to be recovered by the Doctor, who,
once again a time traveller and once again a person, places it in his
buttonhole.

Published one year after Cornell's novel, Steven Moffat's 1996
short story 'Continuity Errors' imagines the Doctor as a transformative
presence in texts already written. The basic plot elements of the story
have now become familiar through its redevelopment for a 2010
Dickens-themed television Christmas special, but Moffat's original
work is more explicitly about texts and their instability in the hands
of those who care about them. Confronting a Scrooge-like librarian
who persistently refuses him access to a restricted text, the Doctor
functions in the story as a metaphor for the 'continuity errors' that
the protection of canon from fandom purportedly serves to prevent.
Although the Doctor does get his book – and changes it – most of
the plot, as in the 2010 Christmas special, concerns the Doctor's
interventions in the librarian's own story that bring about this result.
These typically Doctor-ish acts – including a two-month career as a
substitute teacher; the return of the librarian's absconding husband
in a mysterious blue lorry; and the rescue of her daughter from a
plant monster – arguably restore 'continuity' to the librarian's life
rather than disrupting it. Whether these interventions are permitted
for a time traveller, however compassionate and expert, is of course
a fictional problem, but Moffat certainly seems to suggest that they
are allowed for Doctor-inspired fans. Introducing himself at the
beginning of the story as a doctor of history, the Doctor adds, 'I mean
I make it better', and it would be difficult to argue that Moffat and
other fans have not done the same for him.[39]

Written over a decade after *Human Nature* and 'Continuity Errors',
Steven Hall's *A Death in the Family* nevertheless builds on both works,
along with an immense wealth of inspiration from other stories. This
integrative achievement, breathtaking in its complexity, is already
a kind of midrash. Even more remarkably, however, Hall's story is
arguably about midrash itself. Battling a 'Word Lord', who travels
in a CORDIS (Conveyance of Repeating Dialogue in Spacetime), the
Doctor and other characters in *A Death in the Family* face challenges
framed by the limitations and possibilities of texts, language and
imagination. Realising that he requires a text 'huge and branching,
contradictory yet singular and coherent, made of living thoughts', the
Doctor uses his own narrative to defeat the Word Lord but loses his

life in the effort. It is his companions, remarkably, who resurrect him, using an inventive array of verbal technologies but more importantly the hidden textual and narrative possibilities of their story. Although it becomes clear that a future Doctor has plotted these possibilities himself, his very existence is the result of the choice of his companions to see them and use them. In a brilliant *Doctor Who* paradox that Hall simply allows to stand, the story thus locates midrashic agency in two different Doctors, in the text of the story, and – at last – in his companions, his friends and his fans.[40]

It is perhaps above all in this final sense that the midrashic character of *Doctor Who* may be said to reside in the story itself, or to be the work of the Doctor. To the attentive viewer, the possibility that the Doctor believes profoundly in his fans has been there all along – or at least since the Doctor said goodbye to his first companion, asserting that her journey forward in her beliefs would prove the truth of his own. Significantly, the lines were spoken directly into the camera from within the TARDIS, subjectively breaking the fourth wall and allowing them to speak to audiences across many years. Almost five decades and hundreds of stories later, the point is not even especially subtle. Asked at the end of the 2011 television story 'The God Complex' what he believed in, the Doctor maintained a mysterious silence, only to announce in the next episode ('Closing Time'), 'I've always believed, in all of you, all of my life', imploring a companion once again to 'prove me right!'

Although one can apply something analogous to midrash to virtually any text, the stories that invite and reward the effort are those that credit our intelligence, imagination and potential and through which we extend this confidence to others. *Doctor Who*, for a wide range of reasons, only some of which are in the text, has proved for many of its fans to be this kind of story. Already containing over two decades of imaginative text and space when the programme was discontinued in 1989, it was better than the largest blank canvas. More than a storytelling format, it had become a vast, shared literature. Whether watched alone, among friends, or in families, it was inseparable from the lives and personal stories of its most devoted viewers, who knew its words, like those of a familiar song, by heart. To have imagined in 1989 that they would one day revive *Doctor Who* would have been a hopeful prediction indeed, but they did much more than this. They became innovative curators of the original programme, carefully researching and expanding its stories, repairing its gaps, and reengaging the creative talents behind it. They ensured the continuation of *Doctor Who* not merely as a franchise or a concept but rather in the full richness of its complex history and their own manifold encounters with it.

As *Doctor Who* celebrates its fiftieth anniversary and enters the second half of its first century this year, one can hope that it will continue to grow with its audience, embracing the many readers and writers whose stories it has only begun to tell and correcting the continuity errors that have left their stories out. In writing these chapters of *Doctor Who* history, future authors can certainly draw inspiration not only from the programme but also from the extraordinary achievement of a community of fans who took its expansive invitation boldly to heart and extended it to future generations. The second midrashic mystery of texts, television boxes and TARDISes – never very well hidden in Doctor Who – is that they are bigger on the outside. With this universe of stories still to explore and with only 497 regenerations left – if that's even canon – the Doctor, as always, has no time to waste.

Epilogue

James F. McGrath

As one of the editors, let me say that trying to put together a single volume that did at least some justice to the richness of this show's 50 years was a challenge. And so trying to bring the threads of the volume together into a concluding summary, as well as looking ahead to what the future might hold, should we be fortunate enough to get another 50 years of *Doctor Who*, might well be daunting for a Time Lord. As it is, I'm only human. But hopefully I can offer a few reminders of themes that have come to the fore in the chapters of this book, highlight some questions the show still keeps us asking, and offer some suggestions about useful topics that Whovians interested in the intersection of religion and *Doctor Who* might talk about and reflect upon.

Many people, when they think about religion and *Doctor Who*, think only of the Doctor as a Christ or saviour figure. Yet a major focus of recent episodes has been on the Doctor's 'God complex' being deflated. And while the Doctor has regularly appeared in the role of a debunker of foolish superstitions, in the very process he frequently demonstrates their reality. For instance, the Doctor says about the idea that all life in the universe might stem from Akhaten, 'It's what they believe. It's a nice story.' Yet the Doctor soon finds himself confronting an entity that is real, powerful, and extremely dangerous, to which he says, 'You're not a God, you're a parasite'. What, if anything, would make a being a 'god' in the *Doctor Who* universe? This is not a new question for the show. When the Third Doctor was asked (in the episode 'The Time Monster') 'Are you trying to tell us that the classical gods are real?' his response was, appropriately, 'Well, yes and no.' And beyond these individual entities that might or might not be appropriately referred to as 'gods,' there is also the question of whether there is something even greater that encompasses them – whether one can bargain with the universe, as in 'The Snowmen'.

Does the distinction between the natural and the supernatural disappear in a universe in which the seemingly miraculous happens? The last season of *Doctor Who*, as of the publication of this book, the seventh series of the revived show, has focused on one such phenomenon: a seemingly impossible girl, a person who seems to be instantiated multiple times across the universe. It has been a characteristic of recent series to present a mystery (often but not always at the beginning of a season) which gets explored and eventually solved. Bad Wolf, River Song, the crack in the universe, the Doctor's death and Clara the impossible girl, to name a few examples. Yet while this might seem not to be characteristic of the show in its earlier days, that depends how one thinks about the show's episodes. When the show first began, it featured half-hour episodes which could be grouped together into larger story arcs, and it was only later that these came to be thought of as multi-part episodes. And even then, we were kept in suspense for four to six weeks at a time, each part ending with a cliffhanger. And so, far from being a radical change of format, the fact that the current forty-five minute episodes have often been parts of a larger whole is in keeping with an element of suspense and mystery that has been part of the show from the beginning.

Whatever the format of the mystery or cliffhanger that drives the story forward over a couple of hours or an entire season, many of the mysteries and threats to the universe have some intersection with religion: the need for absolute faith as in 'The Curse of Fenric', or the need to shake that faith as in 'The God Complex'; the danger posed by a rather unimpressive-looking Kronos or a Daemon from ancient mythology, or a rather large and genuinely threatening-looking Satan or parasite sun-god. And while on rare occasions it is only the people on one planet or one spaceship that are in danger, the number of ways that the entire cosmos can apparently be destroyed in the *Doctor Who* universe is genuinely staggering. It might be worth investigating how this sense that not merely an individual's existence, but existence itself, is extremely fragile came to be a part of the show's outlook, and what has led to its continued presence as part of the *Doctor Who* mythology.

Recent episodes and seasons have focused attention on the Doctor's secrets. This too was in keeping with the show's earlier heritage. Many fans who watched the show in the 1980s may think of the so-called 'Cartmel masterplan', which was exploring the possibility that the Doctor was more than just another Time Lord, that he was in fact the third of the three key Gallifreyans who, along with Rassilon and Omega, made the Time Lords what they are and achieved a god-like status among them. But the original background notes for the show[1] planned to make the mystery of the main character's identity a central and ongoing theme, with possible answers to the question 'Doctor Who?' being proposed regularly, only to be found to be wrong. The precise original idea was not the direction the show would eventually take. But the mystery coming to the fore on the show recently is in keeping with the original proposal. If, on one level, the Doctor initially seemed less the main character, and more the classic old wizard or trickster god whose presence leads to adventure for others, the intention was always for his identity to drive the ongoing story, with eventual revelations to be offered if the show continued long enough.

When the title of the series 7 finale was revealed to be 'The Name of the Doctor', many fans debated whether they wanted to know his name. Is 50 years long enough for a show to keep its fans in suspense before revealing the name of the central character? The biggest fear seems to have been that the name, if revealed, would seem too mundane, insufficiently satisfying after such a long wait. As it turned out, the Great Intelligence sought to get the Doctor to utter his name in order to get into his tomb and access his timeline – it wasn't the sound of the name itself that was to the fore in the episode, but the access that the name granted when uttered. Secrecy regarding one's true name is a facet of much ancient religion and magic, in which knowing the name of a god, angel or demon was thought to grant the knower power over the entity. A connection between name and nature of this sort is in fact proposed not merely in the aforementioned season finale, but much earlier, in 'The Beast Below,' when the Doctor says that if he murders the star whale, he will have to find a new name, because he 'won't be The Doctor anymore'.

The show has now tantalisingly given us a deeper glimpse of the Doctor's chosen self-designation as 'a pledge' which one of his selves broke. And Clara's glimpse of the Doctor's name in a volume entitled *The History of the Time War* suggests one context within which that might have occurred.

The Doctor's darker side has always been with the show – indeed, there were proposals before the show ever aired to have his character be even harsher than William Hartnell eventually depicted him.

Ambivalence about the Doctor's darker side and his fallibility have continued, and we see the impact of this in the abruptly-ended era of Colin Baker's Doctor, when the Doctor's instability at the beginning, and appearance in a malevolent form as the Valeyard at the end, led to a shake-up on the show and Baker's departure. The recent focus of the show perhaps suggests that *Doctor Who* was ahead of its time in the 80s, rather than having gone off course, as some then felt.

Looking ahead to the future, there is no way to predict the direction the show might take. But that in itself can lead to interesting discussions at the intersection of *Doctor Who* and religion. For those steeped in the study of religion, the impossibility of essentialising the show or neatly defining the boundaries of its canon comes as no surprise. Religious traditions and their canons of sacred texts (when they have such things) are never a simple given, never static, never with boundaries that are permanently impermeable. Science-fiction traditions and canons are very much the same, in this regard.

Back in 2011, I began blogging through the classic *Doctor Who* series from the beginning on my blog Exploring Our Matrix, highlighting the themes of religious interest in each episode. Now it is 2013, and I am still not finished. Someone has calculated that it would take around 370 hours to watch every episode from 'An Unearthly Child' through 'The Name of the Doctor.' While that is a mere 16 days without any significant breaks to sleep or do other necessary activities, it is more than a year if one watches an hour a day. If one were to include all of the audiobooks, novels, TV specials, documentaries, supplements and spin-offs, one might not manage to partake of them all in a single human lifespan. And so the most a volume of this size can hope to accomplish is to celebrate this cultural phenomenon, study it, and hope to generate continued discussion. One can readily discuss very serious topics related to religion using *Doctor Who* as a jumping off point, and one can also find thought-provoking treatments of such topics in its episodes themselves. This book illustrates that amply. But it does not exhaust the discussion. And that is as it should be. The show is, after all, about the extent of space and time. As the Doctor put it in the episode 'The Power of Three,' the universe is full of so many ephemeral things that are worth seeing, and he is 'running to them before they flare and fade forever'. The fictional universe of *Doctor Who* teems in a similar way with an incredible richness of material to watch, read, listen to and discuss.

The Doctor's eloquent words about the beauty and extent of the cosmos, about the value of human life, about the need to be true to our chosen identity, illustrate the reason the show is so important to so many fans, and of natural interest for those who study religion. *Doctor Who* does not merely explore topics like religion in some sort of historical or polemical manner. It contextualises its explorations within the producers' and writers' visions of the broader framework of human existence, which in turn is placed within the broader context of our ever-changing universe. When we explore our place in the universe as human beings, we tell stories, creatively weaving older stories into the fabric of new ones. *Doctor Who* does that with classic historical, mythological and spiritual motifs. This book has sought to do something along the same lines with religious traditions and the stories of the *Doctor Who* universe. What will come next, we do not know. But we look forward to it, and hope you will join us in taking the Doctor's hand, running to see and explore, and reflecting on what we find!

Notes

Andrew Crome, Introduction

1   Linda Woodhead, 'Introduction' in Linda Woodhead and Rebecca Catto (eds), *Religion and Change in Modern Britain* (London: Routledge, 2012), pp.1-33.

2   For example, Steve Bruce, *Secularization: In Defence of an Unfashionable Theory* (Oxford: Oxford University Press, 2013).

3   'The Rings of Akhaten' (2013).

4   Robert Pope, *Salvation in Celluloid: Theology, Imagination and Film* (London: T&T Clark, 2007), pp.1-19.

5   John Tulloch and Manuel Alvarado, *Doctor Who: The Unfolding Text* (London: Macmillan,1983), pp.249-268.

6   Ian Chesterton responds to a robot's question of why Barbara has set off 'dangerous vibrations in the perceptor coils'. Ian's answer would surely have changed our own perceptions of him forever: 'I bet they have. They are women, old mechanical chum... w-o-m-e-n. And if you think your perceptor coils are the only ones affected...'. See Anthony Coburn, *Doctor Who: The Scripts: The Masters of Luxor* (London: Titan Books, 1992), p.51.

7   Coburn, *Masters of Luxor*, p.90.

8   'The Face of Evil' (1976).

9   'The Parting of the Ways' (2005).

10 Piers D. Britton, *TARDISbound: Navigating the Universes of Doctor Who* (London: I. B. Tauris, 2011), pp.10-28.

11 Callum G. Brown, *The Death of Christian Britain: Understanding Secularisation 1800-2000* Second Edition (London: Routledge, 2009), p.1. For the most recent debate on when (or if) Britain was secularised see S. J. D . Green, *The Passing of Protestant England* (Cambridge: Cambridge University Press, 2010); J. C. D. Clark, 'Secularization and Modernization: The failure of a "Grand Narrative"', *The Historical Journal* 55:1 (2012), pp.161-194; Jeremy Morris, 'Secularization and Religious Experience: Arguments in the Historiography of Modern British Religion', *The Historical Journal* 55:1 (2012), pp.195-219. Also of note are the alternative viewpoints explored in chapters of Woodhead and Catto's volume. See particularly Mathew Guest, Elizabeth Olson and John Wolffe, 'Christianity: Loss of Monopoly' in Woodhead and Catto (eds), *Religion and Change in Modern Britain*, pp.57-78 and Callum G. Brown and Gordon Lynch, 'Cultural Perspectives' in Woodhead and Catto (eds), *Religion and Change in Modern Britain*, pp.329-351.

12 Christopher Partridge, *The Re-Enchantment of the West: Alternative Spiritualities, Sacralization, Popular Culture, and Occulture* 2 vols., (London: T&T Clark, 2004-5).

13 John D. Beckwith, 'Honest to Doctor Who' in Terrence Dicks, *The Making of Doctor Who* (London: Pan, 1972). We are grateful to Gordon Blows for bringing this source to our attention.

14 Stephen Kelly, 'Does *Doctor Who* offer a God for our times?', *The Guardian Online*, 24th December 2011, [http://www.guardian.co.uk/commentisfree/belief/2011/dec/24/doctor-who-god-christmas]. Last accessed 13th April 2013; Liel Liebovitz, 'Doctor Who? Doctor Jew', *Tablet Magazine*, May 9th 2013, [http://www.tabletmag.com/jewish-arts-and-culture/131751/doctor-who-doctor-jew]. Last accessed 24th May 2013.

15 'Spirituality and *Doctor Who* Day', [http://www.churcharmy.org.uk/pub/nc/News/News2008/0802DoctorWho.aspx]. Last accessed 13th April 2013. It is tempting, but probably facetious, to see the quite literal Church Army of the fifty-first century in 'Time of Angels' as a tongue-in-cheek response to this.

16 Jonathan Wynne-Jones, 'The Church is Ailing-Send for *Dr Who*', *Daily Telegraph* 4th May 2008, [http://www.telegraph.co.uk/news/newstopics/howaboutthat/1925338/The-church-is-ailing-send-for-Dr-Who.html]. Last accessed 13th April 2013.

17 Rowan Williams, 'Archbishop of Canterbury's 2011 Easter Sermon', [http://rowanwilliams.archbishopofcanterbury.org/articles.php/1926/archbishop-of-canterburys-2011-easter-sermon]. Last accessed 13th April 2013.

18 Anthony Thacker, *Behind the Sofa: A Closer Look at Doctor Who* (Eastbourne: Kingsway, 2006).

19 'Epiphany Prizes: Purpose', [http://www.epiphanyprizes.com/purpose.html]. Last accessed 13th April 2013.

20 Russell T. Davies and Benjamin Cook, *Doctor Who: The Writer's Tale, The Final Chapter* (London: BBC Books, 2010), pp.55-56.

1. Courtland Lewis, Why Time Lords Do Not Live Forever

1   Bernard Williams, *Problems of the Self: Philosophical Papers 1956-1972* (Cambridge: Cambridge University Press, 1973), p.89.

2   Paul Edwards, *Immortality* (New York: Macmillan Publishing, 1992).

3   Michael Hand, 'Regeneration and Resurrection ' in Courtland D. Lewis and Paula Smithka, (eds), *Doctor Who and Philosophy: Bigger on the Inside* (Chicago and La Salle, IL: Open Court Press, 2010), pp.213-224.

4   Hiroshi Obayashi, *Death and the Afterlife: Perspectives of World Religions* (New York: Greenwood Press, 1991), ix.

5   'The End of Time, Part Two' (2010).

6   Obayashi, *Death and the Afterlife*, p.16.

7   Obayashi, *Death and the Afterlife*, p.25.

8   Obayashi, *Death and the Afterlife*, p.68.

9   Houston Smith, *The World's Religions: Our Great Wisdom of Traditions* (San Francisco: Harper Collins, 1991[1958]), p. 24.

10 Smith, *The World's Religions*, p.241.

11 Smith, *The World's Religions*, p.241.

12   Obayashi, *Death and the Afterlife*, pp.136-138.

13   Smith, *The World's Religions*, p.242.

14   A. Charkrabarti, 'Is Liberation (*mokṣa*) Pleasant?' in Charles Taliaferro and
      Paul J. Griffiths (eds), *Philosophy of Religion: An Anthology* (Malden, MA and
      Oxford: Blackwell Publishing, 2003), pp.589-590.

15   The four schools of theological thought just described are taken from
      Charkrabarti, 'Is Liberation (*moska*) Pleasant?', pp.591-592.

16   Plato, *Apology*, XXXII.

17   Plato, *Phaedo*, In *The Collected Works of Plato*. Edited by Edith Hamilton,
      Huntington Caims, and Lane Cooper (Princeton: Princeton University
      Press, 2005).

18   Friedrich Nietzsche, *The Will to Power*, Trans. Walter Kaufmann and R.J.
      Hollingdale (New York: Random House, 1967), Book I, Section 5.

19   Nietzsche's eternal recurrence is sort of an outlier, since the category in
      which it fits depends on how one understands Nietzsche's philosophical
      position. If we can be aware of our place in the eternal recurrence, and
      simply be limited in our ability to change things, then we have a type of
      subjective immortality. However, if this 'awareness' is merely a recurrence
      of something that happened during a previous occurrence, then we are not
      having any new experiences: hence, our immortality is objective, instead
      of subjective. If it is the latter, then the motivational force that Nietzsche
      suggests by the eternal recurrence loses its force, since if everything has
      already happened, and we cannot change it, then there is no reason to
      even try to be a better human. If this implication is true, then the first
      interpretation is correct, and the eternal recurrence deserves to be part of
      the first type of explanations regarding subjective immortality.

20   Tat Wood, *About Time: The Unauthorized Guide to* Doctor Who, *Expanded
      2nd Edition. 1970-1974: Seasons 7 to 11* (Chicago: Mad Norwegian Press,
      2009), p.299.

21   Randall Auxier, 'Why One Hundred Years is Forever: Hartshorne's
      Theory of Immortality', *The Personalist Forum* 14:2 (1998), pp.109-132.

22   Ronald E. Bishop, 'Is This It? Immortality in Charles Hartshorne's Neo-
      Classical Theology', *Addresses of the Mississippi Philosophical Association*
      102 (2000), p.268.

23   Charles Hartshorne, 'Time, Death, and Eternal Life', *The Journal of Religion*
      32:2 (1952), p.102.

24   Hartshome, 'Time, Death, and Eternal Life', p.92.

25   Bishop, 'Is This It?', p.267.

26   Donald Wayne Viney, *Charles Hartshorne and the Existence of God* (Albany,
      NY: State University of New York Press, 1985), p.41.

27   Auxier, 'Why One Hundred Years is Forever', p.114.

28   Albert Camus, *The Myth of Sisyphus and Other Essays* (New York: Vintage, 1991).

29   'The End of the World' (2005).

2. Gabriel McKee, Pushing the Protest Button: *Doctor Who's* Anti-Authoritarian Ethic

1 Quoted in John Tulloch and Manuel Alvarado, *Doctor Who: The Unfolding Text* (New York: St. Martin's Press, 1983), p.149.

2 Tulloch and Alvarado, *Doctor Who: The Unfolding Text*, p.31.

3 Tulloch and Alvarado, *Doctor Who: The Unfolding Text*, p.31.

4 Tulloch and Alvarado, *Doctor Who: The Unfolding Text*, p.100.

5 Melissa Beattie. 'Life During Wartime: An Analysis of Wartime Morality in Doctor Who' in Anthony S. Burdge, Jessica Burke, and Kristine Larsen (eds), *The Mythological Dimensions of Doctor Who* (Crawfordville, FL: Kitsune Books, 2010), p.101.

6 See Vincent O'Brien, 'The Doctor or the (Post) Modern Prometheus' in Anthony S. Burdge, Jessica Burke, and Kristine Larsen (eds), *The Mythological Dimensions of Doctor Who* (Crawfordville, FL: Kitsune Books, 2010), pp.185-188.

7 Una McCormack. 'He's Not the Messiah: Undermining Political and Religious Authority in New Doctor Who' in Simon Bradshaw, Antony Keen and Graham Sleight (eds), *The Unsilent Library: Essays on the Russell T. Davies Era of the New Doctor Who* (London: The Science Fiction Foundation, 2011), pp.61-62.

8 Leo Tolstoy, *The Kingdom of God is Within You* (Mineola, NY: Dover Publications, 2006), p.167.

9 Tolstoy, *The Kingdom of God*, pp.203-204.

10 Tolstoy, *The Kingdom of God*, p.208.

11 Jacques Ellul, *Anarchy and Christianity* (Grand Rapids: Eerdmans, 1991), p.11.

12 William Lloyd Garrison, 'Declaration of Sentiments (1838)', *Internet Archive*, [http://archive.org/details/DeclarationOfSentiments]. Last modified March 10th 2001.

13 Paul Cornell, *No Future* (London: Virgin Publishing, 1994), p.142.

14 A strong case could be made, however, for an anarchist interpretation of *Blake's 7*, the science-fiction programme created by Terry Nation, the creator of the Daleks, in 1978. This programme followed a revolutionary group led by escaped criminal Roj Blake as it attempted to overthrow an oppressive galactic government. Incidentally, a major character on *Blake's 7* was played by Michael Keating, who had previously appeared as a member of the band of outlaws in the *Doctor Who* serial 'The Sun Makers'.

15 Martin Luther King, Jr., 'My Pilgrimage to Nonviolence', *The Martin Luther King, Jr. Papers Project*, [http://mlk-kpp01.stanford.edu/primarydocuments/Vol4/1-Sept-1958_MyPilgrimageToNonviolence.pdf], p.479.

16 George Fox, *George Fox: An Autobiography*, 'Christian Classics Ethereal Library', [http://www.ccel.org/ccel/fox_g/autobio.html], p.47. Last modified June 1st 2005.

17 A stranger similarity between George Fox and the Doctor is the fact that, on several occasions in his life, Fox fell seriously ill, and underwent drastic physical and emotional changes connected to his recovery, undergoing what could fancifully be termed 'regenerations'. (Fox, 38n).

18 Quoted in Christopher Hill, *The World Turned Upside Down: Radical Ideas During the English Revolution* (London and New York: Penguin Books, 1991), p.223.

19 Dee Amy-Chinn, 'Davies, Dawkins and Deus ex TARDIS: Who Finds God in the Doctor?' In Christopher J. Hansen (ed.), *Ruminations, Peregrinations, and Regenerations: A Critical Approach to Doctor Who* (Cambridge: Cambridge Scholars, 2010), p.28.

3. K. Jason Wardley: Divine and *Human Nature*: Incarnation and Kenosis in *Doctor Who*

1 Paul Cornell, *Human Nature* (London: Virgin, 1995), p.93.

2 The Christian/Greek synthesis 'constantly justifies a certain notion of hierarchy that placed the integrity of the good in question'. Greek philosophy meanwhile 'gave rise to a view of self-abnegation that brought the wholeness and integrity of the human good into question'. Philosophical schools – such as Stoicism – preached the 'foolishness of loving things in this world' and were 'hard to reconcile with the Jewish-Christian doctrine of creation'. Andrew O'Shea, *Selfhood and Sacrifice: Rene Girard and Charles Taylor on the Crisis of Modernity* (London: Continuum, 2010), p.150; p.149.

3 This practice is particularly well illustrated by the behaviour of the school Captains towards the younger boys: 'At that moment, the Captains were beating Timothy with a tarred and knotted rope. "Gag him, for God's sake […] We don't want Wolvercote to think we're squealers." Timothy looked over his shoulder, clutching the cold metal of the radiator which he was bent up against. "I had a dream, Hutchinson, a nightmare. Death was in it. We all died. We were all killed." "We all have nightmares from time to time", Hutchinson told him, "but one learns not to wake up screaming. Only four more now. If you can refrain from making a noise, we shan't gag you. D'you think you can?' Cornell, *Human Nature*, p.21.

4 Marilyn McCord Adams, *Christ and Horrors: The Coherence of Christology* (Cambridge: Cambridge University Press, 2006), p.271.

5 Maurice Wiles, *The Making of Christian Doctrine* (Cambridge: Cambridge University Press, 1967), p.111.

6 Frank R. Leavis, *The Great Tradition: George Eliot, Henry James, Joseph Conrad* (London: Chatto & Windus, 1962).

7 Paul Cornell, Martin Day and Keith Topping, *The Discontinuity Guide* (London: Virgin, 1995), p.2.

8 Cornell, *Human Nature*, p.46.

9 Lance Parkin, 'Canonicity Matters: Defining the *Doctor Who* canon', in David Butler (ed.), *Time and Relative Dissertations In Space: Critical*

perspectives on Doctor Who (Manchester: Manchester University Press, 2007), pp.246-262; p. 256.

10   'Interview with Paul Cornell' cited in Dale Smith, 'Broader and Deeper: The Lineage and Impact of the Timewyrm series', in Butler (ed.), *Time and Relative Dissertations In Space*, pp.263-279; p.269.

11   Parkin, 'Canonicity Matters', p.259.

12   Conversely, Davies seems happy to exert a 'papal role' elsewhere, reacting to '...the broadcast of *Human Nature* on Saturday, to be honest – in a really, really selfish way. I had a whole Sunday of people saying, "That was brilliant", and specifically, "What a brilliant script. Paul Cornell is a genius." Which he is. But I'm thinking, if you only knew how much of that I wrote!' Russell T. Davies and Benjamin Cook, *Doctor Who: The Writer's Tale: The Final Chapter* (London: BBC Books, 2010), p.130.

13   Russell T. Davies, 'Production Notes: The Evasion of Time', *Doctor Who Magazine* 356 (2005), pp. 66-7, cited in Lance Parkin, 'Canonicity matters', p.258.

14   Cornell, interviewed for the twentieth anniversary of Bernice's appearance in the *New Adventures*, lamented that the mainstream television audience and purely fan audience were 'never reconciled ... these approaches fought and fought, and no end was ever come to'. Dan Tostevin, 'The Secret Companion', *Doctor Who Magazine* 453 (December 2012), pp.60-63; p 60.

15   René Girard, *Things Hidden Since the Foundation of the World* trans. Stephen Bann and Michael Mettee (London: Continuum, 2003), p. 294.

16   Cornell, *Human Nature*, p.124.

17   'A Brief History of Time [Travel]: Human Nature' [http://www.shannonsullivan.com/drwho/serials/2007hi.html] Last accessed 2nd October 2012.

18   Cornell, *Human Nature*, p.193.

19   Symcox is married to *Human Nature* writer Paul Cornell and is an ordained Anglican priest.

20   Maurice Wiles, 'Omooyzioe hmin [Homoousios emin]', *Journal of Theological Studies* 16:2 (1965), pp.454-461, p.454.

21   Davies and Cook, *The Writer's Tale*, p.323.

22   Other examples would include nationalist expression and sporting competitions – the very things in fact that defined the English public school. It is also imperative that judicial and military systems are developed to the extent that the state – as a *katēchon* – has an official monopoly on violence and punishment. Similar sentiments can be found in Constantine's attempts to preserve the unity of the Empire.

23   Thomas Hobbes, *Leviathan* (Cambridge: Cambridge University Press, 1991), p.87; p.91.

24   René Girard, *Violence and the Sacred* (London: Continuum, 2005) trans. Patrick Gregory, p.156.

25   One commentator observes that the Doctor doesn't confront them 'until it's absolutely necessary, instead choosing to hide, waiting for them to die of natural causes'; 'an act of kindness' from someone who has overcome

'the desire for vengeance' and 'is strong enough to treat his enemies with kindness and respect ... Nietzsche's Overman'. Adam Riggio, 'Overcoming Evil and Spite, and Resentment, and Revenge', in Courtland Lewis and Paul Smithka (eds), *Doctor Who and Philosophy: Bigger on the Inside* (Chicago: Open Court, 2011), pp.249-259; p.257. This is a misreading of the *Übermensch* and overlooks the mercy denied their victims had the Doctor chosen to resist earlier; elsewhere in the same volume other contributors argue that while the Doctor ran from them 'not out of fear, but out of kindness' hiding 'in human form so they couldn't track him down' once discovered 'in his fury he did punish them', succumbing 'to the temptation to make godlike judgments'. See respectively, J. J. Sylvia, 'Doctor, Who Cares?', p.162 and Laura Geuy Akers, 'Empathy, Ethics and Wonder', p.146.

26 Girard, *Things Hidden*, p.294.

27 Cornell, *Human Nature*, p.122.

28 Cornell, *Human Nature*, p.123.

29 Cornell, *Human Nature*, p.158.

30 Girard, *Violence and the Sacred*, p. 157. However, exposure to the Doctor's Time Lord nature reveals to one boy that, despite all the sacrifice and killing, their future *can* be changed: 'I thought that I knew how Rocastle was going to die. [...] But he blew himself up to kill Serif.'; 'Then that means that the future's wide open. We can change it ... [i]sn't that wonderful?' Cornell, *Human Nature*, pp. 225-226.

31 Giambattista Vico, *The New Science of Giambattista Vico* (Ithaca: Cornell University Press, 1984), § 215.

32 As Bernice observes, 'that terrible male triumphalism ... that causes boys to line up and be slaughtered'. Cornell, *Human Nature*, p. 34.

33 Cornell, *Human Nature*, p.216.

34 Cornell, *Human Nature*, pp. 217-218.

35 Cornell, *Human Nature*, p.218.

36 In the eBook of the novel Joan Redfern is troubled by the peculiar combination of religion, ethics and patriotism the school embodies: 'She wasn't tremendously fond of the open declamation of ethics and, while watching all those young boys destined to be military officers mixing chemicals, she often associated the two. Two parts this to one part that, God and country and a straight back. No inner knowledge of what made these things elements, no questioning of how God's goodness translated into things like patriotism and bravery.' Similar sentiments are expressed in the print version (pp.118-119).

37 Cornell, *Human Nature*, p.227.

38 Girard, *Violence and the Sacred*, p.292.

39 This would still be a mimetic extension: '"We are Aubertides [...] shape-changers... We can eat anything organic and can duplicate the appearance of anything that we take in that has its genetic material reasonably intact. If we have so much as one complete cell, we can take on the memory of what we eat, also." "Wonderful, isn't it?" Greeneye took a pinch of Bernice's hair in his fingers and sniffed it. "We are what we eat, as I'm

sure you were about to observe. Haven't you ever looked in the mirror and wished to be different: thinner, stronger, more beautiful? Or met somebody and wanted to be whatever they needed, old or young, man or woman?"' Cornell, *Human Nature*, pp.120-121.

40 Girard, *Violence and the Sacred*, p.292.

41 Cornell, *Human Nature*, p.125.

42 Cornell, *Human Nature*, pp.228-229.

43 Cornell, *Human Nature*, p.197.

44 Gianni Vattimo, *Belief* trans. Luca D'Isanto and David Webb (Oxford: Polity, 1999), p.63.

45 Cornell, *Human Nature*, p.203.

46 Cornell, *Human Nature*, p.228.

47 Cornell, *Human Nature*, pp.237-8.

48 Colin Gunton, *The Actuality of Atonement: A Study of Metaphor, Rationality and the Christian Tradition* (Edinburgh: T&T Clark, 1998), p.77.

49 Contrast this with the death of Shockeye of the Quawncing Grig at the hands of the Sixth Doctor in 'The Two Doctors'; see 'A battle of wits...' *Doctor Who Magazine* 453 (December 2012): pp. 58-59.

50 Cornell, *Human Nature*, p.253.

51 Cornell, *Human Nature*, pp.210.

52 Girard, *Things Hidden*, p.445.

53 Girard, *Things Hidden*, p.429.

54 Gunton, *Actuality of Atonement*, p.80.

55 William Temple, 'The Divinity of Christ', in Burnett Hillman Streeter, et al, *Foundations: A Statement of Christian Belief in Terms of Modern Thought by Seven Oxford Men* (London: Macmillan & Co., 1913), pp.211-263; 219.

56 Cornell, *Human Nature*, p.190.

57 Cornell, *Human Nature*, p.166.

58 René Girard, *Evolution and Conversion: Dialogues on the Origins of Culture* trans. João Cezar de Castro Roch (London: Continuum, 2007), p.237.

59 In the novel 'Doctor Smith' visits his local church: 'His parents had been Presbyterians, very strict and conventional, and thus he'd grown up without religion. Sometimes, it would be nice to have some. So he tried. "God?" he asked the roof. Something in him expected an answer. "What is it inside me that hurts so?" "Can I help?" asked a voice from the vestry. A kind looking vicar was smiling at Smith, extending his hands, welcomingly. Smith glanced ruefully back at the ceiling. "No", he muttered. "I was just a little lost."' Cornell, *Human Nature*, pp.104-5.

60 David Brown, *Divine Humanity: Kenosis Defended and Explored* (London: SCM Press, 2010), pp.208-9.

61 The question of *kenosis* and the subordinate role of women in the type of patriarchal society in which the story is set is explored by Sarah Coakley in 'Kenosis and Subversion: On the Repression of 'Vulnerability' in Christian Feminist Writing', in Daphne Hampson (ed.), *Swallowing a Fishbone? Feminist Theologians Debate Christianity* (London: SPCK, 1996).

62 Cornell, *Human Nature*, p.193.

63 Girard, *Things Hidden*, p.429.

64   Indeed, at one point in the novel, finding himself alone 'John Smith' closes
      his eyes and begins to recite the Lord's Prayer. Cornell, *Human Nature*,
      p.203.
65   Adams, *Christ and Horrors*, p.142.

4. Tim Jones, Breaking the Faiths in 'The Curse of Fenric' and 'The God Complex'

1   Ian Briggs, 'Shattering the Chains' on the DVD of 'The Curse of Fenric'
      (BBC, 2003).
2   Richard A. Epstein, *The Theory of Gambling and Statistical Logic* (London:
      Academic Press, 2009), p.52.
3   Paul Tillich, *The Dynamics of Faith* (New York: Perennial Classics, 2001),
      p.1.
4   Richard Hofstadter, 'The Paranoid Style in American Politics' in *The
      Paranoid Style in American Politics and Other Essays* (New York: Vintage
      Books, 2008), p.29.
5   David Aaronovitch, *Voodoo Histories: How Conspiracy Theory Has Shaped
      Modern History* (London: Vintage Books, 2010), p.324.
6   Hans Maier, 'Concepts for the Comparison of Dictatorships:
      "Totalitarianism" and "Political Religions"' in Hans Maier (ed.),
      Totalitarianism and Political Religions, Volume I, trans. Jodi Bruhn (London:
      Routledge, 2004), p. 204.
7   Klaus-Georg Riegel, 'Marxism-Leninism as political religion' in
      Totalitarianism and Political Religions, Volume II, ed. Hans Maier and
      Michael Schäfer, trans. Jodi Bruhn (London: Routledge, 2007), p.73.
8   Terry Eagleton, *Reason, Faith, and Revolution: Reflections on the God Debate*
      (London: Yale University Press, 2009), p.37.
9   Surah 2: 119 and Surah 104: 4. See *The Holy Qur'an*, trans. Abdullah Yusuf
      Ali (Birmingham: Islamic Dawah Centre International, 2010), pp.13, 360.
10   Surah 15: 44. *The Holy Qur'an*, p.147.
11   Sam Harris, *The End of Faith: Religion, Terror, and the Future of Reason*
      (London: Simon and Schuster, 2005), p.45.
12   Richard Dawkins, *The Selfish Gene*, Second edn., (Oxford: Oxford
      University Press, 1989), p.198.
13   Richard Dawkins, *The God Delusion* (New York: Houghton Mifflin, 2008),
      p.346.
14   Dawkins, *God Delusion*, p.347.
15   Christopher Hitchens, *God is Not Great: How Religion Poisons Everything*
      (New York: Grand Central Publishing, 2007), pp.4-5.
16   Callum G. Brown, *The Death of Christian Britain: Understanding Secularisation
      1800-2000* (London: Routledge, 2001), p.1.
17   Brown, *Death of Christian Britain*, p.1.
18   Brown, *Death of Christian Britain*, p.3.
19   Jean-Francois Lyotard, *The Postmodern Condition: A Report on Knowledge*,
      trans. Geoff Bennington and Brian Massumi (Manchester: Manchester
      University Press, 2001), xxiv.

20   Keith Ward, *Why There Almost Certainly is a God* (Oxford: Lion, 2008), p.146.
21   DVD Commentary, 'The Curse of Fenric' (BBC, 2003).
22   Dawkins, *The God Delusion*, p.348.

5. Michael Charlton, The Doctor Working on God's Time: Kairos and Intervention in 'The Waters of Mars' and 'A Christmas Carol'

1   Jack Finegan, 'Of Time and History' in Jerry Vardaman and Edwin M Yamuchi (eds), *Chronos, Kairos, Christos: Nativity and Chronological Essays Presented to Jack Finegan* (Winona Lake, IN.: Eisenbrauns, 1989), xiii.
2   Phillip Sipiora, 'The Ancient Concept of Kairos' in Phillip Sipiora and James S. Baumlin (eds), *Rhetoric and Kairos: Essays in History, Theory, and Praxis* (Albany, NY: State University of New York Press, 2002), pp.2-3.
3   Phillip Sipiora, 'Kairos: The Rhetoric of Time and Timing in the New Testament' in Sipiora and Baumlin (eds), *Rhetoric and Kairos*, pp.121, 120.
4   Sipiora, 'Kairos', pp.120-123.
5   William Gallois, *Time, Religion, and History* (Edinburgh: Pearson, 2007), p.109.
6   Notably, this verse comes while the epistle is discussing the central kairic moment in God's time as described in the New Testament: the judgement or 'day of the Lord', in which human history will end and only divine time will continue to exist (2 Peter 3:10).
7   Robert R.N. Ross, 'Hegel, Tillich, and the Theology of Culture' in John J. Carey (ed.), *Kairos and Logos: Studies in the Roots and Implications of Tillich's Theology* (Macon, GA.: Mercer University Press, 1984), p.206.
8   William Henry Warren, 'Kairos and Liberation: A Critical Comparison of the Theologies of History of Paul Tillich and Selected Latin American Theologians' (Unpublished PhD Thesis: Emory University, 1989), pp.35,37.
9   David Schnasa Jacobsen and Robert Allen Kelly, *Kairos Preaching* (Minneapolis: Fortress Press, 2009), p.108.
10   Stephen Usher, 'Kairos in Fourth-Century Greek Oratory' in Michael Edwards and Christopher Reid (eds), *Oratory in Action* (Manchester: Manchester University Press, 2004), pp.60-61.
11   John Poulakos, 'Kairos in Gorgias' Rhetorical Composition' in Sipiora and Baumlin (eds), *Rhetoric and Kairos*, p.89.
12   James L. Kinneavy, 'Kairos in Classical and Modern Rhetoric' in Sipiora and Baumlin (eds), *Rhetoric and Kairos*, p.70.
13   Amelie Frost Benedikt, 'On Doing the Right Thing at the Right Time: Towards an Ethics of Kairos' in Sipiora and Baumlin (eds), *Rhetoric and Kairos*, p.226.
14   Aristotle, *On Rhetoric*, trans. George A. Kennedy (Oxford: Oxford University Press, 1991), p.48.
15   Isocrates, 'Panathenaicus' in George Norlin (ed.), *Isocrates* Vol. 2 (Cambridge MA.: Harvard University Press, 2000), p.393.

16   Steven Savitt, 'Time in the Special Theory of Relativity' in Craig Callender
      (ed.), *The Oxford Handbook of the Philosophy of Time* (Oxford: Oxford
      University Press, 2011), p.561.

17   Savitt, 'Time in the Special Theory of Relativity', p.565.

18   Jean-Pierre Luminet, 'Time, Topology and the Twin Paradox' in Callender
      (eg.), *Oxford Handbook of the Philosophy of Time*, p.529.

19   This sentence, of course, would be a perfectly acceptable quiz answer to
      the question: 'What is kairos?'

20   Richard Feynman, *Six Not-so-easy-pieces: Einstein's Relativity, Symmetry,
      and Space Times* (New York: Basic Books, 2011), p.101.

21   Lawrence Fagg, *The Becoming of Time: Integrating Physical and Religious
      Time* (Durham, NC.: Duke University Press, 2003), p.254.

22   For an interesting discussion of such paradoxes, see Michael Lockwood's
      The Labyrinth of Time: Introducing the Universe (Oxford: Oxford University
      Press, 2005).

23   Of course, given the series' original mandate to teach history to
      schoolchildren, there were also pedagogical reasons why the Doctor
      could not, for example, intervene in the St. Bartholomew's Day Massacre.

24   Paul Cornell, Martin Day and Keith Topping, *The Discontinuity Guide* (Los
      Angeles: MonkeyBrain Books, 2004), p.152.

25   For example, consider 2 Corinthians 1:7: 'And our hope of you is steadfast,
      knowing, that as ye are partakers of the sufferings, so shall ye be also of
      the consolation'.

26   For another interesting subversion of this cliché, consider 'Kinda', where
      the threat is less monsters breaking into the sealed environment (as in
      stories like 'The Ark in Space' or 'The Wheel in Space') as it is the threat of
      a spiritual or philosophical invasion by 'primitive' forces.

27   See the ambivalent 'Chronovore' Kronos in 'The Time Monster' (1972).

28   Co-writer Russell T. Davies notes a similar dilemma in the *Doctor Who
      Confidential* episode on 'The Waters of Mars', arguing that the Doctor fails
      to recognise that his 'bigger responsibility' in the story is to time itself and
      not to the people of Bowie Base One.

29   Of course, this incarnation of the Doctor does not evade his judgement
      for long, as he dies in the very next story (the suitably eschatological
      'The End of Time') while finally making a choice that respects his own
      foretold doom and sees a moment of genuine self-sacrifice. In his book
      The Writer's Tale, Davies describes it in strikingly similar terms of hubris
      and confrontation: 'He has been too arrogant, and Time is calling him
      in for his final story, in which he'll pay the price' (Russell T. Davies and
      Benjamin Cook, *Doctor Who: The Writer's Tale, The Final Chapter* (London:
      BBC Books, 2010), p.427).

30   It is possible that these two pasts (the original one without the Doctor,
      the new one with the Doctor) are intended as completely separate
      timelines. Yet, with the rare exception of a parallel or alternate universe
      story ('Inferno', for example), there is little tradition in *Doctor Who* of
      independent and branching timelines.

6. Brigid Cherry, 'You're this Doctor's companion. What exactly do you do for him? Why does he need you?': *Doctor Who*, Liminality and Martha the Apostle

1   Anton Karl Kozlovic, 'Sacred Cinema: Exploring Christian Sensibilities within popular Hollywood Films', *Journal of Beliefs & Values* 28:2 (2007), p.203.

2   Matt Hills, '*Doctor Who*' in David Lavery (ed.), *The Essential Cult TV Reader* (Lexington, KY: The University Press of Kentucky, 2010), p.98.

3   See, for example, Michelle Cordone and John Cordonw, 'Who is the Doctor? The Meta-Narrative of *Doctor Who*' in Christopher Hanson (ed.), *Ruminations, Peregrinations and Regenerations: A Critical Approach to Doctor Who* (Newcastle: Cambridge Scholars Publishing, 2010).

4   Jonathan Wynne-Jones, 'The Church is Ailing – Send for *Doctor Who*', *Daily Telegraph*, May 4 2008, [http://www.telegraph.co.uk/news/newstopics/howaboutthat/1925338/The-church-is-ailing-send-for-Dr-Who.html]. Last accessed 30th April 2013.

5   Wynne-Jones, 'The Church is Ailing'.

6   David Rafer, 'Mythic Identity in *Doctor Who*' in David Butler (ed.), *Time and Relative Dissertations in Space: Critical Perspectives on Doctor Who* (Manchester: Manchester University Press, 2007), p.135.

7   Russell T Davies and Benjamin Cook, *Doctor Who: The Writer's Tale* (London: BBC Books, 2008) pp.35-36.

8   For more on this see Dee Amy-Chinn, 'Davies, Dawkins and Deus ex TARDIS: Who Finds God in the Doctor?' in Chris Hanson (ed.), *Ruminations, Peregrinations and Regenerations : A Critical Approach to Doctor Who* (Newcastle-upon-Tyne: Cambridge Scholars Publishing, 2010), pp.22-35.

9   Matt Hills, '*Torchwood*' in Lavery (ed.), *The Essential Cult TV Reader*, p.278.

10   Adam Sherwin, 'Christians Protest as *Doctor Who* is Portrayed as 'Messiah', *The Times*, December 21st 2007.

11   Sherwin, 'Christians Protest'.

12   See, for example, Thomas Bertonneau and Kim Paffenroth, *The Truth is Out There: Christian Faith and the Classics of Television Science-Fiction* (Grand rapids: Brazos, 2006).

13   Wynne-Jones, 'The Church is Ailing'.

14   Wynne-Jones, 'The Church is Ailing'.

15   David Layton, *The Humanism of Doctor Who: A Critical Study in Science Fiction and Philosophy* (Jefferson, NC: McFarland, 2012), pp.134-135.

16   Hills, '*Torchwood*', p.281.

17   John Williamson, *The Oak King, the Holly King and the Unicorn: the Myths and Symbolism of the Unicorn Tapestries* (New York: Harper and Row, 1986), p.94.

18   Walt Kowalski, 'A Christ Figure?: Christic Resonances in *Gran Torino*', *Journal of Religion and Film* 15:2 (2011), [http://digitalcommons.unomaha.edu/jrf/vol15/iss2/5]. Last accessed May 19th 2012.

19   Adele Reinhartz, 'Jesus and Christ-Figures' in John Lyden (ed.), *Routledge Companion to Religion and Film* (London: Routledge, 2009), pp.430-431.

20   This is true also of Amy Pond under Stephen Moffat, Amy not only being the Doctor's best friend but a member of his family unit when she effectively becomes his mother-in-law.

21   The Doctor in his eleventh incarnation continues to feel guilt towards his companions, including Martha, in 'Let's Kill Hitler' (2011).

22   Caesar Montevecchio, 'Framing Salvation: Biblical Apocalyptic, Cinematic Dystopia, and Contextualising the Narrative of Salvation', *Journal of Religion and Film* 16:2 (2012), [http://digitalcommons.unomaha.edu/jrf/vol16/iss2/7]. Last accessed 30th April 2013.

23   Davies and Cook, *The Writer's Tale*, pp.35-36.

24   Montevecchio, 'Framing Salvation'.

25   David Bakan, *The Duality of Human Existence: An Essay in Psychology and Religion* (Oxford: Rand McNally, 1966).

26   J. L. Austin, *How to Do Things with Words* (Cambridge, Mass.: Harvard University Press, 1962), pp.5-6.

27   Amy-Chinn, 'Deus ex TARDIS'.

28   Timothy Mark Robinson, 'Agency, Action and Re-action: The Black Female Presence in *Doctor Who*' in Hanson (ed.), *Ruminations, Peregrinations and Regenerations*, pp.150-163.

29   Charles C. Ryrie, *The Role of Women in the Church* (Nashville, TN: B&H Publishing, 2011), p.55.

30   Eldon Jay Epp, *Junia: The First Female Apostle* (Minneapolis, MN: Fortress Press, 2005).

31   Hills, '*Doctor Who*', p.99.

7. Laura Brekke 'Humany-Wumany': Humanity vs. Human in *Doctor Who*

I have to thank two people who helped me especially in the writing of this chapter: Diane Codding for all her help in writing the original abstract, and Phil Wall for all his support and encouragement from beginning to end.

1   John Plunkett, 'TV ratings: David Tennant's final Doctor Who watched by more than 10m', *The Guardian*. 4th January 2010.

2   Riazatt Butt. 'Church of England Attendance Falls For Fifth Year in a Row', *The Guardian*. 22nd January 2010.

3   Typing that phrase into any internet search engine reveals dozens of fan websites passionately discussing the Doctor's ethics and on-line stores selling bracelets and t-shirts asking the same question.

4   William Placher (ed.), *Essentials of Christian Theology* (Louisville: Westminster/ John Knox Press, 2003), p.137.

5   The concept of *Imago Dei* is drawn from Genesis 1:26-27, where human beings are created 'in the image and likeness of God'.

6   'Rise of the Cybermen' (2006).

7   'Age of Steel' (2006).

8   Serene Jones, 'What's Wrong With Us?' in Placher (ed.) *Essentials of Christian Theology*, p.146.

9   Daniel L Migliore, *Faith Seeking Understanding*, Second Edition (Grand Rapids: Eerdmans, 2004), p.141.

10   It is important to note here that there are varying opinions on the relation of the 'soul' and the body. Generally speaking, however, the orthodox understanding of the soul to the body is that they are inseparable. Bodies are made good by God; they are not shells to be discarded. We are better to talk of human beings as 'embodied souls' rather than strictly dividing the two. See Shirley C. Guthrie, *Christian Doctrine*, Revised Edition, (Louisville: John Knox Press, 1994), p.195.

11   Placher, *Essentials of Christian Theology*, p.137.

12   Guthrie, *Christian Doctrine*, pp. 194-196.

13   Karl Barth, *Dogmatics in Outline* (New York: Harper and Row, 1959), p.89.

14   Karl Barth, 'True Humanity' in Clifford Green (ed.), *Karl Barth: Theologian of Freedom* (Minneapolis: First Fortress Press, 1991), p227.

15   John 11:30-37; the well-known phrase 'Jesus wept' comes from verse 35.

16   Mark 8:2.

17   Migliore, *Faith Seeking Understanding*, p.144.

18   Matthew 22:37-39.

19   Luke 4:2.

20   Matthew 27:26-31.

21   Matthew 27:50.

22   Guthrie, *Christian Doctrine*, p.198.

23   Catheirne Cornille,. *The Im-Possibility of Interreligious Dialogue* (New York: Crossroads Publishing Company, 2008), p.137.

24   Cornille, *Im-Possibility of Interreligious Dialogue*, p.138.

25   The Star Whale from 'The Beast Below' (2010) is a rare example, and the Doctor has especially vibrant compassion for him.

26   'The Poison Sky' (2008). This is an excellent basis for a discussion on the Doctor's ethic of war, but that will be left for another chapter!

27   'Evolution of the Daleks' (2007).

28   'Dalek'. The Doctor is unyielding in his desire to destroy the final Dalek, only stopped by Rose's plead for mercy on the dying Dalek's behalf.

29   The Doctor's initial reaction to the loss of the Master, 'The Last of the Time Lords' (2007).

30   'I'm burning up a star just to say goodbye'. The Doctor to Rose, 'Doomsday' (2006).

31   Like disguising himself as a human being in order to avoid a violent confrontation with the Family of Blood ('Human Nature' and 'The Family of Blood').

32   All of these characteristics make for a compelling discussion of the Doctor as a Christ figure; but I shall not get into that discussion here.

33   'More Young People Are Moving Away From Religion, But Why?' *NPR. org*, 5th January 2013 [http://www.npr.org/2013/01/15/169342349/more-young-people-are-moving-away-from-religion-but-why]. Last accessed 30th April 2013.

34   Philippians 2:7.
35   This is not to say that the Doctor is flawless – he is imperfect and struggles
      throughout the series with his own anger and rage.

8. Jennifer L. Miller, The Monstrous and the Divine in *Doctor Who*: The Role of Christian Imagery in Russell T. Davies's *Doctor Who* Revival

1   David Rafer, 'Mythic Identity in *Doctor Who*' in David Butler (ed.), *Time
      and Relative Dissertations in Space: Critical Perspectives on Doctor Who*
      (Manchester: Manchester University Press, 2007), p.124.
2   Aristotle, *Politics* (Chicago: University of Chicago Press, 1985), I.1253a27.
3   Todd Comer, 'Who Needs Family? I've Got the Whole World on My
      Shoulders: How the Doctor's Non-domesticity Interrupts History' in
      Christopher J. Hansen (ed.), *Ruminations, Peregrinations, and Regenerations:
      A Critical Approach to Doctor Who* (Newcastle upon Tyne: Cambridge
      Scholars Publishing, 2010), pp.36, 38.
4   Comer, 'Who Needs Family?', pp.38-39.
5   Certainly, as many critics have noted, other religious imagery and
      mythical elements appear throughout both the original *Doctor Who* and
      the show's 2005 revival. For instance, as Rafer notes, 'Writers and analysts
      of *Doctor Who* have therefore often identified the Doctor with the Trickster
      archetype' (p.124), pointing to the inherent contradictions in the figure of
      the Doctor as well as his unpredictability, changing faces, and tendency
      to get into trouble as support for this argument. This chapter is not
      discounting such elements in the show, nor is it denying that there are other
      alternatives for interpreting divinity than the Christian understanding of
      God as omnipotent and omniscient. Given this chapter's focus on the
      treatment of the imagery of Christmas, however, as well as the show's
      general cultural context of being made and taking place in a Western
      society in which Christianity has traditionally been the dominant religion,
      this chapter will proceed with the Christian understanding of divinity as
      its starting point.
6   Dee Amy-Chinn, 'Davies, Dawkins and Deus Ex Tardis: Who Finds
      God in the Doctor?' in Hansen (ed.), *Ruminations, Peregrinations, and
      Regenerations*, p.23.
7   Amy-Chinn, 'Davies, Dawkins and Deus Ex Tardis', p.29.
8   Amy-Chinn, 'Davies, Dawkins and Deus Ex Tardis , p.22.
9   John Paul Green, 'The Regeneration Game: *Doctor Who* and the Changing
      Faces of Heroism' in Melissa Beattie, Una McCormack, and Ross P. Garner
      (eds), *Impossible Worlds, Impossible Things: Cultural Perspectives on Doctor
      Who, Torchwood and The Sarah Jane Adventures* (Newcastle upon Tyne:
      Cambridge Scholars Publishing, 2010), p.16.
10   Green, 'Regeneration Game', p.17.
11   Rafer, 'Mythic Identity', p.123.
12   Green, 'Regeneration Game', p.17.
13   Green, 'Regeneration Game', p.17.

14 Sigmund Freud, 'The Uncanny' trans. Alix Strachey, in David Sandner (ed.), *Fantastic Literature: A Critical Reader* (1919; Westport, CT: Praeger, 2004), p.77.

15 Freud, 'The Uncanny', p.78.

16 Freud, 'The Uncanny', p.78.

17 Freud, 'The Uncanny', p.79.

18 Granted, the Doctor often draws attention to the true nature of these perverted Christmas images because he is the one on the show with the most knowledge. As the cliché about not shooting the messenger implies, however, this does not prevent him from being associated, in the mind of the viewer, with the uncanny.

19 Some might argue that the Christian God admits being wrong as well—when negotiating with Abraham for the fate of the cities of Sodom and Gomorrah, or after the flood, when God puts the rainbow in the sky. Such events, however, are a far cry from actually admitting fault, and while they might provide interesting fodder for theological debate, the popular conception of God in the Christian context is defined, in large part, by the ideas of perfection and infallibility.

20 Amy-Chinn, 'Davies, Dawkins and Deus Ex Tardis', p.128.

21 This is a theme that has been carried into later seasons of *Doctor Who* as well. For instance, in the episode 'A Town Called Mercy' from the 2012 series of the show, Amy tells the Eleventh Doctor that travelling alone for an extended period has changed him for the worse. The figure of The Gunslinger in this episode, a Frankenstein's monster-like cyborg, serves as a visual reminder of the theme of monstrosity, while the experimentation of the scientist named Kahler-Jex introduces the theme of moral monstrosity. While this chapter focuses exclusively on the Russell T. Davies years of the show, more recent examples such as this one demonstrate how the monstrosity of the Doctor and the humanising effects of his companions continue to be recurring themes in the show as a whole.

9. John Vohlidka, 'With proof, you don't have to believe': *Doctor Who* and the Celestials

1 John Tulloch and Manuel Alvarado, *Doctor Who: The Unfolding Text* (New York: St. Martin's Press, 1983), p.116.

2 Not that scepticism and faith are at odds. Migliore argues that true Christian faith is concerned with inquiry and dares to ask questions. Daniel Migliore, *Faith Seeking Understanding: An Introduction to Christian Theology*, 2nd ed. (Grand Rapids: Eerdmans, 2004), p.2.

3 I am borrowing this term from comic book writer and artist Jack Kirby who used it this way in several of his comic series, including *The New Gods* and *The Eternals*.

4 Christine Cornea, 'British Science Fiction Television in the Discursive Context of Second Wave Feminism', *Genders* 54 (2011) p.22.

5   Peter B. Gregg, 'England Looks to the Future: The Cultural Forum Model and *Doctor Who*', *The Journal of Popular Culture* 37:4 (2004), p.652.

6   For a discussion of the historiography of religion in Modern Britain see Jeremy Morris, 'Secularization and Religious Experience: Arguments in the Historiography of Modern British Religion', *The Historical Journal* 55:1 (2012), pp.195-219.

7   Stuart Clayton, 'Television and the Decline of Deference', *History Review* 68 (Dec. 2010), p.4.

8   Although Britton and Barker argue that the show was essentially magical and that the scientific aspect was 'window dressing'. Piers D. Britton and Simon J. Barker, *Reading Between Designs: Visual Imagery and the Generation of Meaning in The Avengers, The Prisoner and Doctor Who* (Austin: University of Texas Press, 2003), p.133.

9   Kenneth O. Morgan, *Britain Since 1945: The People's Peace*, 3rd ed. (Oxford University Press, 2001), p.479; Grace Davie, *Religion in Britain Since 1945: Believing Without Belonging* (Cambridge: Blackwell, 1994), p.37.

10   Britton and Barker, *Reading Between Designs*, p.149.

11   The reference to seasons in this matter can be seen to relate to Ecclesiastes and its discussion of time and seasons. In the case of the Solonians, there is a time to be reborn.

12   Hugh Ruppersberg, 'The Alien Messiah' in Annette Kuhn (ed.), *Alien Zone: Cultural Theory and Contemporary Science Fiction Cinema* (New York: Verso, 1990), p.33.

13   Ruppersberg, 'The Alien Messiah', p.32.

14   The Doctor fulfils a similar but more direct function as a liberator in 'The Time Monster' (1972). While the Master and the Doctor talk of Kronos in scientific terms, the people of Atlantis clearly identify Kronos as a god. Kronos describes herself thus: 'I can be all things. A destroyer. A healer. A creator. I'm beyond good and evil as you know it'. Despite this claim of amorality, Kronos demonstrates a desire to exact revenge against the Master, who imprisoned her, and gratitude towards the Doctor for freeing her, albeit accidentally. By freeing Kronos, the Doctor subtly diminishes her absolute power, as she was still trapped in a crystal and needed freeing.

15   This can be seen as a corrupted version of God's proclamation before Moses 'I am'. Exodus 3:13-14 NSRV.

16   James Chapman, *Inside the TARDIS: The Worlds of Doctor Who* (New York: I.B. Tauris, 2006), p.77; Britton and Barker, *Reading Between Designs*, p.150.

17   Britton and Barker, *Reading Between Designs*, p.150.

18   Bernice Martin, 'Dark Materials? Philip Pullman and Children's Literature' in Jane Garnett, Matthew Grimley, Alana Harris, William Whyte, and Sarah Williams (eds), *Redefining Christian Britain: Post-1945 Perspectives* (London: SCM Press, 2006), p.185.

19   '...for I the Lord your God am a jealous God'. Exodus 20:5 NSRV.

20   Migliore, *Faith Seeking Understanding*, p.302.

21   Joel Marcus, 'Idolatry in the New Testament', *Interpretation: A Journal of Bible and Theology* 60:2 (Apr. 2006), p.152.

22   Migliore argues that Christian faith causes us to think and that the opposite, unquestioning faith leads to idolatry. See Migliore, *Faith Seeking Understanding*, pp.2, 4, 6.

23   I argue elsewhere that this story was also a warning about the dangers of blind worship of technology. John Vohlidka, '*Doctor Who* and the Critique of Western Imperialism' in Lindy Orthia (ed.), *Doctor Who and Race* (Bristol: Intellect, 2013). Note that the Tesh who remain in the spaceship with Xoanon appear less human, paler and more rigid than the Sevateem, who lived in a more natural environment. The Tesh are also less human because of their blind faith. See Migliore, *Faith Seeking Understanding*, p.6.

24   One wonders if writer Chris Boucher chose the name Tomas as a play on the Apostle Thomas. John 20:24-29. NRSV.

25   Chapman links this era of *Doctor Who* with other costume serials as a vogue for a romantic sense of 'Englishness' from the past. Chapman, *Inside the TARDIS*, p.143.

26   Idolatry in the Judaic tradition is personal: Israel is the faithless wife who turns away from her husband, God, and is seduced by the gods of the other great powers of the ancient world (Egypt, Assyria, etc.). See Ian Buruma and Avishai Margalit, *Occidentalism: The West in the Eyes of its Enemies* (New York: Penguin, 2004), p.103.

27   Leela also made a choice of friendship when she joined the Doctor at the end of 'The Face of Evil'. Loyalty to one's friends trumping loyalty to family or the tribe is a Christian ideal. See Martin, 'Dark Materials?', p.187.

28   It is suggested, although not stated, that Monarch is killed by this action. The virus was originally Monarch's, with which he planned to wipe out Earth's population.

29   Kings 18:36 NSRV.

30   This active killing underlines the idea that Monarch was an evil that had to be destroyed. It also echoes the action in C.S. Lewis' *Perelandra*, where the hero, Ransom, physically and violently confronts evil.

31   'You shall not make gods of silver alongside me, nor shall you make for yourselves gods of gold'. Exodus 20:23 NSRV.

32   Marcus, 'Idolatry in the New Testament', p.8.

33   Martin Luther, *Luther's Large Catechism* (Minneapolis: Augsburg Publishing House, 1967), p.11.

34   'for the love of money is a root of all kinds of evil, and in their eagerness to be rich some have wandered away from faith and pierced themselves with many pains'. 1 Timothy 10 NSRV.

35   Utopian communities are often motivated chiefly by religious ideology. See Timothy C. Baker, 'Scottish Utopian Fiction and the Invocation of God', *Utopian Studies*, 21:1 (2010), p.94.

36   Monasteries began as a counter-culture movement that criticised contemporary life. See Joseph H. Lynch, *The Medieval Church: A Brief History* (New York: Longman, 1992), p.30.

37   '...I appoint you over nations and over Kingdoms, to pluck up and to pull down, to destroy and to overthrow...' Jeremiah 1:10 NSRV.

38   Patricia Berlyn, 'Elijah's Battle for the Soul of Israel', *Jewish Bible Quarterly*, 40:1 (2012), p.57.
39   Migliore, *Faith Seeking Understanding*, p.43.
40   Ruppersberg, 'Alien Messiah', p.33.
41   Morris, 'Secularization and Religious Experience', p.210. See also Callum G. Brown, *The Death of Christian Britain: Understanding Secularization 1800-2000* (New York: Routledge, 2001).
42   Morris, 'Secularization and Religious Experience', p.210. See also Bernice Martin, 'Dark Materials?', p.186.
43   Nicholas J. Cull, '"Bigger on the inside…" *Doctor Who* as British cultural history' in Graham Roberts and Philip M. Taylor (eds), *The Historian, Television and Television History* (Luton: University of Luton Press, 2001), p.97.

10. Kieran Tranter, 'Her brain was full of superstitious nonsense': Modernism and the Failure of the Divine in *Doctor Who*

The quotation in this paper's title is taken from a Sontaran commenting on an old woman whom he killed as she prayed to a statue of the Virgin Mary in 'The Two Doctors' (1985).

1   Anne Cranny-Francis and John Tulloch, 'Vaster than Empire(s), and More Slow: The Politics and Economics of Embodiment in *Doctor Who'* in Pat Harrigan and Noah Wardrip-Fin (eds), *ThirdPerson: Authoring and Exploring Vast Narratives*, (Cambridge, MA.: The MIT Press, 2009).
2   Alec Charles, 'The Crack of Doom: The Uncanny Echoes of Steven Moffat's *Doctor Who'*, *Science Fiction Film and Television* 4:1 (2011), pp.1-24.
3   John Tulloch and Manuel Alvarado, *Doctor Who: The Unfolding Text* (London: Macmillian Press, 1983).
4   For example see James Chapman, *Inside the TARDIS: The Worlds of Doctor Who* (London: I. B. Tauris, 2006), where separate chapters are devoted to specific Doctor/producer/script editor eras.
5   Darwin's medical degree is well known. I will accept that the mostly self-taught Huxley did not earn a medical degree or other doctorate. In my defence with respect to calling Huxley 'doctor' is that he was awarded honorary doctorates from Oxford, Cambridge, Edinburgh and Dublin. Cyril Bibby, *Scientist Extraordinary* (Oxford: Pergamon Press, 1972), p.2.
6   Kieran Tranter, '"Frakking Toasters" and Jurisprudences of Technology: The Exception, the Subject and Techné in Battlestar Galactica', *Law and Literature* 19:1 (2007), p.49.
7   Jennifer Stoy, 'Of Great Zeitgeist and Bad Faith: An Introduction to *Battlestar Galactica'* in Roz Kaveney and Jennifer Stoy (eds), *Battlestar Galactica: Investigating Flesh, Spirit and Steel*, (London: I. B. Tauris, 2010).
8   See 2009 episode 'Daybreak Part II'.
9   In this I draw inspiration from Fiske's fabulous structural reading of 'The Creature from the Pit' (1979). See John Fiske, '*Doctor Who*: Ideology

and the Reading of a Popular Narrative Text', *Australian Journal of Screen Theory* 14-15(1983), 69-100.

10   See Marcus Harmes's article in this volume for more on the role of the Church.

11   Melody Green, '"It Turns Out They Died For Nothing": Doctor Who and the Idea of a Sacrifical Death' in Anthony Burdge, Jessica Burke, and Kristine Larson (eds), *The Mythological Dimensions of Doctor Who*, (Crawfordville: Kitsune Books, 2010), pp.105-109.

12   'The Talons of Weng-Chiang' (1977)

13   Arthur C Clarke, *Profiles of the Future*, Rev. ed. (New York: Harper and Row, 1973), pp.12-21.

14   See 'The Celestial Toymaker' (1966) and 'The Mind Robber' (1968).

15   'Tooth and Claw' (2006).

16   'The Unquiet Dead' (2005).

17   'State of Decay' (1980); 'The Curse of Fenric' (1989); 'The Vampires of Venice' (2010).

18   'Pyramids of Mars' (1975).

19   'Curse of the Black Spot' (2011).

20   'The Chase' (1965).

21   Paul Cornell, Martin Day, and Keith Topping, *The Discontinuity Guide: The Definitive Guide to the Worlds and Times of Doctor Who* (Austin, Texas: MonkeyBrain Books, 1995), pp.83-84.

22   Martin Heidegger, 'The Question Concerning Technology' in *The Question Concerning Technology and Other Essays* (New York: Harper and Row, 1977).

23   Heidegger, 'The Question Concerning Technology', p.19.

24   On the Frankenstein archive see Donald F. Glut, *The Frankenstein Archive: Essays on the Monster, the Myth, the Movies and More* (Jefferson, North Carolina: McFarland, 2002). On the anti-science of much within the archive see Kurt W Back, "Frankenstein and Brave New World: Two Cautionary Myths on the Boundaries of Science", *History of European Ideas* 20: 1-3 (1995), pp.327-332.

25   The representations of the 'Fourth Great and Bountiful Human Empire' in series 1 of New Who – e.g. 'The Long Game', 'Bad Wolf', 'The Parting of the Ways'.

26   For example, 'Colony in Space' (1971); 'The Face of Evil'; 'State of Decay'; 'The Mysterious Planet' (1986); 'The Doctor's Daughter' (2008).

27   'Full Circle' (1980).

28   'Image of the Fendahl' (1977); 'Four to Doomsday' (1982).

29   'The Ark' (1966); 'The Ark in Space' (1975); 'The End of the World' (2005).

30   H. G. Wells, *The Time Machine* (London: J M Dent, 1995).

31   Tulloch and Alvarado, *Doctor Who: The Unfolding Text*, pp.121-126.

32   Piers D Britton and Simon J Barker, *Reading Between Designs: Visual Imagery and the Generation of Meaning in The Avengers, The Prisoner, and Doctor Who* (Austin: University of Texas Press, 2003), pp.184-189.

33   See also 'The Ark'.

34   H. G. Wells, *The War of the Worlds* (London: Pan, 1975); 'The Ark' (1966); 'The Ice Wariors' (1967).

35   H. G. Wells, *The Island of Doctor Moreau* (London: Heinemann, 1896), Pigs seem to be particularly favoured in *Doctor Who* for hybridisation. See the pig brained 'Mr Sin' in 'The Talons of Weng-Chiang'; the quasi-sentient pig in 'Aliens of London'; and the Dalek pig slaves in 'Daleks in Manhattan' (2007).

36   Mark R Hillegas, *The Future as Nightmare: H.G. Wells and the Anti-utopians* (Carbondale and Edwardsville: Southern Illinois University Press, 1967), p.31; John Huntington, *The Logic of Fantasy: H. G. Wells and Science Fiction* (New York: Columbia University Press, 1982), p.45.

37   Darko Suvin, *Metamorphoses of Science Fiction: On the Poetics and History of a Literary Genre* (New Haven: Yale University Press, 1979), p.223; Adam Roberts, *The History of Science Fiction* (Houndmills, Basingstoke, Hampshire: Palgrave Macmillan, 2005), pp.142-146.

38   Wells, *The Time Machine*, p.17.

39   Wells, *The Time Machine*, p.59.

40   Wells, *The Time Machine*, pp.72-76.

41   Frank McConnell, *The Science Fiction of H.G. Wells* (New York: Oxford University Press, 1981), p.72.

42   On Wells' engagement with Marxism and alternative future utopian thinking see Patrick Parrinder, 'Imagining the Future: Zamyatin and Wells', *Science-Fiction Studies* 1:1 (1973), pp.18-19; Robert Crossley, 'The Letters of Olaf Stapledon and H.G. Wells, 1931-1942' in Gary K. Wolfe (ed.), *Science Fiction Dialogues* (Chicago: Academy, 1982), p. 29.

43   Paul K Alkon, *Science Fiction Before 1900: Imagination Discovers Technology* (London: Routlegde, 2002), 50; David J Laker, 'The White Sphinx and the Whitened Lemur: Images of Death in *The Time Machine*', *Science-Fiction Studies* 6:1 (1979), p.78.

44   Mark Rose, 'Filling the Void: Verne, Wells and Lem', *Science-Fiction Studies* 8, no. 2 (1981), p.129.

45   McConnell, *The Science Fiction of H.G. Wells*, p. 61.

46   For example 'Fear Her' (2006); 'Vincent and the Doctor' (2010).

47   'City of Death' (1979)

48   From the earliest episodes the Doctor had been seen as unable to pilot the TARDIS with any degree of certainty. This was made explicit with the fitting of a 'Randomiser' to the TARDIS at the end of the 'The Armageddon Factor'. A further suggestion in 'The Doctor's Wife' was that the TARDIS takes the Doctor to where he needs to be.

49   'The Ultimate Foe' (1986); 'The End of Time'.

50   Thomas H. Huxley, *Evolution and Ethics* (Princeton, NJ.: Princeton University Press, 1989), pp.139-140.

51   Huxley, *Evolution and Ethics*, p.140.

52   Huxley, *Evolution and Ethics*, p.143.

53   McConnell, *The Science Fiction of H.G. Wells*, pp.62-63.

54   Huntington, *The Logic of Fantasy: H. G. Wells and Science Fiction*, p.51.

55   Wells, *The Time Machine*, pp.179-180.

56   Wells, *The Time Machine*, p.80.

57   Huntington, *The Logic of Fantasy: H. G. Wells and Science Fiction*, p.84.

58 Wells, *The Island of Doctor Moreau*, p.176.

59 Robert M Philmus, 'The Satiric Ambivalence of the Island of Doctor Moreau', *Science-Fiction Studies* 8 (1981), p.9.

60 Paul K Alkon, 'Cannibalism in Science Fiction' in Gary Westfahl, George Slusser, and Eric S Rabkin (eds), *Foods of the Gods: Eating and the Eaten in Fantasy and Science Fiction* (Athens, Georgia: University of Georgia Press, 1996), p.146.

61 Wells's precise relationship to socialism, the Fabians and social liberalism was complex. Edward Mead Earle, 'H.G. Wells, British Patriot in Search of a World State', *World Politics* 2:2 (1950), pp.183-186.

62 See for example 'The Girl in the Fireplace' (2006).

63 Fiske, '*Doctor Who*: Ideology and the Reading of a Popular Narrative Text'; Alan McKee, 'Is Doctor Who Political?' *European Journal of Cultural Studies* 7:2 (2004), pp.201-217.

64 Dee Amy-Chinn, 'Rose Tyler: The Ethics of Care and the Limit of Agency', *Science Fiction Film and Television* 1:2 (2008).

65 Melissa Beattie, 'Life During Wartime: An Analysis of Wartime Morality in Doctor Who' in Budge, Burke and Larsen (eds), *The Mythological Dimensions of Doctor Who,*, pp.85-104.

66 Lindy A Orthia, '"Sociopathetic Abscess" or "Yawning Chasm"? The Absent Postcolonial Transition in Doctor Who', *The Journal of Commonwealth Literature* 45:2 (2010), pp.207-225.

67 Richard Tuerk, 'Upper-Middle-Class Madness: H. G. Wells' Time Traveller Journeys to Wonderland', *Extrapolation* 46: 4 (2005), 520-521; Roberts, *The History of Science Fiction*, 152.

68 Lynnette Porter, *Tarnished Heroes, Charming Villains, and Modern Monsters* (Jefferson, N.C.: McFarland, 2010), p.229.

69 'The Runaway Bride'.

70 See for example 'Terror of the Autons' (1971); 'Last of the Time Lords' (2007).

71 Kieran Tranter, 'In and Out of Time: Memory and Chronology of *Doctor Who*' in Gillian Leitch (ed.), *Doctor Who In Time and Space* (Jefferson, N.C.: McFarland, 2013), pp.82-96.

72 Thomas Hobbes, *Leviathan* (New York: Pearson Longman, 2008), pp.113-117.

73 'Doctor Who and the Silurians' (1970); 'Warriors of the Deep' (1984); 'The Hungry Earth/Cold Blood' (2010).

74 For example, 'The Savages' (1966); 'The Sun Makers' (1977); 'The Happiness Patrol' (1988).

75 'The Power of Three' (2012).

76 In 'The Ark', 'The Face of Evil', and 'Bad Wolf' the Doctor is confronted with the negative effects of his previous involvement.

77 'The Waters of Mars' (2009).

78 Through the Doctor participating in the plot to kill him ('The We''ding of River Song' (2010) and then systematically removing the traces of his past from the universe, a process that is seemingly complete with the wiping of the Daleks' collective memory of him in 'Asylum of the Daleks'(2012)).

79 'The Power of Three' (2012).

11. Karma Waltonen, Religion in *Doctor Who*: Cult Ethics

1   Terry Pratchett, *Small Gods* (New York: HarperTorch, 1994), p.69.

2   Even when the Cybermen create a CyberKing in 'The Next Doctor' (2008),
     they do not seek to worship it. Miss Hartigan's language concerning the
     other humans remains regal rather than religious: 'My people. Why do
     they not rejoice?'

3   'The Parting of the Ways' (2005).

4   Harold Pinter, 'The Echoing Silence', *The Guardian*, December 30th 2008
     [http://www.guardian.co.uk/culture/2008/dec/31/harold-pinter-
     early-essay-writing]. Last accessed 30th April 2013.

5   'The Time of Angels/Flesh and Stone' (2010).

6   For more on this see Marcus Harmes's chapter in this volume.

7   From the point of view of the Silence, who do not know of the Doctor's
     trick.

8   Terry Pratchett, *Small Gods* (New York: HarperTorch, 1994), p.89.

9   'Man' is used in a non-species specific way throughout.

10   This paper presumes that pantheon gods are in fact mythological. The
     author apologises to any actual gods who may in fact be real and reading
     this chapter.

11   This paper isn't making the formal distinction between gods and demi-
     gods. It should be noted, however, that seeing the Doctor as only a demi-
     god may be tempting, given his ability to die and his status as a hero to
     humanity (both qualities of the hero/demi-god archetype).

12   If one wanted to extend this example, one might note that archaeologists
     believe part of the decline of the Easter Island civilisation was caused by a
     stripping of natural resources from the island to create the famous totemic
     heads. In the world of the show, then, a devotion to the cult of the Doctor
     has a direct correlation to a civilisation's destruction.

13   Many Biblical scholars note that The Old Testament, with its numerous
     references to other gods, shows the Abrahamic God as part of a pantheon.

14   See also Brigid Cherry's chapter in this volume.

15   The seventh series also resets the Doctor's history with the Daleks, as he
     is erased from their knowledge base. River Song says in the mid-season
     finale ('The Angels Take Manhattan') that she has been pardoned for his
     death because he no longer exists – she implies that he has been deleting
     himself from many databases. These moves serve three purposes – to
     exonerate River for the crime we now know she didn't commit, to make
     the question 'Doctor Who?' funny again, and to further the idea of the
     Doctor as a mythic figure. Immediately after his death (and resurrection),
     he fades from the real lives of all but the true believers.

16   Even the reluctance to take on the badge is a cliché.

17   This dilemma in this episode is like the philosophical thought problem
     developed by Philippa Foot and Judith Jarvis Thomson called the Trolley
     Problem, in which people are asked about sacrificing one to save many.
     The level of personal active engagement in sacrificing the one changes
     people's answers, though the morality of the moment doesn't really
     change.

18   'Cold Blood' (2010).

19   'The Wedding of River Song' (2011).

12. David Johnson, Mediating Between the Scientific and the Spiritual in *Doctor Who*

1   Marvin Perry, Joseph R. Peden and Theodore H. Von Laue, *Sources of the Western Tradition, Volume 1*, Seventh Edition, (Boston: Houghton Mifflin Company, 2008), p.52.

2   Cecil Maurice Bowra, *Periclean Athens* (London: History Book Club, 1971), p. 194.

3   David C. Lindberg, *The Beginnings of Western Science: The European Scientific Tradition in Philosophical, Religious, and Institutional Context, 600 B.C. to A.D 1450* (Chicago: University of Chicago Press, 1992), p.42.

4   James Hannam, *The Genesis of Science: How the Christian Middle Ages Launched the Scientific Revolution* (Washington D.C.: Regnery Publishing, 2011), xviii.

5   Lindberg, *Beginnings of Western Science*, p.151.

6   James Hannam, *Genesis of Science*, xix.

7   Hannam, *Genesis of Science*, p.50.

8   Hannam, *Genesis of Science*, p.30.

9   Hannam, *Genesis of Science*, p.296.

10   Andrew D. White, *A History of the Warfare of Science with Theology in Christendom* (New York: D. Appleton and Co., 1897), p.9.

11   Daniel C. Dennett and Alvin Plantinga, *Science and Religion: Are They Compatible?* (Oxford and New York: Oxford University Press, 2011), chs. 1 and 2.

12   Michael Majerus, *Melanism - Evolution in Action* (Oxford and New York: Oxford University Press, 1998), p.116.

13   Hannam, *Genesis of Science*, p.165.

14   Frank Eltman, 'Scientist: Evolution debate will soon be history', *AP News Online*, 26th May 2012, [http://news.yahoo.com/scientist-evolution-debate-soon-history-155252505.html]. Last accessed 20th June 2012.

15   *Futurama*, 'Godfellas' directed by Susie Dietter (2002).

16   Dennett and Plantinga, *Science and Religion*, p.4.

17   Bruce Murray and Christopher J. Wickham, *Framing the Past: the historiography of German Cinema and Television* (Carbondale: Southern Illinois University Press, 1992), pp.58, 75.

18   For more on this see Alexander Cummins's chapter in this volume.

19   Stephanie Pappas, '"Twilight" Stands In For Religion for Some Teens', LiveScience.com, 23rd May 2012, [http://news.yahoo.com/twilight-stands-religion-teens-105559027.html]. Last accessed 20th June 2012.

13. Kristine Larsen, Karma, Conditionality, and Clinging to the Self: The Tennant Years as Seen Through a Tibetan Buddhist Lens

1   Tenzin Gyatso, *Illuminating The Path to Enlightenment*, trans. Thupten Jinpa (Long Beach, CA: Thubten Dhargye Ling, 2002), p.14.

2   Tsong-kha-pa. *The Great Treatise on the Stages of the Path to Enlightenment*, vol. 1, trans. The Lamrim Chenmo Translation Committee (Ithaca, NY: Snow Lion Publications, 2000), pp.130-33.

3   For more information on the Buddhism of 'Kinda' see David Layton, *The Humanism of Doctor Who* (Jefferson, NC: McFarland, 2012). For a list of Buddhist references in the classic series, see Ziro, 'Buddhism in Doctor Who: A Detailed Analysis' [http://homepages.bw.edu/~jcurtis/Z1R0_3. htm]. Last accessed 30th April 2013.

4   For more on emptiness, see Tenzin Gyatso, *The Essence of the Heart Sutra*, trans.Thupten Jinpa (Boston: Wisdom Publications, 2002). Note that there is a special class of phenomena which also dependently arise yet are said to be uncaused, such as uncompounded space. For more information see Pabonka Rinpoche, *Liberation in the Palm of Your Hand*, trans. Michael Richards (Boston: Wisdom Publications, 2006), pp.646-7.

5   Gyatso, *Essence of the Heart Sutra*, p.34.

6   Peter Harvey, *An Introduction to Buddhist Ethics* (Cambridge: Cambridge University Press, 2000), p.135.

7   Tsong-kha-pa, *The Great Treatise*, pp.299-300.

8   Gyatso, *Essence of the Heart Sutra*, p.36.

9   Mark Morris, *Ghosts of India* (London: BBC Books, 2008), p.51.

10   Pabonka Rinpoche, *Preparing for Tantra: The Mountain of Blessings*, trans. Lobsang Tharchin and Michael Roach (Howell, NJ: Classics of Middle Asia, 1995), p.135.

11   Tsong-kha-pa, *The Great Treatise*, p.265.

12   Morris, *Ghosts of India*, p.51.

13   'Rise of the Cybermen' (2006).

14   'The Age of Steel' (2006).

15   See Courtland Lewis's chapter for a further exploration of immortality in *Doctor Who*.

16   It is possible to compare the disembodied consciousnesses of CAL and River Song to the *bardo*, the intermediate state between rebirths, but that analysis is beyond the scope of this chapter. For information on the bardo, see John Powers, *Introduction to Tibetan Buddhism* (Ithaca, NY: Snowlion, 2007).

17   In the classic Buddhist cosmology, the destruction of one cosmos would lead to the creation of another. For more information on Buddhist cosmology, see Tenzin Gyatso, *The Universe in a Single Atom* (New York: Morgan Road Books, 2005).

18   'Utopia' (2007).

19   For more on Rose's relationship with the Doctor, see Kristine Larsen, 'Doctor Who and the Valkyrie Tradition, Part 1: The Valiant Child and the

Bad Wolf' in Anthony Burdge, Jessica Burke, and Kristine Larsen (eds), *The Mythological Dimensions of Doctor Who* (Crawfordville, FL: Kitsune Press, 2010), pp. 120-39.

19   Tsong-kha-pa, *The Great Treatise*, p.143.

20   Tsong-kha-pa, *The Great Treatise*, p.149.

21   Tsong-kha-pa, *The Great Treatise*, p.146.

22   'Planet of the Ood' (2008).

23   Tsong-kha-pa, *The Great Treatise*, p.158.

24   Tsong-kha-pa, *The Great Treatise*, p.163.

25   Rinpoche, *Liberation*, p.306.

26   'The End of Time, Part One' (2009).

27   Tsong-kha-pa, *The Great Treatise*, p.168.

28   Tsong-kha-pa, *The Great Treatise*, p.281.

29   Rinpoche *Preparing*, p.55.

30   Tsong-kha-pa, *The Great Treatise*, p.307.

31   Tsong-kha-pa, *The Great Treatise*, pp.277-8.

14. Andrew Crome, 'There never was a Golden Age': *Doctor Who* and the Apocalypse

1   For a recent example of applying this approach see Caesar A. Montevecchio, 'Framing Salvation: Biblical Apocalypse, Cinematic Dystopia and the Narrative of Salvation', *Journal of Religion and Film* 16:2 (2012). [http://digitalcommons.unomaha.edu/jrf/vol16/iss2/7/]. Last accessed 30th April 2013.

2   The classic study is Norman Cohn, *The Pursuit of the Millennium* (London: Mercury, 1962), which remains controversial. Two excellent recent works on the subject are Richard Landes, *Heaven on Earth: The Varieties of the Millennial Experience* (Oxford: O.U.P., 2011) and Catherine Wessinger (ed.), *The Oxford Handbook to Millennialism* (Oxford: Oxford University Press, 2011).

3   Frank Kermode, *The Sense of an Ending: Studies in the Theory of Fiction* (Oxford: Oxford University Press, 2000), pp.3-67.

4   'The Angels Take Manhattan' (2012).

5   'The Caves of Androzani' (1984).

6   Piers D. Britton, *TARDISbound: Navigating the Universes of Doctor Who* (London: I. B. Tauris, 2011), pp.16-21, although Britton sees this deferral as achieved through a general exploration of character as opposed to specific reference to the title. Mark Seton explores this further in terms of the appeal of apocalyptic prophecies relating to the Doctor (in the revelatory, rather than the destructive, sense). See Mark Seton, 'Apocalyptic and Prophetic: Revelation and Mystery in the Revival of *Doctor Who*' in James Aston and John Walliss (eds), *Small Screen Revelations: Apocalypse in Contemporary Television* (Sheffield: Sheffield Phoenix, 2013), pp.164-178.

7   Jacques Derrida, 'Of an Apocalyptic Tone Recently Adopted in Philosophy', *Semeia* 23:1 (1982), pp.63-97.

8   John Walliss, 'Apocalypse at the Millennium', in John Walliss and Kenneth
     G. C. Newport (eds), *The End All Around Us: Apocalyptic Texts and Popular
     Culture* (London: Equinox, 2009), pp.71-95.

9   Conrad Ostwalt, "Apocalyptic" in John Lyden (ed.), *Routledge Companion
     to Religion and Film* (London: Routledge, 2009), pp.368-383. Ostwalt
     particularly cites Christian apocalyptic films such as *Left Behind: World
     at War* (2005), or more secular 'revelatory' movies such as *Sunshine*
     (2007). More recent examples might include the active engagement with
     apocalyptic thought seen in *Melancholia* (2011) and *Take Shelter* (2011).

10   See Monteveccio, 'Framing Salvation' for some examples of this in
     practice.

11   A remake of the 1951 classic of the same name, it bears little resemblance
     to its forebear in terms of the judgement which is imagined – in the original
     a warning to stop war or face destruction. The post-electrical society is not
     shown at all on screen – presumably because it would resemble something
     like the dystopia portrayed in NBC's recent *Revolution* (2012-).

12   A good summary of the link between environmental and apocalyptic
     rhetoric can be found in Robin Globus and Bron Taylor, 'Environmental
     Millennialism' in Wessinger (ed.), *Oxford Handbook to Millennialism.*,
     pp.628-646 and Stefan Skrimshire (ed.), *Future Ethics: Climate Change and
     the Apocalyptic Imagination* (London: Continuum, 2010).

13   For more on this see Frederick Buell, 'A Short History of Environmental
     Apocalypse' in Skrimshire (ed.), *Future Ethics*, pp.13-36.

14   I explore this aspect of the serial further in '"Ready to Outsit Eternity":
     Human Responses to the Apocalypse in *Doctor Who*' in Gillian Leitch
     (ed.), *Doctor Who in Time and Space* (Jefferson: McFarland Academic, 2013),
     pp.175-194.

15   While the name 'Save Earth' might appear to recall the environmental
     apocalypticism of the 'Earth First!' movement, the link is coincidental – as
     'Earth First!' did not emerge until the late 1970s. See Bron Taylor, 'Earth
     First!' in Richard Landes (ed.), *Encyclopedia of Millennialism and Millennial
     Movements* (New York: Routledge, 2009), pp.130-133.

16   Landes, *Heaven on Earth*, pp.3-90.

17   'The Power of Three' (2012).

18   The distinction between 'millennial' – as either a distinctly Christian form
     or generally optimistic post-millennialism – and 'millenarian' – as a non-
     Christian or pessimistic form of premillennialism – is largely unhelpful
     and is not followed here. For more on the artificiality of this distinction
     see Ernest Sandeen, *The Roots of Fundamentalism: British and American
     Millenarianism* (Chicago: University of Chicago Press, 1970), pp.1-5, and
     Crawford Gribben, *Evangelical Millennialism in the Trans-Atlantic World
     1500-2000* (Basingstoke: Palgrave, 2011), pp.13-14.

19   See work on secularised millenarian thought in totalitarian movements –
     e.g. David Redles, *Hitler's Millennial Reich: Apocalyptic Belief and the Search
     for Salvation* (New York: New York University Press, 2005).

20   Landes, *Heaven on Earth*, pp.353-88.

21 Catherine Wessinger, *How the Millennium Comes Violently: From Jonestown to Heaven's Gate* (New York: Seven Bridges, 2000).

22 Robert J. Lifton, *Destroying the World to Save It: Aum Shinrikyo, Apocalyptic Violence, and the New Global Terrorism* (New York: Henry Holt, 2000).

23 James Chapman, *Inside the TARDIS: The Worlds of Doctor Who* (London: I. B. Tauris, 2006), pp.42-44.

24 Nicholas Cull, "Bigger on the Inside…' *Doctor Who* as British Cultural History' in Graham Roberts and Philip M. Taylor (eds), *The Historian, Television and Television History* (Luton: University of Luton Press, 2001), pp.95-111.

25 As Britton has argued, the Daleks need to be viewed as simultaneously representing fears of Nazism and contemporary concerns about Communism and the loss of selfhood in the modern world (*TARDISbound*, pp.61-3).

26 Chapman, *Inside the TARDIS*, pp.42-44.

27 For a more in-depth exploration of the themes introduced here, see Crome, '"Ready to Outsit Eternity": Human Responses to the Apocalypse in *Doctor Who*'.

28 Matt Hills, *Triumph of a Timelord: Regenerating Doctor Who in the Twenty-First Century* (London: I. B. Tauris, 2010), pp.25-53.

29 For example – *Queer as Folk* (Channel 4, 1999-2000), *Bob and Rose* (ITV, 2001), *The Second Coming* (ITV, 2003). On the critique of religion in Davies's work see Una McCormack, 'He's Not the Messiah: Undermining Political and Religious Authority in New *Doctor Who*' in Simon Bradshaw, Antony Keen and Graham Sleight (eds), *The Unsilent Library: Essays on the Russell T. Davies Era of the New Doctor Who* (London: The Science Fiction Foundation, 2011), pp.45-62.

30 Although the Eleventh Doctor has recently faced threats to the contemporary Earth in 'The Power of Three' (2012) and 'The Bells of Saint John' (2013).

31 Elizabeth Rosen, 'Apocalypse Transformed in *Transformers*', in Lee Quinby and John Walliss (eds), *Reel Revelations: Apocalypse and Film* (Sheffield: Sheffield Phoenix, 2011), p.172.

32 i.e. Dan. 9:27, 11:31, 12:11; Mk. 13:14, Mt. 24:15.

33 The Doctor can also be seen to act as the 'tremendum' for the Daleks. He is hailed as destroyer and 'dark Lord' and pursued by Daleks who – even when he offers himself as a sacrifice – cannot come to kill him (see 'Evolution of the Daleks' (2007)).

34 These critiques are made explicit in Davies's *Doctor Who* spinoff *Torchwood*'s season one finale 'End of Days', in which Ianto Jones reads the Book of Daniel to Captain Jack Harkness and is told 'we can do without the superstition'. Ironically, the world then has to deal with the release of Abaddon the Destroyer (Rev. 9:7-11). Characters repeatedly ask if this is 'the end of the world' and Christians display a paradoxical triumphalism: 'People didn't believe us. Now they should. Judgment Day is finally here. This is the end of days.'

35　Peter Y. Paik, *From Utopia to Apocalypse: Science Fiction and the Politics of Catastrophe* (Minneapolis: University of Minnesota Press, 2010), p.124.

36　Note Davies's *Torchwood: Children of Earth*, 'Day Five' in which Gwen Cooper reflects on the Doctor: 'All those times in history when there was no sign of him, I wanted to know why not... I know the answer now. Sometimes the Doctor must look at this planet and turn away in shame. I'm recording this in case anyone ever finds it so you can see... you can see how the world ended'.

15. Alexander Cummins, 'Qui Quae Quod': *Doctor Who* and the History of Magic

1　Owen Davies, *Grimoires: A History of Magic Books* (Oxford: Oxford University Press, 2009), p.34.

2　Heinrich Cornelius Agrippa von Nettesheim, *Three Books of Occult Philosophy*, ed. Donald Tyson (Woodbury: Llewellyn, 2009), p.558.

3　Agrippa, *Three Books*, p.476.

4　For example, the phrase 'Do My Will Shall Be the Whole of the Law' is a deliberate inversion of the central tenant of the magical system of Thelema developed by English occultist Aleister Crowley: 'Do What Thou Wilt Shall Be The Whole Of The Law'.

5　Adam Fox, 'Aubrey, John (1626-1697)' in *Oxford Dictionary of National Biography*, (Oxford: Oxford University Press, 2004; online edn, May 2008). [http://www.oxforddnb.com/view/article/886?docPos=1]. Last accessed October 31st 2012.

6　Philip Carr-Gomm, *The Elements of the Druid Tradition* (Shaftesbury: Element Books, 1998 [1991]), pp.23-24.

7　*Zecorbeni, sive, Claviculae Salmonis libri IV* (Bodl. Oxf., MS Aubrey 24).

8　For more on early modern magic and science, see for example John Henry, 'Newton, matter, and magic' in John Fauvel, Raymond Flood, Michael Shortland, & Robin Wilson (eds), *Let Newton Be! A New Perspective on His Life and Works* (Oxford: Oxford University Press, 1988), 127-145; Michael Hunter, 'The Royal Society and the decline of magic', *Notes and Records of the Royal Society of London*, 65 (2), 103-119.

9　Darren Oldridge, 'Mother Shipton and the Devil', in Angela McShane & Garthine Walker (eds),*The Extraordinary and the Everyday in Early Modern England* (Basingstoke: Palgrave Macmillan, 2010), pp.211-23.

10　For more on Mother Shipton, see Owen Davies, *Witchcraft, Magic and Culture, 1736-1951* (Manchester: Manchester University Press, 1999), pp.142-147.

11　Agrippa, *Three Books*, p.46.

12　Agrippa, *Three Books*, p.400.

13　For more on 2012-centred apocalypse theories and their relations to Mayan calendrical customs, see Joseph Gelfer (ed.), *2012: Decoding the Countercultural Apocalypse* (Sheffield: Equinox, 2011).

14　For more on millenarianism, see Norman Cohn, *The Pursuit of the Millennium* (London: Secker and Warburg, 1957) and Bernard Capp,

The Fifth Monarchy Men: A Study in Seventeenth-century English Millenarianism (London: Faber, 1972); Catherine Wessinger (ed.), *The Oxford Handbook to Millennialism* (Oxford: Oxford University Press, 2011).

15   For more on female prophets, see Phyllis Mack, *Visionary Women: Ecstatic Prophecy in Seventeenth-Century England* (Berkeley: University of California Press, 1992).

16   The heart itself also played a vitally important part in humoural theory, not least because it was considered the source of innate and natural heat in the body. For more on the humoural heart, see Fay Bound Alberti, *Matters of the Heart: History, Medicine, and Emotion* (Oxford: Oxford University Press, 2010), especially chapters 1 and 2.

17   For more on the recent history of the humours, see Noga Arikha, *Passions and Tempers: A History of the Humours* (New York: HarperCollins, 2007).

18   For more on healing charms, see Jonathan Roper (ed.), *Charms, Charmers and Charming: International Research on Verbal Magic* (Basingstoke: Palgrave Macmillan, 2009). This practice also continued well past the seventeenth century: see also Owen Davies, 'Healing Charms in Use in England and Wales 1700-1960', *Folklore* 107 (1996) pp.19-33.

19   This incantation, referred to as a Disarming Charm, is a signature spell of the eponymous hero of the Harry Potter series by J. K. Rowling, first appearing in *Harry Potter and the Chamber of Secrets* (London: Bloomsbury Publishing, 1998).

20   Brian Vickers, 'Analogy Versus Identity: The Rejection of Occult Symbolism, 1580–1680' in Brian Vickers (ed.), *Occult and Scientific Mentalities in the Renaissance* (Cambridge: Cambridge University Press, 1986), pp.95-164.

21   For more detailed study of chaos magic, see Dave Evans, *History of British Magick After Crowley* (Hidden Publishing: 2007).

22   Aleister Crowley, *The Book of the Goetia of Solomon the King* (Celephaïs Press electronic edition, 2003), p.3. [http://hermetic.com/93beast.fea.st/files/section1/Crowley%20-%20Goetia.pdf]. Last accessed 31st October 2012.

23   Phil Hine, *Prime Chaos* (New Falcon, 1993: 2002 edition), pp.85-86.

24   The term, coined by Timothy Leary, refers to mental and physical contexts for powerful 'soul-revealing' experiences i.e. has been accepted by researchers in psychedelic psychotherapy, as for example, Richard Metzner, 'Molecular Mysticism: The Role of Psychoactive Substances in the Transformation of Consciousness' in Christian Ratsch (ed.), *The Gateway to Inner Space*, (Dorset: Prism Press, 1989).

25   For more on astrological election, see Alexander Cummins, *The Starry Rubric: Seventeenth-Century English Astrology* (Milton Keynes: Hadean Press, 2012), especially chapter 2.

26   'An Interview with Andrew D. Chumbley', *The Cauldron* 103 (2002). Reprinted in Daniel A. Schulke (ed.), *Opuscula Magica: Volume 1 – Essays: Witchcraft and the Sabbatic Tradition* (Richmond, CA: Three Hands Press, 2010), p.129.

16. Marcus Harmes, The Church Militant? The Church of England, humanity and the future in *Doctor Who*

1   Barry Duke, 'Gay atheist *Dr Who* writer sparks religious discussion', *The Freethinker*, 14th September 2007, [http://freethinker.co.uk/2007/09/14/gay-atheist-dr-who-writer-sparks-religious-discussion]. Last accessed 18th September 2012; Cathy Pryor, 'Russell T Davies: One of Britain's foremost television writers', *The Independent*, 22nd October 2006, [http://www.independent.co.uk/news/people/profiles/russell-t-davies-one-of-britains-foremost-television-writers-421182.html]. Last accessed 18th September 2012.

2   Andrew Crouch, 'Time Lord or Messiah?' [http://www.damaris.org/content/content.php?type=5&id=470]. Last accessed 21st September 2012.

3   Such as his comment that learning about the Christian parables in C.S. Lewis's Narnia stories made the tales seem much 'duller'; Benjamin Cook, 'The Doctor, the Widow and the Wardrobe', *Doctor Who Magazine* 442 (2011), p.18.

4   *V for Vendetta* 2006 motion picture, dir. James McTeigue, Warner Brothers Productions.

5   Harry Harrison, 'The Streets of Ashkelon', in *The Best of Harry Harrison* (London: Sidgwick and Jackson, 1976), p.24.

6   John Wyndham, *The Chrysalids* (London: Penguin Books, 1962 [1955]), p.39.

7   Wyndham, *The Chrysalids*, p.18.

8   *The Book of Eli* (Warner Brothers, 2010).

9   Josh Brosnan, *The Primal Screen: A History of Science Fiction Film* (London: Orbit Books, 1991), p.369.

10   Of course the impression is not entirely consistent. In the Davies-produced *Gridlock*, humans in the far future still sing and derive comfort from traditional Christian hymns.

11   The scene was filmed in Brecon Cathedral.

12   Sybil M. Jack, 'The Last Days of the Smaller Monasteries in England', *Journal of Ecclesiastical History* 21:2 (1970), p. 99; Edward Carpenter, *The Protestant Bishop, Being the Life of Henry Compton, 1632-1713, Bishop of London* (London: Longmans, Green and Co., 1956), chap 8.

13   Iris Murdoch, *The Time of the Angels*, (London: Chatto and Windus, 1966).

14   Murdoch, *Time of the Angels*, p.87.

15   Murdoch, *Time of the Angels*, p.62.

16   'Anglican Church Facing Threat of Extinction', *The Globe and Mail*, February 9 2010, [http://www.theglobeandmail.com/news/british-columbia/anglican-church-facing-the-threat-of-extinction/article4352186/]. Last accessed 5th October 2012; Ross Douthat, 'Can Liberal Christianity be Saved?', *New York Times*, July 14th 2012, [http://www.nytimes.com/2012/07/15/opinion/sunday/douthat-can-liberal-christianity-be-saved.html?_r=0]. Last accessed 5 October 2012; 'Women Bishops: Church of England Votes No – As It Happened', *The Guardian*, November 21st 2012, [http://www.guardian.co.uk/world/2012/nov/20/women-bishops-church-england-vote-live]. Last accessed 11 December 2012.

17 Steve Doughty, 'Plans to Allow Gay Marriages "could force Church to split from the state" for First Time in 500 Years', *Mail Online*, 11 June 2012, [http://www.dailymail.co.uk/news/article-2157905/Church-England-Gay-marriage-plan-]. Last accessed 4th September 2012.

18 Adrian Hamilton, 'Will the Last Person to Leave the Church of England Please Turn Out the Lights', *The Independent* 18 April 2011, [http://www.independent.co.uk/voices/faith/will-the-last-person-to-leave-the-church-of-england-please-turn-out-the-lights-2269185.html]. Last accessed 4th September 2012.

19 Stanley Hauerwas, 'Murdochian Muddles: Can we Get Through Them if God Does Not Exist?', in Maria Antonaccio and William Schweiker (eds), *Iris Murdoch and the Search for Human Goodness* (Chicago: University of Chicago Press, 1996), p.193.

20 Iris Murdoch, *Metaphysics as a Guide to Morals* (London: Chatto and Windus, 1992), p.452.

21 'William Hamilton Dies at 87; Theologian Questioned God's Existence'. *Los Angeles Times* March 3rd 2012, [http://www.latimes.com/news/obituaries/la-me-william-hamilton-20120303,0,1455686.story]. Last accessed 10th December 2012; William Hamilton, *A Quest for the Post-Historical Jesus* (New York: Continuum, 1994), p.8.

22 Murdoch, *Metaphysics*, p.419.

23 Murdoch, *Time of the Angels*, p.93.

24 Iris Murdoch, 'On "God" and "Good"', in *Existentialism and Mystics: Writings on Philosophy and Literature* (New York: Penguin, 1999), p.358.

25 Murdoch, *Time of the Angels*, p.67.

26 Elizabeth Dipple, *Iris Murdoch: Work for the Spirit* (London: Methuen and Co., 1982), p.63.

27 Murdoch, *Time of the Angels*, pp.101-2.

28 Murdoch, *Time of the Angels*, p.79.

29 Murdoch, *Time of the Angels*, p.186.

30 Murdoch, *Time of the Angels*, p.187.

31 Murdoch, *Time of the Angels*, p.79.

32 See Sean D. Hamill, 'After Theological Split, a Clash over Church Assets', *New York Times*, October 5th 2008, [http://www.nytimes.com/2008/10/06/us/06church.html?ref=vgenerobinson&_r=0]. Last accessed 30th April 2013; Jonatahn Petre, 'Church of England Faces Court Battle by Gay Clergyman who Claims he was Blocked from Becoming a Bishop', *Daily Mail*, 16th January 2012, [http://www.dailymail.co.uk/news/article-2087173/Gay-clergyman-Jeffrey-John-claims-Church-England-blocked-bishop-role.html#ixzz26xpmXRYt]. Last accessed 30th April 2013; John Bingham, 'New Challenge to Church of England as US Anglicans Approve Gay "Marriage" Service', *Daily Telegraph*, 10th July 2012, [http://www.telegraph.co.uk/news/religion/9389926/New-challenge-to-CofE-as-US-Anglicans-approve-gay-marriage-service.html]. Last accessed September 18th 2012.

33 Murdoch, *Time of the Angels*, p.93.

17. Russell Sandberg, Bigger on the Inside? Doctoring the Concept of 'Religion or Belief' under English Law

I am grateful to Amina Hussain for her research assistance in analysing the case law discussed in this chapter and to Beth Singler at Cambridge University for her valuable comments on the chapter in draft and her advice in relation to 'hyper-real religions' and new religious movements.

1   Linda Woodhead, 'Introduction' in Linda Woodhead and Rebecca Catto (eds), *Religion and Change in Modern Britain* (London: Routledge, 2012), pp.1, 2.
2   To borrow the vocabulary of John Tulloch and Manuel Alvarado, *Doctor Who: The Unfolding Text* (New York: St Martin's Press, 1983).
3   This is, of course, a simplification. Note the inclusion of a primitive religious group in the David Tennant historical episode 'The Fires of Pompeii' (2008). Moreover, little attention is given to the religious beliefs and practices of the military orders, and some representations that are given seem to fall into the primitive category (such as the removal of the heads of the members of the Order of the Headless Monks). Generally, however, it may be observed that it is unlikely that religious orders of the type envisioned in the Matt Smith stories would have appeared in futuristic episodes made as part of the twentieth-century 'classic' series. See Marcus Harmes's chapter in this volume for more on this.
4   See Russell Sandberg, *Law and Religion* (Cambridge: Cambridge University Press, 2011) chapter 10.
5   This was first prohibited by the Employment Equality (Religion or Belief) Regulations 2003 but the law is now to be found in the Equality Act 2010. For a fuller discussion of the law see Sandberg, *Law and Religion*, chapter 6. For discussion of the definition of religion or belief under English law see Sandberg, *Law and Religion*, chapter 3.
6   Employment Equality (Religion or Belief) Regulations 2003, Reg 2(1).
7   [2004] ET ET2306989/2003 (16 June 2004).
8   [2005] ET1400114/2005 (23 March 2005).
9   Section 77 of the Equality Act 2006 substituted the new definition of 'religion or belief' into the Regulations. Lack of belief was now expressly included. The same definition is now to be found in section 10 of the Equality Act 2010.
10   House of Lords Debate, 13 July 2005 col 1109-1110.
11   Compare *Baggs v Fudge* [2005] ET1400114/2005 (23 March 2005), discussed above. For analysis of this point see Russell Sandberg, 'A Question of Belief' in Nick Spencer (ed.) *Religion and Law* (London: Theos, 2012), p.51.
12   There are three distinct (but overlapping) ways in which *Doctor Who* could constitute a 'religion or belief'. First, beliefs concerning *Doctor Who* may constitute a religious belief system in a similar way to which Jedi beliefs have done so. Second, fandom can be seen as a religious activity. Third, *Doctor Who* can be used to inspire discussion of religious themes. This chapter, which is intended to provide an initial exploratory overview, addresses these three ways interchangeably.

13   Adam Possamai, *Religion and Popular Culture: A Hyper-Real Testament* (Brussels and Oxford: Peter Lang, 2005), p.77 *et seq*. The concept draws upon the social theory of Baudrillard.

14   Possamai, *Religion and Popular Culture*, p.58.

15   Possamai, *Religion and Popular Culture*, p.79.

16   Carole M. Cusack, *Invented Religions: Imagination, Fiction and Faith* (Aldershot: Ashgate, 2010), p.141.

17   The term 'hyper-real' is preferable to 'invented' since it is unclear what would constitute a 'non-invented religion ' since all religions must have begun at some point.

18   On which see Cusack, *Invented Religions*, chapter 3.

19   On which see Cusack, *Invented Religions*, chapter 5.

20   Possamai, *Religion and Popular Culture*, p.59.

21   Beth Singler, 'Jedi Ltd. or limited Jedi? Jediism and the Changing Domains of Religious Conflict in New Religious Movements' (Paper presented at the British Association for the Study of Religions Annual Conference 2012).

23   See also the novel *American Gods* (London: Headline Review, 2001) by *Doctor Who* writer Neil Gaiman, which depicts a world whereby the worship of material things takes on the physical form of gods themselves.

24   Cole Moreton, 'Everyone's a Pagan Now', *The Guardian*, 22nd June 2009, [http://www.guardian.co.uk/world/2009/jun/22/paganism-stonehenge-environmentalism-witchcraft]. Last accessed 13th March 2012.

25   Stephen Kelly, 'Does Doctor Who Feature a God for our Times?', *The Guardian Online*, 24th December 2011. [http://www.guardian.co.uk/commentisfree/belief/2011/dec/24/doctor-who-god-christmas]. Last accessed 13th March 2012.

26   The Doctor has also expressed his faith in his Companion: see 'The Impossible Planet / The Satan Pit' (2006). See also stories in which the Doctor has been mistaken as a God (e.g. 'The Face of Evil' (1977)) and stories that touch upon his mythology and standing (e.g. 'A Good Man Goes to War' (2011)). See also Tim Jones's article in this volume.

27   [2009] UKEAT 0219/09/ZT (3 November 2009).

28   *X and Church of Scientology v Sweden* (1978) 16 DR 68.

29   *X v Austria* (1963) 13 CD 42.

30   *Chappell v United Kingdom* (1987) 53 DR 241.

31   *Arrowsmtih v United Kingdom* (1978) 19 D&R 5.

32   *Hazar, Hazar and Acik v Turkey* (1991) 72 D&R 200.

33   *Angeleni v Sweden* (1986) 51 D&R 41.

33   *Plattform "Ärtze für das Leben" v Austria* (1985) 44 D&R 65.

34   *Omkarananda and the Divine Light Zentrum v Switzerland* (1981) 25 DR 105.

35   *X v Austria* (1981) 26 D&R 89.

36   *Campbell and Cosans v United Kingdom* (1982) 4 EHRR 29.

37   [2009] EAT 0434/09/DA (12November 2009).

38   [2011] ET 3105555/2009 (31 January 2011)

39   [2011]ET 1213142/2010 (14 February 2011).

40   [2012] ET 2390772/2011(22 May 2012).

41   [2009] ET 2203854/08 (22 December 2009).

42   [2011] ET 2803805/2010 (24 May 2011).

43   [2011] ET 3300873/2011 (14 September 2011).

44   A poppy is a flower made of paper which has to two red petals and a
      green leaf, which is mounted on a green stem made of plastic. It is often
      worn on clothing and made into wreaths. The Poppy has been used since
      1920 to remember service men and women who have died in war.

45   [2011]ET 1213142/2010 (14 February 2011). At para 20.

46   See Sandberg, *Law and Religion,* chapter 3.

47   [2009] UKEAT 0219/09/ZT (3 November 2009).

48   At para 24.

49   Para 24.

50   *R v Secretary of State for Education and Employment and others ex parte
      Williamson*[2005] UKHL 15.

51   Para 22.

52   [2012] 2390772/2011(22 May 2012). Para 38.

53   For discussion of the impact of Doctor Who fandom, see, for example,
      Brian J. Robb, *Timeless Adventures: How Doctor Who Conquered TV*
      (Harpenden: Kamera Books, 2009), chapter 6.

54   [2007] UKEAT/0223/07/CEA (31 October 2007).

55   [2011] ET 2803805/2010 (24 May 2011). Para 6.9.

56   [2009] UKEAT 0219/09/ZT (3 November 2009). Para 28.

57   [2011] ET 3105555/2009 (31 January 2011).

58   Para 55.

59   Such sentiments have also been frequently expressed in the twenty-first
      century series. See, for instance, 'The Impossible Planet / The Satan Pit'
      (2006) and 'The Power of Three' (2012).

60   [2011] ET 1213142/2010 (14 February 2011). .Para 17.

61   [2009] UKEAT 0219/09/ZT (3 November 2009). Para 27.

62   [2011] ET 1213142/2010 (14 February 2011). Para 18.

63   It is worth noting that the series has moved with the times with the Daleks
      being portrayed as religious fundamentalists in 'Bad Wolf / The Parting
      of the Ways' (2005).

64   E.g. 'The Green Death'(1975).

65   E.g. 'Colony in Space' (1971).

66   E.g. 'Planet of the Ood' (2008).

67   E.g. 'Vengeance on Varos' (1985).

68   E.g. 'Nightmare of Eden' (1979).

69   E.g. 'The Sun Makers' (1977).

70   E.g. 'A Town Called Mercy' (2012).

71   E.g. 'Vincent and the Doctor' (2010).

72   E.g. 'The Curse of Peladon' (1972).

73   Though note the argument that these stories represent a Christianised
      version of Buddhism: see Tulloch and Alvarado, *Doctor Who: The Unfolding
      Text,* chapter 6.

74   *R v Secretary of State for Education and Employment and others ex parte
      Williamson*[2005] UKHL 15.At para 23.

75 At para 24.
76 At para 23.
77 See also the decision in *Lisk v Shield Guardian Co Ltd & Others* [2011] ET 3300873/2011 (14 September 2011) in which Employment Judge George held that belief that one should wear a poppy to show respect to serviceman lacked the characteristics of cogency, cohesion and importance. George gave no reasons to support this conclusion but held that he would characterise the claimant's belief as 'a belief that we should express support for the sacrifice of others and not as a belief in itself and this was 'too "narrow" to be characterised as a philosophical belief'.
78 [2011] ET 2803805/2010 (24 May 2011). Para 6.1.
79 Para 6.3.
80 Para 6.4.
81 Para 6.7.
82 Para 6.8.
83 *R v Secretary of State for Education and Employment and others ex parte Williamson* [2005] UKHL 15.Para 22.
84 *United States v Kuch* 288 F Supp 439 (1968).
85 The court was unimpressed by the fact that the Church had its own symbol (a three-eyed toad) official songs ('Puff, the Magic Dragon' and 'Row, Row, Row Your Boat';) and its own motto ('Victory over Horseshit').
86 Depending upon how the belief is manifested, there may also be issues concerning whether the belief has attained the requisite level of seriousness. A *Doctor Who*-inspired religion may contain an element of irreverence such as eating fish-fingers and custard as a sacrament (as inspired by 'The Eleventh Hour' (2010)). Following *Williamson*, it is suggested that irreverence in itself should not be fatal to this requirement but the focus should be on the subjective beliefs of the claimant. If there is a genuine reason for a seemingly irreverent act which is linked to the claimant's belief (as opposed to the claimant's desire to achieve a legal benefit) then the threshold should be met. This question is of importance in relation to hyper-real religions: Cusack examines satirical religions such as Discordianism and most obviously the Church of the Subgenius and the Church of the Flying Spaghetti Monster and how belief has arisen out of parody (Cusack, *Invented Religions*). It is questionable whether it would be appropriate for courts to determine whether such beliefs are 'serious'.
87 At para 24.
88 *R v Secretary of State for Education and Employment and others ex parte Williamson*[2005] UKHL 15.Para 77.
89 Para 23.
90 [2009] UKEAT 0219/09/ZT (3 November 2009). Para 28. Though note the extent to which English law permits religious groups to have and act upon beliefs concerning sexual orientation that otherwise would be illegal: see Russell Sandberg, 'The Right to Discriminate' (2011) 13 *Ecclesiastical Law* Journal, p.157.
91 House of Lords Hansard (2x009-2010) 23 March 2010,Column 857.

92   It would be interesting to see how this principle would be applied in relation to hyper-religions derived from *Star Wars* given that Beth Singler's research has shown that there are both Jedi and Sith orders: (Singler, 'Jedi Ltd. or limited Jedi?').

93   In parliamentary debates concerning the Racial and Religious Hatred Bill, then Opposition spokesman Dominic Greive put forward a probing amendment which would have provided a list of groups not protected. This list included Satanists, believers in human sacrifice / animal sacrifice / female mutilation / religious violence / racial superiority/ gender superiority, scientologists and Jedi Knights. House of Commons Hansard (2004-2005) 29 June 2005. Column 41.

94   House of Lords Hansard (2009-2010) 23 March 2010, Column 857.

95   [2009] UKEAT 0219/09/ZT (3 November 2009). Para 24.

96   *R v Secretary of State for Education and Employment and others ex parte Williamson*[2005] UKHL 15. Para 22.

97   Para 60.

18. Noel Brown, 'Something woolly and fuzzy': The Representation of Religion in the Big Finish *Doctor Who* Audio Adventures

Quotations from Big Finish audio drama *The Holy Terror* are © Big Finish Productions/Robert Shearman (2000). Quotations from Big Finish audio drama *Bloodtide* are © Big Finish Productions/Jonathan Morris (2001). Reproduced by kind permission.

1   David Layton, *The Humanism of Doctor Who: A Critical Study in Science Fiction and Philosophy* (London and Jefferson, N. C.: McFarland, 2012), pp. 135-37.

2   See John Tulloch and Henry Jenkins, *Science Fiction Audiences: Watching Doctor Who and Star Trek* (London and New York: Routledge, 1995), pp. 67-85.

3   Currently, all new releases are available to purchase on CD via subscription or through specialist retail outlets, or as a digital download from the company's website.

4   Benjamin Cook, *Doctor Who: The New Audio Adventures – The Inside Story* (Maidenhead: Big Finish Productions, 2003), p. 6.

5   Cook, *Doctor Who: The New Audio Adventures*, p. 11.

6   Matt Hills, 'Televisuality without Television? The Big Finish Audios and Discourses of "Tele-Centric" Doctor Who' in David Butler (ed.), *Time and Relative Dissertations in Space: Critical Perspectives on Doctor Who*, (Manchester and New York: Manchester University Press, 2007) [pp. 280-95], p. 281.

7   Cook, *Doctor Who: The New Audio Adventures*, p. 59.

8   This hypothesis has purportedly been put to the test on several occasions, most notably by the Egyptian Pharaoh Psammetichus, and by King James IV of Scotland in the early-sixteenth century. It is also fictionally enacted

- with similarly horrific results - in Jill Paton-Walsh's Booker prize-nominated novel, *Knowledge of Angels* (1994).

9   Grace Davie, *Religion in Britain Since 1945: Believing without Belonging* (Oxford: Blackwell, 1994).

10   Peter Berger (ed.), *The Desecularisation of the World: Resurgent Religion and World Politics* (Washington: Eerdmans, 1999).

11   Callum Brown, *The Death of Christian Britain: Understanding Secularisation, 1800-2000* (London and New York: Routledge, 2001).

12   Steve Bruce, *Religion in the Modern World: from Cathedrals to Cults* (Oxford and New York: Oxford University Press, 1996), pp. 129-67.

13   Cook, *Doctor Who: The New Audio Adventures*, pp. 97; 98-99.

14   For more on the different readings of faith in the series, see Tim Jones's article in this volume.

15   Of course, this is, by necessity, a historically inaccurate account of Darwin's spiritual and intellectual transformation, which was a far more gradual and ambivalent process than this play would imply.

16   Cook, *Doctor Who: The New Audio Adventures*, pp. 98-99.

17   Cook, *Doctor Who: The New Audio Adventures*, pp. 98-99.

18   Cook, *Doctor Who: The New Audio Adventures*, p. 204.

19   Alan Aldridge, *Religion in the Contemporary World: A Sociological Introduction*, 2nd edition (Cambridge: Polity Press, 2007), pp. 111-17.

20   Bruce, *Religion in the Modern World*, p. 147.

21   Bruce, *Religion in the Modern World*, p. 147.

19. Joel Dark, Doctoring the Doctor: Midrashic Adventures in Text and Space

1   'The Dalek Invasion of Earth' (1964); 'The Five Doctors' (1983).

2   Russell T. Davies, foreword in Benjamin Cook, *Doctor Who: The New Audio Adventures – The Inside Story* (Maidenhead: Big Finish Productions, 2003), p.3.

3   Rachel Barenblat, 'Transformative Work: Midrash and Fanfiction', *Religion & Literature* 43:2 (2011), p.171. Barenblat is a rabbi and poet most widely known through her acclaimed blog 'The Velveteen Rabbi' (velveteenrabbi. blogs.com). Although I became aware of her work only in the course of developing this chapter, it owes very significantly to her and to others who have provided effective and engaging introductions to midrash for readers, including myself, within other faith traditions or secular contexts.

4   Barenblat, 'Transformative Work', p.174.

5   For an overview of wide-ranging scholarly efforts to link midrash and literary studies in the 1980s, see especially Geoffrey H. Hartman and Sanford Budick (eds.), *Midrash and Literature* (New Haven: Yale University Press, 1986). The introduction to David Stern's *Midrash and Theory: Ancient Jewish Exegesis and Contemporary Literary Studies* (Evanston, Il.: Northwestern University Press, 1996) provides a retrospective summary of the hopes and limitations of this 'moment of interdisciplinary excitement' (p. 8). Published more recently, chapters 5 and 6 of Leslie Cushing

Stahlberg's *Sustaining Fictions: Intertextuality, Midrash, Translation, and the Literary Afterlife of the Bible* (New York: T & T Clark, 2008) also reflect on and extend the exploration of these connections.

6   On canon in the stories of Sherlock Holmes, see P. J. Campbell, 'The Canon and the Apocrypha' in Charles R. Putney, Joseph A. Cutshall King, and Sally Sugarman (eds.), *Sherlock Holmes: Victorian Sleuth to Modern Hero* (Lanham, Maryland: Scarecrow Press, 1996), pp.234-44.

7   Davies, foreword to Cook, *Doctor Who: The Audio Adventures*, p.3.

8   Michael Saler, '"Clap If You Believe in Sherlock Holmes": Mass Culture and the Re-enchantment of Modernity, c. 1890—c. 1940', *The Historical Journal* 46: 3 (2003), p.607. Saler includes a revised version of this essay alongside chapters on H. P. Lovecraft and J. R. R. Tolkien in his recent book *As If: Modern Enchantment and the Literary Prehistory of Virtual Reality* (Oxford: Oxford University Press, 2012).

9   Saler writes: 'Cultural pessimists have frequently criticised mass culture as a form of false consciousness or dismissed it as a pernicious escape from reality. While both of these positions can have a measure of truth, depending on the situations they discuss, neither takes into account the buffering roles of animistic reason and the ironic imagination, which inhibit complete acceptance or acquiescence into any particular cultural construct' ('"Clap If You Believe in Sherlock Holmes"', p.607). Saler's *As If* further develops this argument and examines the extent to which the imaginary worlds of Conan Doyle, Lovecraft, and Tolkien have, in fact, served this critical function.

10   The recipient of the famous telegraph was the actor William Gilette, who wrote adaptations of Conan Doyle's stories and played Sherlock Holmes on stage in the United States. See Sally Buchanan Kinsey, 'William Gillette: American's Sherlock Lived the Role' in *Sherlock Holmes: Victorian Sleuth to Modern Hero*, p.247.

11   On canon in *Star Trek*, see Michael Jindra, 'Star Trek Fandom as a Religious Phenomenon', *Sociology of Religion* 55:1 (1994), p.45. On *Star Wars* canon, see chapter 5 of Will Brooker's *Using the Force: Creativity, Community, and Star Wars Fans* (New York: Continuum, 2002).

12   For a detailed exploration of all four seasons of these 'Audio Visuals' as well an account of their legacy on audio, in print, and on video, see Alun Harris and Matthew West, *Justyce Served: A Small Start with a Big Finish* (Tadworth: Miwk Publishing, 2012).

13   In a post to a Usenet discussion about the *New Adventures* novels – 'NAs canon? Not to me' on the list 'rec.arts.drwho' – dated 10 April 1996, Moffat wrote: 'Why all this fuss about canon – and, indeed, continuity – in a show about a man who changes history for a living?' Moffat's exploration of this problem in his short story 'Continuity Errors', published the same year, is discussed later in the chapter.

14   James Kugel, 'Two Introductions to Midrash' in *Midrash and Literature*, p.92.

15   This relatively minor problem became more widely known through a reference to it by *Doctor Who* Executive Producer Barry Letts in his

foreword to Jean-Marc Lofficier, *The Doctor Who Programme Guide*, vol. 1 (London: W. H. Allen, 1981), p.6.

16 The referenced television stories are 'Tomb of the Cybermen' (1967), 'Doctor Who and the Silurians' (1970), and 'Pyramids of Mars' (1975).

17 'An Unearthly Child'(1963).

18 This occurred in 'The Three Doctors' (1973), 'The Five Doctors' (1983), and 'The Two Doctors' (1985).

19 Rupert Hine (lyrics and arrangement) and Ron Grainer (composer), 'Who is the Doctor', performed by Jon Pertwee, Purple PUR III, vinyl recording, 1977.

20 Lance Parkin, *Cold Fusion* (London: Virgin Publishing, 1996).

21 James Kugel has developed a lexicon of terms to describe such practices, and others, in the ancient interpretation and development of biblical stories, including 'narrative expansion','narrative resumption', and 'back-referencing'. See especially Kugel's *In Potiphar's House: The Interpretive Life of Biblical Texts* (New York: Harper Collins, 1990).

22 Robert Shearman, *Jubilee*, directed by Nicholas Briggs and Robert Shearman (Big Finish Productions, 2003).

23 David A. McIntee, *The Dark Path* (London: Virgin Publishing, 1997). The quotation, from the 1996 *Doctor Who* television movie, appears on p. xi.

24 Marc Platt, *Spare Parts*, directed by Gary Russell (Big Finish Productions, 2002). The title references 'The Tenth Planet' (1966), in which one of the programme's first Cybermen had explained: 'Our life span was getting shorter so our scientists and doctors devised spare parts for our bodies until we could be almost completely replaced.'

25 Francesca Coppa, 'Girl Genius: Nyssa of Traken' in Lynne M. Thomas and Tara O'Shea (eds.), *Chicks Dig Time Lords: A Celebration of Doctor Who by the Women Who Love It* (Des Moines, Iowa: Mad Norwegian Press, 2010), pp.62-67.

26 The test, named for the cartoonist Alison Bechdel, requires that a narrative include at least two women who talk with each other about something other than a man. See Coppa, 'Girl Genius', pp.63-64.

27 Coppa,'Girl Genius', p.65.

28 'The Edge of Destruction' (1964).

29 Marc Platt, *Quinnis*, directed by Lisa Bowerman (Big Finish Productions, 2010).

30 Russell T. Davies, *Damaged Goods* (London: Virgin Publishing, 1996), pp.154-55.

31 See especially the concluding dialogue of Paul Sutton, *Arrangements for War*, directed by Gary Russell (Big Finish Productions, 2004).

32 This observation draws again on the reflections of Barenblat, who writes: 'Ultimately, I would argue that what matters is the community which is constituted and continued through the conversation of storytelling, and in that sense, midrash and fan fiction are deeply parallel. The stories are how we create and preserve intergenerational global conversations' (p. 176).

33   Audio interview with Louise Jameson included as 'CD Extra 1' in
      Nicholas Briggs, *Destination: Nerva*, directed by Nicholas Briggs (Big
      Finish Productions, 2012).
34   'The Mutants' (1972).
35   Terrance Dicks, *The Eight Doctors* (London: BBC Worldwide Publishing,
      1997). In addition to filling plot holes, Dicks significantly also employs the
      Doctor to confront morally problematic aspects of his earliest character
      development. It was paradoxically the Doctor himself, Dicks writes on
      pp. 34-39, who persuaded the earliest version of the character not to take
      a life in his first television story.
36   Douglas Adams, *Shada*, directed by Nicholas Pegg (Big Finish Productions,
      2003).
37   Paul Cornell, *Human Nature* (London: Virgin Publishing, 1995), p.169.
38   Cornell, *Human Nature*, pp.115-16.
39   Steven Moffat, 'Continuity Errors' in Andy Lane and Justin Richards
      (eds.), *Decalog 3 – Consequences* (London: Virgin Publishing, 1996), pp.214-
      39. The quotation appears on p.219.
40   Steven Hall, *A Death in the Family*, directed by Ken Bentley (Big Finish
      Productions, 2010).

James McGrath, Epilogue

1   These can be found on the BBC website. [http://www.bbc.co.uk/archive/
      doctorwho/6403.shtml]

Appendix: *Doctor Who* Episodes, Writers and Directors

The First Doctor: William Hartnell (1963-66)

Episode title	Writer	Director
'An Unearthly Child' (1963)	Anthony Coburn (with C. E. Webber)	Waris Hussein
'The Daleks' (1963/4)	Terry Nation	Richard Martin/ Christopher Barry
'The Edge of Destruction' (1964)	David Whitaker	Richard Martin/ Frank Cox
'Marco Polo' (1964)	John Lucarotti	Waris Hussein
'The Keys of Marinus' (1964)	Terry Nation	John Gorrie
'The Aztecs' (1964)	John Lucarotti	John Crockett
'The Sensorites' (1964)	Peter R. Newman	Mervyn Pinfield/ Frank Cox
'The Reign of Terror' (1964)	Dennis Spooner	Henric Hirsch/ John Gorrie
'Planet of Giants' (1964)	Louis Marks	Mervyn Pinfield/ Douglas Camfield
'The Dalek Invasion of Earth' (1964)	Terry Nation	Richard Martin
'The Rescue' (1965)	David Whitaker	Christopher Barry
'The Romans' (1965)	Dennis Spooner	Christopher Barry
'The Web Planet' (1965)	Bill Strutton	Richard Martin
'The Crusade' (1965)	David Whitaker	Douglas Camfield
'The Space Museum' (1965)	Glyn Jones	Mervyn Pinfield
'The Chase' (1965)	Terry Nation	Richard Martin/ Douglas Camfield
'The Time Meddler' (1965)	Dennis Spooner	Douglas Camfield
'Galaxy 4' (1965)	William Emms	Derek Martinus/ Mervyn Pinfield

Episode title	Writer	Director
'Mission to the Unknown' (1965)	Terry Nation	Derek Martinus
'The Myth Makers' (1965)	Donald Cotton	Michael Leeston-Smith
'The Daleks' Master Plan' (1965/6)	Terry Nation & Dennis Spooner	Douglas Camfield
'The Massacre of St Bartholomew's Eve" (1966)	John Lucarotti and Donald Tosh	Paddy Russell
'The Ark' (1966)	Paul Erickson and Lesley Scott	Michael Imison
'The Celestial Toymaker' (1966)	Brian Hayles (and Donald Tosh)	Bill Sellars
'The Gunfighters' (1966)	Donald Cotton	Rex Tucker
'The Savages' (1966)	Ian Stuart Black	Christopher Barry
'The War Machines' (1966)	Ian Stuart Black (based on concept by Kit Pedler)	Michael Ferguson
'The Smugglers' (1966)	Brian Hayles	Julia Smith
'The Tenth Planet' (1966)	Kit Pedler and Gerry Davis	Derek Martinus

The Second Doctor: Patrick Troughton (1966-69)

Episode title	Writer	Director
'The Power of the Daleks' (1966)	David Whitaker (and Dennis Spooner, uncredited)	Christopher Barry
'The Highlanders' (1966/7)	Elwyn Jones and Gerry Davis	Hugh David
'The Underwater Menace' (1967)	Geoffrey Orme	Julia Smith
'The Moonbase' (1967)	Kit Pedler	Morris Barry
'The Macra Terror' (1967)	Ian Stuart Black	John Davies
'The Faceless Ones' (1967)	David Ellis and Malcolm Hulke	Gerry Mill
'The Evil of the Daleks' (1967)	David Whitaker	Derek Martinus
'The Tomb of the Cybermen' (1967)	Kit Pedler and Gerry Davis	Morris Barry

Episode title	Writer	Director
'The Abominable Snowmen' (1967)	Mervyn Haisman and Henry Lincoln	Gerald Blake
'The Ice Warriors' (1967)	Brian Hayles	Derek Martinus
'The Enemy of the World' (1967/8)	David Whitaker	Barry Letts
'The Web of Fear' (1968)	Mervyn Haisman and Henry Lincoln	Douglas Camfield
'Fury from the Deep' (1968)	Victor Pemberton	Hugh David
'The Wheel in Space' (1968)	David Whitaker and Kit Pedler	Tristain de Vere Cole
'The Dominators' (1968)	Norman Ashby (pseudonym for Mervyn Haisman and Henry Lincoln)	Morris Barry
'The Mind Robber' (1968)	Peter Ling (and Derrick Sherwin)	David Maloney
'The Invasion' (1968)	Derrick Sherwin and Kit Pedler	Douglas Camfield
'The Krotons' (1968/9)	Robert Holmes	David Maloney
'The Seeds of Death' (1969)	Brian Hayles (and Terrance Dicks)	Michael Ferguson
'The Space Pirates' (1969)	Robert Holmes	Michael Hart
'The War Games' (1969)	Malcolm Hulke and Terrance Dicks	David Maloney

The Third Doctor: Jon Pertwee (1970-74)

Episode Title	Writer	Director
'Spearhead from Space' (1970)	Robert Holmes	Derek Martinus
'Doctor Who and the Silurians' (1970)	Malcolm Hulke	Timothy Combe
'The Ambassadors of Death' (1970)	David Whitaker (Trevor Ray and Malcolm Hulke, uncredited)	Michael Ferguson
'Inferno' (1970)	Don Houghton	Douglas Camfield and Barry Letts
'Terror of the Autons' (1971)	Robert Holmes	Barry Letts

Episode Title	Writer	Director
'The Mind of Evil' (1971)	Don Houghton	Timothy Combe
'The Claws of Axos' (1971)	Bob Baker and Dave Martin	Michael Ferguson
'Colony in Space' (1971)	Malcolm Hulke	Michael E. Briant
'The Dæmons' (1971)	Guy Leopold (pseudonym for Robert Sloman and Barry Letts)	Christopher Barry
'Day of the Daleks' (1972)	Louis Marks	Paul Bernard
'The Curse of Peladon' (1972)	Brian Hayles	Lennie Mayne
'The Sea Devils' (1972)	Malcolm Hulke	Michael E. Briant
'The Mutants' (1972)	Bob Baker and Dave Martin	Christopher Barry
'The Time Monster' (1972)	Robert Sloman (and Barry Letts, uncredited)	Paul Bernard
'The Three Doctors' (1972/3)	Bob Baker and Dave Martin	Lennie Mayne
'Carnival of Monsters' (1973)	Robert Holmes	Barry Letts
'Frontier in Space' (1973)	Malcolm Hulke	Paul Bernard
'Planet of the Daleks' (1973)	Terry Nation	David Maloney
'The Green Death' (1973)	Robert Sloman (and Barry Letts, uncredited)	Michael E. Briant
'The Time Warrior' (1973/4)	Robert Holmes	Alan Bromly
'Invasion of the Dinosaurs' (1974)	Malcolm Hulke	Paddy Russell
'Death to the Daleks' (1974)	Terry Nation	Michael E. Briant
'The Monster of Peladon' (1974)	Brian Hayles	Lennie Mayne
'Planet of the Spiders' (1974)	Robert Sloman (and Barry Letts, uncredited)	Barry Letts

The Fourth Doctor: Tom Baker (1974-1981)

Episode Title	Writer	Director
'Robot' (1974/5)	Terrance Dicks	Christopher Barry
'The Ark in Space' (1975)	Robert Holmes	Rodney Bennett
'The Sontaran Experiment' (1975)	Bob Baker and Dave Martin	Rodney Bennett
'Genesis of the Daleks' (1975)	Terry Nation	David Maloney
'Revenge of the Cybermen' (1975)	Gerry Davis	Michael E. Briant
'Terror of the Zygons' (1975)	Robert Banks Stewart	Douglas Camfield
'Planet of Evil' (1975)	Louis Marks	David Maloney
'Pyramids of Mars' (1975)	Stephen Harris (pseudonym for Robert Holmes and Lewis Griefer)	Paddy Russell
'The Android Invasion' (1975)	Terry Nation	Barry Letts
'The Brain of Morbius' (1976)	Robin Bland (pseudonym for Terrance Dicks and Robert Holmes)	Christopher Barry
'The Seeds of Doom' (1976)	Robert Banks Stewart	Douglas Camfield
'The Masque of Mandragora' (1976)	Louis Marks	Rodney Bennett
'The Hand of Fear' (1976)	Bob Baker & Dave Martin	Lennie Mayne
'The Deadly Assassin' (1976)	Robert Holmes	David Maloney
'The Face of Evil' (1977)	Chris Boucher	Pennant Roberts
'The Robots of Death' (1977)	Chris Boucher	Michael E. Briant
'The Talons of Weng-Chiang' (1977)	Robert Holmes (from an idea by Robert Banks Stewart)	David Maloney
'Horror of Fang Rock' (1977)	Terrance Dicks	Paddy Russell
'The Invisible Enemy' (1977)	Bob Baker and Dave Martin	Derrick Goodwin

Episode Title	Writer	Director
'Image of the Fendahl' (1977)	Chris Boucher	George Spenton-Foster
'The Sun Makers' (1977)	Robert Holmes	Pennant Roberts
'Underworld' (1978)	Bob Baker and Dave Martin	Norman Stewart
'The Invasion of Time' (1978)	David Agnew (pseudonym for Graham Williams and Anthony Read)	Gerald Blake
'The Ribos Operation' (1978)	Robert Holmes	George Spenton-Foster
'The Pirate Planet' (1978)	Douglas Adams	Pennant Roberts
'The Stones of Blood' (1978)	David Fisher	Darrol Blake
'The Androids of Tara' (1978)	David Fisher	Michael Hayes
'The Power of Kroll' (1978/9)	Robert Holmes	Norman Stewart
'The Armageddon Factor' (1979)	Bob Baker and Dave Martin	Michael Hayes
'Destiny of the Daleks' (1979)	Terry Nation	Ken Grieve
'City of Death' (1979)	David Agnew (pseudonym for Douglas Adams and Graham Williams)	Michael Hayes
'The Creature from the Pit' (1979)	David Fisher	Christopher Barry
'Nightmare of Eden' (1979)	Bob Baker	Adam Bromly
'The Horns of Nimon' (1979/80)	Anthony Read	Kenny McBain
'Shada' (1980) [Only partially filmed due to strike]	Douglas Adams	Pennant Roberts
'The Leisure Hive' (1980)	David Fisher	Lovett Bickford
'Meglos' (1980)	John Flanagan and Andrew McCulloch	Terence Dudley
'Full Circle' (1980)	Andrew Smith	Peter Grimwade
'State of Decay' (1980)	Terrance Dicks	Peter Moffatt

Episode Title	Writer	Director
'Warriors' Gate' (1981)	Steve Gallagher	Paul Joyce
'The Keeper of Traken' (1981)	Johnny Byrne	John Black
'Logopolis' (1981)	Christopher H. Bidmead	Peter Grimwade

The Fifth Doctor: Peter Davison (1982-84)

Episode Title	Writer	Director
'Castrovalva' (1982)	Christopher H. Bidmead	Fiona Cumming
'Four to Doomsday' (1982)	Terence Dudley	John Black
'Kinda' (1982)	Christopher Bailey	Peter Grimwade
'The Visitation' (1982)	Eric Saward	Peter Moffatt
'Black Orchid' (1982)	Terence Dudley	Ron Jones
'Earthshock' (1982)	Eric Saward	Peter Grimwade
'Time Flight' (1982)	Peter Grimwade	Ron Jones
'Arc of Infinity' (1983)	Johnny Byrne	Ron Jones
'Snakedance' (1983)	Christopher Bailey	Fiona Cumming
'Mawdryn Undead' (1983)	Peter Grimwade	Peter Moffatt
'Terminus' (1983)	Steve Gallagher	Mary Ridge
'Enlightenment' (1983)	Barbara Clegg	Fiona Cumming
'The King's Demons' (1983)	Terence Dudley	Tony Virgo
'The Five Doctors' (1983)	Terrance Dicks	Peter Moffatt
'Warriors of the Deep' (1984)	Johnny Byrne	Pennant Roberts
'The Awakening' (1984)	Eric Pringle	Michael Owen Morris
'Frontios' (1984)	Christopher H. Bidmead	Ron Jones
'Resurrection of the Daleks' (1984)	Eric Saward	Matthew Robinson
'Planet of Fire' (1984)	Peter Grimwade	Fiona Cumming
'The Caves of Androzani' (1984)	Robert Holmes	Graeme Harper

The Sixth Doctor: Colin Baker (1984-86)

Episode Title	Writer	Director
'The Twin Dilemma' (1984)	Anthony Steven	Peter Moffatt
'Attack of the Cybermen' (1985)	Paula Moore	Matthew Robinson
'Vengeance on Varos' (1985)	Philip Martin	Ron Jones
'The Mark of the Rani' (1985)	Pip and Jane Baker	Sarah Hellings
'The Two Doctors' (1985)	Robert Holmes	Peter Moffatt
'Timelash' (1985)	Glen McCoy	Pennant Roberts
'Revelation of the Daleks' (1985)	Eric Saward	Graeme Harper
'The Trial of a Time Lord: The Mysterious Planet' (1986)	Robert Holmes	Nicholas Mallett
'The Trial of a Time Lord: Mindwarp' (1986)	Philip Martin	Ron Jones
'The Trial of a Time Lord: Terror of the Vervoids' (1986)	Pip and Jane Baker	Chris Clough
'The Trial of a Time Lord: The Ultimate Foe' (1986)	Robert Holmes and Pip and Jane Baker	Chris Clough

The Seventh Doctor: Sylvester McCoy (1987-89)

Episode Title	Writer	Director
'Time and the Rani' (1987)	Pip and Jane Baker	Andrew Morgan
'Paradise Towers' (1987)	Stephen Wyatt	Nicholas Mallett
'Delta and the Bannermen' (1987)	Malcolm Kohll	Chris Clough
'Dragonfire' (1987)	Ian Briggs	Chris Clough
'Remembrance of the Daleks' (1988)	Ben Aaronovitch	Andrew Morgan
'The Happiness Patrol' (1988)	Graeme Curry	Chris Clough
'Silver Nemesis' (1988)	Kevin Clarke	Chris Clough

Episode Title	Writer	Director
'The Greatest Show in the Galaxy' (1988)	Stephen Wyatt	Alan Wareing
'Battlefield' (1989)	Ben Aaronovitch	Michael Kerrigan
'Ghost Light' (1989)	Marc Platt	Alan Wareing
'The Curse of Fenric' (1989)	Ian Briggs	Nicholas Mallett
'Survival' (1989)	Rona Munro	Alan Wareing

The Eighth Doctor: Paul McGann (1996)

Episode Title	Writer	Director
'The TV Movie' (1996)	Matthew Jacobs	Geoffrey Sax

The Ninth Doctor: Christopher Eccleston (2005)

Episode Title	Writer	Director
'Rose' (2005)	Russell T. Davies	Kevin Boak
'The End of the World' (2005)	Russell T. Davies	Euros Lyn
'The Unquiet Dead' (2005)	Mark Gatiss	Euros Lyn
'Aliens of London'/'World War Three' (2005)	Russell T. Davies	Kevin Boak
'Dalek' (2005)	Robert Shearman	Joe Ahearne
'The Long Game' (2005)	Russell T. Davies	Brian Grant
'Father's Day' (2005)	Paul Cornell	Joe Ahearne
'The Empty Child'/'The Doctor Dances' (2005)	Steven Moffat	James Hawes
'Boom Town' (2005)	Russell T. Davies	Joe Ahearne
'Bad Wolf'/'The Parting of the Ways' (2005)	Russell T. Davies	Joe Ahearne

The Tenth Doctor: David Tennant (2005-10)

Episode Title	Writer	Director
'The Christmas Invasion' (2005)	Russell T. Davies	James Hawes
'New Earth' (2006)	Russell T. Davies	James Hawes
'Tooth and Claw' (2006)	Russell T. Davies	Euros Lyn

Episode Title	Writer	Director
'School Reunion' (2006)	Toby Whithouse	James Hawes
'The Girl in the Fireplace' (2006)	Steven Moffat	Euros Lyn
'Rise of the Cybermen'/'The Age of Steel' (2006)	Tom MacRae	Graeme Harper
'The Idiot's Lantern' (2006)	Mark Gatiss	Euros Lyn
'The Impossible Planet'/'The Satan Pit' (2006)	Matt Jones	James Strong
'Love & Monsters' (2006)	Russell T. Davies	Dan Zeff
'Fear Her' (2006)	Matthew Graham	Euros Lyn
'Army of Ghosts'/'Doomsday' (2006)	Russell T. Davies	Graeme Harper
'The Runaway Bride' (2006)	Russell T. Davies	Euros Lyn
'Smith and Jones' (2007)	Russell T. Davies	Charles Palmer
'The Shakespeare Code' (2007)	Gareth Roberts	Charles Palmer
'Gridlock' (2007)	Russell T. Davies	Richard Clark
'Daleks in Manhattan'/'Evolution of the Daleks' (2007)	Helen Raynor	James Strong
'The Lazarus Experiment' (2007)	Stephen Greenhorn	Richard Clark
'42' (2007)	Chris Chibnall	Graeme Harper
'Human Nature'/'The Family of Blood' (2007)	Paul Cornell	Charles Palmer
'Blink' (2007)	Steven Moffat	Hettie MacDonald
'Utopia' (2007)	Russell T. Davies	Graeme Harper
'The Sounds of Drums'/'Last of the Time Lords' (2007)	Russell T. Davies	Colin Teague
'Voyage of the Damned' (2007)	Russell T. Davies	James Strong
'Partners in Crime' (2008)	Russell T. Davies	James Strong

Episode Title	Writer	Director
'The Fires of Pompeii' (2008)	James Moran	Colin Teague
'Planet of the Ood' (2008)	Keith Temple	Graeme Harper
'The Sontaran Strategem' / 'The Poison Sky' (2008)	Helen Raynor	Douglas Mackinnon
'The Doctor's Daughter' (2008)	Stephen Greenhorn	Alice Troughton
'The Unicorn and the Wasp' (2008)	Gareth Roberts	Graeme Harper
'Silence in the Library' / 'Forest of the Dead' (2008)	Steven Moffat	Euros Lyn
'Midnight' (2008)	Russell T. Davies	Alice Troughton
'Turn Left' (2008)	Russell T. Davies	Graeme Harper
'The Stolen Earth' / 'Journey's End' (2008)	Russell T. Davies	Graeme Harper
'The Next Doctor' (2008)	Russell T. Davies	Andy Goddard
'Planet of the Dead' (2009)	Russell T. Davies and Gareth Roberts	James Strong
'The Waters of Mars' (2009)	Russell T. Davies and Phil Ford	Graeme Harper
'The End of Time' Parts One and Two (2009/10)	Russell T. Davies	Euros Lyn

The Eleventh Doctor: Matt Smith (2010-2013)

Episode Title	Writer	Director
'The Eleventh Hour' (2010)	Steven Moffat	Adam Smith
'The Beast Below' (2010)	Steven Moffat	Andrew Gunn
'Victory of the Daleks' (2010)	Mark Gatiss	Andrew Gunn
'The Time of Angels' / 'Flesh and Stone' (2010)	Steven Moffat	Adam Smith
'The Vampires of Venice' (2010)	Toby Whithouse	Jonny Campbell

Episode Title	Writer	Director
'Amy's Choice' (2010)	Simon Nye	Catherine Morshead
'The Hungry Earth'/'Cold Blood' (2010)	Chris Chibnall	Ashley Way
'Vincent and the Doctor' (2010)	Richard Curtis	Jonny Campbell
'The Lodger' (2010)	Gareth Roberts	Catherine Morshead
'The Pandorica Opens'/ 'The Big Bang' (2010)	Steven Moffat	Toby Haynes
'A Christmas Carol' (2010)	Steven Moffat	Toby Haynes
'The Impossible Astronaut' / 'Day of the Moon' (2011)	Steven Moffat	Toby Haynes
'Curse of the Black Spot' (2011)	Stephen Thompson	Jeremy Webb
'The Doctor's Wife' (2011)	Neil Gaiman	Richard Clark
'The Rebel Flesh'/ 'The Almost People' (2011)	Matthew Graham	Julian Simpson
'A Good Man Goes to War' (2011)	Steven Moffat	Peter Hoar
'Let's Kill Hitler' (2011)	Steven Moffat	Richard Senior
'Night Terrors' (2011)	Mark Gatiss	Richard Clark
'The Girl Who Waited' (2011)	Tom MacRae	Nick Hurran
'The God Complex' (2011)	Toby Whithouse	Nick Hurran
'Closing Time' (2011)	Gareth Roberts	Steve Hughes
'The Wedding of River Song' (2011)	Steven Moffat	Jeremy Webb
'The Doctor, the Widow, and the Wardrobe' (2011)	Steven Moffat	Farren Blackburn
'Asylum of the Daleks' (2012)	Steven Moffat	Nick Hurran
'Dinosaurs on a Spaceship' (2012)	Chris Chibnall	Saul Metzstein
'A Town Called Mercy' (2012)	Toby Whithouse	Saul Metzstein
'The Power of Three' (2012)	Chris Chibnall	Douglas Mackinnon

Episode Title	Writer	Director
'The Angels Take Manhattan' (2012)	Steven Moffat	Nick Hurran
'The Snowmen' (2012)	Steven Moffat	Saul Metzstein
'The Bells of Saint John' (2013)	Steven Moffat	Colm McCarthy
'The Rings of Akhaten' (2013)	Neil Cross	Farren Blackburn
'Cold War' (2013)	Mark Gatiss	Douglas Mackinnon
'Hide' (2013)	Neil Cross	Jamie Payne
'Journey to the Centre of the TARDIS' (2013)	Stephen Thompson	Mat King
'The Crimson Horror' (2013)	Mark Gatiss	Saul Metzstein
'Nightmare in Silver' (2013)	Neil Gaiman	Stephen Woolfenden
'The Name of the Doctor' (2013)	Steven Moffat	Saul Metzstein

Notes on Contributors

Laura Brekke is a Presbyterian preacher by day and a reluctant theological writer by night. A graduate of the Candler School of Theology, she is interested in comparative religious studies and how popular culture can be a meeting ground for interreligious dialogue. During a year studying at the University of Cambridge, she encountered the strange man in a blue box and has been enamoured with him ever since.

Noel Brown received his PhD in Film from Newcastle University in 2010, where he has taught several courses on film and literature. Currently an independent scholar, he is the author of *The Hollywood Family Film: A History, from Shirley Temple to Harry Potter* (I. B. Tauris, 2012), and the co-editor of *Beyond Disney: Children's Films and Family Films in Global Cinema* (I. B. Tauris, 2014). He has written for various journals and other publications on aspects of youth culture.

Michael Charlton is an assistant professor at Missouri Western State University, where he teaches professional writing and rhetoric. His work has previously appeared in journals such as *Alphaville*, *Programmatic Perspectives*, and *Composition Studies*. Students frequently ask about the Dalek pencil sharpener on his desk.

Brigid Cherry is a Research Fellow in Communication, Culture and Creative Arts at St Mary's University College, Twickenham, UK. Her research focuses on fan cultures, and she has recently published work on *Doctor Who* fans' responses to the return of the series. Her Film Guidebook on *Horror* was published by Routledge in 2009, she is co-editor of *Twenty-First-Century Gothic* published in 2011, and had an edited collection on *True Blood* published by I. B. Tauris in 2012.

Andrew Crome is Lecturer in the History of Modern Christianity at the University of Manchester, where he teaches and writes on English religious history and apocalyptic thought. His students are frequently surprised to discover the ways in which *Doctor Who* can be worked into teaching the history of Victorian Christianity and related subjects. His first book, *The Restoration of the Jews: Early Modern Hermeneutics, Eschatology, and National Identity in the Works of Thomas Brightman*, will be published by Springer Academic Press in 2014.

Alexander Cummins received both his BA and MA by Research in History from the University of Leeds, and is currently finishing his doctoral research into the history of early modern magic and the emotions at the University of Bristol, where he also teaches. His first book, *The Starry Rubric: Seventeenth-century English Astrology and Magic*, was published last year. Along with writing on the history and philosophy of occultism, Alexander is a published performance poet and creative writing coach.

Joel Dark is a professor of history and the interim associate dean of the College of Liberal Arts at Tennessee State University in Nashville, Tennessee. He first encountered *Doctor Who* on PBS as a teenager during the 1980s and still seems to think that it is educational programming. He is deeply inspired by *Doctor Who* fans – including close friends, family, and many strangers – and aspires to be one himself.

Marcus Harmes lectures in the Faculty of Arts at the University of Southern Queensland, Australia. His major research focus is the history of the Anglican Church in a number of contexts, including the sixteenth and seventeenth centuries and in science fiction.

Tim Jones is (hopefully) very near the end of a PhD about the Czech author Milan Kundera at the University of East Anglia, where he also teaches Literature. His earliest memory of *Doctor Who* being the cliffhanger to Part 1 of "Remembrance of the Daleks" signifies him as a relative newbie, though this hasn't adversely affected his love of all eras of the show, classic and new. His favourite Doctors are, somewhat confusingly, William Hartnell and Matt Smith.

David Johnson is a professor of history at Colorado Northwestern Community College. He has a Master's degree in history from the University of Colorado at Colorado Springs, where he was named the Outstanding Graduate Student of the Year in history for 2011. David grew up with *Doctor Who*, and was a founding member of the Los Angeles-based fan group The Time Meddlers as well as running the hospitality suite for the first two years of the Gallifrey One convention. He currently lives in Craig, Colorado with his wife and two children

Courtland Lewis is currently Visiting Assistant Professor at the University of Alabama at Birmingham. He received his PhD from the University of Tennessee, where he specialised in Ethics and Social/Political Philosophy. He co-edited *Doctor Who and Philosophy* with Paula Smithka.

Kristine Larsen is Professor of Physics and Earth Sciences at Central Connecticut State University. Her research focuses on the intersections between science and society, including science and gender, science education, and scientific motifs in science-fiction, fantasy and horror media (especially the works of J. R. R. Tolkien). She is the author of *Stephen Hawking: A Biography* and *Cosmology 101*, and co-editor of *The Mythological Dimensions of Doctor Who* and *The Mythological Dimensions of Neil Gaiman*.

James McGrath is the Clarence L. Goodwin Chair in New Testament Language & Literature at Butler University. His books include *The Only True God* (University of Illinois Press, 2009) and *John's Apologetic Christology* (Cambridge University Press, 2001), as well as having edited the volume *Religion and Science Fiction* (Pickwick Publications [Wipf and Stock], 2011). He has taught and spoken widely on religion and science fiction. You can read his thoughts about the latest episodes of *Doctor Who* on his blog Exploring Our Matrix.

Gabriel McKee is the author of *The Gospel According to Science Fiction: From the Twilight Zone to the Final Frontier*, the blog SF Gospel, and *Pink Beams of Light From the God in the Gutter: The Science Fictional Religion of Philip K. Dick*. An independent scholar specialising in the intersection of theology and popular culture, he also works as a librarian and archivist specialising in rare books and counterculture ephemera.

Jennifer Miller received her PhD. in English from the University of Minnesota, and she is currently an instructor at Normandale Community College in Bloomington, Minnesota. Her current book project, entitled *Fantastic Borderlands*, looks at the hesitation between the supernatural and the real as a way of reconsidering race in contemporary popular fiction. Jennifer is also the editor of *Fantasy Matters*, a website dedicated to bridging popular and academic discussions of fantasy and science fiction.

Russell Sandberg is a Lecturer in Law at Cardiff University where he researches at the Centre for Law and Religion. He is author of *Law and Religion* (Cambridge University Press, 2011).

Kieran Tranter, PhD, is based at Griffith Law School, Gold Coast campus, Griffith University. He researches the cultural mediations between law and technology. He is particularly interested in the formative location of science fiction in this mediation and his favourite Doctor is Jon Pertwee.

John M. Vohlidka, PhD, is an Assistant Professor of History at Gannon University. There he teaches a multitude of courses ranging from his Tudor-Stuart speciality to History of the Future.

Karma Waltonen, PhD, teaches various writing and literature courses at The University of California, Davis, including *The Simpsons*: Satire and Postmodernism, The Graphic Novel, Writing in International Relations, and Writing and Performing Stand-Up Comedy. She is the editor of *Prized Writing* and *Margaret Atwood Studies*. She co-authored *The Simpsons in the Classroom: Embiggening the Learning Experience with the Wisdom of Springfield* with Denise Du Vernay. If you have the chance to see her wandering around WonderCon or ComicCon, where she presents as a professional geek, she will likely be dressed as Zuul.

K. Jason Wardley is a librarian at the University of Edinburgh, where he also recently completed a PhD in the School of Divinity, New College. His research interests are in phenomenology and theological anthropology, and in Continental philosophy of religion, in which he has published articles on metaphysics and liturgy, most recently in *Looking Beyond?* (Rodopi, 2012) and *Intensities: Philosophy, Religion and the Affirmation of Life* (Ashgate, 2012).